The

BUDDHIST
HANDBOOK

The
BUDDHIST
HANDBOOK

A Complete Guide to Buddhist Schools, Teaching, Practice, and History

John Snelling

Inner Traditions
Rochester, Vermont

Inner Traditions International
One Park Street
Rochester, Vermont 05767
www.InnerTraditions.com

Library of Congress Cataloging-in-Publication Data
Snelling, John, 1943–1992
    The Buddhist handbook: the complete guide to Buddhist schools, teaching, practice, and history/John Snelling
        p.   cm.
    Includes bibliographical references and index.
    ISBN 0-89281-319-9
    1. Buddhism.   I. Title.
BQ4012.S64   1991   91-3504
294.3—dc20   CIP

Printed and bound in Canada

10 9 8 7 6 5 4 3 2 1

Contents

Acknowledgments

I should like to sincerely thank the following for their kind help, advice, information, support, and encouragement:

Geshe Namgyal Wangchen, Phiroz Mehta, Francesca Fremantle, Robert Beer, Maurice O'C Walshe, Garry Thomson, Stephen Batchelor, Frances Wood (British Library), John Stevens, Eric Cheetham, Ven. Amaro Bhikkhu, Richard Hunn (Upasaka Wen Shu), Arthur Burton-Stibbon, Arthur Dyer, Rev. Jack Austin, Ven. Ajahn Sucitto, Jim Pym, Nick Cook, Phuntsog Wangyal, Shenpen and Mike Hookham, U Ba Maw, Ken Wilber, Dr. Nina E. Coltart, Dr. A. Piatigorsky, Patrick Gaffney, Ven. Dr. H. Saddhatissa, Jim Belither, Ven. Chushin Passmore, Nick Ribush, Brian Hickman (SOAS Library), and all those who kindly supplied biographical details for the Who's Who section.

In particular, Russell Webb's great kindness in substantially assisting with the compilation of the Who's Who section of the book in addition to his help and guidance in other areas must be mentioned, with gratitude.

Finally, I should like to register my sincere and affectionate appreciation of my first editor, the late Oliver Caldecott, for his professionalism and staunch support on both this and other of my books.

Gill Farrer-Halls would like to thank Stephen Batchelor, Russell Webb, and everyone else who kindly assisted in this work.

A Note on Language

The scriptural language of Theravada Buddhism is Pali, that of Indian Mahayana Buddhism in Sanskrit—both dead Indian languages. In many cases, the spellings of names and terms in the two languages are similar: *bodhisatta/bodhisattva, kamma/karma, dhamma/dharma, arahat/arhat, Gotama/Gautama, kapilavatthu/kapilavastu.* I have not opted for a single standardized spelling throughout but generally have tended to use the appropriate spelling in the appropriate place, i.e., Pali when discussing Theravada Buddhism, Sanskrit when discussing Mahayana and Tantra. In gray areas where either might be used I have tended to use Sanskrit, but have usually tried also to give Pali equivalents. In the case of Tibetan names and terms, I have not employed the tortuous Wylie system but have opted for simpler phonetic forms. Finally, I have used the old Wade-Giles Chinese transcriptions rather than the new Pinyin ones.

As regards accents, I have retained the use of some but have not used diacriticals, for which I will surely be castigated by sticklers but would argue in return that, as they are unfamiliar to the Western general reader (for whom this book is intended), they are not very helpful. I have also introduced minor changes of spelling in the interests of making particular words and names phonetically comprehensible.

Caveat

Mention of any group or teacher in this handbook does not imply endorsement of them by the author. This is in line with the traditions of Buddhism, which is not an authoritarian religion with centralized authority that bestows or withholds the seal of approval. It is therefore up to the individual to test the ground for him or herself, guided by common sense and the advice given by the Buddha himself, for example in the *Kalama Sutta*.*

---

* See pages 3–4.

P·A·R·T 1

Prologue

O·N·E

Why Buddhism?

Buddhism has gained enormous ground in the West during the past thirty years. Recently it was hailed as the fastest growing religion in Britain. There are over one hundred groups and centers established here by now, more in the United States, and an ever-increasing number in Europe too. There is every indication that the interest in Buddhism will continue to grow, for it clearly supplies some deep spiritual need in the people of the Western world that their established religious traditions fail to fully supply. One might well ask, then: "What does Buddhism possess that is especially valuable and helpful?"

FREEDOM FROM DOGMA AND FINDING THE TRUTH FOR ONESELF

Buddhism does not demand that anyone accepts its teachings on trust. The practitioner is instead invited to try them out, to experiment with them. If he finds that they work in practice, then by all means he can take them on board. But there is no compulsion; and if he happens to find the truth elsewhere or otherwise, all well and good. This essential freedom from dogma is enshrined in the Buddha's words to the Kalamas, a people who lives in the vicinity of the town of Kesaputta:

> Come, Kalamas, do not be satisfied with hearsay or with tradition or with legendary lore or with what has come down in your

scriptures or with conjecture or with logical inference or with weighing evidence or with liking for a view after pondering it over or with someone else's ability or with the thought "The monk is our teacher" *When you know in yourselves* "These ideas are unprofitable, liable to censure, condemned by the wise, being adopted and put into effect they lead to harm and suffering," then you should abandon them. . . . (And conversely:) *When you know in yourselves* "These things are profitable . . ." then you should practise them and abide in them.*

TOLERANCE

If one reserves the right to find the truth for oneself, one must logically accord the same right to others—and also respect them if they arrive at different conclusions. From this comes that basic tolerance that the world so acutely needs today. There have inevitably been exceptions—some Buddhists have fallen short of the very high standards set by the Buddha himself—but on the whole Buddhism has kept its record remarkably clean of inquisitions, pogroms, religious wars and massacres, heresy-hunting, and burning of books or people.

A LIBERAL TRADITION OF FREE INQUIRY

If Buddhism is a nondogmatic tradition, not founded on a book or articles of faith, what makes a Buddhist a Buddhist rather than nothing in particular? To start with, there is respect for the Buddha himself and for the manner in which he conducted his own search for spiritual truth. From this directly stems a sense of belonging to the tradition that the Buddha established: a liberal tradition of free inquiry into the nature of ultimate truth. Then too there is a sense of community with others of a similar (though not necessarily identical) outlook.

PRACTICAL METHODS

If the Buddhist emphasis is on finding out for oneself, this necessarily places primary emphasis upon direct religious experience, as opposed to belief or blind faith. However, one doesn't in the normal course of events just receive deep religious experience as manna from above. Though that can of course happen, one generally has to make a conscious effort. So Buddhism does not so much offer things to believe as things to do: a vast array of spiritual practices, ranging from moral

---

* Ñanamoli, *The Life of the Buddha* (Kandy: B.P.S., 1978), 176–7. My italics.

precepts that one can apply in everyday life and virtues that one can cultivate, to meditative practices (a profusion of these) which help to develop untapped spiritual resources: faculties like profound wisdom or clear-seeing and an all-embracing, selfless compassion. Put in Western terms, the ultimate aim of Buddhist practice is to engineer mystical experience: to penetrate the great mystery at the heart of life and find the answers to the knotty problems that have perennially engaged the most developed minds of the human race. This implies a complete spiritual transformation of the person as well.

HEALING AND TRANSFORMATION

C. G. Jung once wrote: "The whole world wants peace and the whole world prepares for war. Mankind is powerless against mankind. And the gods, as ever, show us the way of Fate."

This is a succinct summary of our contemporary dilemma. The world today is beset by many grave problems—social, psychological, ecological, economic—and of course the threat of nuclear destruction casts its shadow over all. Our planet has now very literally become a great time-bomb, and it is five minutes to zero-hour. As the final seconds tick away we seem hopelessly in the grip of deep dark forces that we don't understand and over which we have no control.

Sometimes we project the evil outwards and lay the blame on other people and groups. Sometimes too politicians and social scientists claim to have solutions; but these are invariably partial and temporary, touching the surface and relieving superficial symptoms rather than getting down to the root causes. If we are honest, these root causes lie in the individual human heart, in *our* hearts, where a primitive but fanatical self-centeredness holds sway. It is our own personal greed, hatred, and delusion, collectivized and amplified on a massive scale, that cause our planet's grave problems. Yet just to see this is not enough. The dark forces within each of us must be acknowledged and brought up into the light. Then, through awareness and understanding, they can be transformed into the stuff of true wisdom and compassion. Buddhism offers us ways and means of doing this.

So we need Buddhism. And our world needs it as never before.

T·W·O

The Heart of the Matter

What is the essence of Buddhism?

Quite simply, it is the great question of who or what we are, right here, now, at this very moment.

For you, the reader, this means nothing other than *who* or *what* is *right now* looking at *these* printed words on the page of *this* book.

Reflect on that for a moment. You see the letters of each word printed in clear black type on the bright white paper. As you stare they begin to vibrate a little, perhaps. The letters seem to stand out with super clarity for a second or two and then go unstable. . . .

But who is the reader that is looking at them?

Your initial reaction to this might be one of mild irritation. You have no doubt at all about who it is that is reading these words. You call that person "I" or "me." You have a name, a life history, a profession or job, relationships, a nationality. If you were to turn away and seek out a friend or a member of your family, they'd know instantly who was confronting them.

But don't turn away. Continue to look at the words on the paper. If you're really concentrating on the book, your name isn't in your mind at the moment, nor your life history; you're probably away from your job and your nationality isn't something of which you've been

conscious since you last went abroad; and if you don't seek out anyone, you're not in a relationship. So what then is the "I?" Right now,
does it amount to anything more than a collection of thoughts and
memories which are just transitory and insubstantial things that come
and go in the mind like clouds in the sky?

So, if you really concentrate single-pointedly on what's before your
eyes at this very moment, there are only the words on the paper. Thin
black on flat white. As for who's reading them, that's after all not
really so very easy to say, is it? Perhaps you're now beginning to feel
a little uneasy. Things are not what you thought they were. Something that you always took to be self-evidently present has gone—or
at least is not so solid. Or perhaps you feel a slight sense of amazement,
as though you've touched upon the edges of a great mystery.

Actually, you've touched the deepest mystery of all. Scientists may
send spacecraft to distant planets or probe remote quarters of space
with radio-telescopes. They may investigate the mysteries of the sub-
atomic world with electron microscopes. But the thing that in fact
they know least about is this great mystery that is right here with each
one of us all the time. Like everyone else, they subscribe to the consensus view and don't give the matter a second thought. Thus in a
very real sense they fail to see what's right under their noses.

Buddhism, however, is centrally concerned with this mystery and
how to unravel it. In the first instance it is necessary to see through
the great delusion of "I," of the so-called person. Then it's a matter
of finding out what is really there. And now the plot thickens, for to
penetrate this mystery is to penetrate the ultimate mystery, the mystery at the heart of all things, and confront what the Christians call
God, the Muslims *Allah,* the Hindus *Brahman* or *Atman*—and it goes
by other names in other religions. Buddhists, however, hesitate to put
a name to it or say anything at all about it. It is, they maintain, something that cannot be grasped by the intellect or described in words. It
can only be seen directly; but that seeing brings about something truly
miraculous: a total transformation, no less. The veils of delusion fall
away and at last the world is perceived as it really is. At the same time
a deep compassion also crystallizes: a pure, selfless kindliness and caring born of an understanding of the unity of all beings.

In essence, then, Buddhism is quite simple. But simple things are
often hard to fully realize, so people need all kinds of aids and sup-
ports. A vast superstructure has therefore grown up around the basic
heart-core of the Buddha's teaching: mountains of philosophical
speculation, a voluminous literature, monastic codes and ethical systems, histories, cosmologies, different types of ritual and meditation

practice, institutions, and hierarchies. All or any of this may be helpful in enabling the sincere practitioner to zero in upon the central issue—who or what is here, now—and to keep doing so until that great mystery has been completely realized. But it can also become a massive hindrance, entangling the all-too-errant mind in a thick undergrowth of secondary accretions.

When Shuan Chinken wrote his preface to the *Mumonkan,* a great textbook of the Ch'an (Zen) school of Buddhism produced in China in the early thirteenth century, he complained that he had been practically forced to take up his brush. "Don't use it, don't use it, for it will be yet another drop in the great lake," he urged,* implying that the true practice of Buddhism is about getting rid of thoughts and other mental bric-à-brac and confronting the central matter starkly and squarely; books, however, just contain more potential clutter for the attics of the mind.

This should be borne in mind when reading the present book. When the reader's mind begins to bulge and ache with useful facts, perhaps it might then be as well to let them all go for the time being and just return to the present moment and the great mystery of what is here, now. When we are fully aware and awake to this, then we confront the very heart of the matter.

* R. H. Blyth, trans., *Mumonkan,* vol. 4 of *Zen and Zen Classics* (Tokyo: Hokuseido Press, 1972), 11.

P·A·R·T 2

The Buddha

T·H·R·E·E

The Indian Background

Buddhism is a child of India, a uniquely spiritual country. A concern for truth and a respect for that basic instinct in us that, if we heed it, urges us to reach for the highest spiritually—these have been and remain aspects of the Indian scene since time immemorial. Fundamental to the Indian religious outlook at its best* is a basic liberalism that comes from an understanding that there are many paths by which the great mystery of ultimate reality may be approached. Allied to this is a fundamental tolerance: a willingness to listen, to learn, to change, and to coexist with others with whom one may not necessarily agree. Mahatma Gandhi, the father of modern independent India, exhibited these noble qualities in his own life and work.

About 1500 B.C., a race of nomadic herders who had long since migrated from the central Asian steppe thrust their way into northwest India. They spoke an Indo-European language, an early form of Sanskrit, and for this reason are popularly known as Aryans. In the valley of the River Indus, which lies in present-day Pakistan, these Aryans found the remains of what had once been a civilization as advanced for its day as those of Egypt and Mesopotamia. The great cities of

---

* I say "the Indian religious outlook at its best" because of course there have been instances when it has manifested at less than its best; for instance during the terrible fighting between Hindus and Muslims following independence from British rule.

Mohenjodaro and Harappa had stood here but had sadly long since begun to crumble into the dust. The Aryans were well-armed warriors. They thus had little difficulty in dominating northwest India and establishing supremacy over the people they found there. These included the once proud creators of the Indus Valley civilization. It was the age-old story of energetic, patriarchal barbarians colliding with a more sophisticated but essentially decadent, matriarchal people. But the Aryans did not destroy pre-existing culture; they learned from it, and they no doubt reinvigorated it. The civilization that afterwards developed and spread throughout India is therefore the result of the dynamic interaction of the Aryans with the other peoples of India.

The period of Indian history ushered in by the coming of the Aryans is known as the Vedic Age (c. 1500-500 B.C.), after a series of literary compositions of great antiquity known as the Vedas (Veda means knowledge).* The oldest is the Rig Veda, a collection of one thousand and twenty-eight poetic hymns. Of it Phiroz Mehta has written:

> What is the Rig Veda? A collection of hymns, the earliest document of the human mind, representing, according to most scholars, the religion of an unsophisticated age, the creation of inspired poets and seers. Many of the hymns, it is said, are simple and naïve, in praise of nature gods and goddesses; some deal with formal ritual; and others, especially the last book . . . present the results of conscious reflections on the origin of the world and on the Supreme Being. . . . They embody penetrating intuitions. But no system of philosophy is presented at this stage, for mythology and poetry precede philosophy and science.†

Three other Vedas later came into being:

1. The Yajur Veda—concerned with sacrificial formula
2. The Sama Veda—which is purely liturgical
3. The Atharva Veda (the last)—mainly a book of spells

At the center of religious life during the Vedic Age lay the ritual of sacrifice. The world had been created by sacrifice and was maintained

---

* Strictly speaking, the Vedas consist of three parts: the Samhitas, the Brahmanas, and the Upanishads. The Samhitas consist of the collections of hymns listed in the text. The Brahmanas, on the other hand, are prose texts dealing with brahmanical sacrificial rites. Finally, the Upanishads are discourses concerning Brahman (Ultimate Reality) and other lofty philosophical topics—they are discussed later on.

† Phiroz Mehta, Early Indian Religious Thought (London: Lusac, 1956), 32–3.

by sacrifice, it was thought. This was, however, completely controlled by the hereditary brahmin priesthood, who claimed that they alone were fitted by birth to perform sacrifice, and jealously guarded the secrets of its rituals. The most elaborate sacrifice was the Ashvamedha or "Horse Sacrifice," which went on for about a year and involved a small army of specialist priests and the ritual slaughter of a large number of animals. It was an exceedingly costly affair.

At the social center of the new culture, on the other hand, there developed a caste system, which divided the population up into various hierarchical groups: the priesthood (*brahmanas*); the warriors and aristocrats (*kshatriyas*); the traders and other professionals (*vaishyas*); and the cultivators (*shudras*). Later a subcaste appeared: the untouchables (*harrijans*), who were probably of aboriginal stock and strictly speaking did not have any caste at all. Caste probably existed in the Indus Valley civilization and rested on a racial basis—the Aryans merely adapted it to their own purposes, taking care to reserve the higher echelons for themselves!

The caste system was a closed system; once born into a caste, there was no leaving it; upward or downward mobility was unknown. And underpinning the whole thing was the notion of *dharma,* a word with a range of meanings. Used in its widest, impersonal sense it can have connotations of universal law. Related to people, on the other hand, it can imply duty to family, to the surrounding sociopolitical matrix, and religious duty. If a person lived dharmically, then, in his next incarnation, he might receive the reward of birth into a higher caste. This of course implies acceptance of the notion of personal rebirth of reincarnation.

The caste system has survived to a large extent down to the present time, and has had both its critics and its apologists. In its favor, it has been said that it helped establish a stable and well-organized society and fostered the virtues of patience, respect, and responsibility. On the other hand, it is often criticized as being rigid, inhumane, unjust, and the root cause of that pernicious malaise known as oriental fatalism.

The spiritual health and richness of India owe rather less to brahminism than to an alternative tradition that had its roots in pre-Aryan culture. This was essentially an ascetic tradition and its exponents were not *brahmanas* as a rule but rather *kshatriyas* of the warrior or aristocratic caste. They would renounce the world and go off either singly or in small groups into the solitude of forest and mountain retreat. It has been suggested that some were merely drop-outs, casualties who had failed to adapt successfully to conventional social life. Others may have been in search of paranormal powers—the forerunners of the legendary fakirs who later astonished European travellers in India by magically charming snakes, levitating and performing the Indian rope trick. The best of them, however, certainly withdrew from their social duties for only the highest spiritual purposes. They no doubt practiced meditation and other mystical disciplines, including forms of yoga. Such practices may date back to pre-Vedic times, for images of figures sitting cross-legged in yogic posture have been unearthed by archaeologists working in the remains of the lost cities of the Indus Valley. It has also been suggested that shamanistic influences transported by the Aryans from their northern homelands may also have been at work here. By means of such practices, the ascetics were able to gain direct knowledge of exalted spiritual states (*jhanas* in Pali; Sanskrit, *dhyanas*). An elite few came to know *Brahman*.

Brahman was ultimate reality, no less. It is said to be one and all-pervading, but formless and ineffable: a great mystery. Thus it is often referred to in negative terms: "*Neti, neti*"—"Not this, not this." It is identical, however, with the great mystery at the heart of every human being, so if a man asks what his true nature is, he might receive the classic answer: "*Tat tvam asi*"—"You are That." In this, its immanent aspect, *Brahman* is known as *Atman*.

These noble teachings, which really touched the spiritual heights, were recorded, though not in systematic form, in the two hundred or so Upanishads, which were composed between about 800 and 400 B.C.The most important are the *Isa, Kena, Katha, Prasna, Mundaka, Mandukya, Svetasvatara, Chandogya, Brihadaranyaka,* and *Taittiriya.* Like the Vedas, the Upanishads are the work of great poets but ones whose lyrical inspiration was fully informed by profound insight.

Some of the ascetics who had gained direct knowledge of *Brahman* must have left their mountain caves and forest hermitages to return to the world to share their wisdom with their fellow men. They must have impressed the ordinary people very much, and made the *brahmana* priests look little better than self-serving traffickers in mumbo-jumbo. The *brahmana* were sensible, however. They may have scorned these ascetics and discouraged the ordinary people from listening to them, but they did not launch any kind of violent campaign against them; rather they sought to incorporate aspects of the alternative wisdom into their own teachings. Also, alarmed at the number of young men who were throwing up their family duties to take to the homeless ascetic life, the *brahmanas* began to propound the notion of Four Stages of Life. Firstly one is a student, then a householder, later one retires and gradually loosens the bonds that tie one to the world, and finally, only when one has discharged all one's other dharmic debts fully, can one become a renunciate or *sanyassin* and go off in search of religious truth.

Unfortunately, even the highest teachings seem invariably to undergo a fall when they are packaged for popular consumption by a professional priestly class. Thus it was with the Upanishads. The formless *Brahman* became formalized and eventually came to wear an anthropomorphic face, that of the great god Brahma. And the equally elusive *Atman* that once great sages had hesitated to mention save in negative terms, that too congealed into a permanent personal entity or immortal soul, the *jivatman*. It was part of the Buddha's project to point out these debasements of the once noble teachings of the Upanishads, which in their original and highest forms were quite consistent with his own teachings.

By the time that the Vedic Age was drawing towards its close, Vedic culture had spread down the plain of the River Ganges and the restless Aryan invader had been long since transformed from a pastoral nomad into a settled agriculturist. He had also integrated, insofar as the caste system facilitated integration, with the other peoples of the area. The clearing of the great Gangetic Plain for agriculture had also unleashed a vast untapped economic potential. The population grew and prosperity burgeoned, great trading cities emerged and with them a sophisticated urban culture and a new individualism. New forms of political organization developed too as the old tribes began to be replaced by more highly organized groupings. Tribal republics appeared, ruled by elected aristocracies drawn from the *kshatriya* caste, and these may have been less well disposed towards the prevailing *brahmana* orthodoxy than the kingdoms that also appeared at this time. These were more expansionistic than the republics and two of them, Magadha and Kosala, vied for domination of "Middle Country," the central heartland of the Ganges Plain, which by the time of the Buddha's birth (563 B.C.) was the main center of civilization in India.

Wealth and social change generate stress, and from stress come psychological and spiritual problems. At the same time the necessary leisure and surplus resources are also available for solutions to those problems to be sought. Thus the changes outlined above probably increased the numbers of people taking to the homeless life as followers of the alternative spiritual tradition. But as life became more organized it also became expedient for those ascetics to abandon their old anarchic ways and become more organized themselves. They had also to demonstrate their seriousness and usefulness to society. Thus we find identifiable sects emerging, each with its own philosophy and practices, and centered around a *shramana* or teacher. The ascetics themselves were at first called *ajivakas* or *parivajakas* ("homeless ones;" "ones who had gone forth"). Five main sects can be determined:

1. *Ajivakas.* (As well as referring to ascetics generally, the term also referred to the followers of this particular sect.) The root teacher was Makkhali Gosala and he seems to have taught a philosophy of utter determinism: the universe was a totally closed causal system but it was inexorably moving each person towards ultimate perfection, though the process would take untold aeons of time.

2. *Lokayatas.* (The Materialists.) As propounded by Ajita Keshakambalin, a contemporary of the Buddha, the philosophers of this sect held that a human being was composed of the four elements and into those his constituent parts would be resolved at death, which was an utter finality: "When the body dies both the fool and the wise alike are cut off and perish." In life then a man should seek the maximum of pleasure possible.

3. *The Sceptics.* These held that brahmanical doctrines were mutually contradictory and that truth was utterly unattainable. They are said to have wriggled like eels out of every question put to them, but believed in cultivating friendliness and peace of mind.

4. *The Jains.* The Jains held life to be an extremely painful business and aspired to attain *moksha* or liberation from the painful cycles of endless rebirth by withdrawing to a high, rarefied spiritual state. To do so they sought to amass the necessary karmic merit by the practice of extreme forms of austerity and impeccably moral conduct. They were particularly preoccupied with the karmic consequences of killing or causing suffering to living beings, even microscopic ones. They thus took the virtue of *ahimsa* (harmlessness) to extreme lengths and some would sweep the ground ahead of them when they walked and wear gauze masks over their faces. The Jain philosophy, which was systematized around the time of the Buddha by Mahavira, has followers in India to this day, though few of them are extreme ascetics.

The fifth sect, which was in time to spread so widely that for a time it became the predominant religion of all Asia, was founded by Siddhartha Gautama, the Buddha, whose life and work we will look at in the next two chapters.

The Buddha:
The Early Years

Biographies of the Buddha were comparatively late arrivals. There is no biography as such in the earliest Pali scriptures, but a skeletal one might be pieced together from scattered references. The Ven. Ñanamoli Thera (Osbert Moore) did just this in his *Life of the Buddha* (Kandy, Sri Lanka, 1972). One of the first true biographies was the *Buddhacarita* ("Acts of the Buddha") of the first or second century A.D. by the Sanskrit poet Ashvaghosa. A condensed translation of this appears in Dr. Edward Conze's anthology, *Buddhist Scriptures* (Harmondsworth, 1959, a Penguin Classic). Various other versions of the life were subsequently produced. Many of them contain additions and embellishments not found in the earliest sources.

A BRIEF OUTLINE OF THE LIFE

The man who was to become the Buddha was born about 563 B.C. of *kshatriya* stock at a place called Lumbini. This is situated in the Terai region of what today is the kingdom of Nepal, immediately below the Himalayan foothills on the northern edge of the plain of the River Ganges, due north of the holy city of Benares. He was given the name Siddhartha and took the clan name Gautama. His father, Shuddhodana, has been variously described as the king or leader of a local people known as the Shakyas or even just as a prominent citizen of Kapilavastu, the Shakyan capital. The Shakyas were in fact just one of the number of more or less independent peoples then inhabiting this part of northern India, who were politically organized into tribal republics ruled by elected aristocracies.

A remarkable man is deemed to require a remarkable birth. So it is said that prophetic dreams heralded the great event; that the Buddha-to-be was not conceived in the usual way but descended from the Tushita Heaven and entered his mother's womb in the form of a white elephant; that she carried him for ten months and then gave birth to him from her side and standing up; that he was born clean, unstained in any way but that nevertheless streams of water poured from the sky to wash both mother and child; and finally:

> As soon as born, the Bodhisatta (Buddha-to-be) firmly standing with even feet goes firmly to the north with seven long steps, a white parasol being held over him (by the gods). He surveys all the quarters, and in a lordly voice says, "I am the chief in the world, I am the best in the world, I am the first in the world. This is my last birth. There is now no existence again."*

Unfortunately, Siddhartha's mother, Mahamaya, died a week after giving birth to him, and her place in his life was taken by her sister, Mahapajapati, who in the polygamous society of the day was probably also one of Shuddhodana's wives.

Not long after the birth, a wise sage named Asita came to Kapilavastu. He gasped with wonder and smiled when the infant was laid before him, for he at once noticed that there were thirty-two special signs on his tiny body. But then Asita began to weep and when asked why replied that he was not weeping for Siddhartha but for himself. Siddhartha would certainly grow up to be a fully enlightened buddha, a teacher of men and gods, but he, Asita, was old and would not live long enough to hear Siddhartha's profound teaching.

Shuddhodana was far from delighted when he heard this. He therefore determined to do whatever he could to prevent Asita's prediction coming true. Reflecting that it would be experience of the hard, ugly, and painful things of life that would turn Siddhartha's mind towards religion, Shuddhodana decided that he would create a hermetic environment of comfort, beauty, and pleasure for Siddhartha. The real world would be utterly shut out.

Probably while Siddhartha was still a boy it was sufficient for Shuddhodana to see to it that he was just closely chaperoned. As he grew towards manhood and was more disposed to take independent action, more elaborate

* E. J. Thomas, *The Life of the Buddha* (London: Kegan Paul, 1949), 31.

security arrangements became necessary. So Shuddhodana ordered three splendid marble palaces to be built: one for the hot season, one for the cool season, and one for the rainy season. Siddhartha was confined in the upper stories of these, and every kind of pleasure and luxury was laid on to make sure that he would not become bored. He lolled around in splendid robes of Benares silk, anointed by oils of the finest quality. He ate the most delicious foods, and armies of musicians, dancing girls, and the most sensuous courtesans were on hand to amuse him.

One might have thought that such an environment would have produced a decadent hot-house plant, but by all accounts Siddhartha grew up to be a splendid young man. He was good at his studies, very handsome, just and kind, and he also excelled at all kinds of sports and martial arts. Those last talents helped him to win the hand of Yashodhara, his beautiful young cousin, who was desired as a wife by many young noblemen and princelings. Siddhartha trounced all these other suitors easily in a series of contests and he and Yashodhara were married when he was only sixteen. However, the mores of the day would no doubt have allowed him to enjoy the pleasures of numerous concubines as well. One child resulted from Siddhartha's marriage to Yashodhara—a son, Rahula, born when Siddhartha was about twenty-nine.

No doubt information about life in the world beyond the walls of his pleasure palaces filtered through to Siddhartha and aroused his natural curiosity. He was probably getting restless anyway. So a trip to the outside world was arranged, either with his father's knowledge or without it.

Siddhartha made four fateful trips to the outside world, driven each time by his groom, Channa. On the first they encountered an old man, on the second a sick man, and on the third a corpse being carried away to be cremated on the burning *ghat*. Having lived in pleasure palaces, completely insulated from such sights for nearly thirty years, the effect of these three encounters upon Siddhartha was traumatic. Here were the true facts of the human condition: that men are susceptible to sickness, old age, and death—all men: even Siddhartha himself.

In order that life be tenable, most people suppress the reality and inevitability of death. Those who have been forced to confront it, however, will bear witness to the profound effect that it can have. A vital shock it always is, but one that can also bring about a sudden maturing of the whole personality by summarily clearing the mind of its usual clutter of trivial preoccupations and bringing into focus that which is of real importance. The cloistered Siddhartha received such a vital shock and at once all the pleasures and delights of palace life lost their charm.

But he also made a fourth visit to the outside world with Channa. On that occasion they saw a *sadhu,* a wandering holy man such as one can see on the highways and byways of India even today. It is also significant that this man, who was to awaken Siddhartha's dormant spirituality, was not a *brahmana* priest but follower of the alternative *shramana* tradition. He was alone and dressed in rags, and clearly possessed nothing; yet there was a quality about his whole demeanor that deeply impressed Siddhartha—a tranquillity that other men, for all their possessions and family connections, clearly lacked. *Perhaps,* Siddhartha wondered, *he has discovered some secret; perhaps old age, sickness, and death are no longer frightening for him?*

And now the conflict within Siddhartha's heart became really intense. He had been awakened to the central problem of human existence, the problem of suffering, and also been shown a potential way of finding a solution to it. This would, however, mean not only giving up all the material riches that he enjoyed but also walking out on his family: his father, who expected him to do his duty, and his wife and son, whom he loved deeply. His heart was wrenched this way and that. A large part of him longed to stay, and yet at the same time there was a powerful force within him, a force that *could not* be denied, that was pushing him out into the unknown.

This conflict eventually reached its inevitable climax. Around midnight on the very night that his son, Rahula, was born, Siddhartha rose from his bed and dressed. Waking up Channa, Siddhartha asked him to saddle up his horse, Kanthaka. Then they rode through the night until they came to the River Anoma, which divided the land of the Shakyas from the neighboring kingdom of Magadha. On the far bank of the river a poignant ritual took place. Siddhartha hacked off all his handsome jet-black hair, exchanged his silken robe for the ragged yellow one of a wandering holy man, and took off all his rings and ornaments. Handing these to Channa, he asked him to take them back to Kapilavastu along with the horse. Then the two of them said their farewells and Siddhartha walked off alone. His great spiritual quest for the solution to the problem of suffering had begun.

Siddhartha went and sought out the most distinguished *shramana* teachers of the day: Alara Kalama and Udraka Ramaputra. Both taught him all that they knew and he for his part studied and practiced assiduously. But though he obtained a great deal of intellectual knowledge and became proficient in the attainment of *dhyanas* (Pali, *jhanas*), he was still unsatisfied, for a complete solution to his spiritual problem still eluded him.

So then Siddhartha took himself off into the jungle near Uruvela and began to submit himself to the most grueling forms of asceticism. The rationale for this was that by mortifying the body, subjecting it to the most extreme forms of privation and suffering, suffering itself could be finally overcome. He spent long periods living alone and naked in eerie forests and in charnel grounds. He slept on beds of thorns. He burned in the heat of the midday sun and suffered cold at night. At the same time he tried to burn and crush all thoughts from his mind, and experimented with holding his breath for long periods until there were violent pains in his head and he lapsed into unconsciousness. He also starved himself into a state of extreme emaciation:

> All my limbs became like the knotted joints of withered creepers, my buttocks like a bullock's hoof, my protruding backbone like a string of balls, my gaunt ribs like the crazy rafters of a tumble-down shed. My eyes lay deep in their sockets, their pupils sparkling like water in a deep well. As an unripe gourd shrivels and shrinks in a hot wind, so became my scalp. If I thought, "I will touch the skin of my belly," it was the skin of my backbone that I also took hold of, since the skin of my belly and back met. The hairs, rotting at the roots, fell away from my body when I stroked my limbs.*

It is a gruesome picture, but it also portrays a virtuoso performance of its kind and it impressed five other ascetics, who asked if they could join him. However, in the long run Siddhartha had to admit to himself that it had not provided him with a fully satisfying answer to his problem, and he realized that if he went on abusing his body in that way he would die before finding one. He therefore took a little food in order to give himself enough strength to make a new start. Witnessing this, his five fellow ascetics walked off in disgust, declaring, "Gautama has taken to the easy life!" This in itself gives a hint of the spiritual one-upmanship that so often underlies that sort of ascetic athleticism.

Siddhartha was now a man *in extremis*. He had renounced social role, material support, family—everything. Now even his fellow ascetics had rejected him. He had also experienced the extremes of sensual indulgence and of self-mortification, and found that both ultimately led nowhere.

There was one thing that he had not really tried, however—a middle way between the luxurious and the ascetic ways. He also recalled an incident during a ploughing festival when as a child he had sat beneath the rose-apple tree and entered a state of meditation. He thought: "Might that be the way to Enlightenment?"

At a place nowadays called Bodh Gaya in the modern Indian state of Bihar, Siddhartha made himself a cushion of grass beneath the spreading branches of the famous bodhi tree, a tree of the species *ficus religiosa*. He determined to sit in meditation here until he found an answer to the problem of suffering—or died in the attempt.

What next took place is sometimes recounted in high dramatic form. Besides Siddhartha, the other protagonist is Mara, supported by his

---

* *Majjhima Nikaya*, 245–6, quoted in Garry Thomson, *Reflections on the Life of the Buddha* (London: The Buddhist Society, 1983), 7.

demonic hordes. Mara is a kind of Buddhist Satan, a tempter whose role within the scheme of things is to maintain delusion and desire and all those wisdom-inhibiting factors that keep *samsara*, the world of illusion, in endless cyclic motion. When Mara saw what Siddhartha was trying to do, he naturally became very perturbed. The last thing he wanted was that a way out of suffering and *samsara* be discovered. He had in fact been keeping a close eye on Siddhartha's activities right from the time he had embarked on the homeless life six years before and had already tried to tempt him to give up his quest. He had whispered insinuations into Siddhartha's ear, suggesting, for instance, that his energy would be better spent earning merit for himself by doing good works. Now that he saw that Siddhartha was getting perilously close to success, however, he decided to launch an all-out attack with his army of hideous demons, supported by elephants, horses, chariots, infantry, auxiliaries, and all—and he himself cheered them on with "*Seize him, drag him, slay him . . . !*" But Siddhartha was quite unshaken by all this and the attack collapsed. Poor Mara, knowing that he was beaten, slunk away, "pained, dejected, depressed and sorrowful." Still, he was to keep up his watch on Siddhartha for another year and made further attempts to undo him, on one occasion deploying his ultimate weapon: his superseductive daughters.

We might interpret all this to mean that there were times during Siddhartha's quest when he was tempted to give up. He may occasionally have felt that he had done enough and should go home and discharge his social duty. At other times perhaps powerful fears rose up within him. He may have become worried that he might go mad, that what he was doing might project him into some outlandish psychic state. Fear of the supernatural may also have hit him, or fear of death, or even an *angst* more frightful than that of death: a kind of existential terror of utter annihilation or non-being. We can take it, however, that he did not succumb to any of these. Sexual desire also reasserted itself with great force from time to time.

Other accounts of the final push for enlightenment are less mythological and more informative. It would firstly appear from them that Siddhartha went into *samadhi,* a state of meditative concentration in which he attained various *dhyanas*. It was proficiency in this that he had learned with his first teachers, Alara Kalama and Udraka Ramaputra. But then, with a mind fully clear and concentrated, he began to practice *vipassana* or insight meditation and thereby gained certain special kinds of knowledge:

1. He "remembered many former existences."

2. He gained knowledge of the workings of karma: how those who acquire bad karma by performing evil actions are reborn in miserable

states, while those who acquire good karma by performing meritorious actions are reborn in happy states.

3. He gained knowledge of the destruction of the *asavas*, the "cankers" or "taints." Three *asavas* are often identified: sensual desire, desire for existence, and ignorance. Later a fourth was added: addiction to views—or even to holding any views at all.

Garry Thomson has pointed out how thin this account seems of what to Buddhists is regarded as the greatest event of human history. We must remember that at its core lies a radical transformation of perception, indeed of being itself, that cannot be adequately grasped by the intellect or described in words. It is truly ineffable. Yet we might propose certain pointers, understanding that these can only be tentative and provisional until we can gain direct insight into these things for ourselves.

We might suggest that Siddhartha now finally *saw through* his "I" or ego, saw that in an ultimate sense it was an illusion, a creation of thought rather than anything with a more solid existence. Moreover, with "I" removed from the center of the arena, there was no identifiable *subject* perceiving the world in a dualistic (subject-object) manner. Consequently, "the world" became a unity.

Siddhartha must also have become aware that the world of manifestation was an apparent outpouring of energy from a mysterious, unlimited source. During deep meditation, his mind perfectly still and quiet, he could feel the presence of this source, in totality, in his own heart-core. It was similarly in all other beings. Thus it was the true nature of all things, the basic ground of being itself. Never having been born, however, it was not subject to suffering or death; thus it could be called the deathless. It was also fully conscious; it was "the one who knows"— though paradoxically it could not know itself.

So, abandoning identification with the illusion of his "I" (there is no reason to believe that a conventional sense of ego identity did not to some extent persist), Siddhartha from then on identified himself primarily with his true nature and sought to rest in that mysterious center.

At dawn following the night of the full moon of May, this great spiritual hero looked up and saw the morning star rise. As he did so he saw the world for the first time with undeluded eyes. He felt like a man who had just woken up from a long and confusing dream. He was Siddhartha no more, but the Buddha—The Awakened One. Touching the earth, he called upon it to bear witness to his great achievement.

F·I·V·E

The Buddha:
The Teaching Career

Following his great breakthrough to enlightenment, the Buddha is said to have remained in meditation under the bodhi tree for a while (seven days, four weeks, seven weeks—accounts vary), enjoying the supreme bliss of his great spiritual liberation. As for trying to communicate this great discovery, however, he felt that it would be a waste of energy even to try. Human beings were simply too deeply caught up in worldly attachments and pursuits to want to hear about it. But then the great god Brahma Sahampati appealed to him, saying that there were some people with "just a little dust in their eyes" who could be released from the coils of suffering if he would consent to teach. The Buddha's deep compassion was aroused and he agreed to the idea.

But who was he to teach? Alara Kalama and Udraka Ramaputra had died by this time and the only other potentially interested people still alive that he could think of were the five ascetics who had spurned him earlier. It would therefore have to be them and he located them in a deer park at Isipatana (modern Sarnath, near Benares). Recalling his earlier lapse, they decided to give him a cool reception, but then they noticed that his whole appearance had changed. He possessed a new spiritual radiance. This won them over in spite of themselves and made them receptive to his teaching.

So at Isipatana the Buddha preached his first sermon to the five ascetics on the subject of the Four Noble Truths; he also told them about the Middle Way that he had found between the extremes of sensual indulgence and self-mortification. One of the five ascetics, Kaundinya, understood at once.

"Kaundinya knows!" the Buddha exclaimed, and immediately ordained him the first Buddhist monk (*bhikshu*). This was done according to a very simple formula. Kaundinya's four companions followed suit shortly afterwards. And so, in Buddhist parlance, the Buddha began to turn the wheel of the dharma; and so too was born the *sangha,* the community of Buddhist monks, to which later nuns were also admitted.

The Buddha was about thirty-five when he became enlightened. He lived until he was about eighty, and those last forty-five years of his life were given over to teaching. He walked the hot and dusty roads of central-northern India, going from village to town to city, addressing himself to all who wanted to hear what he had to say, regardless of distinctions of sex, caste, vocation, or religion. He was a truly liberal and generous teacher.

He was also apparently a very inspiring teacher, for right from the start large numbers of people were ready to give everything up in order to follow him and devote themselves wholeheartedly to the practice of his teachings. There was Yashas, the worldweary son of a well-to-do Benares business family, four of Yashas' friends, and later fifty more, all young men of good social connections. Yashas' mother and wife became the first female lay followers, while his father became a lay follower too.

Another early convert was the fire-worshipping ascetic Kshyapa. The Buddha so impressed his with a series of virtuoso demonstrations of supernormal powers that Kshyapa and his five hundred followers, matted-haired ascetics to a man, all entered the Buddhist fold. Kashyapa's two ascetic brothers joined the *sangha* soon afterwards too, bringing with them three hundred and two hundred followers respectively.

Two important new additions to the early *sangha* were Maudgalyayana and Shariputra, who became the Buddha's chief disciples. They had formerly been disciples of another spiritual teacher, Sañjaya, but had not gained complete understanding through his teachings. On hearing a brief summary of the Buddha's *dharma*, however—"All that is subject to arising is subject to cessation"—all their difficulties were resolved. They also brought with them two hundred followers. In time Shariputra was to become highly respected for wisdom, Maudgalyayana for paranormal powers.

These mass conversions led to certain misgivings in the kingdom of Magadha, where they took place, which is not to be wondered at since families were being broken up: husbands were leaving wives, sons were leaving parents, and disciples were also leaving their gurus. These misgivings soon evaporated, however, as the Buddha predicted.

The Buddha eventually decided to introduce a more formal ordination ceremony for his monks, which consisted of shaving the hair and beard, donning the yellow robe, and reciting the Refuge three times: "I go for refuge to the Buddha; I go for refuge to the *dharma;* I go for refuge to the *sangha.*" Later a more complicated formula evolved.

A code of monastic rules (*Pratimoksha*) was not set up straight away. Apparently, in the early days, the *sangha* was so strong and true that there was no need to do so. As all things mortal are subject to degeneration, however, the Buddha was eventually obliged to establish one.

The monks of this rapidly growing *sangha* lived the homeless life, wandering from place to place, carrying the Buddha's teachings out into the world "for the welfare and happiness of the many folk." During the monsoon, however, the rainy season in India, they were allowed to go into retreat. This was not least because the rains are a time of new growth and to walk abroad then would have meant trampling green shoots and other forms of new life underfoot.

If the Buddha himself was impressive and inspirational to a wide spectrum of people, it is clear that the *bhikshus* of his *sangha* were so too. On one occasion King Prasenajit of Kósala contrasted them with other monks and *brahmanas,* who appeared to be "lean, wretched, unsightly, jaundiced" and so forth. The Buddhists, on the other hand, were "smiling and cheerful, sincerely joyful, plainly delighting, their faculties fresh, unexcited, unruffled . . . dwelling with minds like the wild deer" (Ñanamoli, 1972, p. 285).

The Buddha's early wanderings in the kingdom of Magadha eventually brought him to the capital, Rajagrha. Here the king, Bimbisara*, came to see him accompanied by a large number of citizens. The Buddha gave them teachings, which they all understood, and then they too all became lay followers. King Bimbisara was particularly moved by the experience of receiving teachings from a *buddha* as it fulfilled a lifelong wish. He himself waited on the Buddha and his *bhikshus* at the next day's alms meal; and afterwards, with truly regal largesse, he donated the bamboo grove, a pleasure-garden lying just outside the city, to the *sangha.* A rich merchant later put up shelters there and so created the first proper Buddhist monastery. The Buddha spent his second and third rains re-

---

* Bimbisara was the first important king of Magadha and has been described as a man of determination and political foresight. His conquest of Anga extended his power over the trading routes, and he was also one of the earliest Indian kings to see the need for efficient administration. In about 493 B.C. he was murdered by his son, Ajatasattu, who then became king and was determined to continue his father's aggressive expansionist policies.

treats there, the first having been spent at Benares. Up until its foundation the *bhikshus* had lived "in the woods, at the roots of trees, under overhanging rocks, in ravines, in hillside caves, in charnel grounds, in jungle thickets," or just out in the open on heaps of straw.

Other generous donations were to follow. One came from Anathapindika, a layman so renowned for his generosity that he had been given the title "Feeder of the poor." He first heard the Buddha preach the *dharma* in Rajagrha. Inspired by what he heard, he invited him to spend the next (fourth) rains retreat at his own city of Shravasti, the capital of the neighboring kingdom of Kosala, which was then ruled by King Prasenajit. Returning there in advance, Anathapindika looked around for a suitable place nearby where the *bhikshus* could stay. He lighted upon a pleasure-garden owned by a certain nobleman named Jeta and accordingly known as the Jetavana or Jeta's Grove. On being asked to sell, however—perhaps half in jest, not really wanting to let the property go—Jeta named a preposterous price: the entire grove was to be covered with gold pieces. Anathapindika held Jeta to his price, however, and cartloads of gold pieces were brought; they covered all but a tiny space. Impressed by Anathapindika's piety, Jeta said, "Enough, do not cover that space. It shall be my gift." In due course another monastery was built here; and later, also near Shravasti, a third monastery: the Purvarama or Eastern Park. This was donated by a generous laywoman named Vishakha. When the Buddha settled permanently at Shravasti, he spent alternate rains retreats at the Jetavana and the Purvarama.

These generous bequests demonstrate how, from the very start, the *sangha* was supported by a sympathetic lay community. In return the Buddha gave discourses to lay people and, the general monastic bias of early Buddhism notwithstanding, certainly encouraged them to practice to as great an extent as they were able. His qualified *bhikshus* of course gave teachings too. This reciprocal relationship, which so clearly illustrates the Buddhist virtue of *dana* or giving, survives in many Buddhist countries to this day. Besides food and shelter, the laity may donate cloth for robes, medicines, and other requisites to the *sangha*.

It was only natural that the Buddha should one day pay a visit to his own people at Kapilavastu, and they for their part must have been very excited and curious to see this native son of theirs who had made such a great name for himself in the wider world. At Kapilavastu, he stayed with a large number of *bhikshus* at Nigrodha's Park and gave talks on *dharma,* which had the usual profound effect. Even his father, Shuddhodana, was established on the path, though the visit was not without its heartaches for Shuddhodana. For one thing, the proud old *kshatriya* nobleman was deeply offended when he saw his son going out on alms round (*pindapat*).

"No one in our family has ever lived by begging!" he protested.

"You belong to a noble line of kings," the Buddha replied "but I belong to the lineage of buddhas, and thousands of those have lived on alms food."

Then plans to simultaneously install the Buddha's half-brother, Nanda (Mahapajapati's son), as heir to the throne and marry him off as well were scotched at the last minute when the Buddha ordained him into the *sangha*. And to cap that, when his own son, Rahula, was sent along by Yashodhara to claim his inheritance, the Buddha simply turned to Shariputra and said: "Ordain him, Shariputra."

Quite understandably, Shuddhodana complained bitterly to the Buddha about these ordinations. The bonds that tie father to son run deep; the loss of a son is painful beyond measure, but he, Shuddhodana, had lost three sons: Siddhartha, Nanda, and now Rahula (who had become like a son after Siddhartha's departure). He suggested that ordinations should not take place in future without parents' consent. The Buddha agreed to this.

It is also possible that Ananda, the Buddha's cousin, who became his faithful personal attendant during the latter part of his life, was ordained about this time.

During the fifth year of the Buddha's ministry, Shuddhodana died, though happily as he was by then an *arhat,* a worthy one. Later, his widow, Mahapajapati, came to see the Buddha, who was again staying at Nigrodha's Park, and begged him to ordain her as a nun. She repeated her entreaty three times, but each time the Buddha refused it. Such was her commitment, however, that she cut off her hair, donned the yellow robe and followed him when he traveled on to Vaishali, the capital of the adjacent state of Videha. At Vaishali, when Ananda saw Mahapajapati and the other Shakyan ladies who had accompanied her, he was so moved by their tear-stained faces, dusty clothes and swollen feet that he spoke to the Buddha on their behalf. On being reminded of the motherly care that Mahapajapati had selflessly lavished upon him when he was a child, the Buddha very reluctantly agreed to ordain her, but only if she would agree to submit to eight very stringent rules, one of which was that a nun (*bhikshuni*) of one hundred years' seniority would still be junior to a *bhikshu* who had only been ordained that very day and must accord him deference. Mahapajapati gladly accepted these terms, so she was fully admitted into the *sangha;* the ladies with her were also admitted in due course. Afterwards, however, the Buddha lamented to Ananda that the admission of women would seriously weaken his *dharma:* it would now only last five hundred instead of one thousand years. This of course implies a certain prejudice against women, though it probably more closely reflects the prejudices current at that time and place than the Buddha's own views. After all, he had admitted to Ananda during their discussions about

Mahapajapati's admission that women possessed the same spiritual potential as men.

Another relative of the Buddha who later joined the *sangha* was Yashodhara, his ex-wife, the mother of Rahula. Indeed, it would appear from the records that she adopted an ascetic way of life from the time that the Buddha first left Kapilavastu.

The crowds that were drawn to hear Buddha's teachings and the enormous moral and material support that the early *sangha* attracted naturally aroused the jealousy of the other ascetic sects that existed in northern India at this time. The Buddha for his part never tried to win converts by demonstrations of low-grade magical tricks; in fact, he forbade the use of such gimmicks by his followers, though he did give a few remarkable demonstrations of paranormal powers himself when he felt that the particular situation justified them. He also never set out to poach devotees from other sects, as witness the case of the prominent Jain, Upali, who had asked to join the *sangha*. As Upali himself remarked, other religious leaders would have paraded him through the streets, boasting of having made an important convert, but the Buddha just urged him to think things over very carefully before transferring his loyalties.

But even though the Buddha himself always behaved according to the highest principles, there were others who were not so scrupulous and some were even prepared to resort to foul means to try to discredit both Buddha and *sangha*.

The Buddha's attitude to the orthodox *brahmana* priesthood was characterized by his usual tolerance and liberality. Sometimes *brahmana* came to him for advice or teaching. He did not believe that ritual sacrifices involving the slaughter of animals served any useful spiritual purpose whatsoever, and he did not conceal the fact. Sometimes he expressed the view that sacrifice should be interpreted figuratively—that the real sacrifice was a giving up of selfishness, or a giving of donations to the *sangha* and other ascetics. As regards Brahma and his fellow gods, goddesses, demigods, demons, and the other denizens of the Vedic pantheon, he did not so much deny their existence as hint more or less broadly that they were of little real importance.

(It should perhaps be noted by the way the modern Hindus do not regard the Buddha as an outsider to their tradition. In fact he is considered by them to be a manifestation of the great god Vishnu, one of the Hindu trinity, who descends into the world in various forms at particularly difficult times to help set things right. The Hindu system certainly derived much from Buddha's teaching, and indeed Buddhism, during the more than fifteen hundred years during which it was a significant part of the Indian spiritual scene, also derived much from

Hinduism. Buddhist Tantra, for instance, has a great deal in common with the Shiva-Shakti tradition of Hindu Tantra.)

The Buddha's problems were not solely from without, however. Quite early on the *sangha* was rocked by dissension when the *bhikshus* at Kaushambi grew litigious with each other over a minor infraction of the monastic rules. The Buddha himself counseled a forgiving line but, being ignored, withdrew to the Parileyyaka forest, where he was looked after by a lone bull elephant who, like himself, had retired into solitude to get away from the vexations of the herd. Eventually, the quarrelsome *bhikshus* at Kaushambi resolved their difficulties and harmony was restored.

Potentially more disastrous for the Buddha and the early *sangha* were the machinations of the Buddha's unpleasant cousin, Devadatta. At first Devadatta joined forces with Ajatashatru, the son of King Bimbisara of Magadha, in a double plot that involved the murder of both King Bimbisara and the Buddha as a prelude to the seizure of their respective roles and prerogatives. The plan misfired, however, so Devadatta resorted to various direct methods of dispatching the Buddha: he hurled boulders down onto him as he was preaching at Vulture Peak Mountain; and later he loosed a savage elephant in his path. Both stratagems of course failed utterly.

Finally, Devadatta managed to engineer an open schism and lured five hundred new *bhikshus* away. Maudgalyayana and Shariputra followed them, and Devadatta in his triumph thought that they had come to join his cause as well, so he invited them to sit down. He then embarked on a long discourse that lasted most of the night. When his back eventually began to pain him, he asked Shariputra to take over and settled down for a nap. Needless to say, Shariputra and his friend Maudgalyayana used this opportunity to advise the schismatic *bhikshus* of the error of their ways; they also preached true *dharma* to them. Therefore when Devadatta woke up he learned to his considerable chagrin that he had lost his following. Hot blood then gushed from his mouth, we are told.

Obviously Devadatta's crimes had piled up a great stock of black points in his karmic account, which he inexorably had to suffer out in the hell realms, where he languished until the end of the age. The Buddha himself proclaimed, however, that he would eventually regenerate spiritually and become a *buddha* himself, for eternal damnation is a concept unknown in Buddhism, where every being is ultimately destined for nirvana, even the most foul-hearted reprobate.

This forgiving aspect of Buddhism also comes out in the story of a desperado named Angulimala, or Finger Necklace. It was his habit to sever the fingers of his victims and wear them on a string around his neck, hence his gruesome nickname. One day down a lonely stretch of road he gave chase to the Buddha. However, he found that he simply could not catch up with Buddha. He therefore shouted, *"Hey! Stop, monk!,"* whereupon the Buddha replied, "But I have stopped, Angulimala. Isn't it time that you stopped too?" and went on to explain that he meant *stopped using violence.* This somehow touched a tiny residual spark of decency in Angulimala's black heart and, throwing away his sword, he begged to be allowed to become a follower of Buddha.

The story of Kisa Gautami, on the other hand, well illustrates the Buddha's sensitivity as a teacher. She turned up one day with a dead child in her arms and begged the Buddha for medicine to bring him back to life. The Buddha saw at once that she simply could not accept her child's death, so he told her, "Yes, I can help you. First you must bring me a mustard seed, but it must come from a house in which no death has ever taken place." Of course, Kisa Gautami searched all day but could not find such a house, so in the evening when she came back to the Buddha she learned a deep lesson. "I know now," she told him, "that I am not alone in my grief. Death is common to all people."

The Buddha's kindness also comes out very strongly in the incident of a *bhikshu* who was suffering from dysentery. The poor man was lying in his own mess with no one at all looking after him. The Buddha himself, assisted by Ananda, washed him and laid him out on a bed. Afterwards the Buddha admonished the other *bhikshus* there in terms very reminiscent of Jesus Christ:

"Bhikshus, you have neither mother nor father to look after you. If you do not look after each other, who will look after you? Let him who would look after me look after one who is sick."

The Buddha was also a skillful peacemaker. One day he settled a dispute between the Shakyas and the Kraudyas over water rights on the River Rohini. Tempers had apparently risen to such great heat by the time that he appeared on the scene that hardly anyone could remember the root cause of the quarrel. Then someone remembered: it was water.

"But how much is water worth?" asked the Buddha.

"Very little," came the reply.

"And how much are the lives of people worth?"

"They are beyond price."

In this way sense was made to prevail and the two armies which had been brought up were sent away.

On another occasion, the Buddha managed to dissuade King Ajatashatru of Magadha, King Bimbisara's son, from attacking a peaceful neighboring people called the Vrjis. At the same time he held up the enlightened social and political practices of the Vrjis as a model for the *sangha* if it was "to prosper and not decline."

This last incident took place in the final year of the Buddha's life, of which a comparatively detailed chronology exists. He was then about eighty and the long ministry of forty-five years had begun to take its toll. He still, however, wandered from one place to another, waited on by the faithful Ananda.

He apparently started out from Rajagraha and went to Venuyastika (Pali, Ambalatthika), and thence to Nalanda, where later a great Buddhist university was built. At Nalanda, Shariputra uttered a "lion's roar" and proclaimed that the Buddha was the greatest spiritual teacher ever—only to be admonished by the Buddha on the grounds that he really didn't have the necessary breadth of direct knowledge to be able to make such a sweeping statement. Then it was on to Pataligrama, where the Buddha foresaw the building of the great city of Pataliputra (modern Patna).

The Buddha and Ananda proceeded via Kutigramaka and Nadika to Vaishali, where they received alms food from the courtesan Ambapali, who also donated a park to the *sangha*. After that it was on to Beluva, where the Buddha planned to pass the rains retreat. Here, however, he was overtaken by "violent and deadly pains," but he suppressed these symptoms because it was not fitting that he should die without having taken proper leave of the *sangha*. Recovering temporarily, he spoke to Ananda, stressing that it was not his intention that the community should become dependent upon him personally. Each *bhikshu* should try to be as self-reliant as possible and when in need of guidance should turn to the *dharma*. He, the Buddha, had in fact taught them everything that they needed to know; there were no secret or esoteric dimensions; he had not maintained any "teacher's clenched fist." By the latter he was possibly referring to devious teachers who kept their students in a dependent state by withholding certain vital teachings.

The Buddha's next port of call was Shravasti, where he stayed at Jeta's grove. Here he heard of the death of Shariputra; Maudgalyayana died at about the same time. Addressing the *bhikshus* at Ukkacela shortly afterwards he used their passing as an object lesson in his teaching that everything that is born must die.

Shortly afterwards the Buddha was at Vaishali again. There, he and Ananda sat in the Capala Shrine after going out on alms rounds together. Now the Buddha hinted to Ananda that, if asked directly, it was possible for him to prolong his life more or less indefinitely. Ananda, however, failed to seize the opportunity—a slip for which he was later sternly reprimanded by the *sangha,* for the Buddha now let go of the will to live and the death process was set irreversibly in motion. Thus when Ananda did ask the Buddha to prolong his life, his request was greeted with a fateful, "Too late." This is certainly an apocryphal touch and does poor justice to Ananda, whom the Buddha himself praised as being exemplary in his devotion: "Your acts of love and kindness have been invariable and are beyond measure."

Having spent some time at Vaishali, the Buddha cast a last—sad?—look at the city and proceeded to Bhandagama. Thence he made his way to Papa by way of Hatthigama, Ambagama, Jambugama, and Bhoganagara, giving teachings as he went. It was at Papa that Cunda the smith gave him the meal that was to precipitate his final and fatal illness. Scholars have debated the precise nature of the dish—*sukaramaddava*—that poisoned him: minced pork has been suggested, also mushrooms. It caused sickness, bleeding, and great pain, but still the Buddha was able to set out with Ananda for Kushinagara, an insignificant wattle-and-daub village in the country of the Mallas. He managed to reach the outskirts of Kushinagara, but then his suffering became so intense that he had to lie down in a grove of *shala* trees.

The final scene has been encrusted with mythological accretions, and understandably so, for the Buddha was an exceptional person; but he was also very much a human being, not any kind of god or superman, so at the heart of it there is a very human and touching drama. Thus while the *shala* trees rain blossom even though it is out of season and the gods of the ten world-systems crowd round so densely that a hair could not be slipped between them, Ananda also goes away and weeps, and indeed there is a great grief in every sphere of existence, even among the animals, for a *buddha,* a fully enlightened one, is born into the world only very, very rarely. The local people also arrived in large numbers to pay their last respects, and even though he is nearing the end Buddha still carries on teaching. He agrees to see an ascetic named Subhadda—and converts him. And of course he gives advice to his *sangha.* Indeed his very last words are ones of advice and encouragement to them: "Impermanent are all created things. Strive on mindfully."

Then he passes into meditation and, having traversed the hierarchy of trance states, arrives at ultimate nirvana or Parinirvana. If the true nature of that which he discovered beneath the bodhi tree at Bodh Gaya some forty-five years before is a great mystery that cannot be conceived in conventional terms, how much more so this final fulfillment:

> *As a flame blown out by the wind*
> *Goes to rest and cannot be defined,*
> *So the wise man freed from individuality*
> *Goes to rest and cannot be defined.*
> *Gone beyond all images—*
> *Gone beyond the power of words.**

* *Sutta Nipata,* 1074, 1076, quoted in Thomson, *Life of the Buddha,* 22.

The Basic Teachings
and Practices

S·I·X

The Buddhist World View

Before we set out to explore the Buddha's teachings in detail, it is important to get a clear picture of his view of the world. By "world" we do not merely mean the physical world, but the psychological and spiritual worlds as well, which in traditional Buddhist cosmology are regarded as interlocking.

The Buddhist view of the material world has been decisively superseded by that which modern science with its more sophisticated methododology has given us. What is really of interest here, therefore, are the spiritual and psychological aspects, and the underlying outlook.

In Buddhist cosmology, innumerable world-systems similar to our own are thought to float in infinite empty space, each one founded on a two-layered basis of air and water. Each world-system can be divided into three main realms: *Kamadhatu,* the realm of desire; *Rupadhatu,* the realm of form; and *Arupadhatu,* the realm of no-form.

Within this three-tier system there are broadly six "destinations," two good and four bad, into which it is possible for beings to enter. These are the realms of the gods (*devas*), of humans, of animals (including birds, fish, reptiles, insects, etc.), of titans (*asuras*), of hungry ghosts (*pretas*), and various hell realms. The *pretas* or hungry ghosts are disembodied spirits, who are often shown in Buddhist pictures as having hugely bloated bellies and tiny mouth-openings, signifying their enormous and utterly insatiable desires.

At the core of each world-system rises the massive bulk of Mount Meru, the axial mountain, from which seven concentric ranges of golden

mountains radiate outwards, each separated from the next by an inter-
vening sea. Between the last range and the outer boundary wall of iron
mountains (*Chakravala*), there is a great ocean in which four great continents are situated, one at each of the cardinal points of the compass.
These are the abodes of human beings and the southern continent,
Jambudvipa, is clearly identical with India as we know it. Later Buddhist
cosmologists moved the four great continents closer to Meru, probably
so that people should not be exiled so far away from the vital center.

In the human sphere there are periods of progress and decay. Virtue
advances and declines, and life expectancy can vary from eighty thousand
years at the beginning of an age (*kalpa*) down to ten years at the end of
one. Of all the ages into which one might be born, the most fortunate is
a *Bhadra Kalpa*. No less than one thousand buddhas will appear during the
three hundred and twenty million years of such an age; each will redis-
cover the *dharma,* teach it, and the way will remain fully open for a time
(five hundred, one thousand, or five thousand years); then a period of
decline will set in and finally a dark age will descend when the teaching,
hopelessly undermined by corruption, is lost completely. The doors to the
deathless realm then remain closed until another *buddha* appears on the
scene to open them again. We currently live in a *Bhadra Kalpa,* Shakyamuni
Buddha being the *buddha* of our time, though we would appear to be in
the second kind of phase, when the *dharma* is in decline. The *buddha* of
the previous age was Dipamkara and the next *buddha* will be Maitreya.

Mount Meru was thought to rise to a mind-boggling height above the
terrestrial zone and to penetrate to the even greater depth beneath it.
Down in the bowels of this subterranean world various hot and cold
hells are disposed in tiers, rather as in Dante's *Inferno,* the lowest and
hottest being the *Avici* hell. The torments of the Buddhist hells equal if
not exceed any- thing conceived by Hieronymous Bosch and other Western infernologists. The human imagination seems to become unusually
inspired when it comes to devising extreme forms of horror and tor-
ment, and the early Buddhists were no exception. In Buddhism there
is no such thing as eternal damnation, so sojourns in any of the hells,
though possibly extremely long, are not forever.

Above the hell realms, at the tope of the subterranean zone, are to be
found the caves in which the titans or *asuras* dwell. They are the "old
gods": inflated, hot-tempered, and congenitally prone to jealousy. Periodically they sally out of their dark labyrinths to join battle with the
gods (*devas*) who inhabit the upper portions of Meru, the cause of their
ongoing feud being the Great Wish-fullfilling Tree that grows half-way
up the mountain.

The first three of the four upper terraces on Mount Meru are inhabited by different kinds of powerful spirits known as *yakshas*. On the

fourth dwell the Four Great Kings, the guardians of the four quarters, who rank as gods. They keep a watch over goings-on below on earth and send in periodic reports to the superior gods who live above them on the summit, who rejoice or lament accordingly.

The realm of the superior gods, who are headed by Shakra, is called the Heaven of the Thirty-Three (Trayastrimshas) and among its delightful features are a beautiful city of palaces and jewelled parks called Sudarshana. Every kind of pleasure and luxury is at the disposal of the gods who live here; in particular they enjoy the services of heavenly nymphs (*apsarases*), who are highly skilled in the arts of love and music. The lives of the gods are exceedingly long—reputedly one thousand years, and each day is equal to one hundred human years. The bitter pill, however, is that the day will inexorably dawn when the floral garlands they wear begin to wither and their bodies give off an odor that makes them unattractive to their fun-loving consorts. Then they know that they are about to die and be recycled through the other realms of existence.

Above the summit of Meru there are four aerial heavens. These, with the lower realms already described, together make up the sphere of desire, which is only the first of the three tiers that comprise a Buddhist world-system. The other two tiers, the sphere of form and the sphere of no-form, which are again sub-divided into various hierarchical levels, rise overhead. These give the key to the whole system, for they are clearly models of graded states of psycho-spiritual experience. As such they would have been explored by yogis engaged in meditation practice and all except the topmost five correspond to the various *dhyanas* (Pali, *jhanas*) or trance states. It was these that the Buddha explored with Alara Kalama and Udraka Ramaputra. Again, existence (if it can be called that) in these increasingly rarefied states, though stupendously long, is nevertheless still of limited duration.

Each world-system is subject to cycles of development and decay and is moreover periodically destroyed, either partially or totally, by fire, wind, or water, then recreated. Images of massive cosmic cataclysm occur in Buddhist literature:

> Worlds clash with worlds, Himalaya Mountains with Himalaya Mountains, and Mount Sinerus with Mount Sinerus, until they have ground each other to powder and perished.*

The Buddhist world view therefore comprises a mind-boggling range of possible literal and psychological states, most of them fraught with more or less terrible forms of suffering, in a universe of equally mind-boggling spatial and temporal dimensions. All is in a constant state of flux

* H. C. Warren, *Buddhism in Translations* (Cambridge, Mass., 1896).

and every now and then undergoes more or less catastrophic convulsions. Merely to be born in this system is very bad news, for the beings that are embroiled in it cannot escape, not even into Keats' "easeful death," for they are subject to continual rebirth through beginningless and endless time. If the bones of all the bodies that a person's consciousness-continuum has inhabited during one age alone were piled up, they would form a cairn higher than Vulture Peak Mountain, where the Buddha taught. All the tears of sorrow that have been shed during the long journey would exceed the waters of the four oceans; and the same might be said of all the mothers' milk that has been drunk.

Nor are all these endless rounds of rebirth confined to one destination alone. It is quite possible, if one has accumulated the necessary bad karma, to regress from, say, the human realm to that of the animals, or even to become a hungry ghost or a denizen of one of the hells. On the other hand, the best that can be hoped for is to sojourn for a few aeons in some relatively peaceful or blissful state. In particular, by long practice of spiritual disciplines, one might be able to project oneself into the *deva* realms, the realms of the gods. But long though one's stay there might be, it is still a mixed blessing, for sooner or later one is certain to be rudely snatched away and recycled through the system, undergoing all the pangs of severence and insecurity in the process, often (usually?) with other more or less extreme forms of suffering thrown in as well. In Buddhist terminology, this is *samsara,* the churning sea of cyclic existence in which beings are ceaselessly thrown about like tide-wrack.

But now for the good news: there is an exit. This is precisely what the Buddha discovered as he sat beneath the bodhi tree on the night of the full moon of May—or rather *re*-discovered, for other buddhas had blazed that particular trail before him. As we saw, he had previously mastered the *dhyanas* (absorbtions), but he saw that they merely led to temporary godlike forms of existence. What he discovered was a way out of the system, one that led to permanent liberation, not just to a temporary resting place.

The nature of that escape and the method by which it may be achieved will be dealt with later, but it is important to note at this stage that it is only possible from one of the destinations in a world-system: that of human beings. The gods in their way are as much trapped in the system as the damned, the *asuras,* the *pretas,* and the animals. Men and women do, however, have a chance of meeting with the teachings of a buddha, studying and practicing them, and thereby achieving release.

The human realm is therefore the center of the action. It is the stage upon which the spotlights are trained and upon which all eyes are concentrated. The performers come on and play their parts. Afterwards, according to how they have done, they are led off to other destinations. Some will be taken up to join the gods in the boxes, galleries, and stalls. Many will be cast into the orchestra pit, or dragged down into the grim labyrinths beneath the stage. A few, however, will go into the wings to make new entrances, and one or two will so refine their performances by dint of the practice of virtue and spiritual discipline that they reach buddhahood. Then the gods in the topmost galleries, break into rapturous applause, for something truly marvelous has happened—something that is not really a personal achievement so much as a great step forward for the totality.

To illustrate the priceless value of human birth, the Buddha told a story about a one-eyed turtle swimming in a great ocean. Floating on the surface of the ocean is a golden yoke. The turtle comes up for air once every hundred years. The possibility of achieving a human birth after having fallen into the lower destinations is statistically less probable than that the turtle should rise to the surface of the ocean and put its neck cleanly through the yoke.

What are we to make of all this? Is it merely the product of dark and superstitious minds that we, children of a more "advanced" age illuminated by the light of modern science, might safely cast away?

It is very hard to say, for there is much here that, unless we have the paranormal vision of a *buddha,* we cannot know directly. That having been said, many people find that the notion of being caught up in vast cycles of painful coming-into-being and ceasing-to-be across untold aeons evokes a psychological resonance. On reflection, perhaps this should not surprise us, for it has taken the evolutionary process millions of years to create human beings and we carry in our genes the imprint of all the struggles that organic life has undergone in the process. We have in a sense known the agony of the first fish to take to dry land; we have died with the lemmings; we have struggled to get up from four feet onto two; we have preyed and been preyed upon, struggled and failed, and succeeded too—but the weariness! And within our present lives, have we not all experienced innumerable forms of suffering: loss of fortune, separation from loved ones, sickness, failure, betrayal, disillusionment, confusion? Perhaps too, at moments of extreme distress, we have known what it is to be in hell. Pleasure there has been too, happiness and other good things, but we know they do not last and that really there is no safe resting place, no lasting haven of security.

The idea, then, of bringing the whole painful and wearying business to a proper conclusion in a nirvana that represents both the full flowering of the potentials of consciousness and ultimate unalloyed peace—this seems to those who have gravitated to the Buddhist path to be as convincing a goal as any offered, and one that lends true meaning and purpose to life.

S·E·V·E·N

The Basic Teachings
and Practices

Buddhism is not a fundamentalist religion. Its teachings are not dogmas or articles of faith that have to be blindly accepted at the cost of suspending reason, critical judgment, common sense, or experience. Quite the contrary, in fact; their basic aim is to help us gain direct insight into the truth for ourselves. We are therefore invited to try these teachings out in our everyday lives. If they work, then we will naturally want to take them on board. If they don't work for us, then we can cast them aside with no qualms.

The nature of the direct experiential knowledge towards which the Buddhist teachings point came out very well many years ago in the interview that John Freeman made with C. G. Jung on the "Face to Face" series on BBC Television. Freeman asked Jung directly if he believed in God. Jung balked a little. "The word believe is difficult for me," he explained. "You see—I *know*." In short, knowledge is direct first-hand experience about which there can be no argument. Belief, on the other hand, arises when you have to take someone else's word for something about which, quite frankly, you know nothing. Of course, knowing may at times imply knowing that one does not know.

THE FOUR NOBLE TRUTHS (*ARYA-SATYA*; PALI, *ARIYA-SATTA*)

Buddhism does not take its starting-point on grand metaphysical questions like *Who made the world?*; *What is the meaning of Life?*; and *What happens to us after death?* It is not concerned with proving the existence of a God or gods. Rather its root focus is on the down-to-earth fact that all existence, including human existence, is imperfect in a very deep way. "Suffering I teach—and the way out of suffering," the Buddha declared.

The Buddha's teaching on this is set out in the doctrine of the Four Noble Truths, which, along with the principle of the Middle Way, was the subject-matter of the first sermon that he preached to his original core of disciples in the Deer Park at Isipatana. It follows a medical pattern: a disease is identified, its cause diagnosed, a remedy is declared to exist, and then that remedy is prescribed:

1. *Duhkha* (Pali, *dukkha*) exists.

2. *Duhkha* has an identifiable cause.

3. That cause may be terminated.

4. The means by which that cause may be terminated.

The Sanskrit term *duhkha* (Pali, *dukkha*) is traditionally translated into English as "suffering" but, though it certainly includes this concept, it possesses a wide spectrum of connotations besides. At one extreme it takes in the most dire forms of mental and physical pain: the agonies of cancer, for instance, and anguish of someone who falls prey to total despair. It covers our everyday aches and pains, our petty dislikes and frustrations too; and it extends to very subtle feelings of malaise: that life is never quite right.

Notice, however, that the Buddha is not saying here that there is only *duhkha*, or the dark side of life. He certainly does not deny that there is a light side: *sukha*, consisting of pleasure, happiness, etc. He stresses *duhkha* because it is problematical, whereas *sukha* is not. At the same time, there is no such thing as perfect, unalloyed happiness or pleasure. Even the most beautiful experience has a melancholy undertone simply because we know that it can't last. So *duhkha* touches everything that exists.

Strangely, however, there is something in us that staunchly resists facing the dark side of life. We have a dogged determination to continue in pursuit of worldly satisfactions even though enormous discouragements are put in our way. Our feeling is that, with a few modifications and adjustments here and there, we can overcome our problems, realize all our dreams and enjoy heaven on earth. Bad times are always provisional and sooner or later we're going to get over the hump and then it'll be downhill all the way.

In a way this shows spirit and could be regarded as entirely commendable—except that there's a quality of willful blindness about it: a refusal to squarely face the true facts of the human condition. The results of this can also be very destructive. How many times have we hurt ourselves and others in the crass pursuit of our own fantasies? Good things do come to us in the course of events and should be accepted and enjoyed while they last, but we tend to want *only* the good and, resisting all else, pursue it exclusively and cling to it desperately if we do get it.

So the beginning of the road to wisdom begins with a realistic (not pessimistic) recognition of the fact of *duhkha*. Life usually has to have bitten us quite deeply, and often many times over, before we reach this stage. But when we do reach it, we have in a very real sense come of age as human beings, for an immature, butterfly existence in pursuit of mere happiness is unsatisfying in the final analysis. When we face up to the dark side of life, on the other hand, we begin to appreciate the full grandeur and challenge of human existence. Now too we can start to do something about changing our lives and putting them on a deeper, more authentic footing.

The second noble truth informs us that *duhkha* has an identifiable cause. This is *trishna* (Pali, *tanha*) which is literally translated as "thirst," but in fact possesses the same kind of spectrum of connotations as *duhkha*. There are gross forms of *trishna,* like obsessive lust for money and sensual pleasures; and there are exceedingly subtle forms, like a desire to do good or to know the truth. And of course there is a whole gamut of middling connotations in between.

Basically *trishna* can be reduced to a fundamental ache that is implanted in everything that exists: a gnawing dissatisfaction with what is and a concomitant reaching out for something else. So we can never be at rest but are always grasping for something outside ourselves. This is what powers the endless cycle-wheeling motion of the Wheel of Life, driving us on from one moment to the next, one life to the next. Here too resides our native clinging to existence.

Trishna is not an aberration. It is entirely natural. But if we want to get off the Wheel of Life and thereby liberate ourselves from *duhkha,* we must do something about it. This brings us to the third noble truth. This tells us that there is a method: a way or path that can be traveled to ultimate freedom.

Freedom from *trishna* is known in Pali as nibbana, the Sanskrit equivalent of which, nirvana, has now entered English parlance. There are two kinds of nirvana:

1. That which has a residual basis
2. That which has no residual basis

The first arose in Shakyamuni Buddha as he sat beneath the bodhi tree at Bodh Gaya on the fateful night of the full moon of May; the second arose when he finally passed away at Kushinagara. In the first case a living being continued to pursue an earthly life; in the second, there was complete extinction (Parinirvana): nothing tangible remained behind.

What is nirvana? Invariably it is stressed that it cannot be grasped via sense experience or by the mind operating in terms of its usual conceptual categories. And it certainly cannot be described in words. To do so would be like trying to describe the color red to a blind person. As it lies wholly outside our normal field of experience, we can and must come to it through direct insight, and this indeed is basically what the Buddha's way is all about. However, bearing in mind that any description must be more or less inaccurate, a few tentative pointers may be given to guide us in the right general direction. The word nirvana itself possesses connotations of blowing out or extinguishing, as a flame may be blown out or extinguished once the fuel that feeds it has been exhausted. It is cool and peaceful. *Duhkha* doesn't touch it, nor the passions of greed, hatred, and ignorance. In the Buddha's own words:

> Monks, there is an unborn, unoriginated, unmade and unconditioned. Were there not the unborn, unoriginated, unmade and unconditioned, there would be no escape from the born, originated, made and conditioned. Since there is the unborn, unoriginated, unmade and unconditioned, there is escape from the born, originated, made and conditioned.*

Finally, even though nirvana is usually described in negative terms— it is obviously easier to say what it is *not* than what it *is*—it is nevertheless lavishly praised in the Buddhist scriptures as amounting to supreme bliss, no less.

At once, of course, the mind starts to create speculative pictures, and stumbles into mistaken views. One classic misconception is to see nirvana as some kind of nothingness. This is to fall prey to the mistaken view of annihilationism (complete non-existence), which is twinned with

* *Udana*, VIII, 3.

the equally mistaken view of eternalism (that something may exist forever). Nirvana lies beyond both existence and non-existence. Another
misconception is to imagine nirvana as a heaven where all good Buddhists go. It is definitely not a place, nor is it "somewhere else."
Paradoxically, though unconditioned itself, it only arises amid worldly
conditions, and in the case of human beings, within the human body:

> In this fathom-long body, with all its perceptions and thoughts, do
> I proclaim the world, the origin of the world, the cessation of the
> world and the path leading to the cessation of the world.*

The fourth noble truth defines this path to liberation by telling us what
practical steps we have to take in order to root out *trishna* and thereby
create the fertile ground in which nirvana may arise. These steps are laid
out in the teaching of the Noble Eightfold Path.

THE NOBLE EIGHTFOLD PATH (*ASHTANGIKA-MARGA;* PALI, *ATTHANGIKA-MAGGA*)

1. Right understanding	(*samyag-dristhi;* Pali, *samma-ditthi*)
2. Right thought	(*samyag-samkalpa;* Pali, *samma-sankappa*)
3. Right speech	(*samyag-vach;* Pali, *samma-vacha*)
4. Right action	(*samyak-karmanta;* Pali, *samma-kammanta*)
5. Right livelihood	(*samyag-ajiva;* Pali, *samma-ajiva*)
6. Right effort	(*samyag-vyayama;* Pali, *samma-yayama*)
7. Right mindfulness	(*samyak-smriti;* Pali, *samma-sati*)
8. Right concentration	(*samyak-samadhi;* Pali, *samma-samadhi*)

The path can be further subdivided into three main elements: wisdom, morality, and meditation.

Although this kind of numerical, hierarchic structure—which was very
much the traditional Indian way of presenting teachings—gives the im-
pression that every step must be approached in due sequence, the three
main elements of wisdom, morality, and meditation in practice need to
be developed together. Without meditation, wisdom remains hollow
and theoretical; at the same time, the insights that arise in meditation
need the informed understanding of wisdom or else they may not be
recognized for what they are. T. S. Eliot talks in the "Dry Salvages"

*Anguttara Nikaya, II, 46.

section of his *Four Quartets* of having "had the experience but missed the meaning." Also, it will be virtually impossible to practice the path without the moral basis.

WISDOM (*PRAJÑA;* PALI, *PAÑÑA*)

The wisdom element features in *right understanding,* which implies the obvious, but perhaps often missed, point that in order to practice we need to have heard (or read) the Buddha's teachings, notably that of the four noble truths, and have not merely understood them theoretically but have actively penetrated their truth by testing them against experience. Our wish to pursue the Buddha's way is therefore founded on informed confidence in the soundness of the teachings rather than on blind faith or misguided attraction to its superficial aspects.

Right thought on the other hand, must include correct motivation. We need to realize that we are practicing, not to acquire greater powers and more possessions for ourselves, but rather to move away from the basic egocentric orientation to a new, wider, more selfless one. In short: there is in the final analysis no pay-off for "me" in practicing Buddhism. That having been said, it has to be admitted that none of us have perfect understanding and motivation at the start. As we continue, however, practice will tend to uncover all sorts of blind spots and subtle forms of self-centeredness. The Buddha's way is an ever-deepening learning process.

An actual change in our thinking processes must begin to take place too. The unreformed (i.e., selfish) mind, like a mill in perpetual motion, is constantly devising plans, plots, and strategies for advancing its own cause, outflanking rivals and undoing enemies. Or else it indulges itself in egoistic or hedonistic fantasies. *Right thought* is about switching over to other- directed mental modes: ones that are more altruistic and benign. We should also become increasingly concerned to act responsibly towards the environment. We think too of religious questions with a view, not to promoting ourselves as *gurus* or pundits, but in order to be of better service to the world.

MORALITY (*SHILA;* PALI, *SILA*)

Buddhist ethics are not codified into a rigid moral code; nor are they about making judgments and arousing sin and guilt, though every willed action produces consequences, as we shall see in greater detail when we examine the concept of *karma.* Rather, Buddhists try to be aware of any particular failing to live up to an ethical principle and resolve to do better next time. They also note in such cases that they have still a long way to go towards finally overcoming their faults, which breeds a healthy humility. There have always been in every religion those self-righteous people who refuse to recognize their own faults but instead nurse delusions of moral superiority. We all fall into these traps at times. Christianity has its "whited sepulchers" who praise the Lord that they are not sinful like other men; Buddhism has its "whited stupas" too. Clearly honesty and keen mindfulness of one's actions are of the essence as a foil to these snares.

Right speech, the third item on the path, is about not telling lies, slandering and backbiting, swearing and using "harsh" language, wasting one's own and other peoples' time with frivolous chatter, and generally not using one's speech faculties in harmful or unproductive ways. It is also about being truthful. This is in fact very important, especially as our modern Western culture has debased truth and facts are wantonly suppressed or twisted to suit self-interest or in order to generate sensation.

Right action, on the other hand, is about decent behavior generally. A lay person may, as a token of their commitment to the Buddha's way, subscribe to Five Precepts—*Pañcha Shila*—and accordingly undertake to train him/herself to:

1. Refrain from taking life.
2. Refrain from taking that which is not given.
3. Refrain from misuse of the senses.
4. Refrain from telling lies.
5. Refrain from self-intoxication with drink and drugs.

Taking life not only includes the murder of human beings, of course, but killing other living beings as well. This inevitably raises the question of whether meat-eating is permissible or not in Buddhism. The members of the original *sangha* were mendicants and as such were supposed to accept whatever food they were given. Thus it was technically permissible for them to eat meat, but only if they knew that an animal, bird, or fish had not been killed specially to provide them with food. Many find this rather permissive attitude unsatisfactory, for to eat meat is in a sense to connive at slaughter, albeit after the event. Later, when the Mahayana developed, strong calls for total vegetarianism were put out.

Under "taking that which is not given" comes stealing and all manner of allied practices whereby money or property, or even more intangible things, are immorally appropriated.

Misuse of the senses embraces a spectrum of vices. There is over-indulgence in food, which not only causes the rich and powerful to gorge themselves at the expense of the underprivileged—in its global aspect, this results in the appalling malnutrition suffered in the third world—but also leads to disease and torpor. The serious Buddhist practitioner is generally encouraged to moderate consumption if only in the interests of maintaining energy and alertness. Strictly observant Theravada Buddhist monks (*bhikkhus*) eat only one meal a day and that before noon.

Then there is glutting the eye with beautiful sights and the ear with beautiful sounds, all of which can become highly addictive as well as unconducive to practice. Similarly, as the mind is also a sense organ in the Buddhist view, one can overindulge in intellectual pastimes with similarly negative results. And, of course, one can abuse the body, both one's own and others', for selfish pleasure.

This brings us to the ever-interesting topic of sex, a matter that generally comes in for a bad press in early Buddhism. As a primary generator of passion, it was considered extremely dangerous by the Buddha. At first he made no training rule about it for his *sangha* but when one of his monks, Sudinna, slept with his former wife in order to satisfy his family's heartfelt wish for an heir, the Buddha dressed him down in no uncertain terms: "Misguided man, it were better for you that your member should enter the mouth of a hideous, venomous viper or cobra than that it should enter a woman," and he went on to make a training rule that those in the *sangha* should henceforth totally refrain from sexual intercourse.

In modern Europe celibacy has become highly unpopular, and those who gravitate to it are popularly thought to be likely candidates for neurosis, or worse. Sigmund Freud and his psychoanalytic school, though in many ways their work was helpful, are much to blame for this, for they did help to instill the notion in the popular mind that regular discharge of the sexual function is essential to mental and physical well-being. Actually, misguided indulgence and overindulgence in sex are as likely to lead to psychological problems as non-indulgence. Celibacy is, in fact, a very healthy state if sexuality, though not expressed, is clearly recognized. It certainly helps to simplify life, and, by freeing a person from the very large energy- and time-consuming duties of supporting and bringing up children, affords them the opportunity of devoting themselves wholeheartedly to spiritual practice.

Lay people, however, are not expected to be strictly celibate, but still their sexual activity should be contained within reasonable constraints. Of course, the vast panorama of sexual diversions that have developed in recent years did not exist in the Buddha's day. He merely had to contend with pretty tame things like adultery and prostitution. We can, however, infer certain basic principles that should be observed: we should firstly try not to hurt others; and secondly we should try to be moderate, for immoderate indulgence of sexual desire will only serve to feed the fires of passion and attachment, which cuts completely contrary to the direction and spirit of the Buddha's way.

The precept to refrain from intoxicating oneself with drink and drugs was formulated because these dull our perceptions and sensitivities. People use them to escape, if only fleetingly, from themselves and from the world. Buddhist training, on the other hand, is directed towards increasing clarity and awareness of what is happening both within and without; it is also very much about facing the world as it is and developing the strength to deal squarely with it using one's own resources.

Novice monks and nuns observe all these precepts and five more besides: refraining from eating more than one meal and that before noon, from attending worldly shows and entertainments, from using perfumes and adornments, from sleeping on a high or luxurious bed, and from possessing money (including gold and silver). Fully-fledged monks observe two hundred and twenty-seven precepts.

Application of the next item on the Eightfold Path, *right livelihood,* has become especially difficult today. In the Buddha's time there were butchers, traffickers in poisons, weapons, and intoxicants, and a few other dubious types, but these were few compared with the legions that contemporary Western society entertains, and often applauds. In our pragmatic society, inspired as it is by commercial advantage rather than ideals or ethics, almost anything goes so long as it makes a fast buck. The fundamental principle at play in *right livelihood* is the classic Indian virtue of *ahimsa:* harmlessness. The serious Buddhist does not wish to compromise his integrity by becoming involved in any activity that is going to cause harm to other people, animals, or the environment, or even outer space. Rather, he/she will wish to use his productive energies in ways that at least cause no harm and hopefully do some good. Such an attitude is not only virtuous and beneficial in itself, but serious Buddhist practice itself becomes impossible if one is caught up in the ramifications, mental, emotional, and/or practical, of corruption of any kind. To be an effective Buddhist, one needs that space and calmness that can only come from being on reasonably good terms with oneself and with the world at large.

Even though it extols gentleness and patience in practice, Buddhism makes it clear that some energy has to be put out too. This brings us to the sixth item on the Eightfold Path: *right effort.* Again, the word "right" is important here, indicating that energy too should be strictly regulated. Too much can be as counterproductive as too little. Also it is not goal-directed energy in the usual sense. One is not trying to obtain anything. As the Ven. (Ven.) Ajahn Chah has said:

> Proper effort is not the effort to make something particular happen.

It is the effort to be aware and awake in each moment, the effort to overcome laziness and defilement, the effort to make each activity of our day meditation.*

MEDITATION (*SAMADHI*)

The seventh and eighth items on the Eightfold Path, *right mindfulness* and *right concentration,* bring us fully into the sphere of meditation. Meditation is the specialized activity that helps us to fully realize the Buddha's teachings, to make them an integral part of our being rather than just a new set of ideas to be entertained theoretically in the mind. It weans us away from our usual habit patterns, particularly our involvement with our thoughts and their emotional sub-themes. At the same time it sharpens and intensifies our powers of direct perception: it gives us eyes to see into the true nature of things. The field of research is ourselves, and for this reason the laser of attention is turned and focused inwards.

Meditation is not something to be toyed with lightly. It involves opening up the psyche and operating with it at depth. Problems, more or less difficult to handle, may arise. Therefore, to begin with at least, it should always be approached in conducive circumstances and with the guidance of an experienced and qualified teacher. The right motivation must also be present. It is a misapplication of meditation to use it to obtain personal benefits like "mind power" or "peak experiences." It is also generally unwise to dabble with it from books. What is offered here is therefore general orientational information for further research, not instructions for experimentation.

The classic Buddhist meditation posture is a cross-legged one, with one leg laid on top of the other (single lotus) or the two legs interwoven (double lotus). Alternatively, if either of these options give pain, an upright chair may be used. The important thing is that the back should be straight and unsupported, and lightly balanced on the pelvis. The head should be squarely balanced on an upright neck. The eyelids are lowered, and the mouth is lightly closed. The hands are laid one above the other in the lap, thumb-tip to thumb-tip, or lightly clasped. There are also forms of walking meditation, and one can even, in extreme circumstances, meditate lying down, though as there is always the danger of falling asleep in the horizontal position, it is not recommended.

* Jack Kornfield and Paul Breiter, eds. and comps., *A Still Forest Pool: The Insight Meditation of Achaan Chah* (Wheaton, Ill.: Theosophical Publishing House, 1985), 51.

Firstly, all personal problems and preoccupations are laid aside; then specialized techniques are brought into play. In basic Buddhist meditation, two elements are usually identified:

1. *Shamatha* (Pali, *Samatha*)—literally "calm abiding."
2. *Vipashyana* (Pali, *Vipassana*)—insight.

In *shamatha,* concentration (*samadhi*) is brought to bear on a single object to the exclusion of all else. It may be the breath, or a colored disc, or the sensations of the body. Many suitable objects are enumerated in the traditional texts; the important thing is that they should be neutral, unexciting, and unevocative. If the breath is used, no attempt should be made to alter it: to make it deeper or more rhythmic; it serves merely as a focus for concentration.

Things rarely go swimmingly in meditation, especially at first. Attention slips and the mind wanders away on beguiling trains of thought and fantasy. When this happens, the fact should be noted and the attention returned to the object of concentration. It will probably have to be brought back time and time and time again. The most important thing is not to set ambitious goals or strive for results—that is more likely to frustrate rather than hasten the development of concentration—but to simply perform the practice patiently and aim first and foremost at remaining aware of what is going on in the now. Sometimes the mind is in turmoil throughout a meditation session and cannot develop any degree of concentration; the practice then is to remain fully mindful of this.

As concentration develops, the mind becomes increasingly tranquil. There are traditionally said to be eight *dhyanas* (Pali, *jhanas*) or absorptions through which the virtuoso *shamatha* practitioner may progress. These are increasingly refined or subtle states of consciousness. As delightful states, the *dhyanas* correspond to the happy realms of the gods and their divine companions, but they are also strictly temporary abodes and do not in any case amount to enlightenment. They also present a special danger: the meditator may become addicted and not want to leave them. The Buddha was enabled to reach the *dhyanas* under the guidance of his Hindu teachers, but he found them unsatisfying, hence his search for something else. He finally found what he was looking for by means of *vipashyana.* However, interesting though it might be to explore these little known reaches of inner space, in modern Western situations, few living outside monastic communities have the time for doing so. Therefore, *shamatha* meditation is usually practiced briefly in the initial stages of a lay meditation session in order to establish a workable degree of mental calm and concentration in preparation for *vipashyana.*

In *vipashyana,* the mind is opened and awareness is directed to all that enters its sphere. Often at first a great deal of hitherto submerged psychological material arises into consciousness. This is a very positive process; the darkness is becoming conscious. Old fears and phobias, traumas and repressions can now be hospitably entertained in full awareness. The meditator is neutral towards them, neither rejecting nor repressing—nor, on the other hand, identifying and hence becoming carried away by them. If merely treated to "bare attention," they will pass away. This is a very real and effective form of psychotherapy.

Later, as the mind quietens down, attention may be directed in a more systematic way. Traditionally there are said to be four foundations of mindfulness:

1. Bodily activity

2. Feelings

3. States of mind

4. Mental contents

Again, whatever enters the field of attention is observed and analyzed. Invariably it will be found to be subject to three conditions or marks.

THE THREE MARKS OF EXISTENCE

1. *Duhkha* (Pali, *dukkha*)—unsatisfactoriness

2. *Anitya* (Pali, *anicca*)—impermanence

3. *Anatman* (Pali, *anatta*)—not self

We have already looked closely at *duhkha,* the flawed nature of all that exists: its inability to give lasting satisfaction or provide us with an unshakable basis of stability and security. *Anitya,* on the other hand, points to the observable fact that the world is a flux; nothing ever stays the same for long and ultimately everything is unstoppably headed—though admittedly at different comparative rates of speed—towards dissolution. *What about the Buddha's way, surely that is exempt?* we may protest. Unfortunately, as the Buddha himself foresaw, even the *dharma* itself is subject to change and degeneration.

The third of the marks of existence, *anatman,* points to perhaps the most profound discovery that can be made in meditation: that, search as hard as we will, we can never point to anything in ourselves that we can definitely say is the self. Neither the body, nor the thoughts, nor the feelings can be self, for they are *duhkha* and *anitya,* unsatisfactory and impermanent. All this we can observe, while the observer, the one who knows, remains ever elusive, standing outside the field of sense perception, outside the world.

To sit in meditation, dredging the depths of the mind for the one who is looking, the one who sees and knows, is rather like searching for a salmon in the deep, dark-green pool of an old river. We know that the great fish is down there; we sometimes think we see his cold eye looking up at us, or the flicker of his shadow on the silt bed, or the flash of his underbelly as he glides away to a deeper, darker place; but in the end he always eludes us—always remains a great mystery. This is *anatman*.

THE EGO OR "I"

If a person called Jill begins to analyze herself, looking for the core in which her Jillness resides, she will find a pattern of ever-changing phenomena—body, emotions, sensations, ideas, etc.—but none of these could be said to be the essential, eternal, and unchanging Jill. But even if in deep meditation Jill can find no solid basis for her idea of herself as a separate individual, the idea of "Jill" still works in terms of the common-sense conventions of the everyday world. Her friends and workmates will call her Jill, and both they and she will know what is meant when she uses the words "I" and "me." In fact Jill needs a reasonably steady "I" or ego in order to be able to function effectively in this world. It is a necessary stage of development.

We erect the idea of "I" as a central reference point around which the world appears to revolve. This is by definition an egocentric view and unavoidably leads to selfishness and all its attendant evils. The world also neatly divides in two: there is the sphere of "I" and the sphere of not-"I." "I," which is really just a more or less unstable fiction anyway, is usually fighting a losing battle to hold its own against not-"I" (i.e., the rest of the world), and this inevitably leads to suffering. "I" can't hold its own for ever, or indeed for long.

The Buddha's way points to a development that leads beyond "I" to wider and larger horizons. It unlocks the door of the cell of individuality and offers freedom, nirvana.

OTHER ASPECTS OF MEDITATION

Through *vipashyana* meditation, the mind arrives at the understanding that "everything that arises passes away and is not self," which is what *buddhas* know. But this, as we have already indicated, is not merely a negative insight: the discovery of a pure nothingness. Nor is it the uncovering of a mysterious "something." It is nirvana—ineffable, infinitely subtle, fleetingly glimpsed at first but returned to again and again until it is fully established as the fulcrum of one's being and lived out in action.

"Real" meditation is direct, formless contemplation of this reality.

Though pure, formless contemplation would seem in itself to be simple, it is not easy. Therefore, as concessions to the errant mind, many types of meditation practice have been developed that use forms to a greater or lesser extent. There are, for instance, meditations involving emotional arousals and imaginative visualizations. One may perhaps try to feel *maitri,* loving-kindness, for oneself and for the whole world. Or one may picture a beautiful person and then, as an antidote to lust, visualize their body full of obnoxious secretions and by-products, as undergoing the processes of aging, death, and decay. One may contemplate the qualities of the Buddha, or the Four Noble Truths, or other doctrinal formulations. When in due course we examine Tantra, we will see how elaborate deities and *mandalas* are created in detail by internal visualization and then dissolved away again into nothingness. A full survey would be very extensive.

The tendency throughout the history of Buddhism seems to have been for vast accumulations to pile up over the formless heat of the matter, not merely elaborations of meditation practice but complex philosophical systems; also ritual, devotional practice, etc., etc. At times it has all conspired to obscure the formless heart towards which, in theory at least, it's all meant to point. However, counter-movements have also sprung up periodically that have sought to sweep all the accumulated accretions and superstructures aside and go back to the basic essentials of pure formless contemplation with a minimum of superfluous trappings. In Tibet (and in medieval India too) there was Mahamudra and Dzogchen, and in China Ch'an, which became known as Zen when it was propagated in Japan.

Meditators also occasionally encounter the *rddhis* (Pali, *iddhis*). These are paranormal powers, like clairvoyance and telepathy, the ability to multiply one's body or transform one's shape, to levitate or walk on water, to recall former lives and such. Although magic has a place in Buddhism—and a very large place in some of its traditions (for instance, that of Tibet)—it is generally speaking thought to be in bad taste to boast of occult powers or to show them off, particularly for worldly gain. The special danger they present is that common to all forms of power: they are open to misuse, may inflate the ego, and may also sidetrack the meditator and cause him/her to forget his main concern: nirvana. The usual advice given is that, if *rddhis* are encountered, the meditator should mindfully observe them, and pass on. They do not in any case indicate any especially high level of attainment and should certainly not be mistaken for true wisdom and enlightenment.

Mindfulness (*smriti*; Pali, *sati*)

The practice of mindfulness is not reserved for the meditation cushion. It should be brought to bear on what is happening at any and every moment. Needless to say, our usual condition is a kind of waking dream. We are almost totally distracted, lost in trains of unreflective thought and fantasy, which are interwoven with beguiling emotional sub-themes. These move us reactively through life according to conditioned habit-patterns. We may be habitual grumblers, for instance, who at every pretext launch into embittered diatribes with all the predictability of Pavlov's dogs.

If we are able to wake up, if only occasionally and for a few moments at first, stand back from the ongoing drama of our lives and take an objective look at the habit patterns in which we are caught, then their compulsive hold over us begins to loosen. We *dis*-identify from them; that is, we begin to see that those thoughts and feelings are not *us*. They come along accidentally. They are neither an organic part of us nor are we obliged to follow them.

There are the beginnings of a remarkable freedom here. Closely observed anger, for instance, need not erupt into disastrous outbursts; its energy may indeed be used for positive purposes. For this reason, mindfulness has been likened to the sun that sheds light where there is darkness and whose warming rays foster life and growth.

When people begin to observe themselves they are often shocked and complain that Buddhist practice is actually making them *worse* human beings. Actually they were that bad all along only they never paused to look! We tend to select data and construct an idealized self-image. Unpleasant characteristics are suppressed because they don't harmonize with this pretty fiction. Once awareness is brought to play, however, the dark, unconfronted side of ourselves has to be faced and that is invariably painful. Mindfulness also brings us squarely up against the world as it is rather than as we would like it to be.

The Aggregates (*skandha*; Pali, *khandha*)

This amounts to the Buddhist theory of man. The Buddha once told a parable about a cart. If the cart were to be dismantled, one would have here a pair of wheels, there a shaft and axle, a body somewhere else—and so forth. But where would the original cart be? It would no longer exist. All that would remain would be the separate components.

It is much the same with a so-called "person." In Buddhism, the theory is advanced that a human being is composed of five "heaps" or aggregates (*skandha*; Pali, *khandha*). These are:

1. *The aggregate of matter.* This includes the body, which is analyzed in terms of four elements (solidity, fluidity, heat, and motion) and their

derivatives, which include our five basic sense organs (eye, ear, nose, tongue, body).

2. *The aggregate of feeling or sensation.* Feelings/sensations are of three kinds: pleasant, unpleasant, and neutral, and arise out of contact between a sense organ and a sense object. One extra sense organ comes into play here: the mind, which apprehends mind-objects (ideas, mental images, etc.).

3. *The aggregate of perception.* Perception is the faculty that actually recognizes an object by picking up its distinctive features. Its data come via the interaction of the five sense organs and the mind with appropriate objects.

4. *The aggregate of mental formations.* This encompasses all the willed activities of mind, plus a few others.

5. *The aggregate of consciousness.* When a sense organ or the mind makes contact with an appropriate object, simple awareness but not actual recognition of that object is the function of consciousness, which arises in dependence on that object. Consciousness is certainly not a kind of pure omnipresent mind-substance that registers impressions while existing independently of them. This was a view held in the Buddha's own day by Sati the fisherman's son, who was severely rebuked by the master for his faulty thinking. "There is no arising of consciousness without conditions," the Buddha unequivocally declared, and he went on to illustrate how, when a suitable set of conditions have arisen, the appropriately tinctured consciousness coincidentally arises.

When all these aggregates come together, the fertile ground exists for the arising of a notion of "I." When the aggregates break up at death, however, where will "I" be then?

KARMA (PALI, *KAMMA*)

The term *karma* has now entered English parlance. When some villain receives his come-uppance, this sometimes elicits a retort like, "That's his *karma!*"Actually, it is the *vipaka,* literally the "fruit"; the *karma* was the seed from which this developed.

Linguistically *karma* means action; specifically it refers to willed actions of body, speech, and mind. All such actions, barring alone those of a *buddha* or *arhat,* produce subtle seeds which in time will spawn further consequences. These will be wholesome, unwholesome, or neutral according to the nature of the original action. Unwholesome, actions like killing or stealing will produce unpleasant results; wholesome actions like giving alms to a beggar or upholding the truth will produce pleasant ones. As the very first verse of the *Dhammapada* puts it: "if a person speaks or acts with unwholesome mind, pain pursues him, even as the wheel follows the hoof of the ox that draws the cart."

Karma is used to explain the differing conditions of people in the world. Some are healthy, strong, and enjoy pleasant circumstances. This is the result of good deeds either performed in the present but more likely in a previous life, for *karma* is a force that can overleap death. In the same way the condition of the wretched of the earth can be put down to bad past deeds. In the East, where the notion of *karma* is general and by no means confined to Buddhist circles, this can result in extreme political *laissez-faire*. After all, rich and poor alike are receiving their just deserts, so why redistribute wealth? In any case, if the unprivileged are virtuous, they will receive their rewards in a future life.

However, these things can be complicated by the fact that various different types of karmic formations may come into play. For instance, a person may be born into a rich, aristocratic family; but due to the influence of a secondary or tertiary strain of negative karmic formations, they may not be able to enjoy the pleasures available to them in such circumstances. They may perhaps suffer physical disability and be in constant pain. Likewise, someone born into adverse conditions may be blessed with a contented disposition that allows him or her to be happy anywhere.

While it is very difficult to check the accuracy of such complicated and long-term ramifications, we can observe in our own lives how particular actions affect the way we subsequently feel and what happens to us. A sudden outburst of anger may sour relations in a particular context for hours, days, or weeks. On a more sensational level, a momentary moral lapse can leave a fortune or a brilliant career in ruins.

Wise reflection on the consequences of actions, even small actions, may give us pause before we plunge ahead on some new course.

According to the traditional view, the kinds of repercussions that can await us for heedless actions may be dire indeed. We can be reborn as poor or sickly people; or we can regress to the animal or even the insect level of existence in a future life; we might find ourselves embroiled in one of the Buddhist hells for several aeons. However, this retributive aspect of *karma* can be overstressed. It can generate unnecessary guilt and fear of life—even terror. Ajahn Sumedho has a lighter, more balanced approach to the subject:

> We worry: "I've done so many bad things in the past; what kind of result will I get from all that?" Well, all you can know is that what you've done in the past is a memory now. The most awful, disgusting thing that you've ever done, that you wouldn't want anyone to know about; the one that, whenever anyone talks about

kamma and rebirth, makes you think, "I'm really gong to get it for having done that"—that is a memory, and that memory is the kammic result. The additions to that like fearing, worrying, speculating—these are the kammic result of unenlightened behavior. What you do, you remember; it's as simple as that. If you do something kind, generous or compassionate, the memory makes you feel happy; and if you do something mean and nasty, you have to remember *that*. You try to repress it, run away from it, get caught up in all kinds of frantic behavior—that's the kammic result.*

How to deal with karmic formations? Ajahn Sumedho maintains that they "will cease through recognition." Thus in mindfulness practice, karmic formations are allowed to rise into the mind and then to pass into cessation, *without being acted upon*. It is the acting out of karmic formation that increases their strength, creating habit and causative patterns that go on and on, continually strengthening themselves.

There is also talk in Buddhist circles occasionally of "burning out one's *karma*." Some practitioners even welcome painful experiences and bear them willingly and patiently because they know that in so doing they are paying off old karmic accounts. I once asked a monk who was engaged in this kind of exercise how he found it. He said that it produced a deep sense of calming down: the old compulsive impulses to action were getting weaker and fainter. However, it is not necessary to burn out all one's *karma* in order to become enlightened. But even then, if the psychophysical organism persists, it still can't escape the ripening of past *karma*. Even the Buddha himself was subject to this. When his nasty cousin Devadatta tried to kill him by dropping a boulder onto him from Vulture Peak, though the boulder was deflected, a splinter wounded his foot, the karmic pay-off for an attempt to kill and steal the property of a step-brother in a previous life.

Various objections can be raised against the notion of *karma*. For instance, if a million people die in a nuclear bomb-strike on a certain city, could they all be said to be equally guilty of unwholesome past-deeds? Statistically, isn't it inevitable that there will be at least a few extremely virtuous people among them, perhaps a saint or two? One answer that may be given is that what is in play here is collective *karma*. Presumably then, collective *karma* can at times override individual *karma*. But if we are to be rigorous and apply basic Buddhist doctrine, who is the karmically-afflicted individual anyway? Haven't we already heard that the notion of an "I," an individual entity, is, in ultimate terms, a false view?

* Ajahn Sumedho, "Kamma and Rebirth," *The Middle Way* vol. 57, no. 1 (May, 1982): 17.

Here indeed lies the nub of the matter. As the *Visuddhimagga* asserts: "No doer of the deeds is found/No-one ever reaps their fruit;/Empty phenomena roll on:/This view alone is right and true."

REBIRTH

Closely linked to the notion of *karma* is that of rebirth. This should not be confused with reincarnation, which is the view that there is a soul or subtle essence imprinted with an enduring personal stamp that transmigrates or commutes from body to body down through the aeons. Buddhism of course rejects that view. What it does admit, however, is *causal connection* between one life and another. Thus the karmic accumulations, good and bad, of a particular life (itself the culmination of an endless series of causally-connected past lives) will condition a new birth. Sequences of such interconnected lives form a continuum. Nothing is handed on, however, but the conditioning: the influences, the karmic charge.

To clarify this notion various standard illustrations have been developed. There is the example of the flame that is passed from one candle to others. It is not exactly the same flame that carries on down the line, but it is not a different one either. Another is the cannoning of billiard balls. One ball strikes another; on impact it stops dead; but the other ball moves on, strikes another ball and itself stops dead; then a third ball continues the process. It is a single movement, passed on through a sequence of temporary vehicles.

It must be stressed that rebirth isn't just something that bridges the abyss of death between one physical life and another. It is something that is happening all the time. As we've already noted, our bodies are undergoing minute cellular changes from moment to moment; our feelings and thoughts change too. What appear then to be our continuous, flowing lives are in reality sequences of essentially separate life-moments, each a death and a rebirth. Take the analogy of a film. It is made up of individual frames, each slightly different from the next. As the film is run through a projector, however, the frames blend into each other and the illusion of flow is created. Our fascination with the ongoing drama obscures the true nature of what is happening.

DEATH

The exact way in which at physical death karmic accumulations condition a new life is a complex matter, though it is treated in the usual detail in the traditional texts. What is considered to be of vital importance is a person's state of mind in their final moments.

The science of death was pursued to considerable depth within the

Tibetan Buddhist tradition. According to this, when a person dies their consciousness-continuum leaves the body and moves into an intermediate or *bardo* state that is full of a bewildering phantasmagoria of powerful apparitions—ghosts, gods, demons, wrathful deities. Ability to stay cool and aware enough to deal with these phenomena depends very much on the amount of spiritual practice performed in the past life. Now, therefore, the diligent meditator (or rather, his karmic inheritance) reaps the fruit of all the years of patient sitting. Help may also be given by friends, who can read the *Tibetan Book of the Dead* (*Bardo Thödröl*) over the corpse.

Firstly, there is a glimpse of a marvelous luminosity. This is none other than the enlightened state itself. If the disembodied consciousness-continuum can see it for what it is and stay with it, then liberation is assured. But if the force of negative *karma* is too strong, all kinds of confusion may rise up, particularly terror. This of course is terror of something untoward happening to an individual entity, to the delusory "I" that contaminates the particular consciousness-continuum. As that sense of "I" has no definite form with which to identify itself, however, there is also a desperate reaching out for a new body in which to be reborn. Thus the deluded consciousness-continuum is swept along. Other lights subsequently appear, offering other chances of liberation, but these too may be lost.

The disembodied consciousness-continuum may spend up to forty-nine days in the *bardo* state. If liberation is not achieved, terror and desire will eventually draw it into a new birth. If it is to be a human one, the future mother and father are seen lying together. In the case of the male birth, attraction for the mother is aroused; vice-versa in the case of a female birth. Heated by lust, the deluded consciousness approaches with a view to intercourse, but is foiled. This generates anger, which seals a connection with the father's semen and the mother's blood. The new life is thereupon initiated.

DEPENDENT ORIGINATION (*PRATITYA-SAMUTPADA;* PALI, *PATICCA-SAMUPPADA*)

If Buddhism makes no appeal to the idea of a creator God and if things are not self-creating, how do phenomena arise? The answer is that they do so as the result of preceding causes and in turn become the causes of future phenomena themselves. All phenomena are thus strictly dependent, conditioned, and relative. The doctrine of dependent origination elaborates the Buddha's teaching on this matter. It shows that, in the case of humans and other sentient beings, a circular chain-reaction consisting of twelve conditioned and conditioning "links" generates one complete life-cycle:

1. *Ignorance* gives rise to

2. *Volitional action,* which in turn gives rise to

3. *Conditioned consciousness,* which in turn gives rise to

4. *Name-and-form,* which in turn gives rise to

5. *The six bases,* i.e., the five senses and mind, which in turn give rise to

6. *Sense-impressions* (contact), which in turn give rise to

7. *Feelings,* which in turn give rise to

8. *Desire or craving,* which in turn give rise to

9. *Attachment,* which in turn gives rise to

10. *Becoming* (the life or rebirth process), which in turn gives rise to

11. *Birth* (or rebirth), which gives rise to

12. *Old age, death*—grief, lamentation, illness, sorrow, and despair.

The final link is circularly connected with a new beginning, thus one life-cycle leads inexorably to another, and so on and on. This is *samsara* as depicted in the Buddhist world-view: the fearful cosmic roundabout upon which myriad suffering beings are trapped for vast aeons of time.

Dependent origination is very central to basic Buddhist teaching, but it is by no means easily grasped in its full implications. When the Buddha's favorite disciple, Ananda, was unwise enough to declare to the master that he felt he had understood it, the Buddha rebuked him soundly, saying:

> Say not so, Ananda, say not so! Deep is this doctrine of events as arising from causes. . . . It is through not understanding this doctrine, through not penetrating it, that this generation has become a tangled skein, a matted ball of thread, like to *munja*-grass and rushes, unable to overpass the doom of the Waste, the Woeful Way, the Downfall, the Constant Round of (Transmigration).*

THE WHEEL OF LIFE (*BHAVACHAKRA*)

The way in which beings are locked into endless cycles is graphically depicted in the great Buddhist image of the Wheel of Life (see following page). The wheel itself is held by Yama, the terrifying Lord of Death,

---

* T. W. Rhys-Davids, trans., "Maha-Nidana-Suttanta" (The Great Discourse on Causation) in part 2 of *Dialogues of the Buddha,* (reprint, London: Pali Text Society, 1977), 50.

The Wheel of Life

who is actually devouring it with his fangs, leaving us in no doubt that in the Buddhist view to be caught on this vicious circle is a supremely wretched plight. The various links in the chain of dependent origination are symbolically represented by twelve small images set along the outer rim. Moving in a clockwise direction from the top, they are:

1. *A blind man*—ignorance: the inability to see the truth.

2. *A potter*—action. With the raw materials of clay and water, the potter creates a new pot on his particular kind of wheel.

3. *A monkey*—conditioned consciousness. A monkey is skittish, wayward, virtually impossible to control. It blindly grasps one branch after another as it swings through the trees. So is a consciousness restless with karmic urges.

4. *Three men in a boat*—the boat is the vehicle that carries the men across the stream; similarly, the body is the vehicle that carries us— or more precisely, our karmic inheritance—through the world.

5. *Houses with doors and windows*—the openings are the "sense-doors" through which sense-data passes.

6. *Lovers*—they signify the contact of sense-organ and sense-data that creates sense-impression.

7. *A man whose eye is pierced by an arrow*—the feelings that arise from sense impressions are so strong that they partially blind us. We thus cannot see the true way but stumble on into desire.

8. *A man drinking*—desire is a kind of insatiable thirst. If the thirst is for alcoholic drink, then it leads to intoxication: it seems to promise all kinds of delights and fulfillments, though in actual fact it must move us on one more notch around the wheel.

9. *A monkey clinging to a fruit tree*—the monkey, symbol of the wayward, desire-ridden mind, has here found a suitable object of desire and has latched on to it. Actually it doesn't look too happy; nor is it apparently enjoying the fruit; it is just clinging on.

10. *A pregnant woman*—the clinging has clearly created an embryo: a new life is on the way.

11. *Woman giving birth*—the new life arrives, but in due course of time it will inexorably lead to

12. *An old man*—he carries a burden, the weight of all the ills that beset human life; and he seems to be walking towards that lake—signifying death, dissolution—from which the blind man in the next panel (the first of the sequence) just seems to have emerged.

Thus the gyre rolls on . . .

But there are wheels within wheels. Inside the outer frieze and comprising the main body of the wheel, are five sections (in some versions six) in which are depicted the various realms into which rebirth is possible. Below there are the lower realms: those of the hungry ghosts (*pretas*), of animals and the hell realm where the damned languish. Above, on the other hand, are the realms of human beings, of titans (*asuras*) and of the gods (*devas*).

Inside this cosmic section of the Wheel of Life is a smaller ring in which beings can be seen falling into lower births and then climbing up into higher ones, only to fall again, and again, and again. . . .

THE THREE FIRES (OR POISONS)

At the very center of the wheel we see three animals: a cock, a pig, and a snake. These represent a teaching known as the Three Fires (or alternatively the Three Poisons). The animals symbolize three fundamental vices that keep the wheel in spin:

1. The pig—ignorance (*moha;* Pali, *moha*)

2. The cock—greed, lust, craving (*raga;* Pali both *raga* and *lobha*)

3. The snake—hatred, anger, aggression (*dvesha;* Pali, *dosa*)

All three are shown either eating each other or vomiting each other up, illustrating the endless cycles of blind compulsion in which those under their power are caught. In a sense, therefore, greed, hatred, and delusion power the Wheel of Life. Also the three fires can initiate each other. For instance, ignorance of the way the world works leads us to desire, for we fondly believe that the attainment of some longed-for object will produce lasting satisfaction and entail no significant karmic cost. Then again, unfulfilled desire often produces frustration, anger, and sometimes violence—consequences which those concerned with whipping up the general public's appetite for consumer goods, entertainment, and pleasure for profit, never seem to wish to recognize.

And so the world goes on, beginninglessly, endlessly, governed, it would seem, by a rigid determinism. The only logical response would appear to be a surrender to utter fatalism—were it not for one thing: *there is a way out.* In the top right-hand corner of the Wheel of Life stands Shakyamuni Buddha, gloriously free from these wheels within wheels. He stands there as a lasting testament to the fact that the power of ignorance, desire, and attachment can be broken by *awareness:* by seeing what is really going on, rather than being compulsively caught up in the endless beguiling shadow-play of it all.

THE HINDRANCES (*NIVARANA*)

The following five factors are regarded as major obstructions to the development of concentration and so to penetration of ultimate truth:

1. Sensual desire—(*abhidya;* Pali, *kamacchanda*).

2. Ill will—(*pradosha;* Pali, *vyapada*).

3. Sloth and torpor—(*styana* and *middha;* Pali, *thina-middha*).

4. Restlessness and worry—(*anuddhatya* and *kaukritya;* Pali, *uddhacca-kukkuacca*).

5. Doubt—(*vichikitsa;* Pali, *vicikiccha*).

The study of the *dharma,* its practice, cultivation of the company of the wise, and profitable discussion all tend to diminish these hindrances, which will gradually fade out as progress is made. Also, specific antidotes may be applied. For instance, to counteract sensual desire one may meditate upon the repulsive aspects of the body; and to counteract ill will, one may consciously direct good will towards an enemy or other particular object of aversion. Cutting down on food intake and taking outdoor exercise may help to diminish sloth and torpor.

Restlessness and worry are said to arise from an uneasy conscience and may be counteracted by repentance of past wrong deeds and a resolve not to repeat them. Moreover, as any Catholic priest or psychoanalyst would no doubt readily confirm, confession can be very helpful in easing the pangs of conscience.

We today are of course familiar with the neurotic form of worry, or chronic anxiety, that expresses itself in a deep-seated and persistent sense of insecurity. This would seem very often to arise from the lack of a sound spiritual or philosophical orientation (not necessarily a Buddhist one) that endows life with meaning and points a way beyond exclusive identification with the illusion of "I." Without such an orientation, the individual ego stands alone, bewildered and under threat; an obsessive concern for self develops in the absence of anything more substantial, and with it a desperate search for a personal security that is not in the very nature of things available. In the modern world, where this unhappy condition has become generalized, and there is talk of a deep *angst* or unease haunting our culture. The antidote to this is obvious.

Finally, the confused form of doubt (rather than healthy skepticism) displays itself in a general inability to decide on any course of action and see it through. Instead there is uncertainty, vacillation, mixed motivation, and muddled thinking. Specifically there may be lack of certainty about the Buddha's teaching, its practice and related matters. This hindrance may be resolved by the increasing clarity that comes from the study and practice of the *dharma,* and from discussions with spiritual friends. Buddhism places very strong emphasis on the importance of spiritual friends and the general company one keeps. After all, the earliest followers of the Buddha consciously grouped themselves into a community, the *sangha,* thus affirming the benefits to be obtained from consorting with like-minded people. The option of joining the *sangha* is still available, and lay people too can gain support from establishing relationships with the *sangha;* they may also join groups and centers.

THE FETTERS (*SAMYOJANA*)

This teaching enumerates the ten factors that bind individuals to samsaric existence:

1. Belief in personality—(*drishti;* Pali, *ditthi*).

2. Skepticism—(*vichikitsa;* Pali, *vicikiccha*).

3. Attachment to rules and rituals—(Pali, *silabbata-paramasa*).

4. Sensuous craving—(*kama-raga*).

5. Ill will—(Pali, *vyapada*).

6. Craving for material existence—(*rupa-raga*).

7. Craving for non-material existence—(*arupa-raga*).

8. Conceit—(*mana*).

9. Restlessness—(Pali, *udhacca*).

10. Ignorance—(*avidya;* Pali, *avijja*).

Of special note here is that craving for *any* form of existence whatsoever, even existence in one of the subtle formless levels of the higher *dhyanas,* is an impediment to liberation, as is attachment to rules and rituals. Rules and rituals certainly have their uses, and they are considerable, but essentially they are means for furthering spiritual development. They can, however, become ends in themselves. Every religion has its legalists, formalists, fundamentalists, and dogmatists. They are quite ready to fight and kill to defend the true way. What they are really defending are empty vessels: pious forms of words and actions from which the living spirit has flown. In such cases, a particularly strong form of attachment has probably been forged, one that is not easily recognized as detrimental because its object is ostensibly so worthy. Fear, ignorance, and a simultaneous grasping for security are more or less certain to be present too.

These "mind-forged manacles" must be broken if development is to take place and freedom be won. Even the *dharma* must be laid aside once its purpose is served. The Buddha himself likened it to a raft that can be used for crossing the river of *samsara* to the further bank of enlightenment. Just as a traveler, once he has crossed a river, will not hoist the boat onto his back and go on carrying it, so a person who has achieved the goal will lay the *dharma* aside. The person of the way travels light and lets no opportunity to further lighten his luggage slip by.

BUDDHA, BODHISATTVA, ARHAT, PRATYEKA-BUDDHA, AND OTHER EXALTED BEINGS

As, through concerted and protracted effort, the fetters are progressively overcome, the practitioner is at last afforded a first fleeting glimpse of nirvana. Then he/she is an ordinary worldling no more but a stream-enterer (*shrota-apanna;* Pali, *sotapanna*). Now there are at most only seven more rebirths before full and complete enlightenment. As the final stages of the path are undergone, he/she becomes a once-returner (*sakridagamin;* Pali, *sakadagami*), then a never-returner (*anajamin;* Pali, *anagami*), and finally an *arhat* (lit. "worthy one").

The *arhat* is the ordinary hero of the Buddha's way as it was first enunciated. He/she is the person who has fully transcended all passion and desire to at last enjoy the cool bliss of nirvana. They do not manufacture any new karmic formations, but old ones still have to be worked out and through their momentum mundane life persists, though they put their remaining time in the world to good effect by teaching *dharma*. To achieve arhatship, the help of an enlightened teacher is necessary; no such help is required by a *pratyeka-buddha* (Pali, *paccheka buddha*), a species of solitary practitioner who attains nirvana alone and unaided. He/she does not teach the *dharma,* however, though they might provide moral example.

Above *arhat* and *pratyeka-buddha* are fully-fledged *buddhas,* who are exponents of supreme enlightenment (*Anuttara samyaksambodhi*). In basic Buddhist teaching, a single *buddha* appears only once about every three hundred and twenty thousand years and restores the *dharma* after it has been completely lost during an immensely extended dark age. Shakyamuni is the *buddha* of our particular *buddha-age*. He combined the qualities of *arhat* and *pratyeka buddha* insofar as he both won enlightenment by his own efforts alone and then proclaimed the *dharma*.

The qualities of a buddha take an immense number of rebirths to forge once the initial resolve to become one has been affirmed. A *buddha*-in-the-making is a *bodhisattva*, literally, an "enlightenment being." A *bodhisattva* remains in the world, not due to the momentum of undischarged karmic debts, but due to the momentum of initial compassionate resolve to help free all beings from the coils of suffering. Later, with the rise of the Mahayana, the *bodhisattva* ideal was to become generalized.

THE PERFECTIONS (*PARAMITA*)

These are the noble qualities that the practitioner actively cultivates during the course of his or her protracted pursuit of *buddha*hood. In early sources only six are mentioned, but these were later stretched to ten, and this listing is retained to the present time in Theravada school. They are (with Pali equivalents):

1. Generosity—*dana.*
2. Morality—*sila.*
3. Renunciation—*nekkhamma.*
4. Wisdom—*pañña.*
5. Energy—*viriya.*
6. Patience—*khanti.*
7. Truthfulness—*sacca.*
8. Determination—*adhitthana.*
9. Loving-kindness—*metta.*
10. Equanimity—*upekkha.*

These perfections or *paramita* are cultivated by a *bodhisattva* in his protracted pursuit of the ideal of buddhahood. Sound reason guides him, and always his motivation is utterly pure: free from all desire, conceit, or misguided views. Thus in the perfection of giving, for instance, he seeks no return for himself and is impartial, like the sun that casts its radiance over all without hint of favor; he moreover knows that, in ultimate terms, there is no giver, no recipient, and nothing is given—yet he still gives.

Although they are often accorded a very high, even transcendental status, these are in fact positive virtues that we can apply in our own lives. Generosity, for instance, is something that we can practice even when time is not available for scholarly study or meditation. It is in fact a very good way of promoting a shift away from a basically ego-centric orientation, for the ego is always trying to expand its province by accumulating, whereas to give freely is to reverse this self-serving habit so that for once the energy flows in the other direction. Of course one may derive merit from giving, but even this can be given away so that there remains "nothing for oneself." Many who start practicing generosity report the sense of joy it brings.

Renunciation is also an important feature of the Buddhist path. Our many possessions are not only great sources of attachment but also tend very much to build up our sense that we are something special and have something to protect. They are also an enormous practical burden. Just think of all the time, energy, worry, and expense that a person can invest in obtaining, maintaining, repairing, protecting, and defending his or her property and its ancillaries. Getting rid of things, by contrast, produces a powerful sense of relief and lightness. It moreover frees resources that can be put to spiritual purposes. The simplicity of the monastic life—as homeless ones, the members of the *sangha* are quite literally "portionless"—is precisely the result of everything not essential to survival having been rigorously cut away.

Impatience is almost invariably the ego's response to adverse experiences or suffering, or indeed to anything that frustrates the fulfillment of its projects and programs. Its opposite, therefore, patience, the sixth *paramita*, represents a willingness to accept and bear conditions that may be painful, unpleasant, or simply not in conformity with what one wants. Actually, life is usually well out of alignment with what we would ideally like.

Finally, equanimity is that ability to accept the vicissitudes of life calmly and dispassionately. Kipling had the same idea when in his poem "If" he talked of meeting success and failure and treating those "two imposters" just the same. This is not a numbed indifference or, still less, a neurotic dissociation from life; rather, it arises from seeing that intrinsically all events are neutral and that it is desire that picks and chooses, grades this as good and that as bad. The adept practitioner, therefore, sits comfortably in any set of conditions, at home in the world whatever happens.

THE BRAHMA VIHARAS

1. Loving-kindness—*maitri* (Pali, *metta*)
2. Compassion—*karuna*
3. Sympathetic joy—*mudita*
4. Equanimity—*upeksha* (Pali, *upekkha*)

These are the four "sublime states." "These virtues tend to elevate man," Narada Mahathera has written.

Loving-kindness represents a warm-hearted concern for the well-being of others. It is not sentimentally or erotically based, nor is it selectively applied to congenial people or one's nearest and dearest. Not that it is wrong to love one's friends and family; although, even so, attachment always ends in sorrow. However, that love should ideally be extended outwards in ever-increasing circles to ultimately embrace totality. *Maitri* almost always expresses itself locally, however, in small and unsensational acts of kindness. As though to emphasize the centrality of *maitri*, H. H. the Dalai Lama has declared: "My religion is kindness."

Ajahn Sumedho has in his practical way pointed out that it is unrealistic to expect to be able to actually *like* every person who happens into our sphere. We can, however, control our impulses to reject or do them harm; and it may be possible to do them some good, even though we don't feel particularly inspired by their presence.

As time went by, compassion (*karuna*) was to become an increasingly highly regarded virtue in Buddhism, for it is the motivating quality of the *bodhisattva*. As the hard carapace of "I" breaks down, the division between self and others weakens and eventually their sufferings come to be regarded as one's own. Ven. Buddharakkhita, a Bengali *bhikshu* who runs the Arogya Institute, a charitable organization that, among other good works, provides artificial limbs for the disabled in Bangalore, south India, believes that mere dharmic study and meditation do not necessarily effect profound spiritual change in themselves; in fact, they can be conducive to egoistic inflation if not combined with some form of altruistic service. He has put this belief into practice in his own life.

Sympathetic joy (*mudita*) is the very antithesis of that hard-hearted competitiveness that is so prevalent today—and which indeed is actively encouraged as an incentive to economic growth. The "normal" view is to experience others as dangerous rivals threatening one's own "legitimate interests"; hence feelings of hostility arise and jealousy at their successes and achievements. Anything that puts another ahead creates a sick, sinking feeling in the gut: a sense of being overtaken, left behind, of becoming a "has-been." Conversely, sympathetic joy celebrates the successes and achievements of others; they become one's own, just as through compassion their sufferings become one's own.

CONCLUSION

The basic Buddhist teachings therefore inform us that our own and the world's ills derive from the fact that, constituted as we are, our perception of the world is distorted. We seek permanence and security where they are not available; and rather than being open and unattached, we postulate a fictitious central reference-point, an "I," and contract around it, whereupon heaven and earth are set asunder and all manner of disjunctions set in motion. The antidote is to watch and understand how these problems arise in the first place; then to proceed to try and cure them by means of morality, meditation, and wisdom. If properly done, the scales should fall from our eyes, we should see things as they really are, and a complete reorientation should take place.

During the last two millennia or so, Buddhism has not remained static. There have been many new developments, changes of emphasis, restatements, and modifications; but a fundamental concern to follow in the Buddha's footsteps to his goal of enlightenment has remained constant. Moreover, the basic teachings are still transmitted in the living Theravada tradition in forms probably reasonably close to the original. We therefore have, amidst so much change, an enduring touchstone against which all other developments may be compared and contrasted.

The Development of Buddhism in India

Four Councils
and Eighteen Schools

Indian Buddhism was dealt the *coup de grâce* by the armies of the prophet Muhammad between the tenth and the thirteenth centuries A.D., and had indeed been in decline for a long time before that. However, for more than a millennium after the Buddha's Parinirvana it was a very active force in the land east of the Indus (and indeed in lands to the west of the great river too) and went through remarkable cycles of development there—far more indeed than anywhere else.

The major features of Indian Buddhism can be broken down as follows:

1. The establishment of the word of the Buddha (*Buddhavacana*) as an oral tradition; its much later commitment to writing

2. The holding of various councils or assemblies of the *sangha,* some of which may be apocryphal; these were:

   i.   the First Council, held at Rajagrha immediately after the Parinirvana

   ii. the Second Council, held at Vaishali about one hundred years after the Parinirvana

   iii. the Third Council, held at Pataliputra (modern Patna) under the patronage of the Emperor Ashoka about two hundred years after the Parinirvana

   iv. the Fourth Council, held under the patronage of King
     Kanishka at Jalandhar or in Kashmir around 100 A.D. (not rec-
     ognized by the Theravadins)

3. The division and sub-division of the *sangha* into numerous schools,
   traditionally numbered as eighteen

4. The emergence of a highly developed Abhidharma, or commentarial tradition

5. The popularization of Buddhism, especially under the patronage
   of the Emperor Ashoka

6. The emergence of the Mahayana and the consequent major division into Mahayana and Hinayana; the development of the
   Madhyamaka and Yogacara schools of Buddhist philosophy

7. The emergence of Tantra

After the Parinirvana (Pali, Parinibbana), the Buddha's mortal remains were cremated and the bones and ashes distributed to a number
of places, where they were enshrined in monumental reliquaries
(*stupa*). How would his followers fare now that the Buddha was gone?
It would seem likely that they fared quite well. The Buddha had,
after all, always encouraged self-reliance. He had not tried to make
himself indispensable by promoting himself as a personal leader; and
in the same spirit he had not appointed a successor. He did, however, let it be known that after his passing the *sangha* would still have
his teaching, his *dharma* to guide it. Soon after the rains retreat following the Parinirvana, therefore, five hundred senior monks (said
to be *arhats*) met together at Rajagrha under the presidency of
Mahakashyapa to recollect the word of the Buddha. Upali recited
the monastic code of conduct or Vinaya as he remembered the Buddha
expounding it; and Ananda recited the teachings themselves, the Sutra.
These renderings were debated and a definitive version agreed upon
(though not unanimously).

   For a variety of reasons, the word of Buddha remained an oral
tradition for more than four centuries. This accounts for certain
stylistic devices—repetitions, poetic flourishes, etc.—which made for
easier memorization.

   The teachings that had been agreed at the First Council were therefore carried away from Rajagrha in memorized form to the various
farflung districts where the scattered *sangha* had established itself. The
next step was their translation from the language used at Rajagrha,
which was probably Magadhi, the language of Magadha, into various

local languages. Then in each locality they would have been broken up into convenient parts and one monk would become responsible for memorizing a particular part and handing it on by word of mouth.

Not everyone who attended the First Council at Rajagrha agreed that what had been recited there was the authentic word of the Buddha; other members of the *sangha* had been absent and, declining to adopt the authorized version, preserved and handed on their own versions of what the Buddha had taught. All this, added to the long oral phase when changes must inevitably have crept in, means that we cannot say with certainty of anything that these are the precise words of the Buddha. Buddhism cannot therefore be a "book" religion in the sense that, say, Islam or Judaism claim to be. It possesses no divinely revealed and hence "infallible" and ultimately authoritative canons.

Nor has Buddhism ever been a centralized religion with a Vatican or Caliphate to regulate its affairs and ensure orthodoxy. The scattered communities of *bhikshus* and *bhikshunis* were thus allowed a healthy latitude to grow organically and creatively, untrameled by authoritarian constraints and pressures. Basically all would have been united in veneration of the Buddha, and would have been concerned to practice his way, at the apogee of which lay the ideal of enlightenment, or liberation from the painful rounds of cyclic existence. But inevitably in this liberal setting variations of discipline, practice, and philosophical orientation began to creep in after the passage of a few decades, which could be construed as rich diversification or dangerous deviation; even degeneration.

About one hundred years after the Parinirvana it was reported that the monks in the Vrjian country were becoming lax about the rules. In particular, they were said to be accepting gold and silver from the laity. This led to the summoning of a Second Council at Vaishali where, after a great deal of difficulty and debate, the Vrjian minority were outvoted, but not outmaneuvered. Unrepentant, they seceded from the orthodox line of the elders or *Sthaviras,* whose school later became known as the Sthaviravada, "The Way of the Elders." The schismatics, on the other hand, called themselves the Mahasangha, "The Great Sangha." They differed philosophically from the Sthaviravadins in that they favored the arguments propounded by one Mahadeva (or Bhadra), which set the standards for *arhats* at a rather less exalted level than the Sthaviravadins. Five points were enunciated:

1. An *arhat* could be seduced by another person.

2. An *arhat* could be ignorant of some matters.

3. An *arhat* might be in doubt.

4. An *arhat* might receive information from (or be instructed by) another person.

5. A person might enter the way as a result of spoken words.

In addition, the Mahasanghikas tended to play down the human aspects of the Buddha and to promote the concept of his being the magical manifestation of a transcendental principle. Conze described the Mahasanghikas as "taking the side of the people against the saints, thus becoming the channel through which popular aspirations entered into Buddhism." Conze also credits the Mahasanghikas with paving the way for the foundation of the Mahayana, the Great Vehicle, of which more later.

This process of fragmentation was to continue. Excluding the Mahayana and Tantric schools, within the Hinayana, the so-called Little Vehicle* or basic tradition of Buddhism, eighteen schools are traditionally said to have arisen in India, though it is in fact possible to trace more than that number. Each had its own version of what the Buddha had taught and different views on how that should be interpreted. How deeply felt these differences were is of course hard to tell at this remove in time. There do seem to have been occasional instances of acrimony when putative heretics were evicted from the order. A. K. Warder also maintains that "in certain cases rivalries of a more personal nature may have been involved, at least in bringing matters to a head."† One would of course hope, however, that basic Buddhist tolerance mostly prevailed!

The Buddha had taught in a practical, *ad hoc* sort of way, giving teachings as and when the need arose. He did not propound a philosophical system, and indeed he seems to have regarded intellectual speculation as something of a red herring, irrelevant to the attainment of liberation. However, attempts began to be made within the various schools to extract certain topics from the basic teachings, to subject them to rigorous analysis and build them into coherent and integrated philosophical systems. These systematizations constitute an extensive philosophical

---

* The term "Hinayana," meaning "Little (or Lesser) Vehicle," was coined by the followers of the Mahayana as a natural contrast to the term they coined for their own "Greater Vehicle." Non-Mahayanists sometimes find the term perjorative and object to it, with obvious reason. However, it is the most useful term for the basic tradition of Buddhism that spawned the Eighteen Schools, and it is used here in a nonsectarian, nonjudgmental spirit.

† A. K. Warder, *Indian Buddhism* (Delhi: Motilal Banarsidass, 1970), 290.

tradition, Abhidharma or "Higher Dharma." At the heart of this lies the theory of *dharmas* (plural with a small *d*). Just as the modern physicist analyzes the world into its basic constituent atoms, molecules, etc., so the Abhidharmist analyzes it in terms of *dharmas,* which are successions of impersonal momentary events. The various schools spawned Abhidharma systems of their own with different classifications and listings of *dharmas.*

The second group to secede from the Sthaviravada became known as the Pudgalavadins or "Personalists," for they challenged the hallowed implications of the *anatman* doctrine by maintaining that the *pudgala* or person does possess ultimate reality: that indeed there is a very subtle transcendental self discernible only by *buddhas* but definitely not to be confused with the false self identified by ignorant people.

Later the Sarvastivadins parted company from the Sthaviravadins too. They are described as realistic in tendency because, while not denying the hallowed *anatman* doctrine or asserting any sort of naïve materialism, they affirmed that things do exist in a real sense, hence the name "All-things-exist School." Past and future also possess real existence, because they are in continuity with the present. They also felt that *arhats* could undergo a fall from grace, a view they shared with the Pudgalavadins.

About two hundred years after the Buddha's Parinirvana, during the third century B.C., Buddhism received a tremendous boost in India when it came under the patronage of the great Ashoka Maurya, the grandson of Chandragupta Maurya, who had by force of arms created a mighty empire in India. Ashoka himself seems initially to have followed in the family tradition of ruthlessness, winning the throne in 268 B.C. in a bloody power struggle, and then in the eighth year of his reign dispatching his armies to deal with the Kalingas, a subject people living in the eastern part of India (modern Orissa) who had rebelled against his authority. The resulting carnage, destruction, and suffering were appalling and affected Ashoka deeply. This experience prepared the ground for a dramatic conversion. A chance meeting with a Buddhist monk named Nigrodha alerted Ashoka to the possibility of using his vast powers for purposes other than waging bloody war; he could in fact use them to promote peace and virtue. In an effort to arouse nonviolence, compassion, and other moral virtues in his people, he ordered exhortations to be carved on rocks and pillars all over his empire—his famous rock edicts:

> Do not perform sacrifices or do anything else that might hurt animals. . . . Be generous to your friends. . . . Do not get involved in quarrels and arguments. . . . Try to be pure of heart,

humble and faithful. . . . Do not think only of your good points;
remember also your faults as well and try to put them right.

He also performed copious good works, setting up hospitals for both
humans and animals, causing wells to be dug, and, as an alternative to
military conquest, he applied himself to spiritual conquest. His new
"soldiers" were missionaries armed with the good news of the *dharma*.
They went in many directions. Some even came to the West: to Egypt,
Syria, Macedonia, Epirus, and Cyrene (in north Africa). These efforts
do not appear to have been very effective in the long-run; on the
other hand, his mission to Sri Lanka was a lasting success.

With good Buddhist open-mindedness, Ashoka showed great interest
in all the religions of his empire and conferred gifts upon them. He also
went on religious tours and held discussions with holy men of all sorts.
But the special liberality of his gifts to the Buddhists, including the founding of many monasteries, attracted hordes of bogus devotees—free-loaders
lacking a sincere vocation for the *dharma* and on the lookout for an easy
meal-ticket. The infiltration of the *sangha* by such charlatans led to great
degeneration in the practice of Buddhism, a situation that concerned
Ashoka very deeply. An assembly of *bhikshus* was therefore called at his
behest and a mass purge of some sixty thousand bogus and heretical ones
was carried out. Then a Third Council is said to have been held at
Pataliputra, Ashoka's capital, consisting of the one thousand genuine
bhikshus that remained after the purge. Some believe this council to be
apocryphal, but sinhalese sources assert that it did take place under the
presidency of Moggaliputta tissa, the emperor's own brother, and that a
new, purified compilation of the teachings was also made. Plans for dispatching missionaries abroad were drawn up as well.

The patronage of Ashoka, who came close to realizing the classical
Indian ideal of a Chakravartin, a great enlightened world ruler, did
much to advance Buddhism as a popular religion, whereas formerly
it had been mainly restricted to the urban educated and privileged
classes. Its subsequent strength at the grass-roots level enabled it to
withstand loss of patronage and even perhaps persecution under the
Shungas, who ousted and succeeded the Maurya dynasty.

As an aid to promoting Buddhism on the popular level, the Jataka
Tales were evolved. A collection of well over five hundred of them
has come down to us. Basically they are moral or cautionary tales,
or they convey a simple aspect of Buddhist teaching.

After Ashoka, Buddhism became adopted by the Greeks in the north
of India, and one of their kings, Menandros (Pali name, Milinda; reigned
c. 155-130 B.C.), was a great champion of the *dharma*. His debate with

a *bhikshu* named Nagasena that led to his becoming a lay disciple is preserved in a celebrated post-canonical dialogue, *The Questions of King Milinda (Milinda-Pañha)*. Royal patronage was also extended to Buddhism by Kanishka, a Scythian king who ruled a wide tract of land in northwest India, probably around the first century A.D. It was under his auspices that a Fourth Council, the last in India, was convoked, though the Theravadins do not accept it. It was reputedly held either at Jalandhar or in Kashmir around 100 A.D. and its purpose again was to resolve differences within the Order. A monastery was built for five hundred monks, and they wrote commentaries on the basic scriptures. A legend survives that the entire canon was engraved on copper sheets and deposited in a *stupa,* but these have never been traced.

Of this entire tradition of Eighteen Schools, only one school survives today. This is the Theravada, which is derived from that branch of the Sthaviravada that was established in Sri Lanka by missionaries sent to the island of Ashoka around 240 B.C.

According to the Theravada view, a Fourth Council was held in the Aloka Cave near the village of Matale in Sri Lanka during the first century B.C. The entire scriptural canon of the school was then rehearsed, revised, and committed to writing on palm leaves (35–32 B.C.), so it comes down to us intact whereas the variant canons of the other schools have been lost to varying degrees. We call it the Pali Canon because it is written in Pali, one of the ancient dead languages of India, akin to Sanskrit. Pali became the scriptural and liturgical language of Theravada Buddhism, but it was not the language in which the Buddha taught, which was probably Magadhi (the language of the kingdom of Magadha). An alternative name for the Pali Canon is the *Tipitaka* (Skt. *Tripitaka*), signifying its basic division into the three *pitaka* or "baskets" of Vinaya, Sutta, and Abhidhamma.

The following is a simplified analysis of the Theravada Pali Canon:

1. *Vinaya Pitaka*. This consists of three main sections:

    i.   *Suttavibhanga*—which explains the 227 rules or precepts listed in the *Patimokkha* which are applicable to monks, followed by a section for nuns

    ii.   *Khandhaka* (lit. "Chapters")—which details the rules; it subdivides into:

        (a) *Mahavagga*—the "Greater Section"; and

        (b) *Culavagga*—the "Lesser Section"

    iii.   *Parivara*—an appendix added at a later date

2. *Sutta Pitaka.* This consists of five main sections of collected discourses or *suttas:*

   i.   *Digha Nikaya*—made up of 34 longer *suttas*

   ii. *Majjhima Nikaya*—152 medium length *suttas*

   iii. *Samyutta Nikaya*—2875 (or 2889—listings vary) "connected" *suttas* arranged in 52 groups

   iv. *Anguttara Nikaya*—2198 (or 2308) *suttas* arranged in an elevenfold numerical categorization

   v. *Khuddaka Nikaya*—15 separate works including, notably, the *Dhammapada*

3. *Abhidhamma Pitaka.* This was a later addition; it consists of seven texts composed at different periods:

   i.   *Dhammasangani*—ennumeration of *dhammas*

   ii. *Vibhanga*—further analysis of *dhammas*

   iii. *Dhatukatha*—discussion of elements

   iv. *Puggalapaññatti*—description of individuals

   v. *Kathavatthu*—discussion of the points of controversy between the Hinayana sects; defense of the Theravada view (probably the latest addition)

   vi. *Yamaka*—"Book of Pairs"

   vii. *Patthana*—"Book of Relations"

A vast post-canonical literature also arose consisting of further commentaries, biographies of the Buddha, and other edifying works.

N·I·N·E

Mahayana

Around the dawn of the common era, a highly significant new wave of development began to assert itself within the spiritual tradition that the Buddha had inaugurated. Its followers called it the *Mahayana* or "Great Vehicle," in contrast to what had gone before, which they rather disparagingly dubbed *Hinayana*: "Lesser Vehicle."

The Mahayana represents a great creative flowering of various potentials latent in the Buddha's basic teachings. South India is generally thought to have been where it originated, though Dr. Edward Conze maintains that the northwest was another focal area. He stresses the importance of non-Indian influences from both the Mediterranean and Iranian worlds on its development, and it was in the south and northwest that those influences were generally most prevalent. Non-Buddhist Indian influences must also have played a part.

The main trends of the Mahayana may be summarized as follows:

THE BODHISATTVA IDEAL

A new type of spiritual hero appears. Instead of the *arhat* (Pali, *arahat*), who seeks release from the painful round of cyclic existence for himself alone, and the *pratyeka-buddha* (Pali, *pacceka-buddha*), who wins it privately and never seeks to impart the *Dharma* to others, we have in the Mahayana the *bodhisattva,* an individual to whom both these highly desirable options are available but who rejects them, and instead aspires to

buddhahood solely that he might help others. This compassionate reso-
lution is called *bodhicitta* or "wisdom mind," and, galvanized by it, he
voluntarily throws himself back time and time again into the raging sea
of *samsara*. Other unregenerate beings will of course be reborn time and
again too, but in their case the process is entirely involuntary.

In other words, the preceding kind of spiritual individualism was replaced in the Mahayana by a more altruistic orientation. This also implies
a very basic difference in attitude to the world. The *arhat* and *pratyeka-
buddha* sought to escape from the Wheel of Life into an ineffable beyond.
The *bodhisattva*, on the other hand, seeks to maintain an enlightened quiescence amid the hurly-burly of life.

THE SIX PERFECTIONS AND THE BODHISATTVA PATH

The aspiring *bodhisattva* strives to master six or ten "perfections" (*paramita*),
including giving, morality, patience, vigor, meditation, and wisdom. He
also passes through ten stages (*bhumi*) on his way to buddhahood. The first
six stages correspond to the six perfections. At the higher four stages,
however, he might become a kind of supernatural being, a celestial
bodhisattva, to the class of which belong Avalokiteshvara, who symbolizes
compassion, and Mānjushri, who wields the sword of wisdom.

COMPASSION AND SKILL IN MEANS

In the Mahayana, compassion (*karuna*) is elevated alongside wisdom
(*prajña*) at the vanguard of the virtues. The two, working together, are
thought to be a supreme combination.

Buddhist compassion has connotations of being able to feel the sufferings of others as if they were one's own, which, indeed, from a high
point that transcends distinctions of self, they really are. Unlike lower
forms of love (if indeed they can be called love), this compassion is not
selective or tainted with attachment but goes out equally to all who
suffer.

Skill in means (*upaya*) is also emphasized, for the mere wish to help
living beings, each of whom is after all unique, would not by itself be
very effective if it were not accompanied by insight into viable and
effective methods of doing so. It would be equally useless to possess
high spiritual ideals and a wealth of theoretical understanding but be
utterly unable to realize the desired qualities in oneself.

All this gives the Mahayana a strong practical emphasis, which had in
fact been present in Buddhism from the beginning, for the Buddha himself
was not merely content with telling people about the blessings of enlightenment; he actually showed them things they could do to get there.

BUDDHAHOOD AS TRANSCENDENTAL PRINCIPLE

As heirs to the Mahasanghikas, the followers of the Mahayana played down the Buddha's historical aspect as Siddhartha Gautama, the man born at Lumbini, and advanced the notion of buddhahood as a transcendental principle which has manifested over untold aeons in innumerable forms and in innumerable places. Various mythical *"buddhas"* consequently emerged in the Mahayana: supernatural beings who held sway in their own heavens or "pure lands"—like Amitabha, the Buddha of Infinite Light, who resides in the western paradise of *Sukhavati,* where followers of the Pure Land sect hope to merit rebirth.

THE TRIKAYA DOCTRINE

As a development of pre-existing notions, the Mahayana accorded the Buddha three bodies:

1. Nirmanakaya: his "Transformation (or Appearance) body." This is the body in which he appears in the world for the benefit of suffering beings. It is not a real, physical body but more a phantom-like appearance assumed by

2. Dharmakaya: his *"dharma* body," wherein he is one with the eternal *dharma* that lies beyond all dualities and conceptions. There is also

3. Sambhogakaya: his "Enjoyment (or Bliss) body." This is the body that appears to *bodhisattvas* in the celestial realm where they commune with the truth of the Mahayana.

FAITH AND DEVOTION

The emergence of celestial *bodhisattvas* like Avalokiteshvara and mythical buddhas like Amitabha gave rise to devotional cults. Formerly the tendency in Buddhism had been distinctly heroic: spiritual progress was possible only through intense personal effort. Now it became possible to direct prayers for help to godlike beings who could intercede on one's behalf. They could also be worshipped through *puja* and other devotional practices. There are similarities here with the *bhakti* cults of Hinduism which were almost undoubtedly an influence on developments.

A NEW ROLE FOR THE LAITY

Originally the bias in Buddhism had been distinctly monastic. Monks (but not so much nuns) were looked up to as the spiritual front-runners: the only ones with a real chance of becoming enlightened and hence the only ones accorded real spiritual status. This of course represented a one-sidedness that begged to be redressed. The emergence of devotional cults was one way in which the aspirations of the laity for a fuller share in the religious life were met.

There were others too. One new Mahayana *sutra,* for instance, the *Vimalakirti-nirdesa,* centered around an enlightened householder who feigned illness as a teaching device. Though not by any stretch of the imagination your average man-in-the-street in contemporary *Vaishali*— great figures in the Buddhist pantheon visited him for instruction— Vimalakirti represents a kind of spiritual hero figure conspicuously lacking in earlier Buddhism.

(There have in fact been various attempts to move the focus of Buddhism away from the monastery over the centuries, but in fairness it must be said that these have achieved little success. Among the world's religions, Buddhism has always gravitated towards the monastic side of the spectrum of orientations.)

NEW BEARINGS IN PHILOSOPHY

At the core of Mahayana philosophy lies the notion of emptiness (*shunyata*). This is very much in the spirit of *anatman* (Pali, *anatta*) as first taught by the Buddha. It implies emptiness of inherent existence or own-being (*svabhava*); that is, that the conventional wisdom that beings create themselves and exist autonomously is false, for in fact they are created by causes and exist in mutual interdependence. Needless to say, emptiness is not to be confused with sheer nothingness or total blankness. Buddhism knows no ultimate vacuum; nor is it a mysterious something. It transcends all dichotomies and can only be understood by direct insight.

Another key Mahayana term is *tathata,* "thusness" or "suchness," which is the way things are before conceptual thought begins to reify and organize them. By extension, the Buddha is often called the Tathagata: the "One Who is Thus Gone." The *Tathagata-garbha* doctrine, meanwhile, puts forward the notion that we are all in a sense wombs in which the seeds of Buddhahood can germinate. The idea of a Buddha-nature, real or potential, was, as many clearly saw, bringing Buddhism close to having a soul doctrine, which is precisely what its basic tenets seemed to so trenchantly deny.

TWO LEVELS OF TRUTH

The structure of our everyday language doesn't allow us to describe things as they really are. It carves the world up into separate bits and pieces and so distorts reality, which isn't in itself fragmented in that way.

Out of this dilemma arose the notion of two levels of truth:

1. Conventional truth—everyday common-sense truth, basically distorted but open to skillful manipulation in order to point to

2. Absolute truth—the way things really are, as *buddhas* behold with enlightened eyes: empty, beyond thought and description.

IDENTITY OF NIRVANA AND SAMSARA

The uncompromising spirit of Mahayana logic tears down all forms of separation, even that which distinguishes nirvana from *samsara*. In terms of absolute truth, nirvana is *samsara,* and vice-versa. There is no split or separation. This, needless to say, throws the ordinary world into a new light: it is indeed the transcendental world of true reality, the world of *buddhas* and *bodhisattvas,* though our defilements prevent us ordinary mortals from seeing it as such.

NEW SCRIPTURES

The new Mahayana ideas, ideals, and orientations were proclaimed in a body of new *sutras,* which Conze has described as "one of the most magnificent outbursts of creative energy known to human history and it was sustained for about four to five centuries."* Often the historical Buddha, Shakyamuni, is cited as author, and fictions have to be advanced to explain why the works in question took so long to come to light. It might be claimed, for instance, that the Buddha had decreed that a particular *sutra* be hidden away until such a time as the world was ready to receive the unusually deep teachings that it contained."†

Possibly the Mahayanists actually believed that these *sutras* came from the same mystical source as the original ones; i.e., from the transpersonal Dharmakaya. They are usually much longer and less immediately accessible than their counterparts in the Pali Canon, more elaborate and mystical, poetic, and often encrusted with rich imagery and other ornate stylistic devices. "Spiritual truths are conveyed, not through the medium of words alone, but symbolically by means of gorgeous phantasmagoria."†† Philosophically, the point of view taken is often very high: that of full enlightenment, no less. Thus:

---

* E. Conze, *A Short History of Buddhism* (London: Allen & Unwin, 1980), 45ff.

† This clearly does not accord with the Buddha's own statement that he did not teach with "the closed fist": i.e., did not hold anything back, or teach an esoteric set of doctrines.

†† Sangharakshita, *The Eternal Legacy* (London: Tharpa Publications, 1985), 96.

They are the Sacred Word which, uttered everlastingly on the heights of existence, reverberates through limitless space and unending time.*

The *Suddharma-pundarika,* "White Lotus of the True Dharma"; the *Vimalakirti-nirdesa* "Exposition of Vimalakirti"; and the vast *Prajñaparamita,* "Perfection of Wisdom" literature are early examples of the new *sutras.*

The word "Mahayana" was coined by the Mahayanists themselves to distinguish themselves from their predecessors, whom they dubbed followers of the "Hinayana" or "Lesser Vehicle." This, of course, implies a value judgment, and indeed it does appear that rivalry did occasionally creep into the relations between the followers of two traditions. Hinayanists were sometimes said to have coldly and selfishly opted for a lesser spiritual goal (i.e., Arhatship), and that even if successful they had not "finished what they had to do." The Hinayana teachings were sometimes dismissed as low-grade *dharma* strictly for beginners and those of limited spiritual understanding and potential. In short, the Mahayana was supreme.

Competitive sectarianism must have been more apparent than real, however, for the more sensitive and sincere would have been keenly aware that it was highly dissonant with the kindly, tolerant spirit set by the Buddha himself. Conze maintains, moreover, that Mahayanists and Hinayanists lived together in the same monasteries and shared much else in common. He also quotes the Chinese pilgrim I-tsing, who visited India around the eighth century:

> The adherents of the Mahayana and Hinayana both practice the same Vinaya, recognize the same five categories of faults, are attached to the same four truths. Those who worship the Bodhisattvas and who read the Mahayana *sutras* get the name of Mahayanists; those who do not are Hinayanists.†

Certainly the Hinayanists remained in the majority until possibly as late as the eighth century A.D. They probably did not view the new *sutras* with much favor, but on the whole they are likely to have maintained a noble silence about Mahayana developments, which must inevitably have influenced them to some extent. Philosophically, they went on quietly developing their own Abhidharma, which reached its apogee around the fourth century A.D.

As already mentioned, the only Hinayana school still extant today is the Theravada. Regrettably, the newcomer setting out to explore Bud-

* *Ibid.,* 96.
† E. Conze, *Buddhism, Its Essence and Development* (Oxford: Cassirer, 1960), 122.

dhism will still find the Theravada/Mahayana division something of a minefield, because vestiges of the old sectarian propaganda in favor of the Mahayana still linger. In practice it would, however, be entirely wrong to think of the Theravada as being for beginners and people of limited spiritual understanding or potential and the Mahayana for the cognoscenti and the spiritual high-fliers. *Both* traditions are pointed in the same direction (though from slightly different angles), and both have a great deal to offer. It may well be that a particular individual might find him or herself more at home in the Theravada than in one of the Mahayana schools, for even though it represents the conservative-traditional orientation as opposed to the innovative one, the Theravada has not stayed still over the past millennia. Moreover, sincere practitioners can be found among the followers of the Theravada who have kept their tradition a living one, while there are certainly Mahayanists who have ossified and lost the vital spiritual spark. The converse is true too.

Here as elsewhere, therefore, the wise thing for the newcomer to do is to keep an open mind, be wary of biased views and opinions, and investigate for him or herself.

Conze distinguishes two phases in the development of the Mahayana:

1. An unsystematic phase; *c.* 100 B.C. to 500 A.D.

2. A systematic phase; after *c.* 150 A.D.

The preceding outline broadly covers the unsystematic phase. The systematic phase, on the other hand, encompasses the emergence of the two main philosophical schools: the *Madhyamaka* and the *Yogacara*. Of these two schools, Conze has written:

> They differ in that they approach salvation by different roads. To the Madhyamikas, "wisdom" is everything and they have very little to say about *dhyana,* whereas the Yogacarins give more weight to the experiences of trance (i.e., meditation). The first annihilate the world by a ruthless analysis which develops from the Abhidharma tradition. The second effect an equally ruthless withdrawal from everything by the traditional method of trance.*

THE MADHYAMAKA SCHOOL

This was founded by Nagarjuna (*c.* 150 A.D.), a south Indian philosopher of genius whose birth was, according to some, predicted by the Buddha himself and who is also reputed to have received instruction

---

* E. Conze, *Buddhist Thought in India* (London Allen & Unwin, 1962), 251.

from the *nagas* (serpent kings) in their palace beneath the sea. His major work is the *Mulamadhyamaka-karika* or "Verses on the Middle Way."

In the great tradition set by the Buddha, Nagarjuna devised new ways for driving us into the arms of the inconceivable. Rather than propounding a philosophy as such, he advocated a method, the technical term for which is *dialectic,* which if rigorously applied ruthlessly negates all pairs of opposites. Shunyata is thus a Middle Path (*madhya* means "middle") dynamically generated by the mutual negation of dualities such as production and extinction, annihilation and permanence, unity and diversity and so forth.

> The right teaching is the Middle Path devoid of name and char-
> acter where no speech or thought can reach. It transcends all points
> of dispute such as "the four forms of argument and the hundred
> negations," thus even going further than Yajñavalkya's famous theory
> of *"neti, neti"* (not this! not this!) in the Upanishads.*

Insofar as *shunyata* depends on the opposites that are negated, Nagarjuna's philosophy is said, for example by Professor Stcherbatsky two forms of truth: worldly truth and higher truth. In terms of worldly truth, the Law of Dependent Origination asserts that the things of the world come into being through causation; in terms of higher truth, however, all is universal relativity—hence *shunyata.* Worldly truth is not without its uses, however, for higher truth can only be reached by going through it.

In the early part of the fifth century, two sub-schools of the Madhyamaka emerged: the Prasangika, founded by Buddhapalita, which maintained the tradition of ruthless dialectics inaugurated by Nagarjuna, and the *Svatantrika,* founded by Bhavaviveka, which attempted to temper the apparently bleak nihilism of Nagarjuna's approach.

THE YOGACARA (OR VIJÑANAVADA) SCHOOL

This flowered in the fourth century A.D., and its principal exponents were Asanga and his younger brother Vasubandhu, who hailed from northwest India.

The Yogacarins took a more positive line of approach than the Madhyamikas. All is mind or consciousness, they maintained, hence their central doctrine of *citta-matra:* "mind only" or "nothing but conscious-ness." According to this view, the objects of the world do not exist *per*

---

* J. Takakusu, *Essentials of Buddhist Philosophy* (Delhi: Motilal Banarsidass, 1975), 104–5.

se but are also created from and by mind. To explain how this is done, they put forward the idea of a store consciousness (*alaya-vijñana*), a kind of collective unconscious in which the seeds of all potential phenomena are stored and from which they ceaselessly pour into manifestation. Delusion, also a creation of mind, consists in taking these for real whereas they are in truth just projections of mind. This cure for this sickness is seeing through the illusion, and by means of the practice of meditation (from which the whole orientation of the school undoubtedly sprang), establishing a pure consciousness devoid of all content. This is called "revolution at the basis."

The Yogacarins are also credited with perfecting the *Trikaya Doctrine*, the theory of the Three Bodies of the Buddha, and with having raised Buddhist logic to a high pitch of development. Their greatest logician was Dignaga (second half of the fourth century A.D.), a pupil of Vasubandhu. Buddhists had in fact debated with each other since the earliest times, and this in itself may have contributed to the subdivision of Buddhism into so many schools. Buddhists also pitted their wits against representatives of Hindu sects in great public debates. In these not only was prestige at stake but often the patronage of the rich and powerful. Buddhist logic was considered so formidable in debate that one Hindu is reputed to have resorted to dastardly underhanded means to learn it for the benefit of his own party. Public debating has survived in the Tibetan Buddhist tradition to this day; it involves highly mannered procedures, including dramatic physical gestures.

The highly sophisticated philosophical ideas summarized here demonstrate how far Buddhism had developed from being the simple path of homeless ascetics living in caves and beneath the roots of trees. Monasteries had of course originated during the Buddha's own time, and as the centuries progressed and Buddhism became favored with the patronage of the rich and powerful—notably, of course, the Emperor Ashoka—those monasteries became large and splendid establishments. To meet the needs of scholarship, some acquired extensive libraries and attracted scholarly monks. The greatest grew into monastic universities of international repute housing hundreds of teachers and thousands of scholars. The greatest of all was Nalanda, near the modern town of Rajgir in the northeastern Indian state of Bihar; it was a Mahayana establishment. The largest Hinayana establishment, on the other hand, was Vilabhi, in western India. Other great monastic universities were Vikramashila, Jagaddala, and Odantapuri.

The Chinese pilgrims I-tsing and Hsüan-tsang visited Nalanda and both have left descriptions. Nalanda was apparently vast and architecturally very fine, graced with beautiful sculpture and grounds; it had "rows of monasteries with their series of turrets licking the clouds." Its campus included schools of study, lecture-halls, residential quarters, and numerous many-storied library buildings to accommodate its wealth of manuscripts. All this was properly administered and subject to close regulation, fixed penalties being imposed for any breach of the rules, and the eight-hour working day was run strictly by a water-clock. The students not only studied Mahayana subjects but the teachings of the Eighteen Schools as well; also the Vedas and other aspects of Brahmanism, and secular subjects like logic, grammar, mathematics, medicine, etc. Degrees were granted to successful students. Nalanda was extremely well-endowed and its monks were not only well fed, but, according to Hsüan-tsang, waited on by two lay servants apiece; moreover, if they went outside they were provided with elephant or litter transport. Nagarjuna is said to have worked at Nalanda.

Sadly, this great establishment, a unique treasury of profound learning, was ruthlessly destroyed during the Muslim depredations. When a Tibetan pilgrim visited its site in 1235, he found only one ancient monk teaching Sanskrit grammar to some students in the burnt-out rubble. Word then came that another raiding party of Turks was on its way, whereupon monk and students wisely made themselves scarce until the danger was past. The Tibetan could find none of the books for which he was looking.

But this is to anticipate. Before the final apocalypse, India was to give rise to yet one more major development in Buddhism.

T·E·N

Tantra

The Mahayana was not the only creative innovation to arise within Indian Buddhism. New dispositions soon began to stir within the Mahayana itself and between the third and the seventh centuries A.D. these constellated into a distinctive new phase of Buddhism: a third turning of the Wheel of the dharma. Tantra is the term usually applied to it by modern commentators, but Mantrayana (Secret Mantra Vehicle) and Vajrayana (Diamond Vehicle) were more usual in the past, though specialists would insist that all these terms are not strictly interchangeable.

Traditionally, the usual kind of explanation is given for the origin of Tantra: that it was originally taught by the Buddha himself, but, because of its highly specialized nature, not for general application. Hence it is sometimes labelled "Esoteric Buddhism." Linguistically a *tantra* is a kind of scripture in which teachings of the kind that have come to be described as "Tantric" are set out. Thus the Tantric scriptures are a kind of late-arriving fourth addition to the original three *pitaka* of Vinaya, *sutra,* and Abhidharma.

In common with all other forms of Buddhism, Tantra is primarily concerned with the attainment of buddhahood. Doctrinally it is founded squarely on a classic Buddhist basis, and philosophically its debt is mainly to the Mahayana, notably for the Madhyamaka teaching on emptiness (*shunyata*). What is original and distinctive is what it has to offer in terms of methods. Tantra is in fact about transforming the gross body, speech, and mind into those of a *buddha* by means of special practices, some of which involve working consciously with extremely subtle processes beyond the range of normal awareness. This must moreover be done within the context of a special relationship with a *guru*. If the ideal of the Hinayana is the *arhat* and that of the Mahayana the *bodhisattva,* the spiritual hero of Tantra is the *siddha* or adept.

This has brought us into the field of yoga, a phenomenon that is as old as Indian civilization itself. There are indeed varieties of Hindu Tantra, notably those which center around the cult of the great god Shiva. In his aspect as "Great Ascetic," Shiva is the prototype of the dedicated *yogi* who, in his ardent pursuit of his spiritual ideal, subjects mind and body to the most extreme austerities. But Shiva also has an antithetical erotic aspect and iconographically he is often depicted as coupling with his consort or Shakti.* Indeed sexual symbolism plays a conspicuous part in Tantra, and understandably so, for it is the self-division of the primal unity into a bipolar dualism and the subsequent dynamic interaction of the two poles that generates the creation of the ten thousand things; and of course that very process of creation can itself be reversed and a conscious return to unity achieved.

Specialists and partisans have hotly debated whether Buddhist Tantra emerged from its Hindu counterpart or was an independent development. Perhaps the most useful approach would be to regard both as outpourings from the general melting-pot of Indian religious creativity. Certainly Buddhist Tantra flourished in India for several centuries before the eclipse of Buddhism in that land and achieved a high state of development there. What we know of it comes mainly from Tibet, however, where it was preserved down to modern times in forms far closer to the Indian originals than is generally supposed. The information given in this chapter is therefore based almost entirely on Tibetan sources, in particular the Gelugpa school. This line of transmission was not only to take root in Tibet itself but throughout the Himalayan region and to reach far up into Mongolia and Siberia as well. Another separate and less important line of transmission ran northwards through China to Japan, where Tantra survives today in the Shingon school.

As Tantra involves a great deal of symbolism and ritual, certain specialist terms need to be clarified before we proceed:

---

* This sexual union symbolizes the process whereby the passive male aspect of ultimate reality is brought into manifestation by the powerfully creative female aspect.

Yidam

Yidam—The Tantric pantheon is composed of a phantasmagoria of incredible deities, both male and female, who are graphically and colorfully depicted in Tibetan religious art replete with all manner of powerful symbolism. Some are benign, wear beatific smiles, and hold up their hands in gentle gestures of benediction. Tara and Avalokiteshvara are examples of these. Others are extremely fearsome: snarling, befanged, wreathed in flames, and wielding skulls, severed heads, daggers, and other gruesome impedimenta—like Mahakala, Yamantaka, Guhyasamaja, and Chakrasamvara. All are archetypal images of primordial energies; they are the passions transformed and personified, or, more precisely, they are emanations of one supreme Tantric buddha sometimes represented in the form of Vajradhara or Adi-Buddha.

Dhyani-Buddhas—Some of the deities of the Tantric pantheon are grouped together in families. Important among these are the families of the Five Tathagatas or so-called Dhyani-Buddhas, Vairochna, Akshobhya, Ratnasambhava, Amitabha, and Amoghasiddhi. These are again invested with dense symbolism and represent five primary energies to whose activity all created phenomena may be attributed.

Mandala—This is a *temenos,* a sacred space. It is also a model of both the cosmos and of the total human being, for there is an equivalence between the two: they are macrocosm and microcosm. Just as the Buddhist cosmos revolves around the axial mountain, Meru, so too in man there is a heart-center where the mystery of ultimate reality is enshrined. Formally *mandala* thus consist of series of concentric precincts converging on a focal sanctum or palace, guarded by dreaded guards, where the presiding *yidam* or some other potent symbol of ultimate reality resides. In a sense, therefore, *mandala* are maps of the spiritual journey itself, and contemplation of them assists in the accomplishment of that journey by awakening latent spiritual potentials buried deep in the subconscious of the practitioner. Carl Gustav Jung observed that mandalic patterns arose spontaneously in the thoughts and dreams of many people, himself included, and saw them as a token of spiritual ripening.

Mantra—These are highly compressed, power-packed formulas, usually of Sanskrit origin, which are charged with deep meaning and magical potency. They may be recited verbally, visualized, or written down. The most famous of course is "Om Mani Padme Hum" (see page 183). The essence of each Tantric deity is encapsulated in his/her own *mantra,* which may have both long and short forms. Recitation of a *mantra* represents a kind of practice that can be readily carried on in everyday situations. It purifies the speech and "protects the mind" by maintaining a constant spiritual connection; and of course it helps disperse mental chatter. Short verbal formula called *dharani* and *paritta* (blessings) were used from early Buddhist times.

Bija (or Seed) Mantra—This is a vowel or consonant which embodies the heart essence of a particular Tantric deity. It may be visualized in luminous form, and the deity then emerges from it.

Mudra—Literally, a "seal" or "symbol;" this is a ritual gesture of the hands imbued with deep symbolic significance. In Tantric contexts the significance again relates to an aspect of a particular Tantric deity.

Mahamudra—Literally, "The Great Seal," this signifies more than just the subjective realization of emptiness. "It is the Buddha nature, the basic mind within all sentient beings" (Khenpo Könchog Gyaltsen); it is "voidness itself . . . the ultimate nature of every single phenomenon"

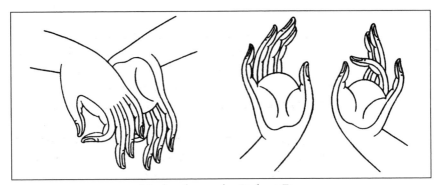

Mudra drawn by Robert Beer

(Geshe Rabten); it is "non-dual awareness that transcends intellect, it is non-dual awareness that transcends intellect, it is non-conceptual, lucid, like all-pervading space" (Maitripa). In short, it is the very apogee of the Tantric path.

Vajra (Tibetan. Dorje, lit. "lord of stones") and Ghanta (Bell)—These are the most important ritual objects in Tantra. Formally, the *vajra* is a single or double scepter and is derived from the thunderbolt of the Hindu god Indra. It symbolizes skillful means, and the adamantine or diamond-like quality of *shunyata*—its indestructible, changeless character—when skillful means are allied to wisdom, which is symbolized by the *ghanta* or bell. Other ritual objects include dagger (*phurba*), skull-cup (symbolizing impermanence), and thigh-bone trumpet.

Dorje, Ghanta (bell), and Phurba (dagger) drawn by Robert Beer

Generally Tantra is divided into four main categories:

• Action Tantra (Kriyatantra)

- Performance Tantra (Caryatantra)
- Yoga Tantra (Yogatantra)
- Highest (or Supreme) Yoga Tantra (Anuttarayogatantra)

The old school of Tibetan Buddhism, the Nyingma, opted for a sixfold classification divided into two main groupings: Inner Tantra and Outer Tantra. Outer Tantra incorporates Action, Performance, and Yoga Tantras; Inner Tantra replaces Highest Yoga Tantra with three new categories: Maha Yoga, Anu Yoga, and Ati Yoga.*

According to most commentators, these different categories exist because of the differing spiritual abilities of human beings. Highest Yoga Tantra is, in Tantric terms at any rate, the apogee of the Buddhist path; but it is not for everyone. Each person must therefore find which level is appropriate to them. It may indeed be that they are suited to no Tantric path at all, in which case they would be advised to practice a *sutra* path. (The Tibetans divided all Buddhist teachings into *sutra* and Tantra. *Sutra* includes both Mahayana and Hinayana.)

Who are the favored people who are qualified to pursue a Tantric path? Basically it is those who have already advanced far upon the Sutra path in both present and previous lives. This means that they have achieved a high degree of mastery over the passions through the exercise of moral restraint, patience, and so on, thus being able to transform the powerful emotions that may arise in ordinary life situations instead of needing to resort to ascetic withdrawal from worldly involvements, which is the classic Hinayana method of dealing with these difficult and dangerous manifestations. They will also have attained an equally high degree of stability and concentration through the practice of *shamatha* meditation; a clear understanding of emptiness should have arisen too. But perhaps most important of all, they must be totally committed to practice, not for egocentric gains, but in order to achieve enlightenment for the benefit of others. This compassionate orientation, *bodhicitta,* which was of course taken over directly from the Mahayana, is of particularly crucial importance.

The Tantric path has its dangers: this is repeatedly stressed in the traditional texts. Improper dabbling may cause psychic damage, perhaps blighting not merely this, but many future lives. Therefore, to prevent fools from rushing in, all manner of safety precautions have been set up.

For a start there is the veil of secrecy that traditionally enshrouds all

---

* One kind person who has cast an informed eye over and commented upon this chapter suggests that this highly formalized systematization of Tantra, though the usual one given in books and disseminated by the more orthodox schools, somewhat misrepresents what happens in actual practice in certain cases. There are less formal approaches to Tantra where things proceed in a more intuitive way.

Tantric matters—hence the name "secret mantra." Tantric texts are written in an enigmatic "opaque" or "twilight" language that renders their contents meaningless to the uninitiated; also those initiated into Tantric cults have to uphold grave vows (*samaya*). Such measures are not merely designed to protect the unwary from getting burnt; they also protect the teachings themselves, for malpractice weakens their effectiveness: the spiritual equivalent of debasing the coinage.

Then it is emphasized that the would-be practitioner should enjoy the guidance of a *guru* who possesses at least the minimal qualifications as set out in the traditional texts. These qualifications vary according to the category of Tantra involved. To teach at the lower categories, the *guru* need not actually be a fully enlightened practitioner himself, but he must have mastered an extensive range of expertise. He will, moreover, have the discernment necessary to see how far the disciple (*chela*) has progressed along the path and whether he is ready for Tantra; he will also be able to steer him past all the pitfalls and point him towards those particular practices that will be most effective in his unique case. Finally, a special compatibility must exist between *guru* and *chela* for an effective "dharmic connection" to be forged.

In view of its many problematic aspects, as well as the fact that buddhahood can be won by other means, what reasons are there for taking the path of Tantra?

Apparently there are some people for whom it is a uniquely suitable way. It also has the distinct advantage of being a very quick one. Those who pursue the *sutra* paths may take many, many lifetimes to reach the ultimate goal; the Tantric practitioner may do so in a single lifetime if he follows Highest Yoga Tantra.

When the *chela* is ready to begin serious practice, this *guru* will initiate him into the *mandala* of his chosen deity. The ritual itself is known as *abhisheka* and possesses connotations of empowerment insofar as it not only authorizes practice but also endows it with special potency. Tantric initiations are often large public events. Many thousands of people have flocked to the Kalachakra initiations that His Holiness the Dalai Lama has given at Bodh Gaya and in the West in recent years. Most of these will not embark upon serious practice under a *guru;* for them, attendance at the initiation represents a way of gathering blessings and of establishing a strong karmic connection with the particular tantra involved that may ripen in a future lifetime.

The seriously committed *chela,* on the other hand, will receive teachings and begin the preliminary practices that are essential for establishing the correct foundation of purity, correct view, and sound motivation. Ethical and other restraints have to be observed, and he will have to perform such strenuous and humbling feats as the legendary one hundred thousand prostrations and similar permutations of *mantra* recitations, offerings, and other devotional actions.

His Holiness the Dalai Lama gives this advice to those wishing to be initiated into a Tantric path:

> Initially, you should take refuge in the Three Jewels from the round orb of your heart, then take a vow of individual emancipation, and after that generate the aspirational and practical minds of enlightenment. Then, when you arrive at the point where it is suitable to hear Tantra, you should receive teachings on Ashvaghosha's *Twenty Stanzas on the Bodhisattva Vow* (*Bodhisattvasamvaravimshaka*) and *Fifty Stanzas on the Guru* (*Gurupañchashika*). Then you may receive initiation.*

Vitally important at this stage is Guru Yoga, which involves practices concerned with developing faith in and devotion towards the *lama*-guide, and with generally deepening the dharmic connection with him. For the *guru* is not just a kindly spiritual chaperone. He must be regarded as identical with the Buddha and with the chosen *yidam*. Tantric practices are moreover actually stated to be quite ineffectual if performed without his empowering blessing. The special nature of the relationship with him can in fact hardly be understated. It is extremely dynamic and powerful.

Another important part of Tantric practice is Deity Yoga. This involves the development of a relationship with the particular *yidam* and the realization of his/her enlightened qualities. The proximity and intensity of the relationship that the *chela* will attempt to achieve will vary according to the level of Tantra at which he is working. At the Action Tantra level, for instance, the deity is conceived as the lord and the practitioner as his devotee, so the relationship is essentially a separate one, and the practices performed are external: the *chela* recites *mantras* and prayers, performs *mudras* and prostrations, makes offerings, and so forth. Actual meditation on the deity is not so important at this stage, but becomes increasingly more so as one ascends the Tantric ladder.

At the topmost level, that of Highest Yoga Tantra, there are two main stages: the Generation Stage and the Completion Stage.

The Generation Stage is essentially preparatory. Here the practitioner learns to conjure the deity and his *mandala* out of the primal emptiness of his mind or out of a seed syllable (*bija*), to visualize the deity in fine detail and to dissolve him/her back into emptiness.

---

* H.H. the XIVth Dalai Lama, "The Essence of Tantra" in Tsong-kha-ka, *Tantra in Tibet* (London: Allen & Unwin, 1977), Introduction.

The Completion Stage is about actualization—specifically the achievement of full buddhahood by special yogic means. A very specialized view of the human organism comes into play here, which sees the gross human body as containing two other bodies of increasing subtlety. These three bodies correspond to the Mahayana classification of the Three Bodies of the Buddha: Dharmakaya, Nirmanakaya, and Sambhogakaya. The most subtle body consists of fine channels called *nadi* along which a number of plexus points or *chakras* are disposed. A so-called wind energy circulates through this system, which is basically inseparable from consciousness, but in its most gross forms manifests as passions like anger and lust. In the unregenerate individual, the *nadi* are knotted up, so the movement of the wind energy is vitiated. Using the virtuoso powers of concentration perfected by means of intensive practice at the Generation Stage, the Tantric yogi seeks to direct and dissolve the wind energy into the minute *bindu* or "droplets" situated in the heart *chakra*. If this is achieved, conceptual thought automatically and instantaneously ceases, and what remains is nothing less than the primordial state itself: *Mahamudra*.

Controversy surrounds Buddhist Tantra—and indeed seems to have done so from its earliest phases—on account of its apparently unconventional methods and symbolism. In a recent conversation, a Western student was discussing the demise of Buddhism in India with a learned Indian Theravadim *bhikshu*.

"The reason can be summed up in one word," the *bhikshu* announced.

"Islam?" ventured the Westerner.

"No, Tantra!" came the unequivocal reply.

Sexual symbolism, which certainly abounds in Tantra, is no doubt largely responsible for such attitudes. Many Tantric deities are shown in passionate union with their consorts. This has different connotations from its Hindu counterpart, for here the masculine denotes the active force of skillful means *(upaya)*, and the feminine the passive quality of wisdom *(prajña)*; enlightenment results from their union. The four stages of relationship between men and women (looking, smiling, touching, and physical union) are also used as analogies for the kinds of relationship that are possible with one's chosen deity.

As for sexual yoga, there is a tradition that this may be practiced in certain very special and closely controlled circumstances during the Completion Stage of Highest Yoga Tantra, but only by advanced practitioners who have transcended egotism and generated perfect *bodhicitta*.

Recently a Western student asked her *guru* whether such practices were still used.

"They're secret practices," the learned *khenpo* replied "so how can I know?"

Finally, what is the modern Westerner to make of Tantra?

Its vast pantheon of deities, its rituals, symbolism, and yogic practiced together indicate that we are here dealing to a very great extent with what in the West is generally classified as magic. But this is not to say that it is primitive superstition; it is in fact highly developed methodologically, and reconciled with the most sophisticated metaphysical notions and the loftiest spiritual aspirations. It works, however, extensively with levels of consciousness that developed back in the mists of history long before the emergence of rationalism and the dualistic view of the world that currently holds sway. These ancient residues, which still actively exist in our multidimensional consciousness, basically operate like dream consciousness. There is no distinction between inner and outer: thoughts and imaginings, feelings, impressions, experiences—all flow freely in and out of each other. This being so, a deity conjured up in the mind is as "real" as a person encountered in the so-called outside world; and in the same way, a picture or a string of words (spell) can possess immense effective power.

Unfortunately, in the West we have tried to cut ourselves off from these dimensions; we fear and repress them. In the ancient East, however, they were rather more humane and sensible. As Buddhism developed—and this is very particularly and clearly brought out in its Tibetan phase—though it engaged in rivalry with the pre-existing traditions that it encountered, it did not attempt to expunge and obliterate them, but instead was wisely prepared to assimilate them. Thus the old animistic gods became "guardians of the *dharma*" and their power was thereby harnessed to the cause of enlightenment.

This, therefore, we tentatively suggest, explains the particular power of Tantra. It embodies all the strengths of all the forms of Buddhism that developed hitherto, and to them it adds the magical dimension. So it could be said to be a logical culmination and completion of the process of development of Buddhism: all aspects of the human being are here mobilized in the great adventure of enlightenment. This also explains the immense popularity currently enjoyed by Tantra among Westerners, for it fulfills a need that is not really met in any of the serious Western traditions. "Magic," as it survived in this hemisphere, is a somewhat dishevelled remnant, and usually attracts the wrong kind of practitioner for the wrong reasons. Tantra, on the other hand, offers people ways and means of integrating the magical into their lives and applying it to authentic spiritual endeavors.

The Spread of Buddhism

E·L·E·V·E·N

The Southern Transmission: Sri Lanka, Burma, Thailand, Laos, Kampuchea, and Indonesia

Fortunately, the fire and fury of the Muslim invasions, which by the thirteenth century had all but expunged Buddhism from the land of its origin, did not totally obliterate the religion from the face of the earth, for by that time it was already firmly implanted in the soil of other countries.

Two thousand years ago, Indian influences spread throughout south and southeast Asia, and these included all forms of Buddhism as well as aspects of Hinduism. Today we find three southern Asian countries, Sri Lanka, Burma, and Thailand, which may still be called Buddhist countries in the full sense of the term. What is locally regarded as a pure form of Theravada has established itself strongly in all of them on a firm monastic basis, with Pali as the canonical and liturgical language. We will, accordingly, use Pali terminology in this chapter. Indonesia, however, is rather different—other developments took place there.

Different groups lived in this general area two thousand years ago and their distribution did not conform to the national boundary lines on any modern map. Later they were supplanted by other racial groups and gradually, over the centuries, a picture more closely resembling the present-day one began to emerge. Of course, being an island, the first country we will look at is an exception to this general rule.

SRI LANKA

Around 240 B.C., the Emperor Ashoka dispatched his *bhikkhu* son, Mahinda, to the beautiful tropical island of Sri Lanka (or Ceylon), which lies in the Indian Ocean just off the southern tip of India. Mahinda was very well received by King Devanampiyatissa and entertained at the royal capital of Anuradhapura. Crowds flocked to hear him preach the *dhamma* and it was early on predicted that, "These *bhikkhus* will be lords upon this island." And so indeed it proved to be. Devanampiyatissa donated to them a tract of land outside Anuradhapura, the former Mahamegha Park, and here a great *vihara,* the Mahavihara, was founded, which in time became the headquarters of Buddhism upon the island.

Seeing the enthusiastic reception that Mahinda evoked everywhere, King Devanampiyatissa asked him whether Buddhism had yet truly taken root upon the island.

"Not yet, Your Majesty," Mahinda is reputed to have replied. "It has certainly sprung roots but they have not yet grown deep into the soil. Only when a *sima** has been established and when a son born in Sri Lanka of Sri Lankan parents becomes a monk in Sri Lanka, only then will it be true to say that the roots of the *dhamma* are deeply embedded here."

Those conditions were fulfilled soon afterwards.

Mahinda's nun sister, Sanghamitta, was also brought over from India to establish an order of nuns. With her came a branch of the bodhi tree, which was duly planted in the grounds of the Mahavihara; later, saplings were transplanted to other sites on the island. These living connections with the basic origins of Buddhism are still to be seen.

It was in Sri Lanka during the reign of King Vattagamani (89-77 B.C.) that the Pali scriptures were first committed to writing on prepared palm leaves at the Aloka Vihara. Another scholarly achievement in Sri Lanka was the translation into Pali of the old Sinhalese commentaries in the fifth century B.C. One of the scholars involved, Buddhaghosa, also produced an important work called the *Visuddhimagga* ("Path of Purification"), of which Conze has written:

> The book is a compendium of the Tipitaka and one of the great
> masterpieces of Buddhist literature which describes authoritatively,

---

* A *sima* is a consecrated area in which ordinations may be performed.

lucidly, and in great detail the principal meditational practices of the Buddhist Yogin.*

Sri Lanka did not escape schism during the following centuries, and some of its dissenting schools were influenced by Mahayana and Tantric developments. A major controversy broke out which resulted in a secession from the Mahavihara and the establishment of the Abhayagirivihara, the monks of the latter taking a more progressive line than the orthodox Sthaviravadins. Thereafter royal patronage flowed now to one side, now to the other, but in the long run the more conservative disposition triumphed. A council held at Anuradhapura in 1160 finally settled the matter by suppressing all non-Theravada schools.

The progress and well-being of Buddhism on the island was inevitably affected by political upheavals, including invasion from south India and, later, European colonialism. From the sixteenth century onwards the Sinhalese suffered the intrusions first of the Portuguese, then of the Dutch, and finally of the British. Efforts at conversion to Christianity were made and Buddhism was often persecuted to the extent that its very survival on the island was at times jeopardized. *Bhikkhus* had even to be imported from other Theravadin countries, notably Thailand and Burma, to ensure continuity.

The revival of Buddhism got fully under way in Sri Lanka towards the end of the last century. Ven. Sri Sumangala and Ven. Dharmananda established two Buddhist monastic colleges, the Vidyodaya and the Vidyolankara Pirivenas (monastic colleges), in 1873 and 1875 respectively. Here traditional education in Buddhism, Pali, Sanskrit, Sinhalese history, and related subjects could be obtained. At about the same time a brilliant young monk named Ven. Mohottivatte Gunananda challenged the Christians to open religious debate. The Christians took up the challenge, most notably at Pandura in 1873, when they bandied arguments rather unsuccessfully with Ven. Gunananda in public for about a week. Reports of these debates got into the foreign newspapers and so reached the attention of the distinguished pioneer Theosophist, Colonel Henry Steel Olcott, in the U.S.A. He came to Sri Lanka with the leader of the Theosophical Society, Madame H. P. Blavatsky, and both of them "took Pansil" (i.e., the Five Precepts) at Galle in 1880. Thereafter the Theosophists worked alongside native Buddhist idealists like Ven. Sri Sumangala and Anagarika Dharmapala (David Hewavitarne, 1864–1933), to regenerate Sinhalese Buddhism.

---

* Conze, *A Short History of Buddhism,* 59.

The movement was very successful. In 1887, after twelve years of effort, there were forty-six schools on the island providing Buddhist education whereas formerly there had been only Christian schools. By 1903 there were one hundred and seventy-four Buddhist schools.

During the present century numerous Europeans have received ordination and/or Buddhist training in Sri Lanka, notably the German-born *bhikkhus* Ven. Ñyanatiloka, Ven. Ñyanaponika, and the British-born Ven. Ñyanamoli. The island hermitage at Dodanduwa (Galle district) has been a notable center for training European *bhikkhus*. Meanwhile the Buddhist Publication Society, founded by Ven. Ñyanaponika, has done much useful Buddhist literary propaganda work in the English language. Its headquarters are in Kandy.

Mention must be made of the noble efforts made by the Sri Lankans themselves to help bring knowledge of Buddhism to the West. A Sri Lankan Buddhist *vihara* was established in London in 1926 by Anagarika Dharmapala, and though closed in 1940, was reopened in 1954 by Ven. Narada Mahathera, who also performed valuable *Dhammaduta* (or Buddhist missionary) work elsewhere, notably in Indonesia and Vietnam. Many important *bhikkhu* teachers have resided at the London *vihara*. Meanwhile, Dr. G. P. Malalasekera, the professional diplomat and scholar, was also a notable ambassador for Buddhism in the West. He became the first editor-in-chief of the Sri Lankan Government-sponsored *Encyclopaedia of Buddhism* (1966–).

Buddhist monks have enjoyed a high measure of social influence, even of political power, right from the early days of Buddhism upon the island. They have also been rich and powerful landowners. Since national independence was won in 1947, the role of the monk as a political animal has been a matter of keen controversy. Ven. Walpola Rahula played a conspicuous part in the debate as an apologist for the politically engaged monk. By contrast, however, there are and ever have been purist monks who have rejected social and political status, and withdrawn to the seclusion of the forest in search of that ascetic simplicity of lifestyle that they see as essential to the proper practice of the Buddha's way.

A significant modern development in Sri Lanka has been the Sarvodaya movement ("The Awakening and Welfare of All") of Aryaratna, which has sought to apply Buddhist principles to social and economic development at the grass-roots level. As Ken Jones wrote in *The Middle Way* (Vol. 59. No. 1, pp 52–3):

> It emphasises self-realisation through compassionate social action
> in creating a simple, egalitarian co-operative commonwealth. The
> purpose of material well-being is to support individual spiritual

growth, with cultural diversity and creativity, local community development, environmental harmony and appropriate technology all directed to the same end.

Sri Lanka is associated with two important relics of the Buddha. In the early days of Mahinda and Sanghamitta, a collar-bone was reputedly brought from India and in 371 A.D. a tooth arrived. The Portuguese claimed to have seized and destroyed the tooth, but the Sri Lankans counter that only a fake was destroyed and that the real one survives to this day. Each year it is paraded with great festivity through the streets of Kandy during the Esala Perahera—a fine and fitting celebration of a religious tradition that goes back such a very long way.

Claiming to be the guardians of the longest surviving continuous tradition of Buddhism, the Theravada Buddhists of Sri Lanka are conscious of having the special role of preserving the original teachings of the Buddha in a pure form. This inevitably implies conservatism and orthodoxy, but it is a conservatism and an orthodoxy that have had the vigor to remain a living force for over two thousand years. Today there are about twenty thousand monks on the island.

BURMA

Lying immediately to the east of India, Burma is carved from north to south by the great river Irrawaddy. The original inhabitants were the Mon people, who also occupied parts of what is today Thailand. The Burmese themselves came down from the mountainous regions to the east of Tibet and established kingdoms in central Burma by about the third century A.D.

It seems that Buddhism did not strongly establish itself here until the fifth or sixth centuries B.C. Afterwards there is evidence of both Hinayana and Mahayana activity. Tantrism also filtered down from the north, and one particularly scandalous sect known as the Aris (after *arya* meaning "noble") is known to have existed.

An important event for the Theravada cause was the conversion of King Anawrahta of Pagan (1044–1077) by a certain Shin Arahan, who was a Mon. Anawrahta attempted to suppress the Aris and then petitioned Manuka, the Mon King of Thaton, for scriptures. When he received an unenthusiastic response, Anawrahta reacted in a somewhat unBuddhist fashion by sending in his troops to simply appropriate what he wanted by force. Manuka was led back to Pagan in chains, and thirty-two elephants carried away his wealth, Buddhist relics, images, and scriptures. His monks, artists, and craftsmen were appropriated as well.

Anawrahta's dynasty was to hold sway for two centuries and during that time a great Buddhist culture blossomed at Pagan. Literally thousands of temples (including the famous Ananda Temple) and *pagodas* were built in a relatively small area, which has caused descriptive images like "a forest of stone" to be coined. Unfortunately, Pagan was attacked by Mongol invaders in 1287.

A turbulent period ensued when Burma was dismembered into warring states. Buddhism of both the Hinayana and Mahayana varieties persisted, however, and great temples and pagodas continued to be built. The most famous Burmese *pagoda* is the gilded Shwedagon in Rangoon, 326 feet high, started in the fourteenth century as a monumental reliquary for some of the Buddha's hair.

During this period there was dissension within the ranks of the Theravada fraternity. One party, which traced its lineage back to a Sinhalese monk named Capata (twelfth century), disputed the validity of ordinations dispensed by other lineages. The matter was resolved towards the end of the fifteenth century when King Dhammaceti of Pegu (1472–1492) introduced a "canonically valid monastic succession" from Sri Lanka. Since then Sri Lankan Theravada has predominated, though a folk religious tradition venerating popular deities known as *nats* continues to exert a hold over the ordinary Burmese.

Burma was united as a single country in the eighteenth century, and during the reign of King Mindon (1853–1878) Buddhism once more enjoyed royal patronage. Between 1868 and 1871, a council was held at Mandalay, King Mindon's capital, when the text of the Tipitaka was revised prior to being formally inscribed on some 729 marble slabs. These were erected in the precincts of the Kuthodaw Pagoda.

The British came to Burma in 1885 during the reign of the last king, Thibaw (1878–1885), and governed the country as a province of their prized Indian Empire. During this colonial period, Buddhism was closely identified with the Burmese national identity: "To be a Burmese is to be a Buddhist." Buddhist monks and groupings like the Y.M.B.A. (Young Men's Buddhist Association) played an important part in nationalist agitation against colonial power. During this period the so-called shoe question became charged with symbolic significance for the Burmese. This arose from the insensitive British habit of disdaining to remove footwear within the hallowed precincts of Buddhist shrines.

Following independence from the British in 1948, Burma has been a socialist state and presently it is a secular one too. Its Buddhist traditions have survived, however, and still exert a strong hold over the people. Ordination into *sangha* is greatly respected, and most men will shave their heads and enter the robe, if only for a short, token period. Another council was held in Rangoon in 1954–1956, when the Tipitaka was again put under close scrutiny by wise *mahatheras*. Traditional Buddhist festivals—Thingyan, Thadingyut, Tazaungdine, Tabaung— are still celebrated enthusiastically in all parts of the country. *Pagodas* continue to be built and embellished: the latest, the Mahavijaya Pagoda, in the vicinity of the Shwedagon, was formally completed in 1986.

In modern times thousands of people, including Westerners, have derived much benefit from the intensive meditation practices developed by masters like Mahasi Sayadaw and U Ba Khin. Mahasi Sayadaw (1904–1982) was an ordained monk who began teaching meditation in Rangoon at the request of the first post-Independence Prime Minister, U Nu, who himself strove hard, though not always successfully, to establish the new Burma on a sound Buddhist footing. Centers teaching Mahasi Sayadaw's method have sprung up all over the world. U Ba Khin (1899–1971), on the other hand, was a remarkable layman who managed to combine serious Buddhist practice with a highly active life involving government service at cabinet level. He had studied *vipassana* meditation under Saya Thet Gyi, a well-known lay teacher who had been a pupil of Ledi Sayadaw. Ba Khin's method involves sweeping the body with the attention, noting the evanescent play of sensations. Many U Ba Khin centers have been set up around the world, and the method has also been vigorously propagated by S. N. Goenka.

Other important modern Burmese masters include Sunlun Sayadaw, Taungpula Sayadaw, U Pandita, Mohnyin Sayadaw, and Mogok Sayadaw. Rena Sircar is a former nun who has taught in the West. Mention must also be made of the good work of the scholarly Sayadaw U Thittila, who spent some years in London, and was for a time librarian at the Buddhist Society.

THAILAND

Thailand, formerly Siam, is a beautiful country about the size of France situated in southeast Asia. Elephants still haul teak in its northern mountains; the central plains, on the other hand, are one of the world's most fertile rice-growing areas; lush tropical beaches abound in the south.

Buddhism is traditionally said to have first appeared among the Mon people, the original inhabitants, in the third century B.C., brought by missionaries sent from India by the Emperor Ashoka. What exactly took place historically is unclear, though a fine Buddhist art evolved in Dvaravati, a Mon kingdom that flourished from about the sixth century A.D. A few centuries later, however, the land fell under the sway of the Khmers of Kampuchea and its religious life was influenced accordingly. There are traces of both Mahayana and Hindu influences from this time.

The Thai people, though not themselves racially Chinese, originated in what is now southern China, and it is therefore highly likely that their first encounter with Buddhism was with one of its Chinese forms. By the fourteenth century, however, having ousted the hitherto dominant Khmers and established themselves both as masters of parts of present-day Thailand and of neighboring Laos, they promoted the Sri Lankan brand of Theravada Buddhism. About 1361 B.C., *bhikkhus*, including one Mahasami Sangharaja, were brought over from Sri Lanka to "purify" local Buddhism, and Pali was established as the religious language. The Thais were able to return the compliment when in the mid-eighteenth century they sent monks to Sri Lanka to revivify the ailing Sinhalese Sangha. This strong Theravada tradition has survived in Thailand down to the present time.

Today Buddhism is the state religion of Thailand and over ninety-two percent of the population adhere to it. The king has to be a Buddhist, though his mandate as Defender of Religion means that his formal protection is extended to all persuasions: Hindu, Muslim, Christian, Confucian, and whatever else, even the Communist Party.

The custom of most young men to spend a period of time during the Vassa (the rainy season) in a *wat* (Buddhist monastery) survives to the present. They learn what it is like to be a monk, rising early to chant and meditate, refraining from eating after noon and abiding by the Vinaya. If the life suits them, they will stay on for a few years—or for life. Young boys also become temporary novices. According to custom, they are given a big send-off and ride away magnificently costumed as little Prince Siddharthas; later their finery is removed, their heads are shaven and they too don the yellow robe.

The present king of Thailand himself spent a fortnight in the robe at the royal Wat Bovornives. His ancestor, King Rama IV (or Mongkut, the inspiration for the musical *The King and I*) also entered the order for a short time, and stayed for some twenty-seven years, becoming a renowned Pali scholar and reformer of the *sangha*. When the king, Mongkut's elder half-brother, died, he harkened to the call of duty and duly ascended the throne. Both he and his son, King Chulalongkorn, did much to modernize the country while respecting its ancient traditions.

Buddhism is highly organized in modern Thailand and subject to a degree of state control. There is a Supreme Patriarch, appointed by the king, who is therefore nominally head of the Buddhist "church"; below ranges a pyramid of ecclesiastical hierarchy radiating outwards into the regions. As a result of King Mongkut's reforms, there is also a basic division of the Buddhist "church" into the Mahanikaya and Dhammayuttika Nikaya "denominations," though the differences between them are very minor today.

In recent years, in common with other southeast Asian countries, Thailand has been launched through an accelerating pattern of disturbing change that has created many complex social and political problems. The role of Buddhist monks within these changing patterns is obviously subject to different interpretations. The conservative *sangha* has in fact received some criticism for its opposition to change and reform. Meanwhile, more radical elements in the *sangha* have argued for a more activist stance.

Many Westerners have derived a great deal of benefit from the living Buddhist traditions of Thailand, especially from the ascetic forest tradition that flourishes in the northeast of the country. Here a strong tradition of highly effective meditation and Vinaya practice has been preserved. Of particular importance has been the influence of Ajahn Cha, a disciple of Ajahn Mun, who has been responsible for training many notable Western *bhikkhus* at Wat Nong Pah Pong in Ubon province. Ajahn Cha's foremost Western disciple is the American-born Ajahn Sumedho Thera, who first helped to establish the international Wat Pah Nanachat under Ajahn Cha's auspices and later Chithurst Forest Monastery in rural West Sussex, the first of a number of highly successful monasteries and centers in Britain. Branch centers are now springing up in other parts of the world too. All these centers derive a high level of support from both Thailand itself and from expatriate Thais. Thai temples have also been established in the West: for example, the Buddhapadipa Temple in London, where a Thai *bot* (meeting hall) has been recently constructed in traditional style.

Other influential modern Thai teachers include the scholarly Buddhadasa Bhikkhu, Ajahn Maha Boowa, and also Dhiravamsa, who first came to Britain in the robe in 1964 as Chao Khun Dhammasudhi, but later resigned monk status to become a lay meditation teacher. He now works mainly in the United States.

LAOS

Laos is a tiny landlocked country sandwiched between powerful neighbors: China, Burma, Thailand, Kampuchea, and Vietnam. Small wonder then that its history has been much marked by strife and foreign domination. During its early period, it fell under the power of the Khmers, who probably introduced Buddhism and Brahminism. Later it became virtually a province of Thailand, and, in consequence, the Thai form of Sri Lankan Theravada became dominant among the Laotians and survived until modern times.

A Communist revolution of the familiar southeast Asian variety took place in 1975, whereupon thousands of monks fled the country, including the Supreme Patriarch of Laos. A few *bhikkhus* who supported the Communist Pathet Lao, however, chose to remain behind. Though the Communist government initially attempted to destroy the *sangha* as an active force in Laotian life, it failed, and subsequently becoming more pragmatic, tried to utilize the monks as teachers of the Marxist creed. The residual *sangha* members have attempted to adapt to the changed situation, but fundamental contradictions existing between the Marxist and Buddhist philosophies have yet to be fully resolved. In the long run, therefore, it is still to be seen whether an authentic form of Buddhism will be able to survive in Laos.

KAMPUCHEA

Kampuchea, formerly Cambodia, is situated in the Mekong valley between Thailand and Vietnam, though unlike Laos it enjoys access to the sea. The Khmer people are the dominant group there. During its early history, which is poorly documented, the area fell, like Burma and Thailand, under Indian cultural and religious influences. Both Brahmanism and Mahayana Buddhism certainly enjoyed favor, and the Sanskrit language was used.

Then, around the ninth century, a great civilization blossomed. It centered on the Angkor region, and over the following centuries the Khmer kings glorified themselves by building numbers of marvelous temples, each an intricately carved stone Mount Meru surrounded by walls, terraces, and moats; some of the larger ones even have palaces and offices within their precincts. The most famous is Angkor Wat itself. Here syncretistic Mahayana-brahmanical rituals were performed with elaborate ceremony; there were also facilities for scholarship. But the cost of building and maintenance bore heavily on the backs of the people and both the inevitable internal unrest as well as attack from outside weakened the dynasty. Finally, Angkor was abandoned to the ministrations of the jungle in the fifteenth century.

It is thought that Theravada Buddhism had meanwhile come into ascendency around the thirteenth century, possibly as the result of Thai influence. It established itself strongly, but was totally destroyed during the tyranny of the Communist Khmer Rouge, who took over the country in 1975, intent upon creating a new order by literally exterminating all representatives of the old, which unfortunately included the Buddhist *sangha*. The Vietnamese invasion of 1979 ousted the Khmer Rouge and religious life was sanctioned again to a limited degree. The present situation is uncertain.

INDONESIA

That Buddhism penetrated the Indonesian archipelago long ago and thrived there is palpably borne out by the fact that Borobodur, the largest Buddhist monument in southern Asia, is situated on the island of Java. Borobodur, which dates from the mid-nineteenth century A.D., is a massive stone replica of the cosmic *mandala*. First there is a series of five terraces, the area of the base terrace being some 403 square feet. Above there are three ascending rings of *stupas,* with a tall *stupa,* symbol of Mount Meru, in the very center; its tip touches a height of 108 feet. The whole edifice is prodigally decorated with some twenty-seven thousand square feet of carvings and over five hundred stone Buddhas.

Buddhism probably came to the archipelago along with other Indian influences around the fifth century A.D. The Theravada may have been favored by the King of Srivijaya, a kingdom on Sumatra. Tantra, however, was later to become very popular on the large island of Java, where it enjoyed the patronage of the Shailendra dynasty. Borobodur is one of its artistic products. Later a cult evolved that combined Buddhist and Shaivite Tantrism, and this persists in Bali and elsewhere to the present time, though on account of the dominance of the Hindu components the Buddhist contribution is often overlooked. That this survived the coming of Islam to the islands from the fifteenth century onwards bears evidence of its vigor and the favorableness of local conditions.

In recent years, Buddhism has begun to re-emerge as a separate religion in Indonesia. This process has been stimulated by Chinese immigrants, by missions sent from Thailand and Sri Lanka, and by the energy of monks like the Ven. Jinarakkhita Thera, who was at one time a pupil of Mahasi Sayadaw. Both the Theravada and Mahayana traditions are therefore now again represented in this part of the world.

T·W·E·L·V·E

The Northern Transmission: The Northwestern Springboard and the Silk Route

A different thrust took Buddhism northwards from India into central Asia, China, Tibet, Mongolia, Korea, and Japan, as well as into the king-doms straddling the Himalayan chain: Bhutan, Sikkim, Nepal, and Ladakh. Both Theravada and Mahayana teachings were disseminated in the process, but in the long run the Mahayana was to prevail—and indeed to undergo exciting new phases of development. Today, however, if not entirely extinguished in places like China and Tibet, where it once flourished, only a drastically truncated remnant of Buddhism survives. We can in fact call none of these northern countries Buddhist countries as we applied the term to Sri Lanka, Burma, and Thailand.

THE NORTHWESTERN SPRINGBOARD

One area played a vital role in the transmission of Buddhism to China and other parts of east Asia. This lay to the northwest of the Indian heartland and encompassed parts of Kashmir and the Punjab, extensive portions of the modern state of Pakistan and neighboring Afghanistan, and even extended through into eastern Iran and the southernmost part of what today is Soviet central Asia (formerly Russian Turkestan). At its heart lay Gandhara, a district of profoundly evocative associations for Buddhists. Gendhara once lay in eastern Afghanistan/western Pakistan, centering on Purushapura, which in its modern manifestation as Peshawar is the first major township that the weary overland traveller to India encounters once he has crossed the Khyber Pass.

This general area lies at what was once one of the world's great crossroads. Here East met West: rich and powerful influences from India converged and mingled with others coming from Iran, western Asia, and the Greco-Roman world, from central and northern Asia, from China and the Far East. Small wonder then that this was to become one of the breeding grounds of the Mahayana as well as the springboard from which Buddhism was launched on its northward and eastward journeys.

Trade routes passed this way, and along them sometimes tramped the feet of conquering armies as well as those of successive waves of migrants. Notable were the Aryans, who had such a profound effect upon Indian civilization. Then around 327 B.C. came Alexander the Great, who cut a swathe through the power of the Persians then dominant in the area. His dreams of glory fizzled out in the Punjab, however, when his weary troops lay down their arms and refused to proceed. Alexander returned home but he left influential pockets of Greeks behind him. Scythians, Parthians, Kushans, and Huns all came afterwards, and much later of course, the armies of the Prophet Muhammad, who were to dispense such violence in India.

Buddhist missionaries are reputed to have been sent to Gandhara not long after the Parinirvana of the Buddha, but the religion did not take firm root in the northwest until the time of the Emperor Ashoka, whose grandfather, Chandragupta Maurya, had extended imperial power in this direction. Ashoka himself had in his youth served as Viceroy in Taxila, a great center of learning and trade that once flourished near Gandhara, and when he came to power he placed great importance upon Buddhist missionary efforts in this corner of his great empire.

After the decline of the Maurya dynasty in the second century B.C., the Greco-Bactrians reasserted their power and pushed their conquests as far as the Punjab. They were Greeks who had settled in Bactria, a fertile region lying between the Oxus river and the Hindu Kush mountains in northern Afghanistan. During this period Buddhism was favorably regarded by one Greek king, Menandros, who was apparently afflicted by some dire spiritual crisis for which he could find no relief until he met a certain Buddhist monk named Nagasena. Menandros's discussions with Nagasena are recorded in the *Milindapañha,* an important noncanonical Pali text. They revolved around the problem of how the Buddha could have believed in rebirth without at the same time believing in a reincarnating "I" or ego. Nagasena was able to masterfully resolve the king's difficulties, and, as a result, Buddhism gained a powerful patron; indeed, Menandros is reputed to have died a member of the *sangha*.

Later the Greeks were supplanted by other people, including the Scythians and the Parthians. Afterwards came the Kushans, a nomadic people who had originated in China (where they were known as the *Yueh-chih*) and thence migrated by a roundabout route through central Asia to Bactria, the Oxus, and the Kabul valleys, and eventually on to the plains of India. The Kushans (who are also sometimes called the Indo-Scythians) established a great empire which extended across northern India, up into parts of Chinese Turkestan, westwards into Afghanistan, and on almost as far as the Sea of Aral in present-day Russia. Though they began by attacking Buddhism, they later became dedicated patrons of the religion and enthusiastic buildings of monasteries and *stupas*. Thus between the first and the third centuries A.D., Buddhism blossomed in this vital part of the world. Its greatest patron was Kanishka (*c.* 78–101 A.D.). Bharat Singh Upadhyaya has written:

> Kanishka's reign . . . marked a turning point in the history of Buddhism and Buddhist literature. It witnessed the rise of Mahayana Buddhism and the magnificent literary activity started by Parshva, Ashvagosa, Vasumitra, and others. It was in this age that Pali gave place to Sanskrit. In the field of art, Gandhara sculptures developed and the figures of the Buddha and Bodhisattvas began to appear. It was during Kanishka's reign and largely through his efforts that Buddhism was successfully introduced into central and eastern Asia. There was ceaseless literary activity throughout his vast empire. . . . A truly integrated Asian culture came into existence at this time, based as it was on the highest purposes of life for which Buddhism stood.*

Apparently Kanishka started out as a bellicose young potentate of the usual sort but underwent an Ashoka-like conversion to Buddhism after witnessing the appalling slaughter caused by his campaigns in Kashgar, Yarkand, and Khotan (modern Chinese Sinkiang). He is reputed to have convened a Fourth Buddhist Council, when the scriptures and commentaries of the Sarvastivadin school were compiled and committed to writing under the presidency of Vasumitra; this, however, is dismissed as a pure myth by many scholars. He is also credited with building numerous monasteries and *stupas*.

* P. V. Bapat, ed., "Some Great Buddhists After Asoka," in *2500 Years of Buddhism* (Delhi: Govt. of India Publications Division, 1959), 199–200.

The Kushan dynasty was ousted by the Sassanids, who came from Iran and professed the fire-worshipping creed of Zarathushtra. They, and the rulers of the petty kingdoms that supplanted the Kushan empire, seem to have been generally tolerant towards Buddhism, however, and the religion continued to flourish between the third and fifth centuries. It was during this period that the cave monasteries at Bamiyan in northern Afghanistan were dug out. Bamiyan also boasts the largest stone statue in the world: a standing Buddha 177 feet high.

Buddhism had reached its apogee in this region by the fifth century; thereafter it declined, hit by the depredations of the White Huns (Hephthalites), by general economic decline, and a resurgence of Hinduism. When the Chinese pilgrim, Hsüan-tsang, passed through en route to India in the seventh century, he encountered much devastation—even in once glorious Gandhara. Only one corner of Purushapura was still inhabited and most of the numerous monasteries were ruined and deserted.

THE SILK ROUTE

If the part of central Asia we have just been looking at was the springboard from which Buddhism was launched into China, then its trajectories followed the courses of the Silk Route, that great international mercantile artery along which from time immemorial the fine silks of far Cathay were transported by caravan to the eager markets of the West. For along with their goods, the merchants carried ideas of all sorts, including religious ideas, and Buddhist missionaries originating in central Asia—Parthians, Soghdians, Bactrians, Kushans, and perhaps a salting of Indians, too—also tramped the same dusty routes.

The first leg of the Silk Route ran through the Tarim Basin, an extremely inhospitable corridor occupied by great sand-dune deserts, notably the Taklamakan, and bounded by soaring mountain ranges (the Tien Shan and the Kun Lun). Nowadays this lies in Chinese Sinkiang (formerly Turkestan) but in ancient times it lay beyond Jade Gate, the entrance to China proper, though the Chinese attempted to assert control here in order to protect their valuable trading connection. Beyond Tun-huang (modern Dunhuang), the Silk Route divided into two: one spur ran northwards through Turfan, Kucha, and Kashgar, the other south through Khotan.

The importance of the ancient communities of this region was not merely as staging-posts on the route along which the *dharma* was transmitted to China. A great Buddhist civilization, now called Serindian or Sino-Indian, once flourished here, brought no doubt by Buddhist missionaries from the central Asian springboard and consolidated by

Kanishka's conquests in the area. It had its own art in which Greco-Roman and Iranian as well as Indian influences were strongly reflected, and of course there were traces of Chinese influence too. Little was known about this Buddhist civilization, however, until the closing years of the last century.

In 1888, a brutal Afghan named Daud Mohammed hacked down a young Scotsman named Andrew Dalgleish in the Karakorams. A redoubtable British agent, Lieutenant Hamilton Bower, who happened to be in Sinkiang at the time, was detailed to track down Dalgleish's killer. This he did, but during the course of his investigations Bower visited Kucha and there was able to purchase an ancient Sanskrit medical text written in Brahmi characters. This was only the beginning; soon the sands of the deserts of Sinkiang were yielding up a wealth of hitherto unsuspected texts in a variety of languages (Sanskrit, Prakrit, Gandhari, Tokharian, Soghdian, Khotanese, etc.) as well as works of art of a very high order, all remarkably well-preserved on account of the extreme aridity of the local climate.

When news of this reached the West and Japan, an archaeological scramble was set in motion. Large expeditions were mounted to plunder the lost cities of the Silk Route for their treasures. Sir Aurel Stein went in for Britain, Professor Paul Pelliot for France, Count Kozui Ohtani for Japan, Professor Albert von le Coq for Germany, and many more besides. Vast hoards of texts and artifacts—sometimes whole walls containing valuable frescoes—were crated up and transported out to foreign museums. The hoard in the British Museum alone is reputed to be so large that much of it still remains in the vaults of the building, unstudied and even uncataloged.

The greatest find of all, made by Aurel Stein, was at Dunhuang. Over one thousand temples and shrine rooms had been hollowed out of a cliff here forming a great monastery complex which had not only served as a settled community and haven for weary Buddhist monks plying the long trail between India and China, but had also in its day been a highly important translation center. Stein found wonderful paintings here, and, in a sealed chamber, a stupendous cache of texts and paintings on silk that had been hidden since the tenth century.

In recent times this area has been staunchly Muslim, and, despite the counter-religious efforts of the Chinese Communists who now control it, still remains so. Apparently, however, many of the ancient Buddhist centers in Sinkiang were abandoned before the Muslim incursions reached their height. The cause was probably the drying up of the glaciers in the high mountains, which rendered irrigation and hence life impossible in the harsh terrain. And so for one thousand years and more the sands of the deserts wafted over those sequestered outposts of early Buddhism.

T·H·I·R·T·E·E·N

The Northern Transmission: China

LATER HAN DYNASTY (25–220 A.D.)

In the first century A.D., because of a prophetic dream in which a great figure 16 feet high and radiant like the sun appeared to the Emperor Ming Ti, agents were dispatched to the west. Somewhere in the wastes of Tokharistan they met two *bodhisattvas* who had with them a white horse, a picture of Shakyamuni Buddha, and a copy of the *Sutra in 42 Sections,* a summary of basic Buddhist doctrines (with Mahayana interpolations) that still exists. The *bodhisattvas,* Kashyapa Matanga and Dharmaratna, agreed to return to the Han capital, Loyang. There they set about translating the *sutra* at a place called White Horse Temple (Pai-ma-ssu), which still exists though the buildings that presently stand on the site are of more recent construction.

In factual terms, however, what probably happened was rather more prosaic. Around the turn of the common era, Buddhism simply began to filter into China from central Asia. It was brought down the Silk Route by merchants, envoys, monks, and other travellers, and nurtured in the expatriate communities in Loyang and a few other northern cities. Down to the end of the Han period, during which China enjoyed a fairly stable centralized government, its progress among the native Chinese themselves was probably fairly slow because a number of important factors stood in the way of its acceptance. There was the deep-seated xenophobia of the Chinese themselves. Self-consciously regarding themselves as citizens of a great empire—the center of the world, no less—with a long and glorious history, a sublime culture, and noble traditions, what use then could they have for an alien cult? Buddhism was also in many ways inimical to the prevailing ideology, which derived from the sayings of the sage Confucius (551–479 B.C.). This upheld the ideal of a stable, harmonious social order in which every human unit, from the Emperor or Empress down to the humblest peasant, played their part according to hallowed custom. Confucianism is very much a this-worldly creed and as such its devotees could only look with disfavor on any religion that seemed to encourage the abandonment of all worldly ties in favor of the pursuit of a remote and vague spiritual ideal. Also the fact that the Buddhist *sangha* did not work, but looked to other people to support them, cut totally against established Chinese values.

Gradually, however, the barriers began to break down, and this process was probably aided by one particular factor: the presence in China of a home-grown mystical tradition called Taoism. This was traditionally said to derive from the teachings of the mythical Yellow Emperor, Huang Ti (2698–2597 B.C.), but it was reformed and revived by the great sage Lao Tzu, author of the classic *Tao Te Ching*. The Taoists were very un-Confucian in their dislike of the social world, which they thought artificial and corrupt. They advocated a return to simplicity and harmony with nature, and their ideal was *wu wei*, a kind of uncontrived mode of being that flowed with all the effortless suppleness of water out of the darkness of the ultimate unknowable mystery and adapted itself to whatever it encountered. The Chinese seem to have found certain points of similarity between the teachings and practices of the Taoists and those of the Buddhists, and this opened up an avenue whereby Buddhism was able to penetrate their culture. In Arthur Waley's words, they could regard Buddhism as "a sort of foreign Taoism."

The existence of a serious Buddhist community in Loyang emerges into the light of history in 148 A.D., when a Parthian missionary named An Shih-kao made his appearance. Other foreigners from central Asia and India followed in the succeeding years, notably a Kushan named Lokaksema. These are credited with bringing the Mahayana teachings. That they imparted them not only to members of expatriate communities but to local Chinese is borne out by the fact that the task of translating the Buddhist scriptures into Chinese was now begun with some energy.

As An Shih-kao and his colleagues were not fluent in Chinese, they used "translation teams" that included not only people conversant with the various relevant languages but also with the subtleties of Chinese literary style. A text would probably have been recited from memory, roughly translated, and then subjected to a process of progressive refinement. Furthermore, a new vocabulary had to be evolved to provide correlatives for specialist Buddhist terms, and though at first crude Taoist equivalents were employed, precise Chinese neologisms were later coined. For convenience, brief texts were chosen in the pioneering stages and often paraphrases were made of longer works. The early appearance of meditation handbooks proves that from the earliest times there was deep interest in this form of practice.

THE PERIOD OF DISUNITY (220–589 A.D.)

Plagued by revolt and court intrigue, the Han dynasty finally expired in 220 A.D. and for more than three hundred and fifty years the Middle Kingdom was riven apart. At first it was divided into three competing kingdoms ruled by independent warlords; there followed a short-lived and precarious period of unity under Western Chin (265–316 A.D.) before war and chaos were again unleashed and eventually barbarian tribes took control of the north. The most powerful, the Toba, who originated in Mongolia, established the northern Wei dynasty and in time became thoroughly sinicized. Meanwhile, successions of native Chinese rulers held sway in the south.

Ironically, it was the decline and fall of the centralized Han empire that created the right conditions for Buddhism to gain popularity and spread to other parts of China.

For one thing, the official Confucianism lost prestige and credibility, and in particular the intellectual and aristocratic elite began to look elsewhere for spiritual inspiration. Taoism and a new mystical metaphysic called the Dark Learning engaged their interest, but Buddhism with its profound teachings on suffering and impermanence had something particularly pertinent to offer amidst the prevailing chaos. The sophistication of its schools of thought probably also attracted many cultured people, as did the notion of withdrawing from the world to the seclusion of a remote temple (preferably set in idyllic pastoral surroundings) in order to quietly contemplate the deepest spiritual mysteries.

Thus was born the genteel scholar-devotee that is so characteristic of Chinese Buddhism. Many of these fled from the north as it was overrun by foreign invaders and found sanctuary in the Yangtse basin and in the south, thus opening up those parts of the country. Gradually distinctive northern and southern types of Chinese Buddhism began to emerge from the resulting cleavage.

124 THE BUDDHIST HANDBOOK

Buddhism also now began to infiltrate court circles in many parts of the fragmented empire. Once it had fallen under the patronage of the mighty of the land its success was assured. It even found favor with some of the barbarian dynasties in the north. The reasons were not entirely spiritual. These very much wanted to undermine traditional Chinese culture and its dominant Confucianism; to advance a foreign religion was a good way of doing this. They may also have felt that the gentle teachings of the Buddha would produce a more tractable kind of subject—the Taoists, on the other hand, were always stirring up trouble. Most importantly, however, they welcomed Buddhist monks at first because of the magical benefits they thought them able to bestow. Later, these monks assumed more dignified roles as wise counselors. Under the northern Wei dynasty, patronage of Buddhism soared and colossal schemes for building monasteries, temples, pagodas, and *stupas* were initiated. The impressive Yun-kang and Lung-men cave temples were begun at this time and still exist to bear witness to the vigor and dedication of the dynasty.

Buddhism was also taken up by native Chinese rulers in the south, notably by the early sixth century Emperor Wu, who tried to make himself into a kind of Chinese Ashoka by suppressing Taoism and squeezing his nobility for substantial contributions towards the cost of building temples and monasteries. One enterprising fund-raising scheme that he devised was to reduce himself to the level of a temple servant, and then have his subjects "ransom" him. Needless to say, though acclaimed in Buddhist literature, the Confucians wrote him off as a feckless fanatic.

One important result of this general success was the emergence of a native *sangha* by the middle of the third century, when a Chinese version of the Vinaya (monastic code of discipline) was produced. Formerly monks and nuns had probably existed on a more *ad hoc* basis. As the period progressed and Buddhism attracted increasing patronage, the numbers of monasteries and temples as well as of ordained monks and nuns fairly soared. Erik Zürcher quotes the following figures for the northern Wei empire alone:

477 A.D.: 6,500 monasteries; 77,000 monks and nuns

c. 514 A.D.: 30,000 monasteries; 2 million monks and nuns*

Unfortunately, as so often with organized religion, power and prosperity led to worldliness and a fall from the high standards originally

* Erik Zürcher, "Beyond the Jade Gate: Buddhism in China, Vietnam and Korea," in *The World of Buddhism,* ed. H. Bechert and R. Gombrich (London: Thames & Hudson, 1984), 201.

professed. The jealousy of the Confucians and Taoists was also aroused, and they were able to exploit the inevitable distrust of Buddhist success felt in official circles to foment trouble. The result was anti-Buddhist backlash, notably in 446 and 574 A.D.

Buddhism also gained ground on the popular level. Sections of the much-abused peasantry were quite ready to seek refuge from the oppressive burdens of taxation, conscription, and forced labor by retreating to Buddhist monasteries, or else to find spiritual consolation in simple acts of humble piety, like making offerings at temples or going on pilgrimage. They also liked to pray for help and protection to benign *bodhisattvas* and buddhas like Akshobhya, Maitreya, or most popular of all, Amitabha.

Chinese Buddhism therefore developed into very much a two-class system, with the sophisticated brand of the gentry contrasting strongly with the popular variety in which there was a strong element of superstition. Even at the height of its prestige, Buddhism was never the sole religion of China, however. It always had to co-exist alongside Confucianism, Taoism, and the folk religions. It underwent considerable modification as a result. This, plus the interaction of the teachings brought from India with the Chinese character itself, ultimately produced distinctively Chinese forms of the religion. But that took time—several centuries, in fact.

During the Period of Disunity, northern China remained in close contact with Central Asia via the Silk Route. A whole new wave of teachers arrived, initiating a fresh burst of activity on the translation front. Among these may be counted Dharmaraksha, a sinicized Indo-Scythian from Tun-huang (late third century), who translated the *Saddharma-pundarika Sutra* or "White Lotus of the True Dharma Sutra," a highly influential Mahayana scripture that was to become the basic text of the indigenous T'ien T'ai school. The other four most influential Mahayana *sutras* in China were the *Prajñaparamita*, the *Vimalakirti-nirdesha*, the *Surangama-samadhi*, and the *Sukhavati-vyuha*. All had been translated by Dharmaraksha's time. Arguably most popular among sections of the Buddhist elite was the *Vimalakirti-nirdesha*, which was admired for its fine literary qualities as well as its sublime philosophy. It held a special appeal for laypeople because it centered around a certain enlightened layman of Vaishali who, out of deep compassion, had taken the sickness of the world upon himself. Such was the perfection of his wisdom, however, that Mañjushri, Subhuti, and other of the highest luminaries of the Buddhist firmament were afraid to visit him for fear of the philosophical put-downs that might be inflicted upon them.

The *Vimalakirti-nirdesha* was retranslated by the doyen of all the translators, Kumarajiva, who was active in the north about a century after Dharmaraksha. He was born around 350 A.D. (some place his birth as early as 344 A.D.), either at Kucha or at Karashahr. His mother, who was ordained as a nun while he was yet young, took him to Kashmir to get him a good Buddhist education. There, among other things, he imbibed Sarvastivadin teachings. He later discovered the Mahayana and his particular penchant, Madhyamaka philosophy, while on a visit to Kashgar. He afterwards spent many years at Kucha and his great reputation for piety spread far and wide. It even reached China.

In 384 A.D., Kucha was taken by a Chinese general, Lü Kuang, who thereby acquired the now famous master as one of the spoils of war. Though not a Buddhist himself, Lü Kuang bore Kumarajiva off to his domains in Kansu. Nothing is known of the next seventeen years, but in 401 A.D. the fortunes of war again caused Kumarajiva to change hands. This time he passed to a Tibetan potentate named Yao Hsing, who transferred him to his capital at Ch'ang-an. His new master being an ardent Buddhist, Kumarajiva was given every encouragement and assistance, including a translation bureau with a reputed personnel of eight hundred. Ten concubines were also allotted to him in the hope that his exceptional talents might be perpetuated. This would of course mean that he would have had to resign monk status. Offspring did apparently appear, but none matched their sire's accomplishments.

In the matter of translations, however, Yao Hsing would have had no cause for disappointment. Kumarajiva was perfectly equipped to be a great translator. Equally at home in both Chinese and Sanskrit, he was also endowed with literary gifts of a very high order. His translations are said by Arthur Waley to be "rather free" but "infinitely more agreeable to read" than the more exact versions of other translators. Besides the *Vimalakirti-nirdesha,* among the numerous *sutras* that Kumarajiva and his team translated or retranslated were the *Saddharma-pundarika,* the *Sukhavati-vyuha* (the so-called "Diamond Sutra"), *Vajracchedika Sutra,* etc. He is also credited with having introduced Madhyamaka philosophy to China.

Two of Kumarajiva's assistants are important. Seng-Chao (*c.* 384–414 A.D.) is said to have literally "held the brush" for the Kuchan Master, for he had been a copyist of Confucian and Taoist texts in lay life and so was possessed of polished literary skills. His own text, *Chao Lun,* in which he tried to put across the Buddhist view of emptiness, was highly influential in awakening the Chinese to Buddhism. He employed Taoist terminology extensively—what the Chinese called *ko-yi*: "extending the meaning" or "borrowing the idea." His colleague Tao-Sheng (360–434 A.D.), on the other hand, wrote an essay on "sudden enlightenment" long before the advent of the Ch'an school. He also wrote a text to the effect that "a good act entails no retribution," that is, in terms of *karma*.

One of the few important translators working in the south was Fa-hsien, who distinguished himself by actually traveling to India (399–414 A.D.) to obtain texts, particularly Vinaya texts. He practically walked the whole way, crossing the Gobi desert and the Hindu Kush mountains in the process and successfully negotiating all kinds of physical and spiritual perils. The outward journey took him six years; he then spent six years in India and finally returned to China by sea via Ceylon and Java—an equally adventurous undertaking that took a further three years.

SUI AND T'ANG DYNASTIES (581–907 A.D.)

Though Buddhism advanced enormously in China during the Period of Disunity, it is generally thought to have enjoyed its golden age during the T'ang dynasty (618–907 A.D.), which followed the Sui dynasty (581–618 A.D.), when the great empire was once again united under a single imperial regime. Having reached its apogee by the ninth century, Chinese Buddhism then began the slow, one-thousand-year decline that has continued to the present.

During the preceding periods, the groundwork had been thoroughly laid; conditions were therefore ripe for a fully-realized Chinese Buddhism to burgeon. In particular, a number of highly developed schools emerged, nearly all of them Indian in origin but to a greater or lesser degree modified and taken on to new heights of development by the Chinese genius. These schools were subsequently transmitted to Korea and Japan, where they underwent further development. Some of them are now being transmitted yet again, this time to the West.

The following are the principal Chinese schools of Buddhism.

THE VINAYA SCHOOL (LÜ-TSUNG)

Principal text: The Vinaya in Four Parts, translated by Buddhayashas and Chu Fo-nien

Mainly concerned with the Vinaya (monastic code of discipline) and the strict observance of both its positive and negative aspects (do's and don'ts), this school played a useful part in raising monastic standards in China. Its foundation is credited to Tao-hsüan (596–667 A.D.).

THE REALISTIC SCHOOL (CHÜ-SHÊ)

Principal text: The Abhidharma-kosha of Vasubandhu

This derived its inspiration from an early text written by Vasubandhu (*c.* 316–396 A.D.), the brother of Asanga and a native of Purushapura (Peshawar) who, before his conversion to the Mahayana, was an ordained member of the Sarvastivada (or "All-things-exist") school, one of the Eighteen Schools of the Hinayana, the teachings of which he studied in Kashmir. The *Abhidharma-kosha,* which represents a critical outline of the Abhidharma system of the Vaibashikas, a group of Sarvastivada philosophers, was translated into Chinese first by Paramartha (563–567 A.D.), Vasubandhu's biographer, and later by Hsüan-tsang. The school that arose in China eventually became an appendage of the Idealist School (*Fa-hsiang,* see below).

THE THREE TREATISES SCHOOL (SAN-LUN)

Principal text: The Madhyamaka-shastra and the Dvadashadvara ("Twelve Gates") of Nagarjuna; also the Shata Shastra ("One Hundred Verse Treaties") of Aryadeva

This was based on the Madhyamaka or "Middle Way" teachings of Nagarjuna and his followers (see pp. 89–90), who sought to advance the perfect wisdom of absolute emptiness by the use of a "transcendental dialect" negating all views. Introduced by Kumarajiva, these teachings were refined by Chih-tsang (549–623 A.D.), the master of Chia-hsiang monastery and a prolific writer of commentaries. In his "Essay on the Double Truth" (*Erh-ti Chang*), Chih-tsang argues that the transcendental can only be discussed in antithetical language, but this does not result in mere negation; in fact, as the dialectic is pushed forward, our usual notions of being and non-being are gradually refined, and an increasingly inclusive, totalistic vision begins to unfold. The school declined after the rise of the Idealist School (*Fa-hsiang*), but was later revived by Suryaprabhasa, an Indian monk who arrived in China in 679 A.D.

THE IDEALIST SCHOOL (FA-HSIANG)

Principal texts: The Vimsatika-karika or "Twenty Stanzas" and other texts by Vasubandhu and his followers

This is the Chinese development of the Indian Yogacara school founded by Vasubandhu and his brother Asanga, which propounded the doctrine of *citta-matra* or "mind only." Its great champion in China was Hsüan-tsang (596–664 A.D.), a kind of saintly innocent of heroic stature who emerges as arguably the most engaging figure in the history of Buddhism in the great empire. His interesting life-story warrants a digression.

Remarkable from an early age for his purity, Hsüan-tsang was ordained as a monk and applied himself to assiduous study. He eventually decided to travel to India himself. He slipped out of China without official permission, and journeyed overland via the Silk Route. That his travels were rich in the stuff of high romance is demonstrated by the fact that they formed the basis for the novel *Monkey* by Wu Ch'ên-ên, which exists in a classic English translation by Arthur Waley. Waley also summarized Hsüan-tsang's life in *The Real Tripitaka,* a book which incidentally gives us a vivid portrait of Buddhism in both China and India during the seventh century.

At the very start of his monumental pilgrimage, the "Great Traveler," as he became called, nearly came to grief at the hands of a spurious guide; then in the great deserts he was harassed by spectral horsemen. In both these and other tight corners he was saved by divine intercession. Then at Turfan the local king was loath to let someone of his prowess slip through his fingers and was prepared to forcibly detain him to enjoy the benefits of his edifying company. Men of wisdom were in those days revered and accorded the kind of celebrity currently reserved for TV soap-opera and sports stars. By threatening to go on a hunger strike, Hsüan-tsang was able to recover his liberty. He then crossed the T'ien Shan mountains, visited Samarkand, looped south into what today is Iran, proceeded on to Afghanistan, and eventually descended onto the plains of India in the vicinity of Gandhara.

In India Hsüan-tsang visited most of the major Buddhist centers and pilgrimage places, studying both widely and deeply as he went. He stayed twice at Nalanda, and on the first occasion was able to study Yogacara philosophy under an ancient master named Shilabhadra, who was reputed to have mastered all the books in the world. He also studied logic, which stood him in good stead during a great public debate in which he triumphantly championed the Mahayana against all comers. The patron on that occasion was Harsha, then Emperor of India, who had jealously snatched Hsüan-tsang from the court of Assam, where he had gone in the hope of reforming the errant king. The favor that he enjoyed with Harsha and the largesse that was heaped on his head were, however, something of a mixed blessing for they delayed Hsüan-tsang's return to China.

Eventually, feted and acclaimed, Hsüan-tsang re-entered Ch'ang-an in 645 A.D. He had been away for sixteen years and had brought back numerous Buddha relics and images and also some 657 texts. He enjoyed the favor of the emperor, who earnestly wished him to surrender the robe and enter public service. Hsüan-tsang tactfully declined, however, for he wished to devote himself to the translation of his collection of texts.

It was Arthur Waley's considered opinion that, while Hsüan-tsang's translations effected a revolution in method and managed a closeness to their originals that earlier translations has failed to achieve, they were nevertheless marred by mistakes, misleading interpolations, and other flaws. They also lacked the literary qualities that had graced Kumarajiva's renderings.

THE MANTREA OR TANTRIC SCHOOL (MI-TSUNG OR CHEN-YEN)

Principal text: The Mahavairocana ("Great Brilliance") Sutra

This is the Chinese manifestation of Tantra with all its esoteric paraphernalia of *yogas, mantras, mandalas, mudras, dharanis,* initiations, and secret doctrines. It was introduced from India during the T'ang dynasty by Subhakarasimha (637–735 A.D.), who arrived in the Middle Kingdom in 716 A.D. and translated the *Mahavairocana Sutra* nine years later. In 720 A.D., another Indian, Vajrabodhi (670–741 A.D.), arrived and began to expound the teachings and initiate neophytes into practice. Special sanctuaries had to be built for the performance of the necessary rituals, which involved the use of complex *mandala.* A third Indian, Amoghavajra (705–774 A.D.), reinterpreted the Tantric teachings in terms of the Chinese classics; he was also active at the imperial court, and is credited with initiating three T'ang emperors. Tantric rites were thought to give magical protection to the empire against catastrophe; they could also influence developments in the after-death state and confer occult benefits. The school flourished for less than a century and was eventually supplanted by Lamaism. It was taken to Japan by Kukai, where it became known as Shingon.

THE AVATAMSAKA OR "FLOWER ADORNMENT" SCHOOL (HUA-YEN)

Principal text: The Avatamsaka Sutra

Although the *Avatamsaka Sutra* originated in India, a full-fledged system developed from its teachings emerged in China and was later transmitted to Japan, where it became known as Kegon.

The plethora of translated texts and commentaries that had become available in China, all collectively propounding an apparent cacophony of differing views, begged for some kind of system of classification that would lend them some measure of coherence. The Hua-yen was one of the schools that responded to this need. It put forward the notion that immediately after his enlightenment the Buddha had preached the Avatamsaka teachings but had met with only blank incomprehension from his listeners. Seeing them standing as if "deaf and dumb," he realized that he would have to compromise and so evolved the simpler Hinayana teachings. In time, as the level of understanding among his followers progressed, he was able to give out increasingly advanced teachings, but the *Avatamsaka Sutra* remained the summation and apogee of his system. Dr. D. T. Suzuki was echoing this to his classes in New York as late as 1951: "Kegon is believed to have been the expression given by the Buddha in his enlightenment," he maintained. "All other teachings were given by the Buddha to his disciples after he had come out of the enlightenment. In Kegon he made no accommodation to his hearers."*

Hua-yen is a creation of cosmic vision on the grandest scale. It evokes a universe where everything freely interpenetrates everything else, where totality may be contemplated and ultimate truth realized in even the tiniest speck of dust. It reinforces its imaginative philosophical arguments with rich poetic images like that of the Jewel Net of Indra: a vast web or network of gems, each of which reflects every other—and also the reflections in every other—and so on *ad infinitum.*

Edward Conze described Hua-yen as a link between Yogacara and Tantra. While providing a "cosmic interpretation to the ontological ideas of the Yogacarins"† it shared with Tantra a fascination with the play of cosmic forces. Unlike Tantra, however, Hua-yen was not concerned with the attainment of liberation by means of the magical manipulation of those forces; its practical bias was rather towards contemplation and aesthetic appreciation of them. By doing this, the devotee would eventually be led to repose in ultimate quiescence.

The outstanding figure in the early history of Hua-yen is Fa-tsang (643–712/3 A.D.), a fully sinicized Soghdian monk who was born in Ch'ang-an. He was at one time a member of Hsüan-tsang's translation bureau but became disenchanted with Idealist philosophy after reading the *Avatamsaka Sutra.*

Hua-yen philosophy attracted the interest of the Empress Wu (ruled 690–705 A.D.—the only female "Son of Heaven") and various emperors, perhaps, it has been suggested, because its all-embracing system appealed to their totalitarian cast of mind. Despite her notorious ruthlessness, Empress Wu was an enthusiastic supporter of Buddhism and even claimed, perhaps to justify her own seizure of power, to be an incarnation of Maitreya. In 704 A.D., she commanded Fa-tsang to lecture to her on the *Avatamsaka Sutra.* The master noticed a golden

* A. Irwin Switzer III, *D. T. Suzuki: A Biography* (London: The Buddhist Society, 1985), 42.
† Conze, *A Short History of Buddhism*, 85.

lion in the throne room and cleverly used it to elucidate Hua-yen philosophy. The gold of the lion symbolized *li* or ultimate principle (noumenal aspect), he maintained, while the lion-form symbolized *shih* or causally-determined characteristics (phenomenal aspect). On the basis of the fact that every distinct part of the lion was made of gold, each phenomenon could be said to embrace every other phenomenon while at the same time being a perfect manifestation of noumenon.

Tu-shun (557–640 A.D.) was the first patriarch of the Hua-yen school; his "Contemplating the Dharmadhatu" (*Ha-Chieh Kuan*) is thought to have set the pattern for subsequent commentaries, its "round view" reflecting the totalistic vision of its subject. Commentaries also flowed from his successor, Chih-yen (602–668 A.D.); for instance, the *Hua-yen Chin Shou Hsuan Chi*: "A Search for the Profound Mysteries of the *Hua-yen Sutra*." The third patriarch was Fa-tsang, and the fourth Ch'eng-kuan (Master Ch'ing-liang, 738–838 A.D.), a giant of a man who was heaped with honors and titles—"Master of the Purple Robe," "National Preceptor," etc., etc.—by his great patron, Emperor Te-tsung. The next patriarch, Kuei-feng Tsung-mi (780–841 A.D.), benefited from similar imperial largesse.

Finally, when a general decline of Buddhism set in in the ninth century, the Hua-yen School also went into eclipse, having flourished for over two hundred years.

THE T'IEN-T'AI OR WHITE LOTUS SCHOOL (FA-HUA)

Principal text: The Saddharma-pundarika Sutra

Although sometimes called the "Lotus" School because of its veneration of the *Saddharma-pundarika Sutra* or "White Lotus of the True Law Sutra," this school derived its principal name from the fact that its true founder and fourth patriarch, Chih-i (538–597 A.D.), lived on Mount T'ien-t'ai in Chekiang. It too was a genuinely Chinese development.

Although accepting the myth that, following his failure to put across his advanced teachings the Buddha had compromised and expounded simpler teachings, the T'ien-t'ai School differed from the Hua-yen in providing alternative classifications of Buddhist scriptures and teachings. These demonstrated, it was claimed, that the *Saddharma-pundarika* was the real "king of *sutras,*" for it alone was fully "round" in the sense that it included the essence of all the other teachings. It was therefore the perfect packet that could ferry all men across the ocean of *samsara* to the far shore of enlightenment, regardless of their level of understanding. Allied to this was the notion of a single vehicle (*ekayana*) in which all other doctrines were united.

The T'ien-t'ai also put forward lofty philosophical doctrines, which owed a lot to those of the Hua-yen and Idealist Schools, but arguably most important was that of the Three Levels of Truth, which bears traces of the influence of Nagarjuna. The three levels are: (1) Void or Emptiness, (2) Temporariness, and (3) Mean. The first signifies that no *dharma* can exist by itself alone but is causally generated and maintained in dependence. However, though *dharmas* are essentially void or empty, they do enjoy temporary existence as perceived by the senses; this constitutes the second level. The third level arises from the fact that emptiness and temporariness are two sides of a dualism that generates a higher third: a mean or middle. This should not be taken as lying between the other two, however; rather, as J. Takakusu puts it: "It is over and above the two: nay, it is identical with the two, because the true state means that the middle is the very state of being void and temporary." (*Essentials of Buddhist Philosophy,* Reprint. New Delhi, 1975, p. 142.)

Because they are perpetually united and harmonious, the Three Levels of Truth must therefore not be treated separately but always as "all in one and one in all." By the same token, phenomena are so interpenetrated by the noumenal that the whole cosmos can be contained in a single instant of thought or in a follicle of hair. This confers a degree of spiritual stature on the ordinary and the everyday that had been largely absent from Buddhism hitherto: the apparently mundane *is* the spiritual; they are not two.

In terms of practice, this school advocated "concentration and insight" (*chih* and *kuan*) as methods of obtaining enlightenment. Concentration puts an end to erroneous thinking by making it clear that all *dharmas* are devoid of self-nature and hence exist without really existing. Insight, on the other hand, means to fully penetrate the phantasmagoric character of all *dharmas* and to become grounded in absolute mind. Incidentally, this absolute mind, or "Womb of the Tathagata," "True and Genuine Suchness," etc., is the repository of all potentialities, both pure and impure, and in its synthetic totality is fully present in all things, whether sentient or insentient. Thus *buddha*-nature and the possibility of enlightenment are utterly unexclusive.

In 577 A.D., the reigning emperor dedicated the revenue of the district adjacent to Mount T'ien-t'ai to the upkeep of Chih-i and his community. The master is said to have promoted non-violence on his monastic domains and to have banned fishing. He went to Ch'ang-an to give discourses to two emperors. A prolific writer of commentaries and manuals, his *Pan-chiao* ("Classification of the Teachings") is very famous. It seeks to harmonize the seemingly contradictory aspects of the Buddha's teachings by dividing them into eight groups and evaluating them in terms of their relevant *upaya* or function. Chih-i also identified five major phases in Shakyamuni's life.

After Chih-i, the T'ien-t'ai transmission line runs: Kuan-ting, Fahua, T'ien-kung, Tso-ch'i, Ch'an-jan, and Tao-sui—the latter being the teacher of Dengyo Daishi, who introduced the school into Japan in the ninth century, where it became known as Tendai.

THE PURE LAND SCHOOL (CHING T'U)

Principal text: The Smaller and Larger Sukhavati-vyuha Sutras

The devotees of this school venerated Amitabha (the Buddha of Infinite Light) and sought not outright nirvana but rebirth in the Western Paradise or "Pure Land" of Amitabha, also called Sukhavati. In that idyllic environment, no new negative karmic accumulations would be created and all existing ones would evaporate; nirvana would be therefore just a short step away.

At root, the school harked back to the notion expounded in early Buddhist cosmology that within a few hundred years of the Buddha's death a degenerate period would set in when enlightenment would no longer be attainable by one's own efforts or "self-power" (in Japanese: *jiriki*). One would therefore have to depend on external grace: in this case, the benign intercession of Amitabha. This represented the opposite of "self-power," namely "other-power" (*tariki*). It was also felt that there was in any case an element of egotism in the very idea of "self-power": that one could win enlightenment by one's own efforts alone. As that was basically the Hinayana outlook, Pure Land Buddhism reflected the Mahayana accommodation to devotional forms of practice. The mantric repetition of the name of Amitabha—"O-mi-to-fo" (in Japanese: "Namu-Amida-butsu")—was the central practice developed here.

A former Taoist named Hui-yüan (334–416 A.D.) promoted the cult of Amitabha in China during the Period of Disunity and in 402 A.D. founded the Fellowship of the White Lotus, from which the Pure Land School eventually developed. Other significant figures in its early history are T'anluan (476–542 A.D.), Tao-ch'o (c. 645 A.D.) and Shan-tao (613–681 A.D.). Its teachings were transmitted to Korea and, more significantly, to Japan, where division into the Jodo and Jodo Shin sub-schools occurred. The Pure Land School in its various forms and derivatives is still very much in existence and today has a following in the West.

THE DHYANA SCHOOL (CH'AN)

Principal texts: Ostensibly nil; actually the *Lankavatarsha, Heart, Vimalakirti-nirdesha, and Vajracchedika Sutras.*

Ch'an represents the finest achievement of Chinese Buddhism: an original and highly creative re-expression of the essence of the Buddha's teaching in terms that are distinctively Chinese. As such it may also be regarded, alongside Abhidharma, Mahayana, and Tantra, as one of the major creations of Buddhism as a whole. It was transmitted to Korea (where it became known as Son), to Vietnam, and to Japan (where it became known as Zen); also in more recent times to the West.

Ch'an is often described as a product of the down-to-earth, practical slant of the Chinese character. Indians, on the other hand, are said to be by nature more airy and metaphysical, and indeed the Chinese were quite fascinated with the marvelous intellectual creations of India for a long time. After the centuries of importation and absorption, however, their own native genius asserted itself resulting in the emergence of Ch'an, which is often described as the complete sinicization of Buddhism.

Ch'an is about a return to essentials. All the teachings, texts, practices, codes of morality, and behavior that had sprung up around the basically simple teaching of the Buddha were intended as aids to progress *beyond:* to enlightenment. But as the years went by, the diligent practitioner might become attached and trapped in them. Just as the *bodhisattva* Mañjushri wields his sword of wisdom to summarily slice through the net of delusions, so the impulse behind Ch'an was to sweep all the training paraphernalia of Buddhism aside and to zero in on the heart of the matter: the direct insight that transformed Siddhartha Gautama into the Buddha beneath the bodhi tree at Bodh Gaya.

The general thrust of Ch'an is typified by its rejection of book-learning and verbalization. Ch'an, it was claimed, was "a special transmission outside the scriptures;" it placed "no reliance on words and letters." What was transmitted was buddhahood, enlightenment itself, no less, which consisted in a "direct pointing to the heart of man," in a "seeing into one's own nature." This was handed on from master to disciple, heart to heart. To authenticate their tradition, the followers of Ch'an traced lines of transmission which showed how, by a process similar to apostolic succession, the teachings had been handed down without interruption.

However, although they often expressed a contempt for the scriptures, the Ch'an masters frequently showed themselves well-versed in them. Indeed the *Lankavatara, Vimalakirti-nirdesha,* and *Vajracchedika sutras* as well as other texts were studied within the school. Furthermore, in time, original Ch'an texts appeared, like the *Platform Sutra* of the Sixth Patriarch, Hui-neng, the *Records of Eminent Monks,* the *Ching-te Record of the Transmission of the Lamp,* and the *Record of the Finger Pointing at the Moon.* The ostensible rejection of scriptures was therefore very much the posture of people well-versed in the traditional texts. One cannot give wealth away if one does not have it, or transcend the ego where no stable, mature ego exists; so, too, with book-learning.

This really goes for the whole of Ch'an: it is intended for practitioners saturated in all aspects of Buddhist teaching and practice. However, the anti-scriptural, unconventional, and sometimes iconoclastic behavior of many Ch'an masters is often mistaken by uninformed Westerners as a cue that the demands and formalities of traditional training can be dispensed with—that Ch'an offers an easy short-cut to enlightenment. Nothing could be further from the case. The Ch'an master who burned a Buddha-image was himself a deeply pious monk, and the Ch'an master who declared that there was no such thing as enlightenment was himself fully enlightened!

The term *Ch'an* is in fact a Chinese corruption of *dhyana,* the Indian term for the absorption or high bliss states achieved through *shamatha* meditation. Sitting meditation was always an important aspect of Ch'an practice as an aid to the development of inner stillness and the accumulation of vital energy or *chi* (a Taoist influence). But in the seminal days in China, sitting was rather less important than it was subsequently to become in Japan, whence most of what we know of Ch'an/Zen in the West today is derived. What the early Chinese masters stressed rather was the "non-abiding mind"—the mind that rests nowhere, beyond all thought and relativity. This is nothing other than our ordinary, everyday mind, and the Ch'an practitioner would seek to remain with it in all situations, not just in sitting. It was to drive this point home that Huai-jang, seeing Ma-tsu sitting in meditation, seized a tile and began frantically rubbing it. When asked what he was doing, he replied that he was trying to polish the stone into a mirror. "*Impossible!*" cried Ma-tsu; whereupon Huai-jang retorted that it was equally impossible to forge a Buddha-mind through sitting alone.

Richard Hunn (Upasaka Wen Shu), a former disciple of the late Charles Luk, has written:

> From all the Chinese Ch'an records, it is easy to determine that at least 80% of the "awakening experiences" in fact took place during apparently mundane activities . . . working in the fields, cooking rice, hearing one's name called, a slap, a kick! And there is reason for this. Continual introspection or "turning back" of the mind arouses an "inner potentiality" (*nei chih*), which even-

tually breaks through into "ordinary" consciousness. One then sees that seemingly conditioned events . . . one's own self . . . all surroundings . . . arise in this marvellous emptiness. . . .

Thus of old the teaching was simple and consisted in "direct pointing." To remove obstructions, the old masters "probed" their disciples to see what their troubles were. If they clung to the "worldly," they stripped that attachment away; if they clung to the "saintly," on the other hand, the master would shout or give them a slap to snap them out of that.

Fa-yung lived in seclusion on Niu-t'ou Mountain. When Tao-hsin went there, Fa-yung offered to put him up in a spot behind his cave. On the way there, they spotted wild animals, whereupon Tao-hsin feigned fear. Fa-yung said, "I see that this is still with you"—meaning the *kleshas* (defilements), in this case fear. Later, Tao-hsin approached the rock where Fa-yung spent all his time sitting in meditation. He motioned as if writing the character *fo* (Buddha) on the rock, saying, "I see that this is still with you"—meaning deep attachment to the very idea of the saintly Buddha-state. Fa-yung got the message, changed his practice, opened a temple and freely interacted with the world.

Initially, however, most disciples withdrew their attention from the play of events in the "world" in order to disentangle themselves from false thinking. But once sure about the underlying (birthless and deathless) nature, they were obliged to harmonize this with their everyday activities. Thus the Ch'an masters used the terms "host" and "guest" for the "numenal" and the "phenomenal," and the terms *ti* and *yung* (principle and activity) in order to make clear both sides of the business . . . Another term coined within Ch'an was *yeh shih* or the "initial consciousness" i.e. the primordial mind that underlies all actions and which mirrors the surface play of phenomena.

Edited letter to the author dated 11/6/87

In a book on rebirth, the Indian sage Sri Aurobindo lamented that Buddhism was just about enlightenment in quiescence. He failed to take account of Ch'an, where the enlightenment attained in quiescence must be brought and tested where the action is. In the classic *Ten Ox-herding Pictures*, which symbolically depict the Ch'an/Zen path, the final picture shows the master coming into the market-place "with bliss-bestowing hands."

The seminal figure in early Ch'an is Bodhidharma, a south Indian master who is said to have arrived in China around 520 A.D. His historicity is often challenged, particularly in the West. Though he was honored as the First Patriarch of Chinese Ch'an, twenty-seven other Indian patriarchs were identified, the first being Mahakashyapa, who reputedly received transmission directly from the Buddha. The way this happened is quite precisely documented. Right from the time of his enlightenment, the Buddha had been unhappy about the capacity of other people to understand his subtle teaching. Usually he compromised and produced verbal teachings, but on one particular occasion he had said nothing but merely held up a flower. Of all the disciples present, only Mahakashyapa got the message. A smile and an answering smile registered that transmission had taken place, and so it went on.

Bodhidharma is depicted in Ch'an and Zen paintings as a grim and glowering figure with huge, bulbous eyes. Legend has it that he sliced off his own eyelids in order to keep awake and aware. Shortly after arriving in China, he visited Emperor Wu of Liang.

"What is the meaning of the *dharma?*" the emperor asked.

"Vast emptiness without holiness," Bodhidharma replied.

"Who is standing before me now?"

"I don't know. . . ."

Evidently neither the master nor the emperor were particularly impressed with the other. The interview ended and Bodhidharma departed for the adjacent state of Wei, where he is alleged to have spent nine years sitting facing a wall in the Shaolin temple. Then one day a monk visited him in search of teaching. Bodhidharma did not gratify his wish, so eventually, as proof of his earnestness, the student chopped off his left arm with a sword. That impressed the master.

"My soul isn't at peace," the student complained. "Please pacify it, master."

"Bring your soul here and I'll pacify it," came the reply.

"I've been looking for it for years, but haven't been able to find a trace of it," the student had to admit.

"*There!* Bodhidharma declared. "It's pacified once and for all."

The history of the Ch'an School begins in earnest, however, with the Sixth Patriarch, Hui-neng (638–713 A.D.). He was an unlettered woodcutter who one day happened to hear the *Vajracchedika Sutra* being recited. Captivated, he longed to study the *sutra* under the guidance of a master. He therefore traveled to see the Fifth Patriarch, Hung-jen (601–674 A.D.), who allowed him to enter his monastery as a lay menial. When the time came for the patriarch to nominate his successor, he announced that his supreme honor would be conferred upon the author of the verse which demonstrated the best understanding of the teaching. His foremost disciple, Shen-hsiu (c. 600–706 A.D.), wrote a very penetrating piece, but this offering was capped by another from the lowly skivvy in the kitchen. This is traditionally cited as the cause of a split in the Ch'an school.

The account that has become prevalent in the contemporary West is that two rival schools subsequently emerged: a southern school led by Hui-neng and a northern school led by Shen-hsiu. Doctrinally the bone of contention was whether enlightenment was gradual, as Shen-hsiu claimed, or sudden—Hui-neng's view. Hui-neng's outlook was, it is usually claimed, the more radical and uncompromising. In his poem, Shen-hsiu had likened the mind to a mirror that had to be continually polished to be kept free of dust. "The mirror bright is nowhere shining." Hui-neng had countered: "As there is nothing from the first/ Where can the dust collect?"

Hui-neng's southern school was eventually to triumph, leaving its rival to go the way of all flesh. Some commentators, however, feel on the evidence of contemporary texts that the significance of the split has been exaggerated and that little of the animosity that is usually described really existed between the two schools. Rather Hui-neng happened to come along at a time when social and historical conditions were right for the reception and a full flowering of Ch'an, and his school attracted the necessary support, notably in pertinent political quarters.

Later there were further sub-divisions and traditionally Five Houses (and Seven Sects) are said to have arisen between the ninth and eleventh centuries, including the Fa-yen, Yun-men, and Kuei-yang. These all died out, however, but two others survived: the Lin-chi (Jap. *Rinzai*) and the Ts'ao-tung (Jap. *Soto*). In their later Japanese forms, both schools place primary stress on sitting practice (Jap. *zazen*) and the Lin-chi/ Rinzai school is popularly distinguished from the Ts'ao-tung/Soto by its use of *kung-an* (Jap. *koan*), a term which possesses connotations of a legal case or precedent. In China, however, *kung-an* were employed within all Five Houses and arose well before the time of Master Lin-chi (d. 867 A.D.). Their origin quite probably lay in the favorite trick of the early masters of suddenly calling out to a student. When the student's head automatically turned, they followed with an urgent, "*What is it???*" Richard Hunn explains:

> In this they were very skillful, for at such moments one is already "half way there" in the sense of the mind being emptied of surface activity. Techniques of this kind are very subtle; they "steal the pearl from under the dragon's chin," seize the "still point" right in the midst of movement.
>
> *ibid.*

Ch'an monks acquired the reputation of being great travelers; even after "breaking through," they might go on foot from master to master, testing the depth of their insight. They also differed from their confrères in other Buddhist schools in that they were not loath to turn their hands to manual labor. Hui-hai (720–814 A.D.) is credited with having introduced this innovation. The maxim, "a day without work is a day without food," is attributed to him. He also formulated other monastic rules aimed at restoring the ascetic way of life practiced by the original Buddhists.

In breaking down the dichotomy between the sacred and the profane, Ch'an also paved the way for lay practice, and indeed a few—though admittedly not many—enlightened laymen and laywomen do grace its annals: for instance, layman P'ang, who discerned the noumenous in the simple tasks of his everyday life:

How wonderful, how miraculous!
I fetch wood, I carry water.

In a similar spirit, some Ch'an masters were disposed to announce that there was nothing special about any of Buddhism. Even enlightenment was no big deal. It was all just a matter of eating when hungry, sleeping when tired, and answering the call of nature.

"Smoothly functioning in response to the moment—what are you lacking?" Master Lin-chi demanded of his followers. And later: "I tell you: There is no Buddha, no *dharma,* no training, and no realization."

There is undeniably something very attractive about Ch'an for all its legendary severity. Its qualities can perhaps be most immediately appreciated in the art that it has inspired. Here simplicity, naturalness, and spontaneity are of the essence. A few deft strokes of the brush, executed (hopefully) without conscious contrivance, evoke an image, say, of bamboos bending in a gentle breeze. This will radiate all the unique magic of the fleeting moment and at the same time indicate the character of the artist—perhaps even, to the cognoscenti, the depth of his insight. Such subtle creations are deceptive, however. Their manifest freedom is not to be confused with the merely anarchic; it is the informed freedom that comes of long and arduous training.

There was generally a great flowering of Buddhist art during the T'ang period, notably of sculpture. In the visual arts, the dominant influence was the style evolved in India during the Gupta period (320–535 A.D.), which was characterized by "restrained sensuousness, with smooth, soft surfaces, and facial expressions exhibiting a certain sweetness."* This

* Elizabeth Lyons and Heather Peters, *Buddhism: History and Diversity of a Great Tradition* (Philadelphia: The University Museum, University of Pennsylvania, 1985), 25.

tempered the austerity that is apparent in images fashioned in the Wei and Sui periods.

The picture that emerges of Buddhism in T'ang dynasty China is a very impressive one. Thousands of temples and monasteries were scattered about the empire, inhabited by a flourishing *sangha* of monks and nuns, among them some of the finest talents of the age. The temples and monasteries ranged from humble provincial establishments or ones situated in remote mountain regions, to truly gigantic and magnificent complexes that were repositories of great wealth and fine art. There were even "official" temples, funded by the state for the purpose of invoking spiritual protection against danger from within or without.

The non-official establishments were of course primarily dedicated to ministering in various ways to the spiritual needs of the lay people to whom most of them looked for their support, but they were also social, cultural, and educational centers. Temple festivals, like the Lantern Festival, the Festival of the Buddha's Birthday, and All Soul's Festival, were great occasions for collective celebration in which all strata of society took part, as were processions, pilgrimages, and vegetarian feasts. Often the *sangha* used these occasions to give talks to the laity, and a popular literature consisting of edifying tales with entertaining and "miraculous" embellishments developed.

Inspired by the Mahayana ideal of compassion, which in China often took practical forms, the *sangha* was very much involved in performing good works like looking after the old and the sick, helping the poor, and distributing food in times of shortage. This public-spiritedness overflowed into the field of useful works: the building of roads and bridges, rest-houses and bath-houses, the sinking of wells, tree-planting, and so forth.

Religious societies also flourished, some of which were secret societies. Both *sangha* and laity participated, and their activities included devotional projects (like copying *sutras* or carving statues) and the provision of various forms of mutual aid.

As a cultural contribution, on the other hand, the invention of printing by Chinese Buddhists is of enormous significance. The earliest example of printing extant is in fact a copy of *The Diamond Sutra,* dated 868 A.D. As this is no crude effort, it is clear that printing had been used as an inexpensive way of reproducing texts and simple images and charms for some time before that date.

Buddhist temples and monasteries also developed into powerful centers of commerce. In fact, Buddhism has been credited (or blamed) for pioneering modern-style capitalism and banking in China. The larger establishments were very rich foundations, often endowed with extensive lands which, as only Ch'an monks performed manual labor, were commercially farmed with the use of slave labor; otherwise a share-cropping system was employed. In addition, the *sangha* owned rolling mills, oil presses, and hostelries, all operated for monetary gain. The profits from these activities (at least some of which may have been tax-exempt), augmented by donations, led to the accumulation of great wealth—the so-called Inexhaustible Treasury—which was used for money-lending and pawn-brokerage. The hoarding of vast quantities of useful and precious metals in the form of images also took place.

Though most T'ang emperors patronized it, the imperial government inevitably felt compelled to exert its control over this affluent, enterprising, extensive, and influential Buddhist church. In characteristic style—bureaucracy was pioneered in China—it placed it under the overall supervision of a government ministry staffed by an army of civil servants. Bowing to expediency, the Buddhist "church" in its turn seems to have come to accept the supremacy of the worldly authority and to acquiesce in a high degree of bureaucratic interference in its internal affairs. Census of the *sangha,* the control of monastic examinations, and the issuing of certificates of ordination were all matters eventually supervised by lay bureaucrats.

Still, church/state tensions persisted and became acute when towards the middle of the ninth century the dynasty was ravaged by civil war. With its coffers sorely depleted, the state naturally looked with envy at the vast wealth hoarded up in the monastic treasuries. The temptation to seize it became great, and whatever scruples might have stood in the way were weakened by a resurgence of classical Confucian values that again stigmatized Buddhism as an alien cult.

In 845 A.D., during the reign of Emperor Wu-tsung (841–847 A.D.), an order was promulgated to the effect that all Buddhist establishments should be destroyed, their lands and wealth seized, their slaves freed, and that all monks and nuns should return to lay life. Buddhism itself was not outlawed, nor was any move made against the laity; moreover the order was quickly lifted. Nevertheless, serious damage was done, damage which, allied to other unfavorable developments, initiated a decline of Chinese Buddhism that sadly has never been effectively reversed.

FROM THE WU-TAI AND SUNG DYNASTIES TO THE PEOPLE'S REPUBLIC (907 A.D. TO DATE)

Aside from the Communists, most of the rulers of China during this very long period were by no means unsympathetic to Buddhism. In fact some were very sympathetic, particularly the foreign dynasties who, as we have seen before, had their own reasons for favoring a non-indigenous religion. As a consequence, the material base of Buddhism did revive and a *sangha* did re-form, temporarily. But the creative spark had gone. During that final millennium the Chinese Buddhist church mainly lived on the achievements of its past and underwent a steady process of decline.

What were the immediate reasons for this?

First there was the resurgence of Confucianism. This was not the old Confucianism either, but a new and improved variety equipped, among other things, with a sophisticated metaphysic that owed not a little to Buddhist philosophy. This neo-Confucianism had the intellectual cachet that its precursor had lacked and, in consequence, Buddhism began to lose its grip on the minds and hearts of the intellectual elite, who in the more settled social climate were anyway more likely to seek a niche for themselves in the imperial service than in a Buddhist monastery. As a result, Buddhism was left to cater to popular spiritual needs, which was not conducive to the expression of its highest potentials. The religion was furthermore diluted by the syncretism that became fashionable.

Another blow was the destruction of Buddhism in India, which meant that no new inspirational impulses came from that direction. At the same time there was a deterioration in the quality and behavior of the Chinese *sangha,* caused in part by the practice inaugurated by the Sung dynasty (960–1279 A.D.) of trafficking in monk certificates in order to raise funds for the relief of its financial embarrassments. These certificates granted the bearers useful exemptions; they could also be purchased by undesirables, even by criminals intent on escaping from justice. "Monks" with wives and children became by no means rare. No doubt sincere monks and nuns still existed, but the prestige of the *sangha* suffered.

This decline was of course quite in keeping with the Buddha's teaching on impermanence as well as with his prediction that the *dharma* would go through repeated cycles of decadence and destruction after every initial period of vitality. In short, the great pitch of creativity and excellence that had been achieved during the T'ang period could not have been expected to have lasted. Of the various schools, those that weathered the decline best were Ch'an and Pure Land. Pure Land was fortified by the undeniable strength of its popular appeal. It spawned numerous societies, some of them claiming membership running into thousands. The very simplicity advocated by Ch'an, on the other hand, lent it a good measure of resilience; also the fact that its monks and nuns were prepared to work. It also enjoyed favor in high places. The prevalent syncretism also touched Ch'an: for instance, some practitioners employed Pure Land practices, like repeating the name of Amitabha.

In many ways, the Sung period was a glorious one for Ch'an. In terms of its art and general cultural importance, this was indeed its golden age, but internally there was impoverishment as the initial unconventional vigor and spontaneity gave way to increasing formalization and institutionalization. There was indeed a tendency to look back nostalgically to the times of the early masters, and the *kung-an* collections made at this time, which anecdotally record their sayings and doings reflect this. Two classic collections appeared, the *Blue Cliff Record* (*Pi Yen Lu;* Jap. *Hekiganroku*), compiled by Hsueh Tou Ch'ung Hsien (980–1152), and the *Gateless Gate* (*Wu-men-kuan;* Jap. *Mumonkan*), compiled by Wu-men Hui-kai (1184–1260), which were commented upon and assiduously studied. Sadly, the *kung-an* lost their original freshness too and, though used as an effective practice aid within the Lin-chi/Rinzai tradition, became, for the most part, mere stock answers to stock questions.

Of the original Five Houses of Zen, only Lin-chi/Rinzai and the Ts'ao-tung/Soto remained by the time of the Sung dynasty. There was some measure of rivalry and mutual criticism between the two, the devotees of the Lin-chi castigating the others for being quietists; that is, taking refuge from the problems of life in sitting stillness. The Ts'ao-tung fraternity retaliated with the criticism that the Lin-chi were hung up on words and concepts—a snipe at the *kung-an*. Nevertheless, the degree of rivalry may have been exaggerated.

A minor but perhaps indicative popular development during the Sung period was the transformation of the dignified Maitreya, the Buddha-to-be, into Pu-tai, the Hemp Sack Monk, often known as the Laughing Buddha. As Pu-tai is depicted as a grinning, pot-bellied hedonist, he suggests the celebration of worldly rather than spiritual values; there is also a hint of decadence about him.

The Mongols established the Yüan dynasty in China in 1280. They made Buddhism their state religion—for the final time. In particular they favored Lamaism, or the Buddhism of Tibet (see chapter sixteen), and thereafter that exotic form of Buddhism was also a part of the Chinese scene and was patronized by the succeeding dynasties. The Lamaist Cathedral, the Yung-ho-kung, is still one of the tourist sights of Peking. However, Lamaism never caught on to any appreciable extent among the mass of the people, though on China's western peripheries, where the empire once blurred into Tibet (now, alas, forcibly incorporated into the Chinese state, but formerly independent), it was strongly in evidence until comparatively recent times.

Subversive or secret societies, not to be confused with the genuine

If you wish to receive a copy of the latest INNER TRADITIONS INTERNATIONAL catalog and to be placed on our mailing list, please send us this card. It is important to print your name and address clearly.

Name _____ Phone _____

Address _____

City _____ State _____ Zip _____

Country _____ Email address _____

Order at 1-800-246-8648 • Fax (802) 767-3726
E-mail: orders@InnerTraditions.com • Web site: www.InnerTraditions.com

Inner Traditions International, Ltd.
P.O. Box 388
Rochester, VT 05767
U.S.A.

religious societies, claiming Buddhist connections were active during this period. They often had a strong messianic element: perhaps proclaiming the advent of some Maitreya who would set the world to rights, according to their own blueprints, of course. The Maitreya Society and the White Lotus Society (no connection with Pure Land) were prominent among them and were responsible for fomenting revolts and rebellions. The popular legacy these groups have left to contemporary Western culture is the myth of the fighting *kung-fu* monks. These are supposed to have practiced the martial arts with superhuman skill and to have been able to defeat all comers brilliantly, and often in droves. Such skills, while they may be feasible given the required training, do not of course indicate any measure of spiritual attainment. Indeed some might argue that no serious Buddhist would engage in martial arts training (excepting perhaps in its gentlest forms, like Aikido, and then strictly for therapeutic purposes), as to do so would cut directly against basic ethical principles, non-violence being the most obvious.

Towards the end of the last century, both China and its Buddhism were in a parlous state. The great empire itself was falling apart and this left the door open for foreign intrusion. Christian missionaries now became active and, while promoting their own creed in a highly organized and energetic way, they singled Buddhism out as the principal target for their attacks. At the same time the modern secular scientific outlook, itself thoroughly inimical to Buddhism, also began to make its presence felt.

These challenges had a positive effect in that they galvanized some sections of the Chinese Buddhist community into action. The initiative had by now passed from the *sangha* to the educated laity, and it was mainly laymen who, around the turn of this century, made a brave attempt to revive Chinese Buddhism and its decadent *sangha*. Influenced in part by the methods of the Christians, Buddhist organizations, some of them active in missionary and educational work, were set up. Contacts were also made with foreign Buddhists and this allowed new and stimulating influences to flow in. Chinese Buddhists also went abroad to study. For instance, around 1930, Wong Mou-lam, who translated *The Platform Sutra* into English and also founded the journal *Chinese Buddhism,* went to Sri Lanka to study Pali and Sanskrit. After Wong's departure, *Chinese Buddhism* was taken over by a Mr. Chen, who has informed the present writer in correspondence of his numerous sympathetic foreign friends in Shanghai in the early 1930s, including "Mr. Goddard, an American, founder of the Followers of the Buddha in the U.S.A." This would appear to be Dwight Goddard, compiler of *A Buddhist Bible.*

However, the tide of history was flowing ever more strongly against Buddhism as this century advanced. Buddhism now encountered its most formidable adversary in Marxism. Though looking with disfavor on Buddhism, as on all religions, the Communists did not initially feel that it needed to be destroyed. The establishment of an ideologically correct state would cause it to wither away naturally, they thought, with a little help in the form of anti-religious propaganda. In the meantime, attempts were made to bring Buddhism under control by organizing it under a central umbrella—the Chinese Buddhist Association. On the face of it, this organization displays a distinctly fellow-traveling complexion, though that might be merely pragmatic: a mask worn in the interests of survival.

The situation deteriorated considerably during the era of the so-called Cultural Revolution (1965–1975). Buddhist temples and monasteries were then sacked, and in some cases destroyed, and the already weakened *sangha* was further depleted. The excesses of this time have since been regretted, however, and a new, more liberal policy introduced.

Certainly the omens do not look particularly promising for Chinese Buddhism; yet, writing in 1986, John Blofeld found cause for optimism. Reflecting on his experiences during a visit to Shanghai that year, he felt that, while the percentage of Buddhists among the population must at present be tiny, and though "knowledge of Buddhism among the masses is almost nil," yet "old values and beliefs persist"; thus "there must be a considerable reservoir of potential Buddhists awaiting the advent of teachers able to put the Buddha *dharma* across to audiences already somewhat favorably disposed towards it." Finally, reiterating his hopes for a "widespread resurgence" that he could vividly picture if not hope to live to see, he concluded: "I possess very little evidence on which to build that dream of the future, but have not the smallest doubt that it will be fulfilled."*

The Chinese part in the transmission of Buddhism to the West has not been great. A few pioneering Westerners, like John Blofeld himself, were able to study in China before the Communist Revolution and have handed on their knowledge. Since 1949, of course, visits for the purpose of study and obtaining training in Buddhism have not been possible. A few Chinese teachers have managed to come to the West, mainly to the U.S.A. Buddhist activity takes place in Hong Kong and Taiwan, as well as in expatriate communities elsewhere in Asia and the United States. Lu K'uan Yü (Charles Luk) has been arguably the most influential writer and teacher living in Hong Kong.

* John Blofeld, "Some Thoughts on Buddhism in China," *The Middle Way* vol. 61, no. 3 (November, 1986): 146ff.

F·O·U·R·T·E·E·N

The Northern Transmission: Vietnam and Korea

VIETNAM

Vietnam, a long, thin sliver of territory lying along the extreme eastern edge of the Indo-Chinese peninsula, has indelibly impressed itself on modern consciousness as the quintessential war-torn southeast Asian country. Though now under a Communist regime, it was also a place where Buddhism once flourished, and indeed one of the unforgettable images of recent times is of Vietnamese Buddhist monks publicly burning themselves as a protest against the corruption of the Roman Catholic elite left behind by the colonial French after their withdrawal.

In ancient times the northern region, Annam, was for many centuries a province of the Chinese empire. To the south lay the Indianized states of Funan and Champa, which then overflowed beyond the present-day frontiers. The Vietnamese themselves originated in the north, and in time came to dominate the whole land. Independence from China was gained in the tenth century, but Chinese influences continued to exert a powerful effect and, in the long run, this meant that the standard brand of Sri Lankan Thervada that triumphed elsewhere in southeast Asia did not do so here; instead, Chinese forms of Mahayana Buddhism, notably a successful amalgam of Ch'an and Pure

Land, prevailed until the country fell to the Communists in 1975. Since then Buddhism has declined enormously and from time to time we hear reports of active persecution.

Many Vietnamese Buddhists now live as refugees in the West. One monk, Thich Nhat Hanh, who currently resides at Plum Village in France, has achieved international fame as a proponent of Engaged Buddhism. In the early 1960s, Nhat Hanh was recalled from his studies at Columbia University in the United States to help with the so-called Third Way of Reconciliation: a brave attempt to provide a viable alternative to the corruption of Saigon and the Communism of Hanoi, then bloodily battling for supremacy. He established Van Hanh University and set up the School of Youth for Social Service, which sent people out into the rural areas where the fighting was taking place to help the peasantry who were caught in the crossfire. Nhat Hanh coined the term "Engaged Buddhism" in his book, *Vietnam: Lotus in a Sea of Fire.*

KOREA

The Korean peninsula is a curving thrust of land reaching down from the northeast corner of China towards the southern tip of Japan. Though its people have staunchly fought for independence over the centuries, they have inevitably come strongly under the influence of the massive neighboring presence of China. The position of their small country, moreover, has naturally made it a kind of bridge whereby Chinese influences have been transmitted to Japan. At times, too, the traffic has flowed in the opposite direction.

It appears that Buddhism was introduced into Korea from China around the fourth century A.D. The transmission continued subsequently and many of the principal Chinese schools were introduced. In terms of development, Korean Buddhism tended broadly to follow the Chinese pattern—with one important difference. Being a small and politically vulnerable nation, the Koreans could not tolerate the same diversity of schools that proliferated in China. Various attempts, none entirely successful, were therefore made to syncretize and harmonize the teachings of various Buddhist schools, though in time the local form of Ch'an/Zen, called Son, was to prevail and has persisted to the present time despite the general rush towards Western-type modernization that has produced a concomitant explosion of Christianity.

Korean Buddhism enjoyed its golden age during the Silla (668–935 A.D.) and Koryo (935–1392 A.D.) periods. It was then favored by the intellectual elite and honored with royal patronage; pilgrims went to China to obtain texts and teachings; monasteries and temples were constructed and a thriving *sangha* established. Five doctrinal schools came into prominence, four of them—the Vinaya, Nirvana, Avatamsaka, and Yogacara schools—broadly emulating Chinese prototypes. The fifth, the Popsong, was an early attempt at syncretism by Wonhyo (617–686 A.D.). Later the Ch'an/Zen school was introduced, traditionally around 630 A.D., and, mirroring the Chinese pattern, it came into conflict with the doctrinal schools on account of its iconoclastic character.

Zen proved too vital to be stifled, however, so efforts to reconcile it with the doctrinal schools were initiated during the Koryo period. An ordained monk of the royal house, Uich'on (1055–1101), attempted a harmonization on the T'ien-t'ai pattern, but his anti-Zen bias hindered his success. A more successful attempt in the same direction was undertaken by Chinul (*a.k.a.* National Master Pojo 1158–1210), a somewhat independent figure who had evolved a personal practice that combined both study and meditation. Chinul's advantage was that he had obtained direct insight into the spiritual authenticity of both paths. He founded the Chogye Zen order, which was plumbed into the main Chinese Ch'an lines of transmission by the monk T'aego (1301–1382), who spent many years receiving Lin-chi (Rinzai) training in China.

Following the Chinese model, from the thirteenth century onwards the growth of neo-Confucianism and other unsympathetic developments led to an anti-Buddhist reaction and concomitant stagnation and decline. Attempts were made to stem the slide, but by the beginning of the present century Korean Buddhism was in a parlous state.

Between 1910 and 1945, the Japanese occupied Korea and attempted to introduce their brands of Buddhism as part of their program of domination. This aroused nationalistic feeling and spurred the Korean Buddhist community into action with the result that the Zen and doctrinal streams were eventually united into a unified Chogye order. This has maintained its pre-eminent position to the present time in South Korea, which was severed from the north by the Korean War (1945–1953). North Korea is now of course a Communist state.

The modern revival traces its roots back to Kyongho Sunim (1849–1912), who, after his major breakthrough at the age of thirty-two, spent twenty years teaching in an orthodox manner, and won widespread renown. His career adopted a more eccentric course during the last nine years of his life, however, when he returned to a secluded village, grew his hair long, and adopted layman's dress. He had numerous disciples, notably Mangong Sunim (1871–1946), who was active during the dark age of the Japanese occupation. In more recent times, the late Kusan Sunim (1909–1983), a disciple of Hyobong Sunim (1888-1966), attracted a certain amount of attention in the West. He established a center for training Western students at his monastery, Songgwang Sa, and also visited the U.S.A. and Europe, and inaugurated Korean Zen temples there. Meanwhile, a few Korean Zen masters have moved permanently to the West, notably Seung Sahn Sunim (*a.k.a.* Soen Sa Nim, b. 1927), founder of the Providence Zen Center, and Samu Sunim (b. 1941) of the Zen Lotus Society, Toronto.

F·I·F·T·E·E·N

The Northern Transmission: Japan

THE EARLY PERIOD (538–1184 A.D.)

Tradition has it that a political delegation arrived in Japan from Korea in the year 538 A.D. Among the gifts it brought for the Emperor were a bronze Buddha-image, some *sutras,* a few religious objects, and a letter warmly praising the most excellent *dharma.* Despite some initial reluctance, these gifts were accepted, and a temple was duly built to house the image and accord it the appropriate respects. However, an epidemic of disease ravaged the land shortly afterwards, and this was interpreted as a sign that the indigenous deities (*kami*) were displeased at the veneration of a foreign deity. To appease them and secure remission of the plague, the Emperor ordered the new temple to be committed to the flames; the *Buddharupa* was meanwhile tossed into a canal.

But Buddhism was an unstoppable force. How could it be otherwise when the Buddha himself supposedly had predicted that it would "spread to the East"? Despite the unpromising start, more scriptures and *sangha* did reach Japan, and, though some resistance still came from some of the conservative followers of Shinto, the native religious tradition, Buddhism began to take hold. Its success was mainly due to the fact that it won favor at court, where it was thought to possess occult powers capable of protecting the state against disease and promoting social harmony. It was also flexible enough to be able to coexist with Shinto, eventually even to merge with it, and it moreover accorded the old *kami* an honorable place and purpose within its own pantheon.

Around the turn of the seventh century, steps began to be taken by the dominant clan towards organizing the country into a centralized state. The great empire of China provided a useful model, and Chinese culture and institutions began to be imported wholesale into Japan at this time. Chinese literary, artistic, architectural, and technical forms were adopted, and a governmental bureaucracy was set up on the lines of the Chinese pattern. The projected centralized state also needed a philosophical sub-structure, and though Confucianism and Taoism had obvious advantages to offer, Buddhism, which had been taken to such a superlatively high pitch of development in T'ang dynasty China, enjoyed special favor at court. The Empress Suiko (reigned 592–628 A.D.) was such a committed Buddhist that she retired to a nunnery shortly after her accession, and her nephew, Crown Prince Shotoku (547–622 A.D), himself an enthusiastic Buddhist, reigned as regent for more than thirty years, during which time the Buddhist cause was advanced considerably in the land.

The initial Korean connection having been largely superceded, increasing numbers of Japanese monastics and scholars began to go to China to partake of Buddhist riches. Initially six of the great Chinese schools were transplanted to Japanese soil in this early period and given Japanese names:

Japanese name	Chinese name	Indian name
Sanron	San-lun	Madhyamaka
Jojitsu	Ch'êng-shih	Satyasiddhi
Hosso	Fa-hsiang	Yogacara
Kusha	Chü-shê	Abhidharmakosha
Kegon	Hua-yen	Avatamsaka
Ritsu	Lü	Vinaya

The Ritsu school, which was imported into Japan in 754 A.D. by the Chinese monk Chien-chên, set procedures for the ordination of monks and nuns on a proper formal footing.

Buddhism tended to remain an elitist persuasion, however, and to be closely bound up with the official state. The Emperor Shomu (724–749 A.D.), for instance, ordered state temples to be set up in every province and prayers for the peace and prosperity of the nation were to be offered in them. His capital of Nara meanwhile burgeoned into a splendid Buddhist capital replete with exquisite temples, sculpture, and artifacts, created mainly at public expense and owing much to Chinese styles in art and architecture. The political power of the *sangha,* many of whom were of the scholar-gentleman type, was considerable in Nara; non-official and popular manifestations of Buddhism, on the other hand, tended to be frowned upon and were sometimes punished. Nevertheless so-called people's priests did appear in the hinterland; they lived wandering and sometimes eremetical lives, dispensing popular religious services; a few of them won a reputation for having miraculous powers.

THE HEIAN PERIOD (794–1184 A.D.)

The groundwork having been laid in the previous period, important changes and developments now began to take place that resulted in the emergence of a more characteristically Japanese form of Buddhism.

First, the capital was shifted from Nara to other sites, eventually being fixed where Kyoto now stands. This effectively undermined the political power of the learned metropolitan *sangha* (which it was fully intended to do) and thereafter the focus of Buddhism in Japan shifted from the political center to the secluded mountain regions where the important new movements chose to establish their headquarters. The Tendai and Shingon schools in particular came very much to the fore now, supplanting the other schools that had established themselves, and laying the foundations for the future development of Buddhism in Japan. Esoteric ritualism became a particularly powerful force.

There was at the same time great rivalry between the various sects, and, following the Chinese pattern, monasteries became centers of worldly wealth and power. Armies of warrior monks (*sohei*) carried on internecine strife and even on occasion stormed the capital to assert their political will there. Buddhism nevertheless continued to enjoy court support, largely on account of its presumed occult powers, but more accessible forms of Buddhist belief and practice did begin to infiltrate other sections of society as well. Finally, Shinto and Buddhism managed to embrace each other into a more or less harmonious unity that persisted until the nineteenth century.

The founding father of the Tendai School, the Japanese elaboration of the Chinese T'ien-t'ai, was Dengyo-daishi (or Saicho, 767–822 A.D.), who established his headquarters at Mount Hiei, not far from the new capital, not too near either. He had entered the *sangha* at an early age, and, after devoting himself to study and practice, eventually became especially partial to the teachings of the T'ien-t'ai School, which were based on the *Lotus Sutra*. Dengyo enjoyed the favor of the Emperor Kammu who in 804 A.D. sent him to pursue his research in China. He spent a few months on a "wild scamper from monastery to monastery" (Arthur Waley), trying to pick up as much as he could of the different kinds of Chinese Buddhism—not only T'ien-t'ai.

Dengyo brought back many *sutras* to Japan from China and an improved knowledge of various teachings and practices. Upon this basis he and his successors developed their school along lines that did not adhere inflexibly to the Chinese prototype; rather, they enriched it with elements borrowed from Ch'an, Shingon, Pure Land, and other forms of Buddhism; a modified Vinaya was also adopted. Dengyo continued to enjoy the favor of the emperor, but he largely succeeded in liberating his school from state interference and from the other schools. Dengyo's disciples further developed Tendai Buddhism and Mount Hiei eventually grew into one of the greatest monastic complexes of all time, with some three thousand temples and halls.

The founding father of the Shingon School, which burgeoned on the basis of Chinese Tantrism, on the other hand, was Kobo-daishi (or Kukai 774–835 A.D.), who occupies a particularly warm place in the hearts of the Japanese people. Scholar, ascetic, traveler, sculptor, calligrapher, educator, and rainmaker he was a man of many parts. He too began his religious and philosophical studies young, became a monk at the age of nineteen and was attracted to esoteric Buddhism. His chief textbooks became the *Mahavairochana Sutra* and the *Vajrashekhara Sutra*. Though some seven years younger, he went to China in the same group as Dengyo-daishi and stayed until 806 A.D. He had the good fortune to study with Hui-kuo (known in Japan as Keika Ajari), who solved all his spiritual doubts and difficulties and also gave him formal transmission; therefore when Hui-kuo died, Kobo-daishi became the eighth patriarch of the esoteric school.

Kobo-daishi returned to Japan with many new skills and accomplishments to impart. He began his activities in Nara, the old capital, but later removed to the mountains and eventually founded his headquarters at Mount Koya on the Kii peninsula.

> Koya is (or rather was) an almost inaccessible place compared to Hiei, but how many pilgrims congregated there every year! On the mountain a little town has come into existence.*

His career was a successful one and he too enjoyed imperial favor, to the extent that he was allowed to build a Shingon temple in the

---

* D. T. Suzuki, *Zen & Japanese Buddhism* (Tokyo: Japan Travel Bureau, 1970), 93.

emperor's palace, where he performed esoteric rituals and ceremonies. He had a great reputation for occult powers, and was heaped with honors for his successful forays into the field of rainmaking. Shingon devotees do not believe him dead to this day but rather sitting in silent meditation behind the closed doors of his retreat at Mount Koya.

Ritualistic Shingon practices were very influential during this period. Indeed no less an authority than Dr. D. T. Suzuki has unequivocally declared that "the Buddhism of the Heian period was flooded with magic ritualism."* Even the highly philosophical Tendai School adopted its own esoteric rituals, which perhaps helped make it more generally palatable.

Buddhism remained essentially an upper class preserve, however, as is palpably demonstrated by the aestheticism that constellated around it. Gorgeous robes, sonorous chanting, dramatic rituals—these stimulated the eventual emergence of *Noh* drama. Buddhism also influenced the arts of poetry, painting, sculpture, and architecture. But the elitist tendency was also restrictive, for as Suzuki has also declared: "aristocracy is a one-eyed child; it sees the refined surface but lacks solidity and frequently sincerity. Real power must grow from life itself."† In short, Buddhism had to reach the ordinary people.

A beginning was made in this direction during the latter stages of the Heian period. Certain teachers did begin to disseminate popular devotional forms of Buddhism, principally derived from the Pure Land cult of Amitabha (Amida in Japan). These devotional cults propounded the notion that salvation was possible through the intercession of benign *buddhas* and *bodhisattvas*. This could be obtained by the repetition of a simple formula such as *Namu-Amida-butsu* (the *Nembutsu*). In this way, the minefields of philosophy and ascetic practice, both of which required special talents and conditions, were effectively bypassed and absolute faith was placed in "other power" (*taviki*): a redeeming action originating from beyond the self.

Two figures are especially important in the popularization of Amidism at this time: Kuya Shonin (902–972 A.D.) and Ryonin (1072–1132 A.D.). Kuya, also known as the Market Sage, quit the rarefied atmosphere of mountain retreat and lacquered temple to take Buddhism among the masses. He lived a peripatetic life and, in addition to his specifically spiritual efforts, was also involved in social welfare and good works. Ryonin, on the other hand, brought Kegon (Avatamsaka) philosophy, with its central notion of universal interdependence, to Amidism. This in turn influenced the Tendai School.

* *Ibid.*, 93.
† *Ibid.*, 95.

THE KAMAKURA PERIOD (1185–1333)

This was a period of crisis, when Japan was both threatened from without and ravaged by internal disunity and violent change. In particular, power was wrested from the hands of the effete imperial aristocracy by the *samurai* or warrior class, and a *Shogunate* (military governorship) was in 1185 established at Kamakura, well away from Kyoto, the capital, by the dominant Minamoto clan. This new climate did not favor the study of abstruse philosophy and the performance of elaborate rituals; rather, more robust and generally accessible teachings and practices became the order of the day. Consequently, the fortunes of the Tendai and Shingon Schools declined, and more earthy, democratic movements advanced, notably the devotional schools and Zen; lay Buddhism also began to come into its own and the spiritual potential of women was recognized. Ultimately, for all its stresses, this was the most highly creative time for Japanese Buddhism—its golden age, no less.

The devotional cults in particular brought Buddhism within reach of the ordinary man and woman. In particular, two major Pure Land schools came to the fore: the Jodo-shu ("Pure Land School") and the Jodo Shin-shu ("The True Pure Land School"). The seminal proponent of the Jodo Shin school was Honen Shonin (1133–1212), who believed that the present state of the world was so dark and desperate that few could practice traditional methods effectively; he therefore advocated as an alternative "easy path," sincere faith in the beneficence of Amida coupled with recitation of the Nembutsu, the Japanese formula "Namu-Amidabutsu."

This highly pared-down formula was taken to an ultimate of economy by Honen's follower, Shinran Shonin (1173–1262), the founding father of the Jodo Shin-shu, who believed that there still remained a vestige of self-power in the Shin doctrine. In his view, the degenerate state of the present age was such that the devotee should forsake all hope that he could achieve anything whatsoever himself, even by repeating the Nembutsu, and should place his fate utterly in the hands of Amida. A dangerous corollary to this was that morality was ineffectual; indeed sinful people, if they fully acknowledged their hopelessness and appealed wholeheartedly to Amida, might be more in line for salvation than those who attempted to live ethically. Ordination into the *sangha* was likewise a vain step and Shinran himself, though a monk initially, married and had children, thus encouraging lay practice by his example. Shinran was particularly active teaching among the common folk.

A highly controversial figure, on the other hand, was Nichiren Shonin (1222–1282), who has attracted a bad press on account of his apparently un-Buddhistic disposition. He in many ways represents a type often to be found in Buddhism: active, energetic, passionate, even obsessive, and highly aggressive—the sort of person who is drawn to the teaching of the Buddha not so much because he exemplifies its gentle virtues and peaceful ideals, but, on the contrary, because, whether he consciously knows it or not, he needs the gentling influence of Buddhist practice to cool his hot nature. Still, the *dharma* has its uses for such people, and indeed Nichiren saw himself as the manifestation of bodhisattvic energies vital to the times. The son of a lowly fisherman, he trained in the Tendai School and came to the conclusion that the *Lotus Sutra* was the key to salvation in the prevailing dark age. He did not advocate that the *sutra* be read and reflected upon, however, but argued that the whole of its teaching was encapsulated in the title; therefore all that was necessary by way of practice was to repeat the formula "Namu-myoho-renge-kyo" which could be roughly translated as "Homage to *The Lotus Sutra*." This would definitely not ensure rebirth in some kind of paradise; it would evoke the enlightenment of Shakyamuni Buddha *here* and *now*. His creed was thus a trenchantly this-worldly one; it was also aggressively of a Mongol invasion of Japan.

Unfortunately, Nichiren did not merely think the other schools completely incapable of saving Japan and the world from impending apocalypse; he considered them downright disastrous and pugnaciously demanded that the state suppress them and rally exclusively behind his own cause. This produced the inevitable counter-reaction, and he was himself persecuted quite viciously, which merely served to reinforce his conviction of his own rightness and galvanize his sense of mission. Although his school has been stigmatized as being the very antithesis of Buddhism (by Edward Conze and John Stevens), it did not finally end up in the graveyard of discarded cults and defunct fads, but survived as a powerful force in Japanese Buddhism to the present time.

Arguably more important than the development of popular devotional forms of Buddhism was the rise of the Zen school at this time. This placed supreme emphasis on self-power: on the active mobilization of all one's energies towards the realization of the ideal of enlightenment. In its more austere forms, Zen also had no time for excrescences (like rituals or philosophical study) and embellishments, but took a no-nonsense, down-to-earth stance. For all these reasons it found favor with the *samurai* class whose fortunes were now in the ascendant and whose members, men who lived constantly under the shadow of death, needed a spiritual way that would not merely reconcile them with their lot in life but take it an authentic path of spiritual development. Zen philosophy and training (especially that of the Rinzai branch) fulfilled their requirements admirably. It equipped the *samurai* to face death with equanimity, while its invocation of a mode of action originating beyond thought and manifesting spontaneously and in perfect harmony with the spirit of the moment, could be applied with effect to military practices—swordsmanship, archery, wrestling, and so forth—thereby transforming them into authentic martial arts. Thus in an actual combat situation, the Zen-trained swordsman could bypass concern for personal safety and intellectual planning, both of which could be crippling, and make his moves freely, guided by this mysterious power. On the other hand, the military ethos, with its tough dedication to training and discipline, itself contributed much to Japanese Zen. All of which might suggest that Japanese Zen lacked an aesthetic side; not so—the Zen virtues of spontaneity, simplicity, tranquility, and aloneness inspired the emergence of a very distinctive aesthetic. This is exemplified in the so-called Zen arts of calligraphy, ink painting, *haiku* poetry, pottery, and flower arrangement (*ikebana*); also in house and garden design and the tea ceremony (*cha-no-yu*).

The two major surviving branches of the Chinese Ch'an School, the Lin-chi and the Ts'ao-tung, known in Japan as the Rinzai and Soto respectively, were introduced during the Kamakura period. Traditionally the Rinzai line is said to have been transmitted by Eisai (1141–1215), and the Soto by Dogen (1200–1253). Both branches place primary emphasis on sitting meditation (*zazen*). There is a slight difference of attitude, however, summed up in the maxim, "Rinzai is for the general, Soto for the farmer." In other words, Rinzai is the more purposeful and militant. In addition to *zazen* practice, it employs the use of *koan*: apparently illogical questions, concerted application to which will (hopefully) precipitate the practitioner beyond normal thinking processes. The Soto disposition, on the other hand, is less goal-orientated. Just to sit in *zazen* is to be in the enlightened state; there is nothing more to be achieved, nowhere else to go.

Originally a Tendai monk, Eisai paid two short visits to China (1168 and 1187–1191). On the first visit, an interest in Zen was awakened; the purpose of his second visit was to deepen his understanding of it. On his return to his homeland in 1191, he attempted to propagate Rinzai Zen in Kyoto, but ran into opposition from the Tendai fraternity. He escaped to the martial atmosphere of Kamakura, where he was better received, and where he established his first temple, Shofukuji, in 1215. He later returned to Kyoto, but had to compromise, and when he did eventually build a temple there, Kennin-ji, it was not exclusively a Zen center of activities. Nevertheless, Eisai laid a basis upon which Daio Kukushi (1235-1308; not to be confused with his pupil Daito) and other Japanese and Chinese Rinzai Zen masters could build. The Japanese masters tended to gravitate to the imperial capital, Kyoto, and were often active in worldly affairs; the Chinese masters, on the other hand, tended to find patronage under the military authorities at Kamakura. Prominent among the Chinese were Daikaku (1203–1268) and Bukko (1226–?), the founders of Kenchoji and Engaku-ji respectively, who evolved an "on-the-instant" "warrior Zen" adapted to the needs of the denizens of Kamakura. They improvised *koan* out of the actual life-and-death situations in which their students were caught up.

Dogen (1200-1253), the seminal master of the Japanese Soto Zen School, came from an aristocratic background but lost his parents at an early age, a traumatic experience that forcefully impressed upon his mind the transitoriness of the things of this world. Intellectually brilliant from childhood, he entered the *sangha* at the age of thirteen and initially trained in the Tendai School. Unresolved questions drove him elsewhere, however, and he eventually gravitated to the Zen School. He spent four formative years studying in China under Master Ju-ching (1163–1228), the Abbot of T'ien-t'ung monastery. Then in 1227, having had his enlightenment confirmed by his master, Dogen returned to Japan, intending to propagate Soto Zen there, but in Kyoto he also came under pressure from the devotees of the older schools. More doggedly independent than Eisai, he refused to compromise, and eventually established a temple, Eihei-ji, in a remote province. This remains one of the two main temples of the Japanese Soto Zen School to this day (the other is Soji-ji, founded by Keizan). Like the Pure Land masters, Dogen was convinced of the degenerate nature of his times but nevertheless felt that it was necessary to struggle for the truth. He himself avoided honors and all the other worldly pitfalls to which so many of his contemporary monks had fallen victim. He did, however, believe that the state should be based on the ideas of Zen Buddhism, and probably tried to impress that view upon the pious Emperor Gosaga.

Dogen earnestly enjoined his own followers to forsake the pursuit of fame and fortune, and, remaining ever keenly aware of death and the general unpredictability of things, to wholeheartedly apply themselves to the practice of sitting Zen. He was less averse to scriptural study than his Rinzai counterparts and in fact left various influential writings behind, notably his classic *Shobogenzo* ("Eye and Treasury of the True Dharma"), in which he wrote the following lines in characteristically terse and direct style:

To study the way is to study the self. To study the self is to forget the self. To forget the self is to be enlightened by all things. To be enlightened by all things is to remove the barriers between one's self and others.*

At the age of fifty-two, Dogen became ill and died soon after arriving in Kyoto for medical treatment.

The monks involved in the transmission of Zen to Japan from China also transmitted neo-Confucian values and ideas. These found favor with the Kamakura authorities, whose military code of honor (*bushido*) elevated loyalty to one's clan lord to the status of a high virtue. Not only were Chinese arts and sciences also brought over in a similar way, tea was introduced into Japan from China, supposedly by Eisai himself.

ASHIKAGA (OR MUROMACHI) PERIOD (1336–1573)

The demise of the Kamakura regime amid fighting and bloodshed inaugurated a new era of internal strife and instability that broadly lasted until the establishment of Tokugawa Shogunate (Shogun means "military ruler") in 1603. More and more power was wrested from the hands of the central government by provincial warlords. At the same time it was a period of economic growth that saw increased rural prosperity, the emergence of a merchant class, and—something hitherto unseen in Japan—the blossoming of an urban culture.

But for Japanese Buddhism the truly creative phase was over. A slide into stagnation or "long narcosis" (Suzuki) now began that was to broadly last until the end of the nineteenth century. According to Dr. Suzuki, all the latent potential seemed to have been realized during the Kamakura period with the result that "what followed was more or less the filling-in and working out of details."†

Of the various Buddhist schools, the Rinzai Zen School fared best, especially during the fourteenth and fifteenth centuries, largely due to the favor it enjoyed with the military rulers. Much patronage was heaped upon it, with the result that many fine temples were built, replete with fine works of art, lavishly endowed, and commanding large estates. In Kyoto the so-called Five Mountains—five splendid temple complexes—came into being and here the arts or "ways" (*do*) of Japanese Zen Buddhist culture were developed to a high pitch of aesthetic excellence. In the strictly religious sphere, however, there was only increasing

* Yuho Yokoi, *Zen Master Dogen: An Introduction with Selected Writings* (New York & Tokyo: Weatherhill, 1976), 39.
† Suzuki, *Zen & Japanese Buddhism,* 103.

hierarchical institutionalization and formalization, but no doctrinal or methodological development.

During this period, all Buddhist schools increasingly sought followers among the ordinary folk. Provincial temples and local organizations were set up; peripatetic priests were also a feature of the times, like Zen Master Ikkyu (1394–1481), putatively sired by the Emperor Gokomatsu, who wandered extensively mingling with all classes and practicing a somewhat iconoclastic lifestyle which embraced many of the pleasures of the flesh. He was, on the other hand, strongly critical of the stuffy hypocrisy of those decadent monks who scrupulously observed the superficial outward forms but neglected inner practice. Ironically, by order of the Emperor, Ikkyu spent the last years of his long life in the highly respectable role of abbot of the Ven. Daitoku-ji monastery in Kyoto.

Towards the end of this period, which closed with a century of civil strife in which the important Buddhist schools took an active part, the first Japanese encounters with Christian missionaries took place.

THE AZUCHI-MOMOYAMA AND EDO PERIODS (1573–1868 A.D.)

Ironically and sadly, in order for Japan to be reunited and pacified, the political and military might of the Buddhist strongholds had to be broken. This task was vigorously undertaken by a ruthless and vengeful warlord named Oda Nubunaga (1534–1582), who was prepared to stop at nothing in order "to bring the whole country under one sword." He violently subdued the Kyoto region and broke the control that the Jodo-Shin-shu school exercised over the vital commercial port of Osaka. But his most devastating act was to destroy the Tendai center in Mount Hiei with its three thousand temples, and slaughter most of its twenty thousand inhabitants.

Nobunaga's reign was short-lived, but his work was carried on by his less vengeful but no less ambitious protege Toyotomi Hideyoshi (1536–1598). It was finally brought to fulfillment by Hideyoshi's successor, Tokugawa Ieyasu (1542–1616), who in 1603 established the Tokugawa Shogunate which ruled Japan from its bastion at Edo (modern Tokyo) for two and a half centuries, the longest period of peace and, for the most part, prosperity in the history of the country. This was achieved by closing the country to the outside world and establishing internally a regime of inflexible authoritarian control that created stability and order, but at the price of effectively stifling all creative change and innovation.

In the religious sphere, neo-Confucianism, which had been transmitted to Japan from China by Rinzai Zen monks, now became the official creed for the simple reason that it promoted those feudal virtues that the new regime wished to inculcate into the subject masses. Buddhism, on the other hand, while not persecuted, was brought under strict state control. The state even interfered in matters of doctrine, invariably coming down on the side of orthodoxy. New teachings and practices were prohibited, nor was it permissible to found a new school or temple. Meanwhile existing major temples and sub-temples were classified according to tradition and all Japanese, regardless of whether they were Buddhist or not, were obliged to register at one of them, though more for demographic than for religious purposes. In the prevailing climate of peace and prosperity Buddhism benefited materially, but spiritually the ongoing process of stagnation that had been inaugurated at the demise of the Kamakura regime was generally consolidated.

The closure of Japan to the outside world also meant that no new stimuli to fresh development were able to infiltrate the country from other Buddhist countries. The one exception was the arrival of Obaku Zen from China via the open port of Nagasaki in 1654. It was brought by Yin-yüan (1592–1673), a Chinese Rinzai Zen Master known in Japan as Ingen. While the Rinzai school had continued along traditional lines in Japan, in China it had been modified. Most conspicuously it was prepared to make concessions to those not able to rise to the full rigors of the pure unalloyed Zen training. So it had adopted devotional practices from Pure Land and sanctioned *sutra* study as a valid form of spiritual endeavor. While Yin-yüan came in the first place as a reformer of Rinzai Zen, he met with resistance and was ultimately obliged to found a separate school, but one which became very successful. He also introduced cultural innovations from Ming China: new styles of ritual, architecture, clothing, and so forth.

Some of the devotional cults were viewed with disfavor by the new regime and were forced underground. Otherwise, as before, the Zen School survived best during this period and a few influential figures did emerge, notably the poet Basho and the Rinzai Zen Masters Bankei and Hakuin, the latter being the most important.

Bankei Yotaku (1622–1693), was something of an iconoclast who challenged orthodox Zen teaching. He himself spent many years intensively pursuing enlightenment. Then at last he realized that he had been in possession of what he had been seeking all along, and decided that the term *the Unborn* best described it. This of course directly echoed the Buddha's pronouncement that there had to be an Unborn, Not-become, Not-made, Not-compounded for there to be release from what is born, become, made, and compounded. At the same time Bankei concluded

Bodhidharma, after Hakuin

that all the sweat and tears of his years of searching had been so much waste of time. Consequently he advocated a simple formula, "Awaken to the Unborn in the midst of everyday affairs," as an alternative to the protracted formal rigors of conventional Zen training. Obviously this was not designed to go down well with the Zen establishment, but Bankei had charisma, and was able to attract a huge following, notably among the ordinary people. Imperial recognition eventually came, but the school that he established did not survive for long after his death.

Matsuo Basho (1644–1694), on the other hand, was not a Zen monk but a poet who consciously transformed the practice of poetry into an authentic religious way. By nature prone to wanderlust, he loved the life of the open road that led him to where he could commune with un-spoiled nature. From these lonely wanderings came his poems. His preference was for the highly economical seventeen-syllable *haiku* form, which he took to unparalleled heights of poetic subtlety. Many of his finest *haiku* are thought to succinctly catch the elusive, often melancholy magic of the passing moment, and thereby express the true spirit of Zen.

Finally, Hakuin Zenji (1685–1768) not only reformed Rinzai Zen and restored the *koan* system, but laid the foundation for the future development of the whole Zen school down to present time. Consequently he is placed in the first rank of Japanese Zen luminaries, alongside Dogen Zenji. He was also a notable painter, calligrapher, and poet in the Zen manner.

Initially it was intense fear of Hellfire that drove the impressionable young Hakuin into the Buddhist *sangha* at the age of fifteen. His doubts and fears were not allayed, however, and he considered quitting Buddhism in favor of poetry, for which he had a certain talent. Unclear as to what to do, he decided to consign his fate to chance. One day he opened a book that had been brought out to be aired. It happened to be a Zen text, and it inspired him to undertake intensive *zazen* practice. This led to his first break-through, which he believed to be the most significant in centuries. His pride in his achievement was unsentimentally smashed, however, when he subsequently came under the hammer of an exceedingly hard master. Then after grappling with the *koan* "*Mu*" for three years, he experienced another illumination after being hit on the head while out on alms round. "You are through," his master told him.

Soon afterwards he was struck by a "Zen sickness" as a result of his extreme spiritual exertions. Fortunately he was able to cure himself with the meditative practice for reviving the spirit-energy described in his text, *Yasenkanna*.* Afterwards he again applied himself intensively to meditation and *sutra* study. He eventually returned to his run-down home temple of Shoin-ji in Hara (Shizuoka prefecture), where one night his mother appeared to him in a dream bearing a robe in which were concealed two mirrors, one bright, the other dull. Suddenly, however, the dull one blazed with a light a million times more bright than the other. Then Hakuin saw that to look at anything was to see his own face, and that it is the Buddha-eye that beholds the Buddha-nature. An even more profound insight followed, hinged around a problem arising from the *Lotus Sutra* and occasioned by his hearing the chirping of a cricket, but utterly devoid of any drama. Then he at last recognized the incompleteness of his earlier enlightenments, great and

* Hakuin Zenji, *Yasenkanna* in *The Tiger's Cave,* trans. Trevor Leggett (London: Routledge & Kegan Paul, 1977).

small and, weeping, declared: "The practice of Zen is not easy!"

Hakuin lived to the advanced age of eighty-four and as his fame grew, increasing numbers of disciples were attracted to him, with the result that rural Shoin-ji became the most influential center of Zen of the period. Nor did he lack the common touch but was greatly concerned to help ordinary people;* he also left many influential writings, notably his *Orategama*. In his teaching he emphasized intensive *koan* practice. He himself invented the famous *koan* of "The Sound of One Hand Clapping." He also placed great importance on the generation of the so-called Great Doubt and on the Great Death, his term for the death of the "I" or ego, beside which natural death is indeed trivial.

FROM THE MEIJI RESTORATION TO THE PRESENT TIME (1868 TO DATE)

As the nineteenth century progressed, it became increasingly clear that the hermetic feudal order established and maintained by the Tokugawa Shogunate was both outmoded and redundant. As the outside world pressed Japan to reopen her doors, internal dissent grew; finally a *coup d'état* restored the imperial regime in 1868, and the modernization process began apace.

Ardent nationalism now asserted itself. The new order elevated the Meiji Emperor to the status of a god while Shinto, detached from Buddhism, was made a state cult. At the same time Buddhism, a foreign religion, was subordinated and subjected to persecution. Estates and endowments were seized and the *sangha* evicted from temples, which were then either closed or destroyed. Buddhism had, however, established itself too deeply in the affections of the Japanese people for this policy to be sustained, so after a short while it was abandoned and religious freedom was promised.

The various pressures that were brought to bear upon Japanese Buddhism at this time, to which the advent of energetic missionary Christianity was later added, in the long run had the beneficial effect of snapping it out of its "long narcosis" and spurring new development. For the first time in centuries contacts with other Buddhist countries, and indeed with Western ones as well, were made. This encouraged Buddhist scholarship, and various Buddhist universities—Ohtani, Ryukoku, Komazawa, etc.—were established in the first part of the present century. Much useful Buddhological work was undertaken and

* John Stevens, "Zen & the Common Man: Social Dimensions of Hakuin Zenji's Art," *The Middle Way* vol.60, no. 1(May, 1985): 32ff.

continues. Critical editions of Pali, Sanskrit, Chinese, and Tibetan texts have been produced, translations made, and in-depth studies carried out. Pioneers in this field include B. Nanjio and K. Kasahara, who studied Sanskrit under Max Müller, and J. Takakusu. In Nishida Kitaro, meanwhile, Japan produced a philosopher of world rank.

The influence of Nichiren played an important part in the militaristic nationalism that developed in the 1920s and 1930s. This caused devastation in Manchuria and Korea and led directly to Japanese entry into World War II. Nichiren devotees were also involved in political assassinations during the immediate pre-War period.

Nearly all the Buddhist schools—except, for example, the lay Nichiren movement, Soka Gakkai—acquiesced in the Japanese involvement in World War II. The *götterdämmerung* of 1945 left the country spiritually devastated, but since then it has of course rallied remarkably, pouring all its energies into development along Western technological lines, and outstripping all its rivals to emerge as an economic power of the first rank.

A significant feature of the post–World War II period has been the enormous success of the so-called New Religions, which in fact represent new orchestrations of traditional themes. Prominent among the Buddhist New Religions are Rissho Kosei-kai, and Soka Gakkai (motto: "Promotion of peace, culture, and education through Buddhism"), both of which take their basic inspiration from Nichiren and the *Lotus Sutra,* though in keeping with the climate of the times they tend to talk vociferously of peace. Lay-orientated, they have recruited mass followings running into millions from among ordinary people, to whom they offer practical support, help with personal problems, and a sense of meaning. Both stress this worldly-success and social involvement. Soka Gakkai, the largest of the New Religions, has strong political connections.

In contemporary Japan, the traditional Buddhist schools, which co-exist alongside the New Religions, have also tried to widen the scope of their appeal and generally regenerate themselves to meet the challenge of the modern world. As we have already noted, however, loyalty to a single religion is not a feature of Japanese religious life; but that life is undeniably rich and diverse—and Buddhism certainly continues to play a very significant part in it.

Japan has also played a large part in the transmission of Buddhism to the West. Japanese *roshis* showed an interest in building bridges to the United States as early as the latter part of the nineteenth century. Some Zen has also been transmitted to Europe, as have the devotional schools of Jodo and Jodo Shin, while some of the Nichiren sects have attracted mass followings.

S·I·X·T·E·E·N

The Northern Transmission: Tibet

Situated mainly on a vast plateau in central Asia at altitudes of thirteen thousand feet and more, Tibet, the "Land of Snows," is curtained on many sides by formidable mountain ranges, like the Himalayas and the Kun-Lun. In this naturally secluded situation a unique culture once flourished: one in which Buddhism, as the dominant factor, was harmoniously integrated into every aspect of life. Sadly, since 1959 that culture has been systematically destroyed by the Chinese Communists, who have taken over the country and sought to forcibly impose their own Marxist ideology upon it. Nowadays there are signs of a change of heart and a certain level of Buddhist observance is again permitted in the so-called Tibet Autonomous Region, but irreparable damage has nevertheless been done.

Although fertile valleys watered by great rivers do occur in Tibet, the country is largely arid, barren, and sparsely populated. Nevertheless, travelers are almost unanimously agreed in finding the primeval landscape compellingly beautiful, especially as the rarefied atmosphere allows colors to reach the eye with primary intensity and distant objects appear close. In such a setting, all kinds of strange, mystical, and magical things—the stuff of Tibetan Buddhism itself—become believable.

THE FIRST TRANSMISSION (C. 640–838 A.D.)

It seems that originally the Tibetans were a primitive, largely nomadic, and pugnacious people whose warlike activities caused more than a few headaches for their neighbors. As their power and organization grew, they were able, for instance, to launch campaigns in China itself and on one occasion captured the capital, Sian. Spiritually they inclined to animism and other primitive magical beliefs and practices. A species of priest existed among them called *bön-po,* who are usually described as shamans, though more specifically the name implies that they recited *mantras* which could be used for exorcism, invoking powerful spirits and so forth. The *bön-po* may also have been concerned with the death rituals of the early kings. In time, as we shall see, Bön was to emerge as an independent religious cult in its own right, deeply influenced by Buddhism but emphatically separate from it.

On the face of it, this does not look like very fertile ground for the lofty teachings of the Buddha, and indeed, the earliest attempts at propagating those teachings in Tibet in their more prosaic forms do not seem to have been overly successful. Tradition has it that it was only with the arrival of the Tantric adept Padmasambhava (or Guru Rinpoché) towards the end of the eighth century A.D. that success was ensured. He alone possessed the occult know-how necessary to subdue the demoniac forces inimical to the transmission of Buddhism. He could counter magic with magic, and emerge victorious. One of his particular feats was to conquer the spirits that hitherto had been frustrating the building of Samyé (completed 787 A.D.), the first Buddhist monastery of Tibet.

It should be noted in passing that the old demons and spirits were not annihilated, as they would have been in the West, with all the grim paraphernalia of witch-hunts and inquisitions; rather they were obliged to submit to the *dharma.* Thereafter they continued to play a tolerated if subordinate role as "*dharma* protectors." Psychospiritually, this could be seen as the assimilation of the magical-mythical in the collective Tibetan psyche, whereas in the West it was ruthlessly repressed.

His seminal exploits won for Padmasambhava a deep and lasting place in the affections of the Tibetans. As regards his life, however, it is hard to disentangle truth from myth, and there have inevitably been those scholars who have questioned whether he visited Tibet at all, although innumerable sites in Tibet and the Himalayan region are mythically associated with him.

By the time of Padmasambhava, Buddhism had of course been flourishing in India for over a millennium. It had also been transmitted throughout southeast Asia and northwards, bypassing Tibet, to China,

Guru Rinpoché (Padmasambhava) drawn by Robert Beer

Korea, and Japan. It is indeed strange that Tibet remained outside the Buddhist fold for so long, though the reasons for this are not hard to find. Once it did take root, however, those roots were to run exceedingly deep and to transform every aspect of Tibetan life. Commentators have often reflected upon the curious enigma that, once adopted—and then against all the apparent odds—Buddhism became for the Tibetan people the one pearl of great price for which they were ready to sacrifice almost anything.

The transmission of Buddhism to Tibet divides into two distinct phases. The first took place during the era of the so-called Three Great

Religious (i.e., Buddhist) Kings: Songtsen Gampo (*c.* 609–649 A.D.), Trisong Detsen (704–797 A.D.), and Ralpachen (805–838 A.D.).

Now, according to Tibetan hagiography, Songtsen Gampo was an incarnation of Avalokiteshvara, the Bodhisattva of Compassion, who in Tibet is known as Chenrezi. He took two wives, one Chinese, the other Nepalese; and these were not only Buddhists but incarnations of Tara (Tibetan. Drölma), Avalokiteshvara's consort. Thus the ideal *dramatis personae* was fortuitously assembled for the enactment of the great drama of the establishment of Buddhism as the state religion of Tibet. To do so, however, the resistance of the *bön-po* who exerted powerful influence among the nobility, had to be first overcome. Also the linguistic apparatus for the translation of Buddhist texts into Tibetan had to be set up. As Tibet had hitherto not developed a system of writing, one of Songtsen Gampo's ministers, Thönmi Sambhota, was dispatched to India. He subsequently evolved an alphabet based on Sanskrit models and composed treatises on grammar. The rambling and magnificent Jokhang, the premier temple in Tibet, often called the Cathedral of Lhasa, also dates from Songtsen Gampo's reign.

Discarding the testimony of tradition, some modern scholars have doubted, not merely that Songtsen Gampo was a *bodhisattva,* but that he was a serious Buddhist at all. They credit him with the foundation of Tibetan power, and see his importance and his interest in Buddhism as primarily political. It has also been disputed that pre-Buddhist Tibet was as benighted as is usually made out. Professor Namkhai Norbu, for instance, has argued that the early Tibetans possessed forms of writing and other cultural assets; also that *bön-po* sages were initiated into advanced spiritual teachings of the kind presently transmitted in the Dzogchen ("Great Perfection") tradition.

All are agreed, however, that King Trisong Detsen was considerably more important than Songtsen Gampo. It was he who invited to Tibet the Indian master Shantarakshita, who in turn inaugurated the building of Samyé, though, as we have seen, he ran into trouble and eventually had to be assisted by Padmasambhava. Other monasteries and temples were also established during Trisong Detsen's reign, and monks were favored with royal patronage. Influential for the future too was the Great Debate held at Samyé between 792 and 794 A.D. under the sponsorship of the King himself. In this the Indian *pandit* Kamalashila defended his conventional Indian brand of gradualistic, ethically-orientated Buddhism against one Ho-shang Mahayana, a representative of the Chinese Ch'an (Zen) school of sudden enlightenment. According to Tibetan accounts, the verdict went in favor of the Indian party and the Chinese departed. Thereafter Tibet took its

Buddhism exclusively from India, though some residual Chinese influence did remain—in Dzogchen, for instance.

The flow of Buddhist wisdom, tangibly represented by a two-way traffic of monks and masters passing between Tibet and India, continued as the period progressed. Meanwhile, the work of translating Indian texts went on apace, and indeed the Tibetans are credited with having achieved great clarity and exactness in their renderings. Teams including both Tibetan and Indian scholars were employed, and a very precise system of equivalents for Sanskrit technical terms was worked out. During the reign of Ralpachen, the last of the Great Religious Kings, the translations hitherto made were revised and reworked.

THE DARK AGE (838–C. 1000 A.D.)

Ralpachen was certainly a pious king, but he was also a weak one. He appears to have been content to leave affairs of state in the hands of chosen monks. Court intrigue eventually resulted in his murder along with that of his chief minister; then his brother, Langdarma, ascended the throne.

Langdarma's name is one that lives in infamy in the annals of Tibetan Buddhism, for he instigated a vicious repression of the *dharma* that effectively terminated its first transmission. His reign was brief, only from 838 to 842 A.D., for he was himself soon murdered by a vengeful Buddhist monk. Langdarma's brief reign of terror ushered in a spiritual dark age that was to last until about the year 1000.

This one-hundred-and-fifty-year dark age is a period about which little is known. Centralized power was broken and Tibet disintegrated politically. Buddhism did not entirely die out, however; it continued to exist underground and among isolated hermits and communities. But the controlling influence of the Buddhist hierarchy and the monasteries was absent and, according to some accounts, this led to deviation from orthodoxy, in particular abuse of Tantric practice.

THE SECOND TRANSMISSION (C. 1000–1959)

According to tradition, an area of great importance in the second wave of transmission was western Tibet (Ngari Khorsum). This is a remote and inhospitable wasteland, in more recent times the domain of hardy nomads and freebooters. One thousand years ago, however, a number of prosperous independent kingdoms existed there, notably Gu-gé in the upper Sutlej valley, with its twin cities of Tsaparang and Thöling; also Purang, just south of the sacred lake Manasarovar. Though far from Lhasa and the central provinces, these kingdoms were well-placed to receive a fresh influx of teachers and teachings from India, Kashmir, and the northwest.

Notable among these agents of regeneration was Rinchen Zangpo (958–1055 A.D.), a great Tibetan *lotsava* (translator) and builder of temples, who made three trips to India and spent in all some seventeen years there, studying, practicing, and collecting texts. Another was the Indian master Atisha (982–1054 A.D.), a teacher at the great monastic university of Vikramashila, who was persuaded to bring the precious *dharma* across the formidable Himalayan mountain barrier. As a token of their gratitude, the Tibetans heaped him with rich offerings—a king's ransom in gold, the story goes—which he donated to his *alma mater*. Atisha arrived in western Tibet in 1042 and later went on to the central provinces, finally settling at Netang, where he died.

Meanwhile, Buddhism was similarly being restored in eastern Tibet, where a Nepalese master named Smrti was active, and in the central provinces, from where Tibetan spiritual travelers like Drogmi (992–1072 A.D.) and Marpa (1012–1096 A.D.) ventured down to the plains of India. The former, who received generous aristocratic sponsorship, spent many years studying with a Tantric master named Shantipa at Vikramashila. Marpa, on the other hand, a less well-funded aspirant, served his spiritual apprenticeship mainly at the feet of a great adept (*mahasiddha*) named Naropa (1016–1100) at his hermitage in Bihar.

Once the second transmission got fully under way, new monasteries were built and old ones were restored. Organizational and spiritual development then proceeded, with the result that a number of distinctive schools emerged, each favoring particular teachings or texts, tracing a lineage back to seminal masters, and having its own particular style and emphasis. With organization and development came cultural (as opposed to strictly spiritual) activity, wealth, and worldly power. In time, Buddhism came to dominate the political life of Tibet, and there evolved that distinctive theocratic, or more accurately, buddhocratic style of government that we have already noted.

Once Buddhism had been all but expunged in the land of its origin, the doors were closed to outside influence and the great plateau of Tibet became a time capsule in which the Mahayana Buddhism of medieval India was reverently preserved by diligent guardians. The teachings were laboriously analyzed, systematized, and codified in terms of graduated stages leading towards an ultimate goal of enlightenment. By the fourteenth century a complete Buddhist canon in Tibetan had been standardized. This achievement, which was masterminded by a scholar named Butön, may be classed as an intellectual achievement of world rank. It divides into two parts:

1. The *Kangyur*, one hundred and eight volumes comprising the teachings (*sutra*)

2. The *Tengyur*, two hundred and twenty-five volumes comprising the commentaries (*shastra*)

The *Kangyur* was printed in Peking in 1410. Various other printings of these massive compilations, together comprising over 4,500 works, were later produced.

The Tibetans also produced over the centuries a vast Buddhist literature of their own, including commentaries, histories, verses, biographies of great masters, and so forth. This was not, however, creative or innovative in the main, but essentially exegetical. In Tibet, self-expression was always subjugated to the higher authority of tradition and the received word.

THE PRINCIPAL SCHOOLS OF TIBETAN BUDDHISM

The Kadam (lit. "Bound by Command") School

This school traced its lineage back to Atisha, who had stressed the need to establish a solid basis of monastic discipline and *guru* devotion before undertaking the adventure of Tantric practice. As the Dalai Lama has written:

> Their trademark was this synthesis of various vehicles (*yanas*), as expressed by their saying, "The external practice is moral discipline (i.e. Hinayana); the inner practice is the *bodhi*-mind (i.e. Mahayana) and, practised in secret, is the secret *mantra* (i.e. Vajrayana);" In the Kadampa Order, these three were taken as interconnected, intersupportive aspects of training.*

Atisha's disciple, Dromtön (1088–1164), who founded the monastery of Reting in 1056 and who shaped the school, seems to have been of a particularly reclusive and puritanical disposition. Kadampas were required to submit to four strict laws which demanded strict celibacy and abstention from intoxicants while at the same time prohibiting travel and the handling of money. Such an austere regime does not seem to have held much appeal for the Tibetans, and the school did not survive long as an independent entity.

The Sakya School

This school was named after its principal monastery, situated to the west of Shigatse in southern Tibet, which was founded in 1073 by Konchog

---

* H.H. the XIVth Dalai Lama, in the introduction to *Atisha, A Biography of the Renowned Buddhist Sage,* Lama Thubtan Kalsang et al. (2nd reprint. New Delhi: Mahayana Publications, 1984), xii.

Gyalpo (1034–1102), a disciple of Drogmi. The latter translated one of the basic texts of the school, the *Hevajra Tantra*, and therefore ranks as one of its founding fathers. Another teaching favored by the Sakyapa is The Way and its Fruit (*Lam-dre*) by the ninth-century Indian adept Virupa, which integrates the teachings of Sutra and Tantra into a course of training designed to induce enlightenment in a single lifetime.

The school was subsequently developed by five great masters and was the first to rise to political power in Tibet. This happened during the thirteenth century, when Mongol power was in the ascendant. Initially, in 1244, Godan Khan invited Sakya Pandita (1182–1251), the foremost Tibetan *lama* of the day, to his court; then later Sakya Pandita's nephew, Pagpa (1235–1280), became the *guru* of Khubilai Khan, the great Mongol emperor of China, who conferred considerable temporal powers in Tibet upon him as a token of esteem. What was established was a unique kind of priest-patron relationship (Tibetan *cho-yün*), whereby the Tibetans became the spiritual teachers of the Mongol *khans* who in return gave temporal protection to Tibet. Ironically, it is now used by the Chinese to support their argument that Tibet has long been an integral part of China. The viceregal status of the Sakyapa patriarchs was eclipsed when Mongol power declined in the fourteenth century, and a little later the school itself divided into its Ngor and Tsar branches.

The succession of the heads of the school, who bear the title Sakya Trizin, is also distinctive. It is basically hereditary, but does not pass directly from father to son, but obliquely from uncle to nephew across the bifurcated Khön family line. The present Sakya Trizin, the forty-first (b. 1945), currently lives in exile. His school, whose noble traditions he strives to preserve, has been successfully transmitted to the West.

The Kagyu (lit. "Transmitted Command") School

This school has separated into a number of branches, but all trace their lineage back to the Indian masters Naropa and Tilopa, and ultimately back to the *buddha* Vajradhara. These great masters were *mahasiddhas*— adepts skilled in various advanced yogic practices—and in fact the emphasis within the school had remained on practical mysticism rather than on, say, scholarship. Notable among its basic teachings are the so-called Six Yogas of Naropa, which include mystic heat yoga (*dumo*) and the yoga of the *bardo* or intermediate state between death and rebirth. These disciplines are famous as particularly speedy routes to the attainment of buddhahood, but they have to be practiced with great energy, and under the guidance of a qualified *guru*.

Marpa the Translator studied and practiced with Naropa in India. When he later returned to Tibet, Marpa married and ostensibly settled down to the life of an ordinary householder; at the same time, however, he discreetly continued to pursue his Tantric path. This was highly significant. The Kagyu School, along with other Tantric traditions, does not require strict celibacy or membership in a religious institution of its followers, though it was later, like the other Tibetan schools, to spawn its own monasteries.

Marpa's foremost disciple was Milarepa (1052–1135), who is one of the best known and most popular figures in Tibetan Buddhism. He too was never ordained or lived in monasteries, but rather represents the type of independent Tibetan yogin who pursues his solitary austerities in mountain caves and other remote places. He started out as a student of the black arts, intent on wreaking horrible revenge on those who had done wrong to his widowed mother, but later saw the error of his ways and, in terror of grotesque karmic repercussions, embarked upon a crash course of authentic spiritual instruction under Marpa. His master gave Milarepa a very hard time, requiring him, for instance, to build, knock down, and rebuild a tall tower several times. He persevered, however, and attained buddhahood. He also became famous for his miraculous powers and would cheerfully take on and subdue all comers in contests of magic. In paintings, Milarepa is often shown with a green tinge to his body, apparently the result of subsisting on an unappetizing diet of nettles for a long time. Also he cups a hand to one ear, which indicates another of his talents: he was a poet as well as a great mystic.

Milarepa's most influential disciple was Gampopa (1079–1153), the Doctor of Takpo, who had originally studied medicine and also the teachings of the Kadampa tradition. He later built a monastery and engaged in literary activities, his most well-known text being *The Jewel Ornament of Liberation*. From Gampopa's disciples stem the various Kagyupa sub-schools, including the Karma, Drugpa, and Drigungpa.

The Karma Kagyu sub-school used to have its headquarters at Tsurphu monastery (founded 1185) in the central provinces, but it enjoyed a considerable following in Kham and other eastern provinces, whence the head of the order, the Karmapa (sometimes called the Black Hat Lama), was frequently wont to go on great visitations accompanied by a large armed cavalcade (*Karmapa Garchen*). The headship of this sub-school passes, not by heredity, but according to a system unique to Tibet. This is based on the notion that a spiritually advanced being is able to consciously choose whether or not to return to the world after death. Thus when a Karmapa dies, he leaves behind a letter containing directions; a search is then begun after an appropriate lapse of time for the child in which the great compassionate spirit that expresses itself through all Karmapas has been reborn. A similar system operates in various Karma Kagyu lineages and in other Tibetan Buddhist schools as well. Beings who have been identified as voluntary reincarnations are known as *tulku* and carry the title *rinpoché* ("precious one"), though these terms have other applications as well. It has been suggested that the system originated in India among a group of highly venerated adepts known as the eighty-four mahasiddhas.

The sixteenth Karmapa set up a headquarters at Rumtek in Sikkim after quitting Tibet in 1959. He was one of the first to appreciate the importance of disseminating the teachings of his sub-school to Westerners, and very early on sent *lamas* to the West, notably Chögyam Trungpa Rinpoché (1939–1987) and Chujé Akong Rinpoché, who together established the first Tibetan Buddhist center in Scotland (Samyé Ling) before Trungpa Rinpoché's departure to North America.

The Drugpa sub-school, on the other hand, was introduced into Bhutan in the seventeenth century and today remains the principal school of Buddhism there and also in Ladakh and other parts of the Himalayan region.

The Nyingma (lit. "Old Ones") School

This name was almost undoubtedly first coined as a convenient umbrella term to describe all those various groups and individuals who, after the second transmission of Buddhism to Tibet, remained devoted to the teachings and practices propagated during the first transmission. As the "Old Ones" they formed a natural contrast to the "New Ones" (*Sarma*) who subscribed to the new teachings that had been brought by Rinchen Zangpo, Atisha, and their colleagues.

Moreover, in the eyes of the Nyingmapa, Padmasambhava came to occupy a uniquely exalted position, being regarded not merely as a manifestation of Avalokiteshvara but as the spiritual equal of the Buddha himself. With his colorful robes, cavalier mustache, and Tantric wand upon which various gruesome severed heads and skulls are skewered, he figures very prominently in Nyingmapa iconography. Needless to say, the school is rich in magical and mystical resonances.

As the new schools organized themselves and flourished in both spiritual and worldly terms, the Nyingmapa began to consciously regard themselves as a distinct school and to emulate them. They too built a few monasteries—Mindroling was the most important in central Tibet—and began to ordain their own monks. They also codified their teachings, many of which, they claimed, had been cunningly hidden by Padmasambhava in caves and other secret places (some were even said to have been hidden in "mind") in anticipation of a time when people would be ready for them. These texts were known as *terma* ("treasures") and those who discovered them as *tertöns*. The classification of Nyingmapa teachings distinguishes nine *yanas* or paths to enlightenment, the first three being based on the *sutras*, and the remaining six on the *tantras*.

Despite efforts at organization, the Nyingmapa remained essentially individualistic, sometimes even anarchic, and their *lamas* tended to be married men who operated independently at the local level. Many of them supported themselves by dispensing occult services like exorcism, rainmaking, divination, and healing that the ordinary, unsophisticated Tibetans required; these are known as *ngakpas*. Others who gained a reputation for proficiency in Tantric practice might gather a few disciples informally around themselves. The school could never have been a match for its newer rivals, especially those with a strong monastic base, but it was generally tolerated, and has survived down to the present. It has also produced many great adepts and masters. The last supreme head of the order, H. H. Dudjom Rinpoché, was considered an incarnation of Dudjom Lingpa (1835–1904), a notable yogi and *tertön*. Rinpoché settled in Darjeeling after quitting Tibet, and paid various visits to the West, where he established centers; he passed away in France in 1987.

The Gelug (lit. "Virtuous") School

The seminal master of this school, which is sometimes called the Yellow Hat Order in the West, was Tsongkhapa (Lobsang Drakpa, also known as Jé Rinpoché, 1357–1419), who is identified as a manifestation of Mañjushri, *bodhisattva* of Wisdom. He hailed from the region of the great Kokonor lake in northeast Tibet. After having traveled and studied widely, Tsongkhapa gravitated to the Kadam School. He earned a high reputation as a writer and teacher, and was later warmly received in the Lhasa region. In 1409 he founded his first monastery, Ganden, in a panoramic natural amphitheater in the hills to the east of Lhasa. Two other great monasteries were later founded, Drepung in 1416 and Sera in 1419, which lay to the west and north of the holy city respectively. Because of their scholarly orientations, and their division into colleges or *dratsang,* these are often described as monastic universities. They certainly grew vastly in size and population. In their heyday Drepung and Sera are said to have housed upwards of seven thousand seven hundred monks each.

Tsongkhapa is also credited with having established the Great Prayer Festival (Mönlam Chenmo), which used to be held over a three-week period in Lhasa immediately after the Losar (New Year) celebrations.

Such was Tsongkhapa's fame that during his heyday the Emperor of China was eager to meet him; the good monk could not go himself, but sent a proxy. On his death, his body was duly embalmed and enshrined in a *stupa* at Ganden. There it remained, venerated and inviolate, until the *stupa* was (reputedly) recently opened by Chinese soldiers, who are said to have been shocked to find the body perfectly preserved with hair and fingernails still growing. The annual festival of Ngachö Chenmo, when thousands of butter-lamps are burned, commemorates Tsongkhapa's death.

Although he is sometimes characterized as a self-appointed reformer of Tibetan Buddhism, Tsongkhapa did not consciously set out to found a school of his own. He certainly uncompromisingly castigated what he deemed to be the dharmically incorrect views prevalent in certain schools, notably the Jonangpa, but his main importance was as an energizer and resynthesizer of existing teachings. In particular he reaffirmed Atisha's stress upon the monastic virtues and upon the need to establish a firm basis in the *sutra* teachings before graduating to the *tantras*. He was also strongly scholastic in orientation and encouraged the study of the great Indian masters of philosophy and logic: Nagarjuna, Asanga, Dignaga, *et al.* Tsongkhapa codified the path to enlightenment in terms of graduated stages and expounded these in his *Lam* and *Lam Rim Chenmo,* which together might be regarded as the *Summa* of Gelugpa doctrine.

In the long run, however, Tsongkhapa's chief disciples were able to evolve a distinct school separate from the Kadam to which Tsongkhapa had originally adhered. From these disciples also came the line of Dalai Lamas, who are also thought to be emanations of Avalokiteshvara. Here again the *tulku* system of succession was employed. The word *dalai* itself is of Mongolian origin and means "ocean," implying an ocean or vast repository of wisdom. The title of the first Dalai Lama was posthumously bestowed upon Gendun-drup (1391–1474), the disciple and putative nephew of Jé Tsongkhapa. Another important reincarnating patriarch within the school is the Panchen Lama, whose seat is traditionally the great monastic complex of Tashilhunpo, near Shigatse in southern Tibet. Later there was to be considerable rivalry between these two grand lamas or, more precisely, between their followers.

In the sixteenth century the Gelug school began its rise to political pre-eminence when it came to enjoy the favor of a new generation of Mongol *khans*. In 1642, Gusri Khan installed Ngawang Lobsang Gyatso (1617–1682), the Fifth Dalai Lama, as the virtual ruler of Tibet under overall Mongol protection, summarily quelling with the sword the ambitions of the other schools and the temporal powers who supported them, in particular the Karma Kagyupas, who were supported by the kings of Tsang province. After obtaining power, however, the Fifth Dalai Lama proved to be a highly effective and tolerant ruler: the other schools were reorganized, and to an extent stripped of worldly wealth and power, but only the Jonang, a Kagyupa sub-school, was suppressed.

Over the ensuing centuries, the regime of the Dalai Lamas consolidated its temporal power over the whole country, and though at times it was necessary, on the basis of the old priest-patron relationship, to accept a measure of Chinese interference, it effectively held sway in Tibet right down to 1950. As the Dalai Lamas came to be regarded by general consensus as the spiritual as well as the temporal leaders of the country, they received teachings in various schools and are not technically heads of the Gelugpa order. That honor is reserved for the Abbot of Ganden monastery, the Tri Rinpoché (or Ganden Tripa).

Besides the Great Fifth, there have been two other outstanding Dalai Lamas. One was the Great Thirteenth (Thubten Gyatso, 1876–1933), who between 1913 and his death made Tibetan independence a full reality. He also attempted to reconcile his country with the realities of the modern world. In this he met with considerable resistance from the conservative monastic element in Tibetan society, which was opposed to all change, however moderate. The other is the present incumbent, the Fourteenth (Tenzin Gyatso, b. 1935), who has had to steer the Tibetans through the greatest crisis of their history: the appropriation of their country by the Chinese. Although now living in exile in the Indian hill station of Dharamsala, he continues to exert a pre-eminent hold over the hearts and minds of his people, both those in exile and those living under Communist rule in Tibet itself. He has also emerged as a spiritual leader of world rank and in 1989 was awarded the Nobel Peace Prize. He would be the first to admit that, prior to the Chinese takeover, Tibet had become socially and politically ossified, and that the old obsessively conservative regime was permeated with numerous faults and abuses. It remains an open question whether His Holiness will ever return to his homeland.

The Gelug was the final school of Buddhism to emerge in Tibet; in fact, the only other development of note during the ensuing years was the emergence of the eclectic Ri-mé (lit. "Not-biased," "non-partisan") movement among some scholarly Nyingma lamas in eastern Tibet during the nineteenth century. Notable figures in the movement were Jamgön Kongtrül the Great (1813–1899), Jamyang Khyentse Wangpo (1820–1892), his *tulku* Jamyang Khyentse Chökyi Lodrö, *et al.*

Despite occasional rivalry, particularly for worldly power and influence, a greater degree of similarity rather than of difference exists between these major schools. They are all basically compounded of the same raw materials: Indian Mahayana and Tantric Buddhism plus an admixture of some native Tibetan elements. What lends each its own individual character, therefore, is the manner in which it organizes the raw material and the particular emphases that are stressed.

While these schools were developing, the *bön-po* tradition was emulating them and emerging as a conscious and, to some extent, organized religion in its own right. It, in fact, adopted and absorbed much from within the Buddhist tradition in terms of teaching, practice, and iconography, either directly or in slightly amended form. For instance, just as the Buddhists venerated Shakyamuni Buddha as the primal originator and inspiration of their tradition, so the *bön-po* elevated one Shenrab Miwo to a similar status. He is a shadowy figure, said to have originated in a western land called Tazik, whose life story was clearly modeled upon that of Shakyamuni. *Bön-po* teachings were also codified into the so-called Nine Ways of Bön, and a goal identical with Buddhist enlightenment was held up as the ultimate fruit of their path. Buddhist influence also prompted the discontinuation of certain old *bön-po* practices, such as blood sacrifice. There were even a few Bön monasteries, though in general style the *bön-po* were closer to the *ad hoc* localism of the Nyingmapas with all its rich magical-mythical nuances, than to the newer schools with their relatively sophisticated organization and worldly interests. Also, a certain anti-Buddhist sentiment, perhaps a lingering resentment at having been displaced from spiritual primacy, can be occasionally detected in their outlook, though this did not erupt into active hostility, and, quietly tolerated or simply overlooked, the Bön religion has been able to survive to modern times.

Finally a word should be said about Dzogchen (lit. "Great Perfection"), which is currently enjoying a certain vogue among Westerners. Although it is transmitted as a Tantric teaching within the Nyingma school—where indeed it is regarded as supreme—it is also propagated as a "wholly self-sufficient path in its own right" by Professor Namkhai Norbu, a married *lama* from the Dérgé district of east Tibet who currently teaches at Naples University and informally guides Dzogchen groups in many Western countries. As presented by Prof. Norbu, Dzogchen seem to have a Zen-like directness,* cutting through the

---

* Professor Norbu and his followers appear to believe that Zen is more superficial than Dzogchen. See review of *The Crystal and the Way of Light* (London: Routledge & Kegan Paul, 1986) by Stephen Batchelor in *The Middle Way* vol. 61, no. 3 (Nov., 1986): 183–4, and John Shane's reply in Letters to the Editor, *The Middle Way* vol. 61, no. 4 (Feb. 1987): 254–5.

usual undergrowth of primary and secondary accretions to zero in on the spiritual core. Dzogchen, he says, "is a teaching concerning the primordial state of being that is each individual's own intrinsic nature from the very beginning." Once perceived, the object of practice is to remain unerringly focused in this state in every aspect of life:

> There was a very great master of Dzogchen living in Tibet and at one point a very learned scholar visited him, saying, "You practitioners of Dzogchen are always meditating—that's it, isn't it?"
> "What is it that "I'm meditating on?" asked the master.
> The scholar then asked, "Ah, so you don't meditate then?"
> The master replied; "When am I ever distracted?"*

Prof. Norbu also characterizes Dzogchen as the essence of all other teachings and traces its origins back to pre-Buddhist times, when, he claims, it flourished among the *bön-po* of Zhang-zhung, an ancient kingdom that existed in the north and west of the Tibetan plateau before the emergence of a unified Tibetan state.

SOME SPECIAL ASPECTS OF TIBETAN BUDDHISM

Important in Tibetan Buddhism is the figure of the *lama*. Basically the term is a Tibetan equivalent of the Indian *guru:* a spiritual teacher. As such, contrary to popular misconceptions, a *lama* does not necessarily have to be a celibate monk, but his guidance is essential if the disciple (*chela*) is to successfully negotiate the difficulties and dangers of the spiritual path, and especially those of its dizzy Tantric heights. So importantly is this figure regarded in this context that, while classic Indian Buddhism speaks of Three Jewels, Buddha, *dharma,* and *sangha,* Tibetan Buddhism sometimes speaks of Four Jewels, the additional one being the *lama.* In some cases, the *lama* should be more highly regarded than Shakyamuni Buddha; indeed he is ultimate enlightenment itself.

Naturally all this places a great deal of responsibility on the shoulders of any *lama* and requires that he behave impeccably. Consequently, the conduct of certain *lamas* who have come to the West and fallen prey to the temptations abundant in this quarter have given cause for concern.

In 1984, His Holiness the Dalai Lama, asked about Buddhist teachers who regularly broke certain precepts, replied unequivocally that it was a teacher's duty to completely practice what he taught to others and

* Namkhai Norbu, "Dharma," *The Middle Way,* vol. 61, no. 2 (Aug. 1986): 89 (slightly rephrased).

182 THE BUDDHIST HANDBOOK

thus be a spiritual example. Therefore, if a teacher enjoined one course of his students and pursued another himself, "this means that the spiritual guide does not have the proper qualifications."* So it was very important for a student to know the requirements of a teacher and to thoroughly check him out before establishing a dharmic or *guru-chela* connection; likewise, a teacher should also check out a prospective student. According to the Tantric system, however, the situation was slightly different. A teacher *could* engage in activities usually prohibited, but only if he had achieved stability; i.e., had the capacity to behave in that way without jarring the faith of others. His Holiness concluded:

> However, if a lama does not have this capacity and we think, "Oh, these are the grand activities of a lama," then we are in a difficult position and must make up our own minds as to how to proceed.†

No member of the Tantric Buddhist pantheon is held in greater regard by the Tibetans than Avalokiteshvara (Tibetan.Chenrezi), who in his various manifestations as *bodhisattva* of Compassion embodies the highest ideal of Mahayana Buddhism, indeed its very "driving force" (Stephen Batchelor): the setting aside of all self-regard in favor of a wholehearted dedication to free all other sentient beings from the coils of *samsara*. His incarnate activities are also mythically woven into the fabric of Tibetan history. The origin of the Tibetan people themselves, for instance, is attributed to his union, in the form of a monkey, with an autochthonous demoness—a myth which neatly accounts for the latent receptivity of the Tibetans to the teachings of Mahayana and Tantric Buddhism, and also for their fiery, passionate nature. Subsequently Avalokiteshvara was incarnate as both King Songtsen Gampo and Padmasambhava, as well as the Dalai Lamas. It was appropriate therefore that the Dalai Lama's majestic main palace in Lhasa should be called the Potala after the abode of the *bodhisattva* in south India.

Highly characteristic too of Tibetan Buddhism, and closely connected with the cult of Avalokiteshvara, is the *mantra,* "Om-mani-padme-hum," which is muttered by all classes of Tibetan Buddhists, inscribed on flags, painted on walls, twirled within prayer-wheels, and even carved on stones and wayside rocks. It is literally translated as "Hail to the

---

* Questions and Answers of the Dalai Lama, "Love, Altruism, Vegetarianism, Anger and the Responsibilities of Teachers" in *The Middle Way,* vol. 60, no. 2 (Aug., 1985): 67.

† *Ibid.,* 68.

The mantra "Om-mani-padme -hum"

Jewel in the Lotus." A volume could be, and indeed has been, written on the infinity of meanings encompassed within these few words. As Stephen Batchelor has said, "the *mantra* . . . functions as a symbolic and highly condensed expression of the entire path to enlightenment."*

In recent years foreign travelers have again been able to enter Tibet. They have been horrified at what they have discovered. Of the more than two thousand monasteries that once adorned the land, treasure-houses of priceless ancient art and profound wisdom, only a handful remain standing. The rest have been wantonly destroyed, their sacred contents either destroyed as well, desecrated, or dispersed, and their occupants humiliated, persecuted, and secularized. It is testament to cultural vandalism on a par with the burning of the great library of Alexandria. Although the present political climate is less extreme, it remains to be seen whether Buddhism will ever again flourish in the Land of Snows. In the meantime, its traditions live on among exiled Tibetan communities, and their ever increasing numbers of Western co-religionists. The modern *lama* is not the denizen of remote mountain solitudes any more; he may be a jet-setter ministering to an international body of students, a man familiar with the workings of modern hi-tech gadgetry as well as the intricate mysteries of the spirit.

* Batchelor, "The Jewel and the Lotus: A Survey of the Buddhism of Tibet," *The Middle Way,* vol. 59, no. 3 (Nov. 1984): 170.

S·E·V·E·N·T·E·E·N

The Northern Transmission: Mongolia, Russia, Himalayan Region, Nepal, and Bhutan

MONGOLIA

Although the Mongols came in contact with Chinese Buddhism as early as the fourth century, it was the Tibetan variety that captured their imagination and long-term allegiance. As in Tibet, Buddhism here had to confront powerful local religious traditions of great antiquity, notably ecstatic shamanism.

Mongolian Buddhism always remained spiritually and theologically dependent on Tibet, and, aside from the incorporation of indigenous elements, no truly local development took place. This does not mean, however, that it is without historical significance. The Mongol Yüan dynasty established Tibetan Buddhism in China, a fact to which the Lamaist Temple in Beijing remains a monument. As we have also seen, Mongol *khans* wielded great power in Tibet itself at various times and advanced the worldly fortunes of, first, the Sakya school, and later the Gelug school. After the sixteenth century, the Mongols remained devoted and enthusiastic Gelugpas, building thousands of monasteries and ordaining a high proportion of their male population as monks. Various *tulkus,* locally known as *khubilgan,* appeared among them, the greatest being the Jebtsundamba Khutukhtu (*khutukhtu* is the local equivalent of the Sanskit *arya,* meaning "noble"), who had his seat at Da Khüree (also known as Urga, now Ulan Bator). The last, the seventh *khubilgan,* died in 1924, having also been temporal ruler of the country after its successful assertion of its independence from China

Nowadays Mongolia is split. Inner Mongolia is part of China, and Buddhism there has suffered much the same fate as in China itself and in Tibet. Outer Mongolia, on the other hand, established itself as an independent people's republic with Russian help in the 1920s. Despite initial repression, the Marxist regime did not manage to expunge Buddhism from the hearts and minds of the people, and it has survived as a living presence into the more tolerant climate of recent years. Now that the country is moving away from the Soviet sphere in the direction of democracy, there is hope that we may before too long witness a Buddhist revival there.

Currently, the chief monastery is Gandan in Ulan Bator, seat of the Khambo Lama, the head of the Buddhists of Mongolia, who is also President of the Asian Buddhists Conference for Peace. This worthy organization puts out an English-language journal, *Buddhists for Peace,* which has a decidedly fellow-traveling slant. His Holiness the Dalai Lama visited Mongolia in 1982 and gave the Yamantaka Initiation to a hundred and forty *lamas* at Gandan; a crowd of twenty thousand are said to have been gathered outside. More recently His Holiness gave a Kalachakara Initiation in 1995, the first time this has been performed here since 1934.

RUSSIA

Tibetan Buddhism was spread to other northern Asian nomadic peoples by the enthusiastic and energetic Mongols. One result of this is that today there are three residual pockets of lamaist Buddhists living in what was Soviet territory, but which are now independent republics since the demise of the Soviet Union in 1989.

One is to be found in Buryatia, which lies in the Lake Baikal region of eastern Siberia. Forty miles from the capital, Ulan Ude, there is a large monastery, the Ivolginsky, "The Buddhist Centre of the USSR" (TASS). This and its fellow, the Aginsky (not strictly speaking in Buryatia but in the neighboring Chita region of Siberia), are the only monasteries now remaining in the region. The chief lama of Buryatia and official head of the Buddhists in Russia is the Bandido-Khambo Lama. Empassioned pleas for world peace also tend to emanate from this quarter; unfortunately, less congenial emanations filter through to the outside world as well. In the 1970s, groups monitoring the persecution of religion in the USSR reported the death in a local labor camp of a distinguished lama named Bidya Dandaron.

Another Tibetan Buddhist group living in this region are the Kalmuks, who originated in Asia but migrated to Europe and were resettled in the lower Volga region around 1630. They remained there until World War II, when they were expelled for collaborating with the Germans; some have since been allowed to return. Geshe Wangyal, a much-traveled Kalmuk lama of the Gelug School, latterly, from about 1955 until his death in 1983, ministered to a group of his fellow expatriates who had emigrated to the USA after World War II and established an exile community in Freewood Acres, New Jersey.

Geshe Wangyal's root guru was none other than the famous and much maligned lama, Khampo Agvan Lovsang Dorjiev (1853–1938), whose journeys between Lhasa and Russia precipitated the Younghusband Expedition (1904), when British troops marched to Lhasa. Later Dorjiev returned to his native land and in the optimistic early phases of the Revolution, when such things seemed possible, actively pursued a vision of reconciling Buddhism and communism. Sadly Dorjiev's hopes were not realized in the long term, and he met his end in 1938, during the dark days of Stalinist repression.

The third Buddhist enclave is in Tuva, a buffer between China and Russia lying east of the Altai Mountains. There are very few temples here, two or three prayer houses and a small number of tantric lamas.

Russia has also produced some fine Buddhist scholars, notably Theodor Stcherbatsky, author of *Buddhist Logic* and *The Central Conception of Buddhism*. In 1923 the first center for Buddhist Studies in Europe was established in St. Petersburg/Leningrad; it ceased to exist in 1938.

The first community of Western Buddhists also appeared in Russia in the 1890s under the inspiration of Karlis Alexis Tennisons (1873–1962), a Latvian who was declared Buddhist Archbishop of Lithuania, Estonia and Latvia by HH the Thirteenth Dalai Lama.

Finally, in 1907, with the permission of Tsar Nicholas II and the blessings of the Thirteenth Dalai Lama, the foundation stone of a Buddhist temple was laid in St. Petersburg. It was probably intended for use by visiting diplomats from Buddhist Countries like Siam (Thailand) and Japan. The construction was supervised by Tennisons, and the temple was finally opened in 1915. It still exists, but has latterly been used as a scientific laboratory. Latest reports suggest that it is to be turned into an "antireligious museum," specializing in Islam and Buddhism.

Rough estimates reckon that there are currently more than half a million Buddhists in these areas, and the numbers are growing now these people have religious freedom in the post–Soviet era.

HIMALAYAN REGION

That magnificent arc of hills and soaring mountains that dominate the northern edge of the sultry plains of India also contains pockets of Tibetan Buddhism. Small communities of Tibetan refugees live in the region too, notably at Dharamsala in the Indian state of Himachal Pradesh, where His Holiness the Dalai Lama conducts his government-in-exile.

To the west, Ladakh, once an independent Tibetan kingdom isolated behind high mountain ramparts, is now an integral part of India. The Gelug and Drugpa Kagyu schools are dominant here; but, while traditional monastic life goes on in great *gompa* (monasteries) like Hemis and Tikse, the ancient local Buddhist traditions are to a degree threatened not from Marxist ideology as in Tibet itself, but from that equally insidious factor, modern development, which includes the blight of tourism. There is also a vigorous Muslim population against which the local Buddhists are not always able to hold their own. Nearby Zanskar and Spiti are also Tibetan enclaves.

To the east lies Sikkim, once an independent kingdom but annexed by India in 1975. In the seventeenth century, Tibetan migrants from Kham entered Sikkim and had little difficulty in subjugating the gentle indigenous Lepchas. They also established Tibetan Buddhism, so Sikkim became a natural haven for Tibetans fleeing from Chinese oppression during the 1950s. In fact, His Holiness the Karmapa, the supreme head of the Karma Kagyu school, established his headquarters at Rumtek near the capital, Gangtok. Even further to the east, in the India state of Arunachal Pradesh, there are also Buddhists among the population.

NEPAL

The kingdom of Nepal can claim the supreme Buddhist accolade of being Siddhartha Gautama's birthplace. Lumbini, which lies just inside its southern frontiers, is therefore one of the four great Buddhist pilgrimage-places. A millennium and a half after Siddhartha's birth, when the Muslims overran northern India, this Himalayan kingdom became a sanctuary for fleeing Indian Buddhists, who brought texts, relics, and sacred artifacts with them and established a *sangha* in the Kathmandu Valley, which is still today dominated by the burnished Buddhist pinnacles of Swayambhunath, the famous Monkey Temple. This *sangha* did not hold its own very well in the local spiritual climate, however, and in a comparatively short time its monks forsook the monastic Vinaya to marry and become a separate caste of their own. Though a Buddhist scholarly tradition centered around four schools of philosophy (Svabhavika, Ashvarika, Karmika, and Yatrika) did survive down to recent times, Buddhism and Hinduism so blurred into each other in the colorful religious melting-pot of the central valley of Nepal that today it is often hard to disentangle the two. In the second half of the present century, however, connections were established with Sri Lanka and attempts initiated to establish a sound Theravada *sangha* on Nepalese soil. Ven. Amritananda Thera, who was trained in Sri Lanka and who has a center at Swayambhunath, has worked energetically to this end. For one thing, he translated numerous Pali *suttas* into Nepalese, before his death in 1990.

Nepal's Buddhist connections with Tibet go back a long way, too— at least to the seventh century when, according to tradition, a local king gave his daughter as a wife for King Songtsen Gampo. During the following centuries much Buddhist traffic passed through Nepal, for it was a major avenue whereby the religion was transmitted from India to Tibet. Newari craftsmen from the Kathmandu region also worked on many religious buildings on the great plateau, and their influence on Tibetan art was considerable.

There have also been reverse movements when Tibetan Buddhism has spilled back over the Great Himalaya into Nepal. The Sherpas of northeast Nepal are in fact a Tibetan people who left their homelands in Khan in eastern Tibet. In their new domains they have built numerous modest *gompa* and *chörtens,* and kept their Tibetan Buddhist traditions alive. More Tibetans arrived in the 1950s, fleeing from the Chinese invasion and takeover of their country. Dolpo and Mustang are also two ancient Tibetan kingdoms in northwest Nepal which, like Zanskar and Ladakh, have until very recently managed to almost totally avoid the intrusions of modernity and progress.

BHUTAN

Finally, Bhutan: in the seventeenth century, Shabdung Ngawang Namgyal of the Drukpa Kagyu sub-school of Tibetan Buddhism established a buddhocracy in this eastern Himalayan kingdom. Numerous imposing *dzongs* (forts) were built which served both as monastic and administrative centers. Succession passed from one Shabdung (or Dharma Raja) to the next by means of the *tulku* system, though, as few incumbents survived to their majority, the reins of power were usually in the hands of a succession of regents, known as Deb Rajas. Earlier this century, these institutions were replaced by a monarchy.

Having observed the disastrous consequences of thoughtless development elsewhere, and appreciating the very real benefits that their spiritually rich traditions confer upon their citizens in terms of intangibles like psychological well-being, the modern political leaders of Bhutan have been very concerned to restrict material "progress" and other modernizing trends at a level consistent with the preservation of their traditional culture.

Buddhism Comes West

E·I·G·H·T·E·E·N

Slow Beginnings

BUDDHISM IN EUROPE TO WORLD WAR II

Sadly, Buddhism has drastically declined, or even in some cases been virtually obliterated, in many of the Asian countries where it once so magnificently flourished. Usually the opposing factor has been a form of materialism, either consumerism or Communism, the origins of which can invariably be traced back to Western sources. This is especially ironic, for as the light of Buddhism fades in the East we see it beginning to shine with increasing brightness in the West. A great new chapter in the history of Buddhism may be beginning: one that may, as it develops, be no less glorious than any that have gone before.

It is impossible to pinpoint exactly when Buddhism first impinged upon the Western consciousness. Back in ancient times, when the Greeks enjoyed connections with northern India and adjacent lands, Buddhist ideas no doubt traveled along the great arteries of trade, notably the Western reaches of the Silk Route, to the Mediterranean world. Theorists have even proposed that Buddhist ideas somehow got into the general melting-pot from which Christian doctrine was extracted. During the Dark Ages, the dominance of Islam in the Middle East effectively blocked European interest in the East, though Arab storytellers did infiltrate the Buddha into Christian legend as St. Josaphat (*Josaphat* being a transmutation of *Bodhisat* or *Bodhisattva*) of the Barlaam and Josaphat story. This tells the familiar tale of a young aristocrat who gives up wealth and privilege to search for spiritual truth, accompanied by a monk.

At the dawn of the modern era, a new expansive energy was unloosed that easily surmounted the Islamic barrier. Voyages and expeditions of exploration to the East got under way, and in their wake followed the traders, the colonialists, and the Christian missionaries. Buddhism was encountered in Mongolia, Tibet, China, Japan, Ceylon (Sri Lanka), Siam (Thailand), Burma, and other farflung and exotic places. Sadly, bigotry prevented most contemporary Westerners from seeing any good in any religious system other than the Christian one. Buddhism was therefore almost invariably dismissed as benighted idolatry, and efforts were made to convert its misguided followers, or even at forcible suppression. When efforts were made by missionaries—by Spence Hardy and Samuel Beal, for instance—to study the religion, it was usually with a view to finding ways of discrediting or undermining it.

THE NINETEENTH CENTURY

It was not until the nineteenth century that European scholars began to make a serious effort to collect Buddhist texts and, having mastered the languages in which they were written (Sanskrit, Pali, Tibetan, etc.), to subject their contents to dispassionate study. Only then did Westerners begin to have a clearer picture of what Buddhism was really about. The establishment of the Asiatic Society of Bengal in Calcutta in 1784 by, among others, Sir William Jones (1746–1794), a judge in the employ of the East India Company and a Sanskritist himself, was a great catalyst. The Society assisted—albeit in a small way—the Hungarian Csoma de Körös (1784–1842), who had gone to the East in search of the mythical lost homeland of his people; he didn't locate that but instead became a great pioneer of Tibetan studies. Substantial Buddhological work was also done by the Frenchman Eugène Burnouf (1801–1852), onetime incumbent of the Chair of Sanskrit at the Collège de France; and by German scholars like Max Müller (1823–1900), Hermann Oldenberg (1854–1920), *et al.* Then in 1881, the Pali Text Society was established by T. W. Rhys Davids (1843–1922), whose interest in that lost Indian language had been aroused when his previous work as a magistrate in the Ceylon Civil Service had produced a case involving a point of Buddhist ecclesiastical law that could only be resolved by reference to Pali texts. The P.T.S. has continued its good work to the present time.

In addition, archaeological field work by Sir Alexander Cunningham and others led to the uncovering of long forgotten Buddhist sites in northern India and elsewhere. Various places mentioned in the texts as having been visited by Shakyamuni Buddha were located, including Lumbini, his birthplace. Such finds tended to confirm the historical accuracy of these old texts, and the Buddha himself could be accepted as a real person rather than dismissed as a mere myth. Some appreciation too began to emerge of just how extensive and highly developed Buddhism had once been.

The nineteenth century was also the time when established religion—that is, the conventional brand of church (or chapel) Christianity—began to lose its grip over the hearts and minds of ordinary people. This created a spiritual vacuum. All kinds of phenomena rushed to fill it: occultism, spiritualism, science, and the religion of art (aestheticism, or bohemianism); but some too, now that accurate information was available, began to look with less prejudiced eyes at Buddhism among the other religions of the East. The apocalyptic writer, Friedrich Nietzsche (1844–1900), author of *Thus Spoke Zarathustra*, who in his famous dictum "God is dead" put into words what was already fact, also spoke sympathetically of Buddhism in his writings, as did the pessimistic German philosopher Arthur Schopenhauer (1788–1860), whose notion of "the will," enunciated in his *The World as Will and Representation*, appears close to the Buddhist concept of *trishna:*

> His general message is evidently close to that of the Buddha: that all life is pervaded by suffering, the cause of suffering is desire or craving, and the way to blessedness is by the extinction of craving. Both for him and the Buddha, the ultimate goal of life cannot satisfactorily be described in language.*

But soon Buddhism was to become more than of mere academic interest. In 1879, the journalist, Sir Edwin Arnold, published his famous epic poem, *The Light of Asia*. This, which Christmas Humphreys has proclaimed "the 'best seller' of all Buddhist books in the West," helped a wider lay public to appreciate that the Buddha's teachings contained spiritual ideas of great depth and beauty. Arnold also drew attention to the sorry state of the Buddhist holy places in northern India, notably Bodh Gaya, and initiated a scheme for buying the site from its (then) Hindu owner. This project was not fully realized until 1949.

The year after *The Light of Asia* appeared, the founders of the Theosophical Society, the formidable Russian, Madame Helena Petrovna

---

* Don Cupitt, *The Sea of Faith* (London: BBC Publications, 1984), 171.

Blavatsky (1831–1891), and her American colleague, Colonel Henry Steel Olcott (1832–1906), declared themselves Buddhists and confirmed it by "taking Pansil"—reciting the Five Precepts—at Galle in Sri Lanka.

Theosophy was one of the cults that sprang up in the vacuum created by the decline of conventional Christianity in the West. Its founders claimed that the known religions of the world merely propagated a superficial spiritual message for mass consumption. Behind this, however, lay a hidden or esoteric dimension strictly reserved for the initiated. This was itself derived from an "Ancient Wisdom-Religion," antedating all the known religions, of which Theosophy was the modern exposition. The cult also—and this no doubt did it no harm when it came to attracting followers—contained stiff admixtures of occultism and other exotic ingredients, and its charismatic leaders regularly commuted to the occult plane to receive guidance from the Mahatmas or "Masters of Wisdom." However, they at the same time claimed that Theosophy was quite compatible with that other fashionable child of the age: science.

The movement caught the mood of the times and won considerable popularity among the spiritually undernourished middle classes of Europe and America. It also caught on in the East, and its headquarters were eventually set up at Adyar, just outside Madras. Its leaders particularly favored Buddhism because they considered it "the noblest and least defiled" remnant of the great ancient wisdom-religion—hence the gesture in Galle in 1880. Madame Blavatsky, Colonel Olcott, and their colleagues subsequently went on to work vigorously for the revival of Buddhism generally, and in Sri Lanka in particular, where they were assisted by a native Ceylonese, Anagarika Dharmapala (David Hewavitarne; 1864–1933), with whom they went to Japan in 1888. In 1891 Dharmapala founded the Maha Bodhi Society in Calcutta: an important step in the direction of reviving Buddhism on its native ground. He also became active in the agitation for the restoration of Bodh Gaya to Buddhist hands.

THE TWENTIETH CENTURY UP TO WORLD WAR I

The pioneer Theosophists often come in for wry critical comment in modern Buddhist circles, and this is understandable, for Western Buddhists have with difficulty disentangled themselves from the subtle (and gross) distortions that Madame Blavatsky and her colleagues projected upon the Buddha's teachings. But, to their lasting credit, the Theosophists prepared the way for Westerners to go deeper into the study and, eventually, the practice of those teachings.

The first Westerner to accomplish the giant step of taking the yellow robe was Allan Bennett (1872–1923), an enigmatic figure whose enthusiasm for Buddhism was awakened by reading *The Light of Asia,* though previously , as a member of the Hermetic Order of the Golden Dawn, he had rubbed shoulders with dubious necromancers like Aleister Crowley and MacGregor Mathers. Possibly funded by Crowley, Bennett went to the East and first studied the *dharma* in Sri Lanka before going on to Burma, where he was ordained as a *samanera* at Akyab in 1901. *Bhikkhu* ordination came the following year, when he took the name Ananda Maitreya, which he later changed to Ananda Metteyya (the Pali form).

By now determined to lead a Buddhist mission to Europe, Ananda Metteyya set up an international organization in Rangoon. A support group was also set up at the British end: the Buddhist Society of Great Britain and Ireland, founded 1907. The pioneer *bhikkhu* arrived back in Britain in 1908, but he was plagued by ill health which obliged him to return to Burma after just six months. Though apparently idealistic, high-minded, and highly energetic in his missionary work, his public speaking was of poor quality and he did not raise much inspiration in his audiences.

In 1914 ill health finally forced Ananda Metteyya to disrobe and return to England. He was by now a broken man. He survived until 1923, supported largely by Buddhist sympathizers, but still active in his Buddhist propaganda work, which he attempted to finance by his inventions. Among his ambitious schemes were a machine for registering the power of thought and another for making oxygen out of fresh air; success, it seems, ever eluded him.

One day in 1904 or 1905 a Scotsman named J. F. McKechnie (1871–1951) picked up a copy of Ananda Metteyya's journal, *Buddhism.* In it he saw an advertisement that changed his life. He sailed out to Rangoon to give editorial assistance to Ananda Metteyya, and it was there that in 1906 he was ordained into the *sangha* as Bhikkhu Silacara. He too wore out his health with strenuous Buddhist missionary work, and in 1925 he disrobed and returned to Britain, spending the last years of his life in a home for the elderly at Bury.

The first German national to enter the *sangha* was a virtuoso musician named Anton Gueth (1878–1957), who ordained as Nyanatiloka Bhikkhu in Rangoon in 1903. He later moved to Sri Lanka, though he came to Europe in 1910–1911 and ordained the first *samanera* on European soil. Returning to Sri Lanka, he lived at the Island Hermitage in Ratgama Lake, Dodanduwa, though being an enemy alien he was interned or otherwise uprooted during the two World Wars. His foremost disciple, Ven. Nyanaponika (Siegmund Feniger, b. 1901), also of

German origin, has been one of the major influences behind the founding of the Buddhist Publication Society. He, like his mentor Nyanatiloka, has produced influential books.

Interest also gained ground in Germany itself. In the early years of this century, Dr. Paul Dahlke (1865-1928) built one of the first Buddhist *vihara* in Western Europe in the grounds of his house at Frohnau, a northern suburb of Berlin. There he lived an ascetic life, closely following the monastic Vinaya. In 1923 George Grimm (1868–1945) founded the "Old Buddhist Community" at Utting in Bavaria. This still exists and claims to be by one year the oldest Buddhist organization in Europe.

Much significant—and forgotten—pioneering work was done in Russia, which of course has Lamaist Buddhists among its Buryat and Kalmuk peoples. The temples built by the Kalmuks in the lower Volga region must rank as the oldest Buddhist foundations in Eastern Europe. Pioneering Buddhological studies were also carried out in Russia by fine scholars like Stcherbatsky, Obermiller, and others. There was practical experimentation too in the community of European Buddhists that built up around the Latvian, Karlis Alexis Tennisons (1873–1962), as early as the 1890s. Tsar Nicholas II, the last of the Romanov line, and some high nobles like Prince Ukhtomsky were probably quite sympathetic to Buddhism. Influential too in Russian court circles was a healer named Badmaev, a Bury at who had studied Tibetan medicine at Chakpori, the Medical College near Lhasa. The Revolution was a setback, however, and later the Stalinist purges resulted in a vicious repression. Many lamas were put on show trial and executed, many monasteries were closed and the religious functionaries who escaped with their lives were forced to return to lay life. During World War II, however, the need to rouse national feeling against the invading Germans led to religious concessions; monasteries and temples were then reopened, monks returned to them and Buddhist life began again.

THE TWENTIETH CENTURY—THE INTER-WAR PERIOD

But Britain, with its close colonial connections with Buddhist countries, not to speak of its political stability, naturally generated the most significant Buddhist activity.

After the first Buddhist Society had been formed, local groups began to spring up, magazines were published, and lectures were vigorously delivered by enthusiastic speakers. The First World War interrupted activities, but afterwards the sight of so many women in black, and the full realization of the horrors of trench warfare, conspired to produce a climate favorable to a peaceful persuasion like Buddhism. Now the movement really started to get under way, and, as so often happens, a natural leader appeared as well. This was Travers Christmas Humphreys (1901–1983), a young man with a quick mind, a poetic turn of phrase, and a flair for dramatic oratory that he put to good effect in his professional calling as a barrister at London's Central Criminal Court, the Old Bailey. The same talents that made Toby Humphreys the star advocate in many a famous murder trial were also, ironically, put at the service of Buddhism. As a speaker, writer, organizer, energizer, and general figurehead, he was to lead the British Buddhist movement for over half a century and to see it develop from an eccentric marginal interest into something that could be fairly counted among the religions of his country.

But Humphreys himself was a product of Theosophy and his Buddhism was one with a distinctly Blavatskian slant. The first organization that he established with his future wife, Puck (Aileen Faulkner), was in fact an adjunct of the Theosophical Society. It was called the Buddhist Lodge, and so it remained from 1924 until 1943, when it became the Buddhist Society, London, and subsequently simply The Buddhist Society, though it had long since parted company with the T.S. due to philosophical differences. The Buddhist Lodge was active in organizing lectures and classes, and in publishing Buddhist books. It also produced its own journal, *Buddhism in England,* founded and edited by Arthur C. March, which later became *The Middle Way.*

In these early days, the sort of Buddhism prevalent was the Theravada variety. With few translated texts available, little was yet known of the Mahayana, and still less of the Vajrayana: the Buddhism of Tibet. However in 1922 a rather strange expedition set out from Britain. It was composed of a number of prominent British Buddhists, including G. E. O. Knight, Captain J. E. Ellam (Hon. Secretary of the original Buddhist Society of Great Britain and Ireland), Frederick Fletcher, and G. Montgomery McGovern (onetime lecturer at London University's School of Oriental Studies). Their intention was to visit the Dalai Lama in Lhasa and obtain permission to study Tibetan Buddhism at first hand in the "Forbidden Land" of Tibet itself. With them they took an imposing silver urn containing an impressive scroll on which the Buddhists of Britain saluted His Holiness, the emanation of Avalokiteshvara. Though these enterprising stalwarts got as far as the southern Tibetan city of Shigatse, they were not allowed to proceed to Lhasa. Reluctantly obliged to return to British territory, they then decided that one of their party, McGovern, should try to slip through to Lhasa in disguise. This he contrived to do, though not without appalling suffering. McGovern spent a short time in the holy city and, though seriously ill, was able to meet the Great Thirteenth Dalai Lama. Eventually, however, when he was strong enough to travel, he was again requested to depart, and perhaps this time he was not too sorry to do so.

While in Shigatse, one of McGovern's colleagues, Frederic Fletcher (1877–1951), became ordained as a novice of the Gelug school—possibly the first Westerner to be so honored. (There is some evidence that a Lithuanian named Kunigaikshtis Gedyminas ordained as a *lama* in the nineteenth century and studied in Tibet.) An Oxford graduate, Fletcher had also been inspired by *The Light of Asia;* he had traveled widely as well, to Sri Lanka and elsewhere; finally his experiences as a major in the First World War convinced him of the futility of worldly life, hence his interest in going to Tibet. Subsequently, he received Theravada *bhikkhu* ordination in Sri Lanka, traveled extensively in India, and finally lived for many years in Burma. His religious name, Lama Dorje Prajñananda, reflects his dual loyalties to both Vajrayana and Theravada.

Rather more well-known are the Tibetan adventures of the great French mystic, traveler, and author, Alexandra David-Neel (1868–1969). Having worked as a singer for the Opéra Comique, and as a journalist, it was the discovery of Oriental religion and philosophy in the Musée Guimet in 1903 that settled the course of her life. After a brief attempt at marriage, she departed for the East in 1904, intending to stay eighteen months; instead she stayed nearly twenty years! She had an audience with the exiled Thirteenth Dalai Lama; then she went to Sikkim, where she met Lama Yongden, her future traveling companion and adopted son. For a time, the two of them lived in a cave-hermitage in the Himalayas, learning Tibetan Buddhist philosophy and Tibetan language from *lama* teachers. They also made three abortive attempts to get into Tibet at this time, which put Madame David-Neel out of favor with the British authorities. Much later, in 1924, though in her mid-fifties, and both ragged and exhausted, she became the first European woman to enter the "Forbidden City" of Lhasa. To do so, she had secretly entered Tibet from the East and laboriously tramped for six months, on foot and in disguise, across some of the most inhospitable terrain in the world. The faithful Yongden had been her sole traveling companion. Later still, during the Second World War, she lived in China along the eastern marches of Tibet. The final phase of her life was lived out in her villa in Digne (Haute Provence). Remarkable to the last, she died at nearly one hundred and one years of age.

Madame David-Neel caught the public's imagination with books like *With Mystics and Magicians in Tibet* and *My Journey to Lhasa*. But she was not alone. At this time almost every traveler to Tibet produced a book, and many of them attempted some kind of account of local religious "beliefs" and practices. The first major pioneering study of Tibetan Buddhism, entitled *Lamaism, or the Buddhism of Tibet,* was made by L. A. Waddell, a British medical officer who began studying the subject in Darjeeling in the fading years of the nineteenth century, employing Tibetan servants and two "very learned *lamas*" to assist him. He even fitted out a private temple for study purposes as well as visiting others in Sikkim and Bhutan. As principal medical officer with the Younghusband Expedition to Lhasa (1904), Waddell had the opportunity of carrying on his studies at first hand in the Tibetan capital. Other pioneering works were produced by Sir Charles Bell, the political officer in Sikkim, who developed a friendship with the Thirteenth Dalai Lama when he was in exile in Darjeeling between 1910 and 1912; between 1920 and 1921, Bell paid an official visit to Lhasa; he was a great enthusiast for all things Tibetan.

We have already mentioned the pioneering Tibetological work of Alexander Csoma de Körös. Better known are the early translations of Tibetan texts made by the American Dr. W. Y. Evans-Wentz (1875–1965) in collaboration with Kazi Dawa-Samdup. Evans-Wentz was an academic folklorist who trained at the universities of Stanford, Oxford, and Rennes. He was influenced by the Irish poet, W. B. Yeats, and his first book was entitled *Fairy Faith in Celtic Lands*. Subsequently, an interest in rebirth took him to the East, where in 1919 he met Kazi Dawa-Samdup, a Sikkimese schoolmaster who had at some time worked for the British Political Officer in Sikkim, for the Tibetans as plenipotentiary in India, and had also been a member of the political staff of the exiled Thirteenth Dalai Lama. Together, Evans-Wentz and Dawa-Samdup produced several useful translations, including *The Tibetan Book of the Dead* and the biography of Milarepa.

In 1925, Anagarika Dharmapala came to England with the intention of founding a branch of his Maha Bodhi Society. Suitable premises were found the following year in the west London suburb of Ealing, and opened with all the usual ceremony. The Buddhist flag designed by Colonel H. S. Olcott was unfurled, and speeches were delivered by the Anagarika, Christmas Humphreys, A. C. March, and others. Two years later a more centrally situated house was obtained near Regent's Park, a three learned English-speaking *bhikkhus* from Sri Lanka took up residence there. This effectively created a branch of the *sangha,* albeit not a native-born one, on British soil. There has been a Sri

Lankan Vihara here in London ever since, except for a hiatus between 1940 and 1954. Anagarika Dharmapala passed away in India in 1933.

The Buddhist Lodge and the British Maha Bodhi Society were the twin poles that sustained British Buddhism down to the Second World War. Despite occasional slight differences, they were in many ways complementary organizations, and often got together to arrange joint functions, like the annual Wesak or Buddha Day celebration.

The Buddhist Society also hosted distinguished Buddhist visitors to London, like Ven Tai Hsü from China, and Dr. D. T. Suzuki from Japan. Dr. Suzuki (1870–1966) is nowadays revered as "the Man who Brought Zen to the West." He trained in Rinzai Zen under Imagita Kosen Roshi and Soyen Shaku at Engaku-ji in Kamakura. Later he worked for the Open Court Publishing House of Dr. Paul Carus in LaSalle, Illinois, where he perfected his knowledge of the English language and of Western thought. A highly gifted writer, teacher, and lecturer as well as a man of very profound spiritual insight, Suzuki in fact made available the hitherto undiscovered treasure-house of Mahayana Buddhism to Westerners, though he is more usually remembered as a great propagator of Zen. He first visited London in 1908, when he met Ananda Metteyya, and again in 1936, when he attended the World Congress of Faiths, which was held under the auspices of Sir Francis Younghusband. The climax of the Congress was a great public meeting when various distinguished speakers were billed to speak on "The Supreme Spiritual Ideal." Suzuki appeared to be dozing, but when he came to speak he dismissed all knowledge of this highfalutin' theme and instead went on to talk about his little house in Japan. His audience was fascinated; they realized that here was very subtle but profound teaching.

One person who was very impressed with Dr. Suzuki at the Congress was a sharp young man-about-town named Alan Watts (1915–1973) who, as a protégé of Christmas Humphreys, had lately assumed the editorship of *Buddhism in England*. Watts, too, possessed communication talents of an exceedingly high order, and went on to make a big name for himself in the United States as a writer and speaker on Zen and related matters.

These slow developments, over so many centuries, prepared the ground for what, following the Second World War, was to be an unprecedented and utterly unexpected flowering of Buddhism in Europe. The great veteran *dharma*-spreader Toby Humphreys intuitively saw it coming. Proclaiming it, he loved to quote from Victor Hugo: "*There is one thing that is stronger than armies: an idea whose time has come.*"

The Flowering of the Lotus

BUDDHISM IN EUROPE FROM WORLD WAR II TO DATE*

Up until the Second World War, and for some years afterwards, Buddhism remained a largely middle-class preserve. One of its twin pillars in London, the Buddhist Society, for instance, had very much the aura of a gentleman's club. Until well into the new era, its front door was kept firmly closed, and anyone who rang the bell would be thoroughly looked over before being granted admittance.

But things were rapidly changing, and no more so than during the 1960s when a new generation came of age. Regardless of class, its members had been brought up in relative affluence and been given good educational opportunities. They also enjoyed new freedoms: to travel, to explore art, politics, sex, and drugs, and to experiment with alternative lifestyles. Inevitably many began to encounter the perennial problems that beset those who have had everything yet still find themselves dissatisfied. In short, they were poised to probe more deeply into the mystery of things. The Western religions could not provide satisfactory answers, so there was a mass turning to the East. Many traveled to India, Nepal, Sri Lanka, Japan, Korea, Thailand, and elsewhere, and spent time there enjoying the local venal pleasures or exploring the religious traditions,

---

*Addresses of many of the groups and centers mentioned in this chapter can be found under Useful Addresses, Appendix II.

by turns. Vedanta attracted some, but in the long term Buddhism proved to be of more considerable influence.

ZEN

Now at last the Mahayana traditions began to come into their own. Springing directly from Dr. Suzuki's pioneering work, Zen became quite fashionable in Britain and other parts of Europe, though it never caught on to the extent that it did in the United States. For a while a kind of intellectual quasi-Zen held the field. Monica Furlong has dubbed it "Christmas Zen" after its main exponent, Christmas Humphreys. Basically it was recycled Dr. Suzuki, put over with verve and more than a little showmanship. Christmas Humphreys' protégé, Alan Watts, also did well with Christmas Zen in the United States, whither he emigrated in 1938.

In 1953 Watts returned for a brief visit to England. The members of the Buddhist Society had, of course, read his eminently readable books and heard all about his exploits across the Atlantic, where he was "setting America alight with his new approach to Zen." They therefore turned out in force to hear him lecture at the Caxton Hall.

Watts, now sporting a crewcut, strode onto the podium, stood stock still for a moment, then cried, "*Wake up!*"

The audience was stunned, but made no special response. Watts was therefore obliged to repeat the gambit. Again no special response. "Direct methods" having fallen rather flat, he then went on to deliver a straight lecture on the theme that we are all asleep to the "zen" within us.

Of course, Humphreys and Watts, both highly gifted communicators, did marvelous work in spreading knowledge of Zen. But it was left to others to go more deeply into the matter. This meant actually going to the East and submitting to long and arduous *zazen* practice under acknowledged masters, which by general agreement is the only viable avenue to genuine Zen realization.

Among the adventurous souls that took this challenging course was another of Christmas Humphreys' protégés, an Austrian woman named Irmgard Schloegl, who received Rinzai Zen training at Daitoku-ji in Kyoto under Sesso Oda Roshi, Goto Zuigan Roshi, and Soko Morinaga Roshi. Zen training is hard, and the Japanese—at this time at least—were not noted for their liking of foreigners, and women did not enjoy great standing in their eyes either; Dr. Schloegl must therefore have needed a lot of determination to stay the course. She did, however, and eventually returned to London and began to teach. Ever since she has guided the large and successful *zazen* class at the Buddhist Society, and has also established an independent organization, the Zen Center, to which Christmas Humphreys with characteristic generosity left his villa in St. John's Wood when he died in 1983. In 1984 the house was renamed Shobo-an, "Hermitage of the True Dharma," and in the same year Dr. Schloegl was ordained as Ven. Myokyo-ni by Soko Morinaga Roshi, who occasionally visits London and the Buddhist Society Summer School.

The London Zen Society has also represented the Rinzai Zen tradition in Britain for many years. It developed from the Hannyakai, a society founded by Kim Wall and others in 1966. Its spiritual director is Sochu Suzuki Roshi (b. 1921), who succeeded Nakagawa Soen Roshi (1907–1984) as abbot of Ryutaku-ji, the famous Zen monastery in Mishima, Japan. Soen Roshi was a respected poet; he also made creative innovations in Zen ritual and took a keen interest in the development of Zen in the West. Another of Soen Roshi's pupils Nakagawa Kyudo Roshi, currently based in New York, also occasionally visits the London Zen Society, which is housed in north London.

All forms of Zen center around the practice of *zazen,* or sitting meditation. In the Rinzai tradition, however, *koan* riddles are also employed. These are profound or enigmatic questions designed to drive the practitioner beyond thought into the arms of a deeper source of wisdom. The progress—or lack of it—one has made, is tested during the *dokusan* or *sanzen* interview with the master or *roshi.* In the Soto tradition, on the other hand, the emphasis is on just sitting (*shikan taza*). To sit is to be a *buddha:* an enlightened person. In the words of Master Dogen, the seminar teacher of the tradition in Japan:

> This type of *zazen* is not something that is done in stages of meditation; it is simply the lawful gateway to carefree peace. To train and enlighten ourselves is to become thoroughly wise; the *koan* appears *naturally* in daily life. If you become utterly free you will be as the water wherein the dragon dwells or as the mountain whereon the tiger roams.*

Another student of Christmas Humphreys' zen class also went east on a Zen quest. Peggy Kennett (1924–1996), a musician by training, was in 1962 ordained by Ven. Seck Kim Seng, Abbot of Cheng Hoon Teng Temple in Malacca, Malaysia. She later went on to study Soto Zen under Chisan Koho Zenji (1879–1967) at Soji-ji, a temple in Yokohama. With

---

* Dogen, *Serene Reflection Meditation* (Carrshield: Throssel Hole Priory, 1987), 4–5.

a license to teach, Jiyu Kennett Roshi (as she had now become) arrived on the West Coast of the U.S.A. in 1969, established the Zen Mission Society in 1970, and then went on to found an abbey at Mount Shasta in California, where she currently presides as abbess. Today Shasta Abbey is the headquarters of the Order of Buddhist Contemplatives of the Soto Zen Church (O.B.C.), which propagates a form of traditional Soto Zen training adjusted to modern Western cultural norms. O.B.C. monks, who may be of either sex and train together, tend to call themselves "reverend" rather than the usual "Ven."; their chanting (which is in English) is also formally based on gregorian plain-chant.

In 1972 Throssel Hole Priory was set up amid eighteen acres of fields and woodlands in the north of England under the auspices of Jiyu Kennett Rochi's British Zen Mission Society. It has developed successfully and enjoys a good reputation as a well-run training monastery. Life there, as in all authentic Zen temples, is simple and disciplined, and centers around the meditation hall, where trainees meditate (it is called "serene reflection" here), attend services and ceremonies, study, eat, and sleep. There are also periods of work. Its abbot at the present time is Rev. Daishin Morgan (O.B.C.) (b. 1951).

Soto Zen has also been represented in Europe by Taisen Deshimaru (1914–1982), a Japanese monk who trained under Kodo Sawaki. Deshimaru lived the householder's life for many years, marrying and begetting children; but the call of Zen drew him away, and, after his teacher's death, he traveled to Europe on the Trans-Siberian Railway. Settling in Paris in 1967, he taught for some fifteen years, and in 1970 founded L'Association Zen d'Europe; this spawned dojos and zazen centers in other parts of France, Belgium, and West Germany, as well as in North and South America and North Africa. Besides his temple in Paris he also had a larger one in the Loire Valley. His student, Nancy Amphoux, has written: "Deshimaru's personality was unique: blustery, sensitive, truculent, subtle, and inimitable. Its greatest strength lay in the boundless universal energy that he transmitted."

The Rinzai and Soto approaches are blended in the teaching of Taizen Maezumi Roshi (1931–1995), founder of the influential Zen Center of Los Angeles (ZCLA). In recent years a branch of the ZCLA, the Zen Practice Centre, has existed in south London under the auspices of Sumi and Colin Buko Barber. Maezumi Roshi has visited and taught in Britain, as has his Dharma heir, Genpo Merzel Sensei, who has branches of his Kanzeon Sangha in various European countries, including Poland, which before the melting of the Iron Curtain was one of the first Eastern Bloc countries to open to Buddhism.

Influential in British Zen, but not a figure to seek the limelight or promote himself as a teacher of any sort, is Trevor Leggett. For many years head of the Japanese Service of the B.B.C., Mr. Leggett not only knows Japanese (and also Sanskrit) thoroughly but has received Zen training at Daitoku-ji as well as having studied with Dr. Hari Prashad Shastri, a Vedantist sage. In recent years Trevor Leggett has brought out a series of books on Zen and translations of Zen texts which have added greatly to general understanding. A consummate storyteller, his lectures at the Buddhist Society's annual summer school and elsewhere have long been greatly appreciated.

All the foregoing of course represent developments from Japanese forms of Zen. There has in fact been little Chinese Zen (Ch'an) activity in Europe, though Richard Hunn of Norwich, who was once a student of Charles Luk (Lü K'uan Yü, 1898–1978) of Hong Kong, is translating texts and occasionally holds Ch'an retreats. John Blofeld (Chu Ch'an 1913–1987), a long-term English expatriate lately domiciled in Bangkok, also provided useful texts (*Huang Po, Hui Hai,* etc.) as well as producing highly readable accounts of his adventures, spiritual and otherwise, in pre-Communist China. He went there as a young man and lived there intermittently for many years, formally becoming a pupil of the legendary Master Hsü Yün (1840–1959), though in fact he received his actual training in Ch'an meditation from Master Hsü Yün's pupils at Hua T'ing monastery near Kunming in Yunnan province.

Stephen Batchelor (b. 1953) and his wife Martine Fages occasionally run what they call "Radical Questioning" retreats in Europe based on the Korean Zen training that they received under Kusan Sunim (1909–1983) at Songgwang Sa, a monastery in Cholla Namdo province, southwest Korea. Strangely, Korean Zen seems to have been embraced most strongly in Poland, where the Ven. Soen Sunim of the Providence Zen Center (Rhode Island, U.S.A) has many devotees; he also has others in West Germany. Genpo Merzel Sensei also teaches in Poland, as does Roshi Philip Kapleau of the Rochester Zen Center (New York State, U.S.A.).

An innovation in recent years has been the *Western Zen Retreats* organized by John Crook, reader in psychology at Bristol University. These usually take place in a secluded farmhouse in mid-Wales and employ a varying combination of *zazen* and other methods, notably the "Communication Exercise" of Charles Berner. They also incorporate the so-called "Enlightenment Intensive" brought to Europe by Jeff Love in the 1970s. The Communication Exercise substitutes for the traditional *sanzen* interview. Instead of confronting the *roshi,* participants break up into pairs and confront each other with the question of self-identity. John Crook says: "The outcome may be profound insight into the 'ground of being'—an event known in Zen as an 'enlightenment experience.' Whether or not this realization happens, participants share a profound experience in new knowledge of self and others."

The West also produces the occasional spiritual original, someone who is able to come up with an entirely new approach to the central enigma of who we are. Douglas Harding (b. 1909) is just such a person. The product of an extremely narrow Plymouth Brethren sectarian upbring-ing, Harding broke away while at London University and began a personal search for spiritual truth. His father and the rest of his family, deeming him utterly hell-bent, promptly turned their backs on him once and for all. Later, while working as an architect in India, he went on a walking tour in the Himalayas. Unexpectedly he saw something at once ex-tremely profound and extremely obvious: from a purely subjective point of view he had no "meatball head" on his shoulders, just pure unbounded space in which the world was happening. Long afterwards, delving into the writings of Dr. Suzuki and Zen masters, he realized that his expe-rience had correlatives in that tradition. At last finding his affinities, he began to write and teach. His book, *On Having No Head,* is a classic of its type: short, lucid, passionate, and original. He has also developed various direct experimental techniques for helping people to "see who they really are." His unconventional approach has, however, hindered his reception in Britain and, though he continues to live in his native county of Suffolk, he now teaches mainly in the United States.

The production costs of *On Having No Head* were borne by another rather remarkable fringe member of the British Buddhist scene, who can really only be placed in this category—though he himself would undoubtedly have heartily rejected any attempt at pigeon-holding. This was Terence Gray (1895–1986). He was an immensely wealthy man of Anglo-Irish ancestry who kept a string of racehorses and is reputed to have won the Ascot Gold Cup. Later he lived in Monte Carlo and would send gifts of wine from his vineyard in the Rhône valley to Christmas Humphreys in London. Privately, however, he addressed himself to the perennial questions and, under the nom-de-plume of Wei Wu Wei, wrote a number of fascinating, impossible books—*Ask the Awakened, All Else Is Bondage, Why Lazarus Laughed*—that seemed designed to precipitate the reader into confrontation with essential nature by so piling paradox upon paradox as to induce a kind of brain seizure.

MAINSTREAM MAHAYANA

The chance discovery around 1937 of one of Dr. Suzuki's books in a bookshop near the British Museum by a scholarly German refugee named Edward Conze (1904–1979) was to have a highly stimulating effect on

Mahayana studies in the West. It revivified an earlier interest in Buddhism, and Conze, an irascible but energetic man with a massive intellect, went on to dedicate the remainder of his life to the study and translation of Mahayana texts. He also produced more popular works, his *Buddhism: Its Essence & Development,* a spirited little monograph, is still probably the best introduction to Buddhism for the general reader. His anthologies helped make the fruits of his scholarship available to a wider, less specialized readership. The other, darker side of his nature, meanwhile, asserted itself in his *Memoirs of a Modern Gnostic,* where he indulged a minor talent for character assassination at the expense of a few luminaries of the Western Buddhist scene.

The tradition of Mahayana studies inaugurated by Edward Conze has been continued in Britain to the present by Eric Cheetham and his colleagues in the Mahayana Study Group. This group dates back to the early 1950s, when several Buddhists began to meet in London under the guidance of Professor Richard H. Robinson, who later went on to found the Buddhist Studies Program at the University of Wisconsin. Whereas so many Buddhists gain their knowledge of the *dharma* from popular interpretations, this group is concerned to seek it out at first hand through the close and careful study of (mainly) Indian Mahayana *sutras:*

> From the beginning we wanted to know what Mahayana Buddhists were supposed to do—and why. The teachings of the Pali texts and the monk exponents of that teaching were much in evidence. Somehow the Mahayana was different but just how and for what purpose we did not know. And we needed to know for the very practical purpose of exercising choice, if there were any, in adopting the Way. Now, many years later, this writer (Eric Cheetham) feels that those early concerns are still valid.*

TIBETAN BUDDHISM

Down to 1959, Tibet remained the "Forbidden Land" from which Westerners were rigidly debarred. But there were a few notable exceptions, among them the eminent Italian Tibetologist Professor Giuseppe Tucci (1894–1984), an aristocratic and immensely wealthy man who established the Istituto Italiano per il Medio ed Estremo Oriente (IsMEO) in Rome in 1933. Between 1927 and 1949, Tucci made a number of well-financed expeditions to Tibet to obtain the manuscripts, books, artifacts,

---

* Eric Cheetham, "Profile of a Buddhist Study Group," *The Middle Way* vol. 60, no. 1 (May, 1985): 36.

and first-hand data that he required for his studies. How exactly he contrived to obtain the necessary official permits, which were notoriously hard to come by, remains something of a mystery, though it does appear that he was a convinced and, to some extent, a practicing Buddhist, and this may have cut some ice with the Lhasa authorities. He also apparently believed that he had been a Tibetan in a previous incarnation.

Another privileged visitor was E. L. Hoffmann (1898–1985), better known by his Buddhist name of Lama Anagarika Govinda. Of Bolivian and German extraction, Govinda studied architecture and archaeology as well as philosophy in Europe; he was also rather a good artist, and lived for a time in an artistic colony on Capri. Having developed an interest in burial mounds, he went to Sri Lanka in 1928 to study the local *stupas* and was bitten by the Buddhist bug. At first he was drawn to Theravada Buddhism, ordained as an *anagarika* and occupied himself with Pali studies. In 1931, however, he encountered Tibetan Buddhism while at a Buddhist conference in Darjeeling. He also met his guru, Tomo Geshe Rinpoché there, and when he died Govinda set up the Arya Maitreya Mandala in his memory. During the 1930s, Govinda pursued his Buddhist studies in Ladakh, Sikkim, and Tibet, and between 1947 and 1949 made two important forays into Tibet. The second took him to western Tibet, where he visited the sacred Mount Kailas as well as Tsaparang and Thöling, the lost cities of the ancient kingdom of Gu-gé in the upper Sutlej valley. His experiences in these wonderful places are recounted in his *The Way of the White Clouds*. His most important book, however, was *Foundations of Tibetan Mysticism,* which was the first comprehensive account of Tibetan Buddhism written from within, so to speak, by a Western practitioner. As a writer, Govinda was always lucid and highly readable, but then there was a strong salting of the artist in his nature.

In 1947 two Englishmen were allowed to cross the high passes and seek Buddhist teaching in Tibet. One was Marco Pallis (1895–1989), a professional musician with an interest in mountaineering who had been born in Liverpool of Greek parentage in 1895. His companion was Ronald Nicholson. They went to Sakya, the great monastic center in southern Tibet about three days' travel west of Shigatse. There they located a qualified *guru:*

> We had to walk a long way to find him. He himself was a recluse: he lived in a little hut. The first time we met, he said, "Well, now, it's best that you should have the bases," and he produced this large loose-leaved book. "Now, you learn that by heart and when you know it we'll start." Well, I conveyed to him that for us this was something very difficult. "Oh, it's not difficult at all," he said; so I said,

"We'll try." And the next time we went, he said, "I've thought about what you've said and so I've found another book which is really the same book reduced to a small formula—a few pages. This you must at all costs learn by heart." We *did* learn it and after a few days we recited it to him correctly. He said, "That's a good beginning."*

But things were to change drastically in 1959. The great diaspora of Tibetan lamas following the Lhasa uprising, and the subsequent flight of the Dalai Lama, made generally available to the West for the first time the rich Tantric heritage of the Vajrayana.

European Buddhists were quick to help the army of Tibetan refugees that spilled over the Himalayas into northern India, Sikkim, and Bhutan, many of them in a very sorry condition. One person who responded with particular wholeheartedness was Freda Bedi (1911–1977), an Englishwoman who had married a Sikh, lived for many years in India, and been given high public office by Prime Minister Pandit Nehru. She was eventually ordained as a Karma Kagyu nun, taking the name Sister Karma Kechog Palmo. As principal of a school for young lamas in Dalhousie, one of her protégés was a young Karma Kagyu *tulku* from Eastern Tibet, onetime abbot of the Surmang group of monasteries; his name was Chögyam Trungpa (1939–1987).

In 1963, Trungpa Rinpoché sailed to England on a P&O liner to study at St. Anthony's College, Oxford. He was accompanied by a fellow Karma Kagyu *tulku* from eastern Tibet: Chujé Akong Rinpoché, the former abbot of Drölma Lhakhang monastery, who went to do medical work at the Radcliffe Infirmary in Oxford.

No Tibetan *lama* who has come to the West has possessed Trungpa's unique blend of qualities. He was certainly charismatic; he also had a wonderful talent for presenting *dharma* to Westerners clearly, lucidly, and creatively; some of his books, like *Meditation in Action* and *Cutting through Spiritual Materialism,* remain lasting classics. Yet Trungpa soon became a controversial figure. His lifestyle, running to excess, disquieted and alienated many; yet at the same time he always retained the loyalty of a vast following, who staunchly maintained to the end that behind the surface problems lurked the true *bodhisattva* nature: compassionate, wise, and capable of giving out profound teachings.

Back in the early sixties, Trungpa soon gathered an entourage of devoted followers in many parts of Europe. It was no doubt quite a strain for him. He was still very young himself, in his early twenties, and here were so many confused people, a lot of them casualties of the permissive

* Recorded interview with the author, 1984.

society and the hippie era, looking to him to sort out their problems. Still, he galvanized himself to the challenge. In 1967, he and Akong Rinpoché were able to establish the first Tibetan Buddhist center in the West at Johnstone House in Dumfriesshire, amid the wet and windy hills of the southern uplands of Scotland. Appropriately it was named Samyé Ling after the first monastery of Tibet. Trungpa himself has written that, for him, Samyé Ling was not "entirely satisfying," for "the scale of activity was small, and the people who did come to participate seemed to be slightly missing the point."*

The early history of Samyé Ling was almost as dramatic as that of its namesake in Tibet, where, it will be remembered, demonic forces frustrated the completion of the building work and had eventually to be subdued by Padmasambhava. Trungpa himself suffered a serious car crash, which left him partially paralyzed; he also shocked some of his followers by deciding to disrobe and marry. Tensions, conflict, and paranoia began to build up, and in 1970 he departed to the United States with his new wife, Diana. There he established various highly successful centers and organizations, and more books appeared. He still retained the loyalty of many of his European followers, including Michael Hookham, who in 1975 founded the Longchen Foundation, of which Trungpa Rinpoché became director and Dilgo Khyentse Rinpoché, patron; also the Nitartha School, which exists to promote contemplative study and practice within a systematic matrix. Meanwhile, Dr. Karl Springer has headed the European arm of Trungpa's Vajradhatu organization (founded 1970), which maintains Dharmadhatu centers in London and other important European cities. Samyé Ling has also raised funds and purchased a small island off of the Scottish coast. Renamed Holy Island, it is in the process of becoming a residential retreat center.

Samyé Ling has successfully outlived its early upheavals and continues to the present time under the guidance of Akong Rinpoché, now its abbot and the spiritual head of associated centers in Spain, South Africa, and elsewhere. It has indeed grown and presently ambitious plans are afoot for its future development. The Samyé Project, now virtually completed, aims at building a splendid Tibetan-style temple with an ancillary college facility endowed with library, lecture halls, translation room, and so forth.

Back in 1975 Samyé Ling was graced with a visit from His Holiness the Sixteenth Gyalwa Karmapa (1923–1981), late supreme head of the Karma Kagyu school, who performed the famous Vajra Crown Ceremony there. That year the Karmapa also visited Kham Tibetan House, a second Karma Kagyu center established in 1973 in the village of Ashdon near Saffron

* Chögyam Trungpa, *Born in Tibet,* rev. ed., (Boulder: Prajña Press, 1981), 252.

Waldon in Essex by Lama Chimé Rinpoché, also a native of Kham, where he was identified as one of the four *tulkus* of Benchen monastery. Lama Chimé, who came to England around 1972, also resigned monk status in order to marry. He now combines his *dharma* work with a full-time career in the Tibetan section of the British Library. He is also spiritual director of a London Center: Karma Kagyu Chö Khor Ling.

A highly respected Karma Kagyu *tulku* who has stayed away from the limelight and avoided groups and centers is Ato Rinpoché (b. 1933). He also hails from eastern Tibet, and in his formative years received Gelugpa and Nyingmapa as well as Kagyupa teachings. In the early 1960s he was the Karma Kagyu representative on H. H. the Dalai Lama's Council for Religious and Cultural Affairs, and later Sister Palmo's assistant at the Young Lamas' School in Dalhousie. Ato Rinpoché married Alethea Martineau in 1967 and came to live in Cambridge, where he worked as a nurse at Fulbourn Mental Hospital until his early retirement in 1981. He teaches privately or by invitation to groups, though in 1986 he departed from his usual practice to begin a monthly meditation group in Cambridge.

The Kagyu School, incorporating as it does the tradition established by Naropa, Marpa, and Milarepa, leans towards the attainment of direct mystical experience. Famous Kagyupa *lamas* have visited Europe from time to time in recent years, notably Kalu Rinpoché, "a modern Milarepa," who has established centers for Westerners in France where three-year retreats are conducted; also Tai Situ Rinpoché, Pawo Rinpoché, Khenpo Tsultrim Gyamtso, *et al.*

The leaders of the "established church" of Tibetan Buddhism, the Gelug School, were rather slower in sending *lamas* to the West than the pioneering Kagyupas. Being in the tradition of Atisha and Tsongkhapa, they also represent a rather more strict tradition that emphasizes monasticism, intensive study of texts, and methodical practice according to a carefully graduated system (Lam Rim). The seminal figure in their work among Westerners was another charismatic *lama* with great warmth, humor, and a talent both for inspiring people and of making *dharma* accessible to them as a living teaching. This was Lama Thubten Yeshé (1935–1984), a monk trained at the great monastic university of Sera (Jé College), near Lhasa. He began teaching Westerners in Darjeeling and later in Nepal, where in 1971 he founded a center at Kopan near Bodh Nath in the Kathmandu valley. His colleague in this enterprise was his chief disciple, Lama Zopa Rinpoché (b. 1946), who, though a native of Nepal, was also trained at Sera. In 1971, Lamas Yeshé and Zopa founded the Foundation for the Preservation of the Mahayana Tradition (F.P.M.T.), which has spawned centers in many countries as well as ancillary ventures like Wisdom Publications, a successful publishing concern now based in London, and Wisdom Books in America. Two of Lama Yeshé's students, Harvey Horrocks and Peter Kedge, managed in 1976 to obtain a vast, rambling, but exceedingly dilapidated medieval-monastery-cum-Victorian-hospital in the north of England named Conishead Priory. Here they established the Mañjushri Institute, the first major center in Europe geared to giving Westerners traditional Gelugpa training right up to the level of the *geshé* degree, the equivalent of Doctor of Divinity. In common with its precursors in old Tibet, it was envisaged that, once the necessary renovation work had been accomplished—a vast task in itself—Mañjushri would become a monastic university accommodating both ordained *sangha*-members and lay students.

Sadly, Lama Yeshé's health was not good and he died prematurely in Los Angeles in 1984, to the great grief of his devoted followers. While his disciple, Lama Zopa, continued his good work around the world, his *tulku* was sought and eventually found among his Spanish devotees. The diminutive Lama Ösel, born to Maria Torres and Paco Hita in 1985, has now been confirmed by the Dalai Lama as Lama Yeshé's new incarnation and duly enthroned. After Lama Yeshé's death, Geshé Kelsang Gyatso (b. 1932), another graduate of Sera, took over as spiritual director at the Mañjushri Institute. He has since founded the New Kadampa Tradition, with its headquarters at Manjushri and numerous other centers worldwide.

In 1983 a metropolitan Gelugpa center was established in a town house in the Finsbury Park area of London. Originally called Manjushri London but renamed Jamyang Meditation Centre after formally dissociating with Manjushri Institute when this became the headquarters of the New Kadampa Tradition, it is under the spiritual direction of Lama Zopa Rinpoché. The resident teacher was Geshe Namgyal Wangchen (b. mid-1930s), a lama with a large smiling face and warm personality, and a graduate of Drepung. Ill health eventually forced him to return to India, but another Gelugpa Lama, Geshe Tashi, eventually took his place. As the center expanded larger premises were needed, and Jamyang now occupies the Old Courthouse at Kennington, South London.

Lam Rim is a Gelugpa center in South Wales. It is accommodated at Pentwyn Manor near Raglan in Gwent. The resident *lama* there is Geshé Damchö Yonten (b. 1930), yet another product of Drepung, who after leaving Tibet in 1959 was for a time abbot of Samtenling monastery in Ladakh (North India). Geshé Damcho was brought to the West by another pioneering spirit, Tsunma Tsultem Zangmo (Connie Bolton, 1929–1984), at one time an art school lecturer, who, like Freda Bedi, responded to the plight of Tibetan refugees in 1959, and in 1971, with her mother, was ordained as a nun. Their original home in Bromley was consecrated by Geshe Rabten (see below), and used as a base by Harvey Horrocks while he was planning the creation of the Mañjushri Institute.

Gelugpa activity has not been confined to Britain by any means. In recent years centers have proliferated all over Europe, even in traditionally Catholic countries like Italy, Spain, and France, not to mention Germany, Austria, Switzerland, and elsewhere. Notable among the many learned lamas that have lived and taught in this part of the world was Geshé Rabten (1920–1986), a monk from Kham in eastern Tibet, trained at Sera monastery (Jé College), who in 1975 came to Rikon in Switzerland and two years later established Tharpa Choeling Center for Higher Tibetan Studies. An austere figure, strict in his adherence to the Vinaya and systematic Lam Rim training, Geshé Rabten in many was epitomized the classic Gelugpa *lama*.

One of Geshé Rabten's ex-students, Stephen Batchelor (formerly Gelong Jhampa Thabkay), is a member of the new generation of European Buddhists who have undergone traditional training and, having become conversant with the Tibetan language in the process, have contributed useful translations of basic texts as well as original works of their own. Keith Dowman and Martin Willson are others. In the United States there are many more, including Jeffrey Hopkins, Robert Thurman, Matthew Kapstein, and Alexander Berzin.

Always a very special event, of course, is a visit to Europe by the Dalai Lama, such as that which took place in 1984. In London that year, as highlights of a strenuous program that took him all over Britain, His Holiness gave a three-day teaching on Buddhism, and a special teaching on Dzogchen at the Camden Center in King's Cross. The sumptuous brocades and *thangkas* (scroll paintings), the robes and ritual, the aroma of incense, the sounds of low chanting, the presence of numerous distinguished *lamas* and scholars, as well as crowds of devoted Western monks, nuns, and laity, all conspired to create a rich atmosphere that was at once deeply spiritual and brightly festive. With apparently inexhaustible energy, patience, and good humor, His Holiness taught and performed ceremonials for hour after hour. He wore his high status and profound wisdom lightly, constantly smiling and breaking into laughter; and he put on no airs and graces but was throughout "the humble monk Tenzin Gyatso." Then at a great public meeting at the Albert Hall, accompanied by the Dean of Westminster, he talked to a more general audience and showed himself to be the spiritual leader of world rank that he has undoubtedly become.

A third Tibetan Buddhist tradition, the Sakya, has also established itself in Europe. In 1977, Ven. Ngakpa Jampa Thaye (Dr. David Scott, b.

1952) was inspired by his teacher, Karma Thinley Rinpoché, a learned *tulku* from Kham, to found Thinley Rinchen Ling in Bristol. Other Sakyapa centers have since been founded in other parts of Britain. Ngakpa Jampa, a lecturer by profession, gained his Ph.D. from Manchester University with a thesis on the history and teachings of the Dagpo Kagyu tradition. He received his qualification as a Dharma-teacher from H. H. Sakya Trizin (b. 1945), the head of the order, who left Tibet in 1959 and is currently based in India. Meanwhile, Phendé Rinpoché (b. 1934), the head of the Ngor sub-school of the Sakya order, came to France in 1969. A "personality of great wisdom and exemplary faith," he married a French woman and has established two centers, Ewam Phendé Ling at Les Ventes-Evereux in Normandy and Ewam Kunzang Ling in Paris.

Traditionally less worldly and well organized than the followers of the other schools, the Nyingmapas have not been so energetic and efficient in founding centers in Europe. Nevertheless, they have not been inactive either. The late supreme head of the order, Dudjom Rinpoché (1904–1987), settled in the Dordogne area of France, where he finally passed away. He had founded two centers in that country: Dorje Nyingpo and Orgyen Samyé Choeling, where he conducted a number of summer retreats. He is succeeded by his son and *dharma heir,* Shenphen Rinpoché.

Dudjom Rinpoché visited London three times at the invitation of Sogyal Rinpoché, a young *tulku* born in Kham in the mid-1940s and raised as a son by Jamyang Khyentse Chökyi Lodrö (1896–1959), one of the luminaries of the non-partisan Ri-mé movement that sprang up among Nyingma *lamas* in eastern Tibet towards the end of the last century. True to the Ri-mé tradition, Sogyal Rinpoché has received teaching and transmissions in all the schools of Tibetan Buddhism, and his Rigpa centers in London, Paris, and Santa Cruz (California) likewise host visits by important *lamas* of all traditions. After his escape from Tibet in 1958, Sogyal Rinpoché himself was educated at Delhi and Cambridge universities, so he is completely fluent in English and thoroughly adept at dealing with Westerners on their own terms. He is in fact one of a new and thoroughly modern generation of jet-setting *lamas* who are as conversant with the electronic gadgetry of the communications age as their forebears were with loose-leaved books printed from hand-cut woodblocks. He has given many appearances on the mass media and attended conferences on psychotherapy, healing, meditation, peace, and also death and dying, a subject in which he has lately specialized.

In recent times an ex-art student born in Farnham, Surrey in 1952, who has taken the name Ngakpa Chögyam Ögyen Pogden, has begun teaching as a shamanistic Tantric adept (*ngakpa*) of the ancient "white" lineage of Tibet. Certainly creative and endowed with infectious enthusiasm, Ngakpa Chögyam has also accurately homed in on a glaring deficiency in Western culture: the lack of spiritually authentic magical dimension; he no doubt aims to fill it.

Finally, Dzogchen. Though this exists as a teaching in the Nyingma school, it is propagated as an independent and self-contained teaching in the tradition of Adjom Drukpa (early twentieth century) by Namkhai Norbu Rinpoché, a married *lama* born in 1938 in the Dergé district of eastern Tibet. Norbu was brought to Europe in 1960 by Professor Tucci and worked for Tucci's IsMEO organization in Rome until becoming a professor in the Oriental Institute of Naples University in 1965. Lately he has guided the Dzogchen Community, an informal association of students scattered through various countries, including Italy, France, Austria, Britain, Denmark, Norway, and the U.S.A.

PURE LAND BUDDHISM

Dr. Suzuki is generally associated with the Zen School, so it is often a matter of surprise to hear that he translated many Pure Land Buddhist texts into English and nourished a belief that Pure Land rather than Zen might be the form of Buddhism most suitable for Westerners.

Pure Land Buddhism, which developed from the cult of Amitabha, represents a flowering of the devotional tendency that arose within the Mahayana in answer to the demand by lay people for a more substantial spiritual role than had been afforded them within the Hinayana schools. It was passed to China and thence to Japan, where during the thirteenth century it divided into two main branches: the Pure Land School (Jap. *Jodo Shu*) of Honen and the True Pure Land School (Jap. *Jodo Shin-shu*) of Shinran.

Both Jodo Shu and Jodo Shin-shu subscribe to the notion of *mappo:* that we are in a degenerate age when it is hopeless (and arrogant) to think that we can be saved by our own efforts alone. We must therefore surrender ourselves to the infinite mercy of Amitabha (or Amida) Buddha, whose "other power" (Jap. *tariki*) can achieve what we ourselves, alone and unaided, cannot hope to achieve. The salvation projected is rebirth in Amida's western paradise of *Sukhavati,* though this may also be discovered here, in the world, while still occupying a human body. Trevor Leggett has retold a forceful story of a great Zen master who one day met an old lady devoted to Pure Land walking along the road.

"On your way to the Pure Land then, Granny?" the Zen man quipped rather condescendingly.

The old lady nodded.

"Amida Buddha will be waiting for you, I suppose?"

The old lady shook her head vigorously.

"What—Amida Buddha not in his Pure Land? Where is he, then?" Gently the old lady tapped her heart twice, then continued on her way. The Zen Master was deeply impressed. "There's a real Pure Lander!" he said to himself.

The difference between the Jodo Shu and Jodo Shin-shu is more one of emphasis than of fundamentals. The central practice in both is the recitation of the *Nembutsu*—the *mantra* "Namu-Amidabutsu." However, what little faith in "self power" (Jap. *jiriki*) remained in Honen's thought was completely discarded in that of Shinran, who called for a more total surrender to Amida's mercy. Shinran also married and thereby set a strong non-monastic tradition which has remained to the present. Shinran's Jodo Shin-shu (often called simply Shin) has been most influential in the West.

There was very little Shin in Britain and the rest of Europe down to the Second World War, though an Englishman born Ernest Hunt in Hoddesden, Hertfordshire (incidentally the home for many years of the Buddhist Society Summer School), was ordained a Jodo Shin-shu priest in Hawaii in 1924. For many years Rev. Shinkaku Hunt (1876–1967) did energetic good work among the expatriate Japanese or *nisei,* many of them Pure Land followers, who form a sizeable community on the Hawaiian Isles. On a return visit to his native land in 1929, he was entertained at the Buddhist Lodge. "The Lodge welcomed back to England on a well-earned holiday one of its noted Buddhist sons," wrote Christmas Humphreys of the occasion. Hunt gravitated to the Soto Zen school towards the end of his life.

A pioneering figure in Britain since the Second World War has been Rev. Jack Austin (b. 1917), though his activities have been in no way limited to this school alone.* In 1976 he co-founded the Shin Buddhist Association in London under the patronage of Abbot Kosho Ohtani of Nishi (West) Hongwan-ji, one of the twinhead temples of Shin in Kyoto. With Abbot Ohtani's help, Rev. Austin went to Japan in 1977 and was ordained a Hongwan-ji priest. He also stayed at the Kobe home of his Shin teacher of some twenty-five years, Rev. Zuiken Saizo Inagaki, who arranged visits and meetings in various parts of Japan.

The son of Sensei Inagaki, Professor Hisao Inagaki, also a Shin priest, spent some time in London during the 1970s as a lecturer at the School of Oriental and African Studies. He was co-founder with Jack Austin of the Shin Buddhist Association. He also established a Pure Land Bud-

---

* For a full listing of his activities and achievements see entry in Who's Who section, Appendix I.

dhist Fellowship in his home in 1977, and this continues to the present as an informal, non-sectarian "network of communicants" that seeks to do without leaders, authorities, chairpersons, presidents, secretaries, constitutions, rules, and principles (apart from this one). Max Flisher, one of its members, has written:

> For us, our Buddha's enlightenment is sufficient for all. We are, I suppose, compassion-orientated and hope that our reliance on the Great Compassion is increasing our own and that the promise of the Pure Land (Nirvana) specified in the Primal Vow of Amita (*sic*) Buddha is being fulfilled in us. All the Buddhas continually say and praise his Name, which we hear as *Namoamitabuddha* (called *Nembutsu* in Japanese). We rely totally on that. The Buddha does everything, including helping us to rely on him. "Namoamitabuddha" is his voice teaching us the Dharma through our blood, heart, body, nervous system, and every fiber of our being. It is calling us to the Pure Land and acculturing us to it. We merely listen (overhear rather). Sometimes it bursts from us in joy and thanksgiving. Who needs an organization? Communication is the name of the game.*

Notable in Shin on the Continent is Adriaan Peel, who was initiated as Shaku Shitoku by Abbot Kosho Ohtani in London in 1977. More recently, a property was purchased in Antwerp and consecrated as the first Pure Land temple in Europe. "The opening was a splendid affair," Rev. Jack Austin reports. "The Chief Abbot conducted it, and all European Shin leaders were present."†

Thee is also a Jodo Shin group in Austria, which has its headquarters in Salzburg. This was set up by Friedrich Fenzl, who was converted to Jodo Shin-shu in 1960 through the influence of Harry Pieper (1902–1978), the original leader of the German Shin movement. In 1966, Pieper founded the first Pure Land Association in Europe (Buddhistische Gemeinschaft Jodo-Shin). His good work is currently carried on by Gerhard Kell (b. 1948). Rev. Jean Eracle and Rev. Jodo Chevrier, meanwhile, are Shin leaders in Switzerland.

NICHIREN SCHOOL

The success of some of the new Japanese Nichiren societies in Britain and other parts of Europe in recent years has been striking, and parallels

---

* Letter to the author dated January 24, 1987.
† Letter to the author dated November 12, 1986.

a similar success on the other side of the Atlantic. Their lay orientation, unascetic character, and simpler approach to practice tend to widen the base of their appeal.

Nichiren Shoshu is the Western wing of the Japanese Soka Gakkai organization, founded in 1930 by Tsunesaburo Makiguchi (1871–1944). It came to Europe in the 1970s where it is known as Soka Gakkai International. Its present U.K. headquarters are in Taplow Court, near Maidenhead, Berkshire, and the first chairman was Richard Causton (1920–1995), a former professional soldier and businessman who came across Soka Gakkai—an "electrifying experience"—while working for the Alfred Dunhill organization in Japan. The present chairman is Richard Baynes. Soka Gakkai International has taken on remarkably, noticeably among many younger people whom in the usual course would not be expected to be attracted to Buddhism, such as stars of show business. Part of its appeal may lie in the fact that it does not disparage this-worldly success. Newcomers are encouraged to chant for what they want in terms of money, material goods, job success, and the fulfillment of other personal desires. On the face of it, this looks a very un-Buddhist approach, more likely to strengthen than to diminish *trishna*. However, within the movement things are viewed differently. There, desire is recognized as having positive uses; in particular it can be used to demonstrate the power of spiritual practice, and this in itself can have a profoundly transformative effect.

Nichiren Shoshu practice breaks down into three parts:

1. *Faith* in the power of the Gohonzon, which is a scroll on which the *mantra,* "Namu-myoho-renge-kyo," is written in the form of a *mandala*. The original, or Dai Gohonzon, of which each member has a copy, was written by the thirteenth-century priest Nichiren Daishonin and is presently enshrined at the Nichiren Shoshu head temple, Taiseki-ji at the foot of Mount Fuji in Japan. (The temple, incidentally, is staffed by a priesthood, so the movement is not exclusively a lay one.)

2. *Study* of Buddhist teaching as restated by Nichiren and his successors within the movement, notably Daisaku Ikeda (b. 1928), the current President of Soka Gakkai International.

3. *Intensive practice* to perform Gongyo twice daily: i.e., chant "Namu-myoho-renge-kyo" in front of the Gohonzon and recite part of the second and the whole of the sixteenth chapter of the *Lotus Sutra*.

Discussion and guidance is also offered and members are now encouraged to share the teachings with others rather than to actively and vigorously proselytize or *shakubuku* non-members, as they once did.

The Reiyukai was founded in Japan in 1919 and registered in 1930 by Kakutaro Kubo (1892–1944) and Kimi Kotani (1901–1971). The current president is Dr. Tsugunari Kubo, the founder's son. A British branch was set up in 1976 by a Japanese educator named Hiromi Hasegawa (b. 1947), who had come to Norfolk some years before to study. Beginnings were modest. A small office was established in a semi-detached house in a Norwich backwater. By 1984, however, sufficient funds had been gathered to open the more ambitious Oriental Arts Center (current secretary, Julian Wilde). Another branch of the movement has also been set up in Liverpool, while in Europe there are centers in Italy, Spain, and France, where it has taken off very strongly thanks to the efforts of Mr. and Mrs. Shinuda.

Reiyukai practice is simple. A typical meeting begins with recitation of portions of the so-called Blue Sutra (the original copies were bound in blue), a compilation derived from the *Lotus Sutra*. Afterwards there may be a period of meditation or chanting "Namu-myoho-renge-kyo," then open discussion. Emphasis is laid on spiritual friendship and on followers positively opening themselves to each other. At one time a form of "ancestor remembrance" was practiced when in true Confucian style family and forebears were remembered, but lately it has declined

Battersea Peace Pagoda

in popularity. This is accepted, for, by the very tenets of Buddhism, all things must change.

Rissho Kosei-kai was founded in 1938 by Rev. Nikkyo Niwano and Mrs. M. Nakaguma. Its central practices include the Hoza (Circle of Compassion) and the Discipline of Veneration. At present there is only one small R.K.K. group in London organized by Jill Sullivan and not more than one or two more in the rest of Europe, though the world-wide membership is said to top five million.

Entirely different in character are the monks and nuns of the Nipponzan Myohoji order, who are strictly ascetic and celibate, and practice frequent ablution rites. Their founder, Ven. Nichidatsu Fujii (1885–1985), who was profoundly influenced by Mahatma Gandhi, saw the world being hustled recklessly towards total destruction by the "power of machines." The remedy he proposed was the ideal of *rissho-ankoku:* the establishment of true religion and the realization of peace on earth. From this developed the radical pacifism of the order. Its monks and nuns march for peace, speak out for peace, and have built beautiful peace pagodas in many parts of the world. There are two in Britain: one at Milton Keynes and another in Battersea Park on the banks of the Thames in London. Another is to be found in Austria, on the banks of the Danube. The central religious practice of Nippozan Myohoji is again the chanting of "Namu-myoho-renge-kyo" (the *Odaimoku*), to the accompaniment of the beating of a hand-drum. Ven. Fujii wrote: "Just chant *Odaimoku* loudly and beat your drum when you are fearful. Nothing is required. Depend on nothing else. Solely chant *Odaimoku* as long as you can, and die when you can chant no longer. That is all. That is all."*

THERAVADA

The remarkable rise of the Mahayana schools in Europe has not meant that the Theravada has been totally eclipsed by any means. It still remains a highly significant presence, and indeed, with the unexpected explosion of interest in Buddhism in the 1960s and after, very impressive new developments have taken place within this tradition too.

Basically one can detect two strands within the Theravada in the West: an ethnic strand and a native Western one. The former consists of activities, notably the founding of temples and centers by expatriate communities from traditional Theravada countries, mainly Sri Lankans, Thais, and Burmese but also more recently Indian Buddhist followers

* Ven. Nichidatsu Fujii, *Buddhism for World Peace,* trans. Yumiko Miyazaki (Los Angeles: Japan Buddha Sangha, 1982), 151.

of Dr. Ambedkar—the former so-called untouchables. The other strand meanwhile is centrally concerned with the foundation of a *sangha* of Western-born monks and nuns.

As we have noted, the British Mahabodhi Society was established by Anagarika Dharmapala in London as far back as 1926, and a Sri Lankan *vihara* materialized soon afterwards and ran until 1940. After the war, in 1948, a group was formed with the intention of founding a new *vihara* where *bhikkhus* might reside. The prominent English-educated Sri Lankan *bhikkhu* Ven. Narada Maha Thera (1898–1983), played an important role in this Buddhist Vihara Society in England, and he himself visited and lectured extensively in Britain in 1949. Eventually a group of wealthy Sri Lankans headed by Sir Cyril de Zoysa obtained the lease of a house in Ovington Gardens, Knightsbridge, and this was opened as the new London Buddhist Vihara with all due pomp and ceremony on Vesak Day, 1954. The Thai Ambassador unfurled the flag and speeches were delivered by Narada Thera himself, the ubiquitous Christmas Humphreys, Miss Grace Constant Lounsbery of Les Amis du Bouddhisme in Paris, and others.

Ven. Narada led the small group of *bhikkhus* resident at the Vihara until 1955. Then in 1957, Ven. Dr. Hammalawa Saddhatissa Thera (1914–1990) came to take over. He remained in London, off and on, till the end of his life. Dr. Saddhatissa was a distinguished scholar who held academic posts at the Universities of London and Toronto; he also lectured widely in Europe, the U.S.A. and Japan, as well as writing, editing, and translating numerous works. In 1964, the Vihara moved to new premises in a modest house in Heathfield Gardens, Chiswick, where it has remained ever since. Two years later Ven. Dr. Saddhatissa revived the British Maha Bodhi Society. The present head of the Vihara is Ven. Medagama Vajiragñana (b. 1928), a very practically minded *bhikkhu,* who previously established himself in London in 1967 and in 1974 became religious director of the British Buddhist Association, a group founded in the same year by A. Haviland-Nye (a professional silversmith), with the aim of:

1. Providing systematic instruction in the *dhamma,* primarily based on Pali sources

2. Promoting textual, canonical, and linguistic studies

3. Advising on matters relating to the *dhamma,* its practice, study, and literature

4. Maintaining close contact with individuals and groups in the West interested in promoting and supporting the foregoing aims

A Thai *vihara,* the Buddhapadipa Temple, backed with Thai government funding, was meanwhile opened in London in 1966 by the King and Queen of Thailand. The first incumbent was Phra Maha Vichit Tissadatto (b. 1934), who was later promoted to Chao Khun and renamed Sobhana Dhammasudhi. *"Chao khun"* is a title that roughly means "noble lord," and is conferred along with a new name when a *bhikkhu* is elevated to a status virtually equivalent to bishophood. Sobhana Dhammasudhi was young monk with a great deal of charm and flair, who soon gathered an entourage of enthusiastic Western followers. He caused a few eyebrows to raise, however, when around 1971 he left the robe. Afterwards he worked as a lay meditation master under the name Dhiravamsa, establishing a center, Chapter House, at Wisbech in Cambridgeshire. Later he crossed the Atlantic and began to experiment with combining traditional *samatha-vipassana* meditation with modern Western psychotherapeutic techniques. For instance, a certain amount of expression might be permissible within the structure of formal silent sitting practice in the interests of releasing repressed emotional energies. Latest information is that he has reverted to more traditional approaches.

In 1975, the Buddhapadipa Temple moved to the more spacious environs of Barrogill House, Calonne Road, Wimbledon Parkside. In the four-acre grounds, a beautiful gilded Uposatha Hall* has recently been built in traditional Thai architectural style, with shining white walls, pillars, and balustrades, steeply pitched roof of red tile, and intricately carved eaves and doorways. Inside, the walls have been decorated with vibrantly colorful murals, the work of gifted Thai artists, depicting traditional scenes from the life of the Buddha, and from Buddhist mythology. The Hall was opened in 1987.

The Buddhapadipa Temple is occupied by five missionary (*dhammaduta*) monks, who are assisted in running the place by various lay groups. The monks, who come under the authority of a senior incumbent, are selected and sent over by the Sangha Supreme Council of Thailand. It offers a very comprehensive program of activities, including Pali and Abhidhamma classes, meditation, and all the traditional reciprocal activities involving *sangha* and laity.

The expatriate Burmese community in Britain did not open a *vihara* until 1978. This enjoys the dual title of West Midlands Buddhist Center/ Birmingham Buddhist Vihara. For the first four years of its existence it shared a house with the local Karma Kagyu group and was honored

---

* An Uposatha Hall is where monks and nuns assemble on full moon days to listen to the reading of the Disciplinary Code.

by the patronage of the late Gyalwa Karmapa, who appointed Dr. U Rewata Dhamma (b. 1929) as spiritual director. Now the Theravada *vihara* has its own premises. Dr. Rewata Dhamma, who first came to Britain in 1975, is a remarkable Burmese *bhikkhu* who has not only developed the scholarly side of his vocation but has also trained in *vipassana* meditation with S. N. Goenka and been appointed a teacher by no less a luminary than Mahasi Sayadaw. At present he has one resident British *bhikkhu,* and together they operate the *vihara* on the lines of a small town temple in Burma, giving Abhidhamma classes, meditation instruction, and retreats, celebrating the feast days, and giving those short-term ordinations that are traditional in the East. These are also given at the Buddhapadipa Temple. More recently, in 1984, a Burmese temple was opened in north London, near Wembley Stadium. The *sayadaw* here is U Nyanika, an Abhidhamma scholar, and he presently has three *bhikkhus* with him, one of them of British birth.

British Buddhist connections with Burma, now Myanmar, go back a long way, however, due to the old imperial link. Many British *bhikkhus,* from the time of the very first, Ananada Metteyya, have gone to Burma for training, though present visa restrictions make this no longer feasible. Burmese *bhikkhus* have also come to Britain from time to time, some of them, like Mahasi Sayadaw (1904–1982) on brief visits, others, like Sayadaw U Thittila (1896–1997), for longer stays. During the Second World War, U Thittila worked as a stretcher-bearer in London during the Blitz; he also lectured widely both then and later, notably on Abhidhamma, and for a while was librarian at the Buddhist Society. In 1952, he returned to Burma to take up the post of Professor of Pali at Rangoon University, though he has returned several times since. Nor should the good work of U Myat Saw (1918–1984) be overlooked. A successful businessman, he came to Britain in 1965, and in 1971 established a Buddhist Center at "Oaken Holt," a large house just outside Oxford, where meditation courses and retreats were held until his death.

British-born Buddhists continued to go East for training and ordination after the Second World War—indeed, the trauma of the War encouraged many to do so. Osbert Moore (1905–1960), for instance, discovered a copy of Julius Evola's *The Doctrine of Awakening* while serving in the Army in wartime Italy. In 1949 he went to Sri Lanka and was ordained the following year as Ñyanamoli Bhikkhu. Thereafter, until his premature death, he did important translation work. Lawrence Mills (b. 1932) also discovered Buddhism through books while with the Army in the Suez Canal Zone after the war. He later received novice ordination in Britain from Ven. Dr. Saddhatissa before going to the East. He was ordained Phra Khantipalo and lived for some eleven years in Thailand before departing for Australia, where he taught for a while at Wat Buddha-Dhamma in rural New South Wales. He later disrobed and married and is currently trying to set up a Buddhist community in a former hippie area in New South Wales.

But the great saga at the heart of all Theravada activity in Britain and Europe since the Second World War has been the ongoing endeavor to establish a native Western *sangha*. This holds great symbolic significance for all those Western Buddhists who would like the satisfaction of knowing that Buddhism has taken firm root on their native ground. The key lies in words spoken during the first Buddhist missionary efforts on the island of Sri Lanka. The convert King Devanampiyatissa was also eager to be assured that the Buddha's Way had taken root in Sri Lankan soil; when he asked Ven. Mahinda for confirmation of this, he was told:

> Only when a *Sima* (consecrated space for ordinations, etc.) has been built and when a son, born in Sri Lanka of Sri Lankan parents studies the Vinaya in Sri Lanka and recites them in Sri Lanka—only then will it be true to say that the Buddha's Way has taken root here.

The man who carried on the torch first lit by Ananda Metteyya into the post-war era was William Purfurst (1906–1971), a small, intense man of many talents. In the war, during the Blitz on London, his duties as a fireman put him in contact with Sayadaw U Thittila, whose pupil he became and with whom he continued his Buddhist studies into the post-war era. His dedication deepened, and eventually he was given permission by his wife to ordain. He became first an *anagarika* and then a *samanera* (novice). He worked vigorously for Buddhism, setting up provincial groups, lecturing, writing, and even establishing the Buddhist Summer School, which survives to the present day under the auspices of the Buddhist Society, for which he also worked. Full ordination was the next obvious step. He therefore took a job as a barman at a hotel in Surrey to obtain the finances to travel to Thailand, where in 1954, at a ceremony at Wat Paknam in Thonburi, he received novice ordination as Kapilavaddho, the Pali name being based on that of the Buddha's home town of Kapilavatthu signifying, appropriately, "he who spreads the *dhamma*." Full *bhikkhu* ordination followed a month later at Vesak.

Having applied himself to an intensive course of *vipassana* meditation, Kapilavaddho returned to London later in the same year with full authority to teach Buddhist subjects. Taking up residence at the Sri Lankan Vihara in Chiswick, he threw himself into the self-appointed task of founding an English branch of the Bhikkhu *sangha*. To this end he established the English Sangha Trust; then, late in 1955, he returned to

Thailand with three recently ordained novice *bhikkhus:* Robert Albison, George Blake, and Peter Morgan (an Englishman, a West Indian, and a Welshman, respectively). They were fully ordained early in 1956 and returned to London as a seminal English *sangha,* taking up residence at 50 Alexandra Road, St. John's Wood.

But the enormous workload that Kapilavaddho had carried in recent years, and continued to carry with unabated vigor, now began to take its toll. Finally in 1957 his health broke down and he was obliged to disrobe and return to lay life. Happily, the grim prognosis his doctor had given that he had only a month to live was not realized, though as far as the Buddhist world was concerned it might have been. Changing his name to Richard Randall for the sake of anonymity, he remarried and for more than ten years dropped out of sight. Those ten years were a lean period for the English *sangha,* for two of the other three *bhikkhus* also left the robe, leaving Ven. Paññavaddho to struggle on for long periods alone. Eventually Ven. Paññavaddho left for Thailand, where he has remained ever since as a disciple of Ajahn Maha Boowa, apart from a brief visit to England in 1974.

In 1962 new premises were obtained at 131 Haverstock Hill in Hampstead; also a meditation center at Biddulph in Staffordshire. These were ably run for two years by the Canadian-born *bhikkhu,* Ananda Bodhi (Leslie Dawson). In 1967, after ten years in the wilderness, Ven. Kapilavaddho returned to the robe and took over the new *vihara.* As Maurice Walshe, then Chairman of the English Sangha Trust, has written:

> Soon the Hampstead Vihara was bursting with activity. The *bhikkhu,* with seemingly his old energy restored, was at work. Meditation cells were built at the back, classes were re-established, plans for a *Sangha* were again formulated. Some young men came forward and received their lower ordination, among them Alan James, who was ordained as Dipadhammo Bhikkhu. Once again, all seemed set fair for the establishing of an English branch of the ancient order of *bhikkhus.**

However, setbacks struck yet again. Alan James returned to lay life and soon after Ven. Kapilavaddho followed suit. He married for a third time, but less than three months later his health gave way completely, and in 1971, he succumbed to a combination of maladies. Meanwhile, with no *bhikkhus* resident, the house in Hampstead could no longer be called a *vihara,* just a Buddhist center in search of a *sangha.*

**Sangha vol. 3, no. 5 (1972): 1ff.

In 1974, Ajahn Maha Boowa visited Hampstead. Shortly afterwards, an American-born *bhikkhu*, Ven. Sumedho, stopped over briefly on his way back from the United States to Thailand, where for some ten years he had been a disciple of Ajahn Cha, a meditation master of the northeast Thai Forest Tradition who had attracted a number of Western disciples. As a result of this meeting, the chairman of the English Sangha Trust, George Sharp, flew to Thailand to meet with Ajahn Cha, an auspicious event, for in 1977 Ajahn Cha came to Hampstead with several of his Western disciples, including Ven. Sumedho and the English-born Ven. Khemadhammo. Ajahn Cha later returned to Thailand but Ven. Sumedho and his fellow Western *bhikkhus* stayed on at the *vihara*.

This turned out to be a highly fortunate turn of events. Ajahn Sumedho, as he has become, has proved himself possessed of leadership qualities of an exceptionally high order, with spiritual qualities to match. He also has the ability to put the *dhamma* across to Westerners in their own terms, and with humor, lightness, and lucidity. He has attracted a vast following of lay disciples, and many have been inspired by his noble teaching to join the *sangha* as monks or nuns.

An important development was the gift of a one-hundred-and-eight-acre tract of woodland in rural West Sussex, Hammer Wood, which has its own lake—a perfect environment for a forest *sangha*. The old Hampstead Vihara was therefore sold, and a large derelict mansion, Chithurst House, situated just a stone's throw away from Hammer Wood, was purchased in 1979 and renovated. Later a nearby cottage was purchased to house the growing community of nuns. In 1981, both houses and forest were officially designated for monastic use, and in the same year a *sima* or "specially defined area in which acts of the Bhikkhu Sangha may take place" was established with the guidance of Ven. Ananda Maitreya. In July that year three *anagarikas* received *bhikkhu* ordination within the new *sima,* thus broadly fulfilling the terms that Ven. Mahinda stipulated to King Devanampiyatissa.

The growth and spread of this new *sangha* has been remarkable. In 1981 a branch monastery, Harnham Vihara, was opened up in the north of England, in 1983 a Devon Vihara was opened in the West County, and in 1997 became the first ever community of western Theravadan nuns. Iin 1984 a vast complex near Hemel Hempstead in Hertfordshire that had once served as a residential school for handicapped children was acquired and opened in 1985 as Amaravati: The Deathless. Thus an English *sangha*—or more accurately an International Western *sangha*—has now been firmly established on British soil, and is sending out tendrils into Europe, America,the Antipodes, and other parts of the English-speaking world. In 1985, two *bhikkhus* were sent to establish a branch monastery in New Zealand, and another is soon to be established in Berne, Switzerland. Ven. Khemadhammo has meanwhile established separate *vihara,* firstly on the Isle of Wight and more recently near Warwick in the Midlands. He has also been very energetic in developing a Buddhist Prison Chaplaincy Service (Angulimala).

A number of people who have received formal Theravada training, sometimes as ordained *sangha* members but not necessarily so, have gone on to establish themselves as lay meditation teachers. Jack Kornfield, once one of Ajahn Cha's *bhikkhus,* is a notable American example. His colleague at the Insight Meditation Society at Barre in Massachusetts, Joseph Goldstein, meanwhile, trained with Anagarika Munindra in Bodh Gaya. In Britain, on the other hand, there are Christopher Titmuss and Christina Feldman, who were two of the founders of Gaia House, a retreat center in South Devon that offers a very full program of events that includes regular *vipassana* retreats. These are occasionally led by Anagarika Vimalo Kulbarz, who was ordained at the old Thai Embassy in London with his twin brother, and later spent many years in Thailand before finally giving up the robe.

Vimalo also taught at and later became a member of the Sharpham North Community, which is situated not far from Gaia House in South Devon. This was an experimental community of non-sectarian meditators, who were concerned to develop a lifestyle in which religious practice is properly integrated, but without the encumbrance of all the usual monastic and institutional trappings. The community wound down in 1996, but the premises are now used for the Sharpham College of Buddhist Studies and Contemporary Enquiry.

Alan James, who was Ven. Kapilavaddho's right hand man for a time at Hampstead, married his teacher's widow, Jacqui (1946–1989), and together they established the House of Inner Tranquility at Bradford-on-Avon in Wiltshire, where lectures, classes, and courses in *vipassana* take place. Other centers have been set up where the intensive meditation methods developed by Sayagyi U Ba Khin and S. N. Goenka are taught.

WESTERN BUDDHISM

From the early days of the Buddhist movement there was talk of the development of a distinctly Western form of Buddhism. The arguments are by now classic. The core of Buddhism is timeless and universal, they run, but around this, all manner of secondary accretions have built up:

230 THE BUDDHIST HANDBOOK

the incidental trappings inherited from the various cultures in which Buddhism has developed. These are not only inessential but often distracting or confusing and so prevent Buddhism from becoming readily assimilated in modern Western contexts. What needs to be done, therefore, is to strip away the inessential and reconcile the essential with modern Western culture: the prevailing religious, artistic, and intellectual traditions, modern science, and psychology—and so forth.

More than half a century ago now, Captain J. E. Ellam, the Hon. Secretary of the original Buddhist Society of Great Britain and Ireland, coined the term *Navayana*—"New *yana* (or vehicle)"—and wrote a book on the subject. Later, in 1951, a Western Buddhist Order was set up in the United States by Ven. Sumangalo (Robert Clifton, 1903–1963). This was "an organization dedicated to interpreting the Dharma to the West and establishing groups where none existed." It was represented in this country by Rev. Jack Austin. More recently, we have seen the emergence in Britain of a Scientific Buddhist Association (founded by Gerald du Pré and Paul Ingram), and also of a movement calling itself the Friends of the Western Buddhist Order (F.W.B.O.)—or simply, the Western Buddhist Order (W.B.O.).

The inspiration behind the F.W.B.O. is Ven. Maha Sthavira Sangharakshita (D. P. E. Lingwood, b. 1925). Having discovered his natural affinities with Buddhism, Sangharakshita joined the Buddhist Society at the age of eighteen. During the Second World War, he saw service in the East and afterwards remained out there, living the homeless life. He took *samanera* ordination in 1949 and *bhikkhu* ordination the following year. He studied Abhidhamma, Pali, and Logic at Benares (Varanasi) University with Ven. Jagdish Kashyap, and later settled in the well-known hill station of Kalimpong, where he set up the Triyana Vardhana Vihara ("Monastery of the Three Vehicles"), a title which indicates his interest in *all* schools of Buddhism. When the *lamas* began to leave Tibet in the 1950s, many passed through Kalimpong and this allowed Sangharakshita to meet and study with several, notably Jamyang Khyentse Rinpoché and Dhardo Rinpoché. The latter gave him Mahayana ordination. During this period he put his considerable scholarly and literary skills to good use, writing *A Survey of Buddhism*—many other books followed—and either contributing to or editing a number of journals. He also became active in Dr. B. R. Ambedkar's movement and is said to have officiated at a mass conversion of some five hundred thousand so-called untouchables (*harijans*).

In 1964, Sangharakshita returned to Britain and took up residence at the old Hampstead Buddhist Vihara. For a time his impressive learning made him the idol of the British Buddhist scene, and he in his turn was apparently impressed that "there was great potential for the Dharma in the West." But problems arose and there was a parting of the ways. In 1967 he founded his own organization, the F.W.B.O. Its first meetings were held in a small room beneath a shop selling Orientalia in central London. Soon, however, the order blossomed and obtained its own premises; then as its numbers grew it was able to branch out in many directions. It now has many city centers scattered across Britain as well as abroad, each offering a full program of classes and meditation sessions. Many of these centers are supported by Right Livelihood Co-operatives based on, for example, whole food shops, vegetarian restaurants, building teams, and gardening businesses. There are also retreat and arts centers, and many of the members (though not all) live in single-sex communities with other members. Books and magazines are published, and a charity, Aid to India, has been set up to support medical, educational, and Buddhist missionary work among the untouchables.

What characterizes the brand of "Western Buddhism" propagated by the F.W.B.O.? In the first place, it disfavors the monastic orientation of traditional Eastern Buddhism, but recognizes the advantages to be derived from close association with spiritual friends within the matrix of community. The term *sangha* has a special use within the F.W.B.O.: it does not merely denote the monastic segment of the Buddhist community but the whole community. Those who live and work together within the order are encouraged to develop "positive and direct communication"* with each other, and to generally strive to coexist in an "ethical, harmonious and altruistic way." Begging as a means of livelihood is regarded as not viable within a Western cultural context, hence the development of Right Livelihood Co-operatives. In terms of study and practice, the approach is essentially eclectic: Pali texts, Mahayana *sutras,* and Tibetan works are all studied, but intellectual activity is always balanced with meditation, devotional *puja,* and often some kind of physical discipline like T'ai Chi or karate. In terms of practice, each individual is encouraged to search for those particular techniques that work in their individual case and then commit themselves to them: a matter of "more and more of less and less":

> All newcomers are taught Mindfulness of Breathing and the Metta Bhavana (Development of Living Kindness) meditation practices, and anyone at all seriously involved practices meditation at least once a day. Order Members at their ordination receive a visualization practice and often take up other insight practices as well.

* Dhammadinna, "F.W.B.O. for the Middle Way," *The Middle Way* vol. 59, no. 4(Feb. 1985): 225ff.

Devotional practices are also regularly performed, especially a Sevenfold Puja derived from Shantideva's *Bodhicaryavatara*. Sangharakshita has said on occasions that many Western Buddhists probably *know* all that they need to know intellectually in order to gain enlightenment. The next step is regular practice of Metta and of Puja so that people can engage their emotions fully in their spiritual lives and create the positive emotional basis necessary for the transformation of Right Views into Perfect Vision.*

F.W.B.O. writings talk much about *commitment*. Indeed, one of their strongest criticisms of most other Western lay Buddhist societies is what they regard as their lack of serious commitment to practice of the *dharma*. Dharmachari Subhuti, a vigorous F.W.B.O. theoretician and organizer, claims in one of his books that these societies "cater for little more than a mild and amateurish interest and . . . their organization is often fraught with intrigue."†

Membership in the F.W.B.O. therefore involves an ever-deepening process of commitment to the order and to Buddhist practice. Those who merely gravitate to the order and frequent its centers informally are known as "friends." Later they may apply to be ordained as *mitras,* and later still as order members. The last stage is preceded by a period of intensive training, at the end of which the readiness of the various candidates for ordination will be judged. If they make the grade, they undergo an ordination ceremony based on the traditional *upasaka* or lay follower ordination, though within the order the old monk-layman dichotomy has been abolished. The ceremony itself centers around the act of Going for Refuge to the Three Jewels of Buddha, *dharma,* and *sangha;* a new name is also given. Finally, if at any stage an order member feels that his spiritual development would benefit from a spell of voluntary celibacy, he may take *anagarika* ordination.

While there is much that is entirely laudable in the F.W.B.O.'s work, and it has certainly been very successful in terms of attracting followers and establishing centers, neither the more conventional lay societies nor the monastic based groups imported from the East have turned out to be as moribund as Dharmachari Subhuti has intimated. Many if not most have done very useful work, not least in encouraging serious practice; so it is as yet unclear what the future shape of "Western Buddhism" will be: whether that prefigured by the F.W.B.O. or something else. Certainly

---

* *Ibid.,* 227.

† Dharmachari Subhuti, *Buddhism for Today* (Salisbury: Element Books, 1983), 25.

the process of westernization will take time—after all, Buddhism took centuries to become fully sinicized in China—and in all probability the process will very largely take care of itself. There are after all distinct dangers in trying to force the pace: in trying to adapt and modify too fast, and on the basis of insufficient knowledge and understanding. The proverbial baby may be thrown out with the bathwater.

Many years ago, when as now these matters were being hotly debated, one wise pundit remarked, "Perhaps before we begin changing Buddhism to suit ourselves we should know what Buddhism really is," and the logical corollary was to study the religion in its traditional Eastern Forms.

CONCLUSION

The Buddhist Society has continued to the present discharging its traditional function as a kind of shop-window in which all forms of Buddhism are, without partiality, displayed for the newcomer. Of course the balance has faltered on occasion, and in 1983 it received a grave set-back when its founder-president, Christmas Humphreys, passed away. For a time, with that towering personality gone, it inevitably drifted for want of definite leadership and direction, but now that its new president, Ajahn Sumedho, has more time at his disposal, there is every hope that a new and positive phase in its history will begin. It continues to offer a full program of lectures and classes; it publishes a journal, *The Middle Way*, runs a Correspondence course and holds a two-week summer school every year. The general week of the summer school provides an excellent opportunity for the newcomer to come in contact with most if not all of the different schools of Buddhism.

Besides the important centers that we have described here and the ones in the major cities, small local centers are springing up in smaller towns and villages right across Britain and the rest of Europe. Specialized Buddhist groups are also beginning to emerge: ones concerned with issues like peace, social action, and animal rights. The issue of women in Buddhism is a frequent talking point too, not least because women are accorded a distinctly secondary place in traditional Eastern Buddhism, and, in addition, the order of nuns has very largely died out, thus denying to half the Buddhist population the advantages inherent in higher ordination. At the same time, Buddhist studies are also beginning to be offered as part of university courses, and the volume of Buddhist books currently being produced in the West, both original works, translations, and editions, has reached the proportions of a major industry.

Surveying all this, it would certainly seem that Christmas Humphreys' optimistic view that Buddhism's time has come has been amply borne out.

T·W·E·N·T·Y

The North American Connection

Like Janus, the Roman god of new beginnings, the North American continent has two faces. One looks towards Europe, the other directly across the Pacific to the Orient itself: to China, Japan, and Korea— three great grounds of Buddhist development.

Some of the same forces that brought Buddhism to Europe, such as trading connections with the Orient, washed Buddhist ideas to the eastern seaboard of the United States during the latter part of the nineteenth century. They were picked up and relayed to a wider audience (though in transmuted form) by a genteel group of New England philosophers called the Transcendentalists, who combined a Taoist-like distaste for the artificialities of the social world with a preference for the uncorrupted world of nature. One of them, H. D. Thoreau (1817–1962), went to live for a time in a lonely cabin in the Massachusetts woods, and out of this experience came his classic work, *Walden*. A simple life with few possessions, a patch of rough ground on which to grow vegetables, trees to chop for wood, and the time and space for quiet reflection, seemed infinitely preferable to the vexed go-getting of the conventional world. Unknown to many, there was a deep strand of Buddhism in all this, for Thoreau drank deeply at the well of Eastern mysticism and, among other things, translated Eugène Burnouf's French version of the *Lotus Sutra* into English.

On the West Coast, meanwhile, Chinese workers were soon arriving in thousands to supply the demand for cheap labor triggered by the great California Gold Rush, the construction of the Union Pacific railroad, and other developments. Chinatowns sprang up in many rapidly growing American cities, and they all had temples in which Confucianism, Taoism, and Buddhism were accommodated in the traditional non-exclusive Chinese way. The Buddhist inclinations of these early Chinese immigrants tended mostly towards Pure Land, though elements of Ch'an were included too. A little later Japanese workers came to labor on contract in the fruit plantations of the Hawaiian islands, which had lately been annexed by the United States, and, before long, they too began to spill over onto the mainland. The Buddhists among them were also, in the main, devotees of Amitabha and the Pure Land. Both the Chinese and Japanese immigrants stayed, and the ethnic Pure Land tradition that they founded over a century ago has flourished in North America ever since. Today it includes various component groupings, notably a substantial Japanese Jodo Shinshu "church"—currently called Buddhist Churches of America and Buddhist Churches of Canada—which was founded in 1899. Hawaii, moreover, now has a Buddhist majority and is recognized as a Buddhist state of the union.

The crucial catalyst to the advance and acceptance of Buddhism in North America came in 1893. That year the great Columbian Exposition took place in Chicago to celebrate America's material achievement. Some of the organizers thought that the spiritual side of things should be represented too, so a World Parliament of Religions was also summoned. The Buddhists who attended this included the Sri Lankan Anagarika Dharmapala and, more significantly, the Rinzai Zen master Soyen Shaku (1859–1919), who had trained with Imagita Kosen Roshi (1816–1892) at the famous Engaku-ji temple in Kamakura and, on Kosen Roshi's death, succeeded to the abbacy there.

At the Parliament, Soyen Shaku made a fortuitous connection with Paul Carus, who ran a religious publishing house called the Open Court Publishing Company in the Illinois zinc town of LaSalle. Carus needed someone to help translate texts, and it so happened that Soyen Shaku had a young student, D. T. Suzuki (1870–1966), who possessed some knowledge of English. Arrangements were subsequently made for Suzuki to go to LaSalle, but before he caught the boat, on his very last *sesshin* at Engaku-ji, he galvanized himself to the full and managed to "break through," so among his "hidden imports" to the U.S.A. was a degree of authenticated Zen insight. Suzuki spent some eleven years over here on his first visit, but later, in the 1950s, advanced in years and equally advanced in wisdom, a new phase began when he undertook a strenuous series of teaching engagements at Columbia University and elsewhere.

Down to the great Tibetan diaspora of the post-1959 era, Japanese Zen was undoubtedly the tradition of Buddhism most strongly represented in North America, thanks in no small measure to D. T. Suzuki's pioneering efforts. Two other Japanese Rinzai teachers also made substantial contributions, both vowing to "bury their bones" in the soil of America. These were Nyogen Senzaki Sensei (1876–1958) and Sokei-an Sasaki (1882–1945).

Senzaki came to the U.S.A. around 1905 to join his teacher, Soyen Shaku, at the home of Mr. and Mrs. Alexander Russell in San Francisco, but something went wrong and he had to leave the house. As he parted from his teacher in Golden Gate Park, Soyen Shaku laid the stern injunction upon him that he should work with Americans and not "utter the B of Buddhism" for seventeen years. Senzaki scrupulously obeyed this injunction, but when the stipulated time was up he promptly started his "floating zendo" on the West Coast. Among his students were Robert Aitken Roshi (b. 1917), who currently guides the Diamond Sangha in Hawaii, and the well-known poet Gary Snyder, who appears in Jack Kerouac's novel, *The Dharma Bums,* as the freewheeling "Zen lunatic" Japhy Ryder. Both Aitken and Snyder are nowadays involved in the Ring of Bone Zendo (named after the title of Lew Welch's collected poems), in the foothills of the Sierra Nevada mountains. Senzaki was also responsible for bringing the innovative Japanese master and poet, Nakagawa Soen Roshi (1907–1984), across the Pacific. Soen Roshi's *dharma heir,* Eido Tai Shimano Roshi (b. 1932), currently teaches at the Zen Studies Society's International Dai Bosatsu Zendo Kongo-ji in the Catskill mountains of New York.

Sokei-an Sasaki (1882–1945), who originally trained in the noble art of carving dragons, was also a pupil of Soyen Shaku. Coming to the U.S.A. in 1931, he worked later on the East Coast, establishing the First Zen Institute in New York City in 1931. In 1944, he married Ruth Fuller Everett (d. 1967), and she carried on his work after his death a year later. While staying in England, Eleanor Everett, Ruth's daughter by a first marriage to a Chicago attorney, met and married Alan Watts (1915–1973), and it was this connection that brought Watts to the U.S.A. in 1938, where he made a great name for himself as a writer and speaker on Zen.

The Zen lunatics of *The Dharma Bums* also met Alan Watts, thinly disguised in the novel as the urbane Arthur Whane. Watts in fact put a name to the brand of Zen that became fashionable on the West Coast in the 1950s: "Beat Zen," he called it, to emphasize a contrast with the "Square Zen" of Japanese temples (for whose formal disciplines he never had much liking), and there was much about it that appealed to the bohemian strand in his own makeup. He went on to play an influential role in the California counter-culture of the 1960s, when Buddhism, along with such strange bedfellows as LSD, pacifism, and rock music, became one of the fads of the moment. Watts had been diligently writing on the *dharma* as well as Taoism and other aspects of Eastern culture for years without causing much stir, but now he found himself in hot demand as a writer and speaker on Zen and allied matters. It was like switching on the light and having the roof fall in, he later remarked.

Of course, as in Europe, much of both Beat Zen and counter-culture Buddhism was superficial or downright spurious, but in time the phoneys and sensation-seekers drifted away, and a few former beats and hippies, like Gary Snyder, who trained in Kyoto under Sesso Oda Roshi, and Allen Ginsberg, who later trained with Chögyam Trungpa, actually began to submit to the demanding requirements of serious study and practice.

Today Zen is still very strongly represented in the U.S.A. and mainly in its now almost traditional West Coast habitat, where there are several large groupings. The San Francisco Zen Center owes its existence to a very remarkable Soto master, Shunryu Suzuki (1904–1971), author of the classic *Zen Mind, Beginner's Mind*. It was under S.F.Z.C.'s auspices that the Zen Mountain Center at Tassajara Springs, the first Zen monastery in the U.S.A. with facilities for long-term practice, was set up. After his death, Suzuki Roshi's work was carried on by his *dharma heir,* Richard Baker, until Baker fell from grace in one of the series of crises that shook American Zen centers in the early 1980s. Tenshin Reb Anderson is currently abbot of S.F.Z.C. The crises of the early 1980s also touched the Zen Center of Los Angeles, founded in 1967 by Taizen Maezumi Roshi (b. 1931), a pupil of Hakujun Kuroda Roshi and Hakuun Yasutani Roshi. Maezumi Roshi, whose lineage incorporates both the Rinzai and Soto transmissions, has two *dharma heirs:* Dennis Genpo Merzel Sensei (b. 1944), who has worked extensively in Europe (including Poland); Bernard Tetsugen Glassman Sensei (b. 1939), who is based in New York. Also active on the West Coast are Jiyu Kennett Roshi (b. 1924), whose Soto-aligned Order of Buddhist Contemplatives has its headquarters at Shasta Abbey, and Kyozan Joshu Sasaki Roshi (b. 1907), who has been in the U.S.A. for nearly thirty years and now heads various centers, including the Cimarron Zen Center in Los Angeles and the Jemez Bodhi Mandala in New Mexico.

Philip Kapleau Roshi (b. 1912) first went to Japan as a court reporter after the Second World War. He went back in the 1950s to train in various Rinzai and Soto monasteries, subsequently returning to the U.S.A. to teach. He was based in Rochester, New York, until his recent retirement. Toni Packer, one of Kapleau Roshi's best-known alumni, maintaining that any religious identity, including a Zen one, fosters attachment, has inaugurated a more open, non-sectarian teaching and practice initiative. More traditionally oriented was Dainin Katagiri Roshi (1928–1990), who came to the U.S.A. in 1963 and worked for a time on the West Coast but later based himself near Minneapolis, where he was spiritual head of Catching the Moon Zen Mountain Center.

The Chinese Ch'an tradition is currently represented on the West Coast by Dhyana Master Hsüan Hua (b. 1908), chairman of the Sino-American Buddhist Association and founder of Gold Mountain Dhyana Monastery and City of Ten Thousand Buddhas. Master Hua, a pupil of Master Hsu Yün, has a reputation for dispensing tough practice. Some of his students are said to sleep in the lotus position; others have gone on arduous pilgrimages, bowing at every third step. Over on the East Coast, meanwhile, Ven. Dr. Sheng Yen Chang, abbot of two monasteries in Taiwan, has opened a branch of his Chung Hwa Institute of Buddhist Studies in New York.

The pioneer of Korean Son in North America is Soen Sa Nim (or Seung Sahn Sunim, b. 1927), who came to the U.S.A. in 1972 and set up in Providence, Rhode Island. He now heads the Kwan Um Zen School, which comes under the banner of the Chogye Order. Another teacher, Samu Sunim (b. 1941), came to the U.S.A. in 1967, but later his Zen Lotus Society has been based in Toronto, Canada. Son is more earthy as well as less formal and martial than Japanese Zen. It has also, unlike most other traditions, preserved its order of nuns, and generally accords the sexes more equality of status. Its practice incorporates three main elements: chanting, study of the Zen records and the Mahayana *sutras,* and sitting meditation, when practitioners may work on a single *hwadu (koan).*

As for Tibetan Buddhism, the Gelugpas were uncharacteristically the first in the field in North America. In 1951, the far-wandering Kalmyks were allowed to settle in Freewood Acres, New Jersey, and the following year they opened the First Kalmyk Buddhist Temple in a remodelled garage. The equally far-wandering Geshé Wangyal (1901–

1983) came to minister to them in 1955, and other *lamas* followed, notably Geshé Sopa (b. 1923), who in 1967 was invited by Professor Richard Robinson, a great promoter of Mahayana studies, to join the Buddhist Studies Program at the University of Wisconsin. Geshé Sopa requested H. H. the Dalai Lama, who was at last granted a visa to visit the U.S.A. in 1979, to give a Kalachakra Initiation at his Wisconsin center, the Deer Park; twelve thousand people are said to have attended the event in 1981.

But as in Britain, the great star of the Tibetan transmission was the prodigal and prodigally gifted Kagyu-Nyingma *tulku* Chögyam Trungpa Rinpoché (1939–1987). Leaving Britain for the U.S.A. around 1970, trailing clouds of controversy behind him, he established important centers in Vermont and Colorado, and a monastic center in Nova Scotia. He also set up the international Vajradhatu organization with headquarters in Boulder. After his untimely death, Trungpa's mantle was assumed by his Vajra Regent, Ösel Tendzin (1945–1990), born Thomas Rich in Passaic, New Jersey, who certainly followed his master's footsteps in respect to controversy. In 1989, a major crisis struck the Vajradhatu community when it was revealed in the national press that Tendzin had contracted the AIDS virus, but, naïvely believing himself to be protected by "some extraordinary means," had failed to modify his lifestyle. The situation was not without its tragic consequences, both for Ösel Tendzin himself, who died in 1990, and for some of his students and their partners. It also again raised thorny questions about the behavior of teachers.

If Trungpa represented Beat Karma Kagyu Vajrayana (to adapt Alan Watts' classic dichotomy), a Square variety that is traditional, stable, and restrained—though necessarily less colorful and adventurous—has also been brought to North America by *lamas* like the impeccable Kalu Rinpoché (1905–89), a great modern *yogi* often compared with Milarepa. He too gave Kalachakra Initiations at large open gatherings, as well as establishing the tradition of three-year meditation retreats in the West. These produced the first crop of Western *lamas*, who in the early 1980s began running their own centers. H. H. the late Karmapa also came to see the American centers falling under the aegis of his tradition. He made three visits, the first in 1974. He came for a fourth time to receive medical attention for cancer. This revered patriarch, a native of the sequestered heights of the Tibetan plateau, quit this life in the completely contrasting milieu of a Zion, Illinois, hospital in 1981.

The Nyingma torch was borne to the U.S.A. by Tarthang Tulku

(b. 1935), a disciple of the great Ri-mé Master Jamyang Khyentse Chökyi Lodrö (1896–1959), who arrived on the West Coast in 1969 and set up the Tibetan Nyingma Institute in Berkeley, California. Dodrupchen Rinpoché (b. 1927) and Sonam Kazi, a Sikkimese layman, are two other teachers active in North America, but many others have paid visits, notably Dingo Khyentse Rinpoché (b. 1910) and the late supreme head of the order, H. H. Dudjom Rinpoché (1904–1987), who established several centers, notably Orgyen Cho Dzong in New York City.

Finally, the Sakyapas gained a foothold in the Pacific Northwest through the good offices of Dr. Turrell V. Wylie (1927–1984), the originator of the phonetically tortuous Wylie System of Tibetan transcription. From about 1960 onwards he brought Dezhung Rinpoche and other Sakyapa scholars to the University of Washington in Seattle. More recently the head of the Order, H. H. Sakya Trizin (b. 1945), thought to be an incarnation of both Mañjushri and Padmasambhava, has visited North America, and a number of Sakya centers coming under the umbrella of his spiritual leadership are now functioning.

Perhaps because the North American countries never enjoyed the same colonial connections with the traditional Theravada countries of southeast Asia that Britain, for instance, enjoyed, and were furthermore not geographically aligned with those areas, this major tradition has not developed as strongly in North America as the others. Nor has a monastic *sangha* arisen; for some reason, most of the outstanding North American Theravadins who have stayed in the robe have either gravitated to Britain, like Ajahn Sumedho (b. 1920) and his confrères (Ajahns Anando, Kittisaro, Pabhakaro, Santacitto, *et al.*); or else stayed in the East, like Bhikkhu Bodhi (b. 1944), born Jeffrey Block in New York City, who currently directs the Buddhist Publication Society in Kandy, Sri Lanka. There are, however, monastic training facilities at the Taungpulu Kaba-Aye Monastery in Palo Alto, California, established in 1981 by Taungpulu Sayadaw but currently directed by Rina Sircar, an ex-nun from Burma who also teaches at the California Institute of Integral Studies, and there are plans for such facilities at the Bhavana Society, a forest meditation center in West Virginia. A few *viharas* have also been set up in North America to cater to the spiritual needs of exiled Sri Lankan, Burmese, Thai, Kampuchean, Laotian, and Vietnamese Buddhists, and interested Westerners also frequent these.

Arguably more significant has been the development of a largely lay *vipassana* meditation teaching effort. Some of the teachers working in this area were originally trained in the East, a few in the robe. Jack

Kornfield, for instance, spent time as a monk with Ajahn Chah in Thailand, while Joseph Goldstein served in the Peace Corps in Thailand and trained with Anagarika Munindra at Bodh Gaya. Kornfield and Goldstein, together with their associates Sharon Salzberg and Jacqueline Schwartz-Mandell, set up the Insight Meditation Center (I.M.S.) at Barre, Massachusetts in 1976, where Salzberg, Goldstein, and Kornfield now guide retreats, including an annual three-month retreat. The Burmese *sayadaw* U Pandita of the Mahasi Meditation Center in Rangoon, Burma, with which I.M.S. has close connections, also leads long intensive retreats there. The latest project at Barre is the creation of a Center for Buddhist Studies, where there will be facilities for students to apply themselves to Pali language and the *suttas*. There also now exists an Insight Meditation West, in the San Geronimo Valley some forty-five minutes' drive from San Francisco; Jack Kornfield and James Baraz are among the guiding teachers there.

An independent lay *vipassana* teacher is Dhiravamsa (b. 1934?), who started out as a monk and was for a time head incumbent at the Buddhapadipa Temple in London, England, where he gained the reputation of being a talented teacher. Later he left the robe, and later still departed for the U.S.A. His main center is now at Friday Harbor, Washington state. Finally, there are also teachers operating in the U Ba Khin/S. N. Goenka tradition, notably Ruth Denison and Robert Hover.

In terms of sheer numbers—though sheer numerical size was never a good index of spiritual quality—the Nichiren Sho-shu (Soka Gakkai) organization has taken off amazingly in recent years, attracting headlines in the press like "The Fastest Growing Religion in the West," and boasting internationally known devotees like the pop singer Tina Turner. Its rise can be traced back to the arrival of one Massayasu Sadanaga, who came to the Los Angeles campus of the University of California to study politics in the 1950s. Changing his name to George Williams, he used his skills to establish an America Soka Gakkai headquarters in 1963, which became Nichiren Sho-shu America (N.S.A.) in 1967. His early converts were mainly Japanese war brides and their American ex-serviceman husbands. Growth was rapid into the 1970s, then tapered off slightly, but is definitely back on the upswing. In the late 1980s N.S.A. was claiming more than five hundred thousand members in the U.S.A., as well as chapters in all the fifty states. In greater Los Angeles alone, one person in every hundred was said to be a member. Whereas Buddhism is mainly a middle-class phenomenon in North America, a substantial proportion of Nichiren Sho-shu members in inner cities come from lower income groups and the Black community, to whom the central chanting offers a way of improving one's life and social lot.

The Nipponzan Myohoji peace monks have also come to North America and built at least one peace pagoda at Lowell, Massachusetts, a traditionally eccentric Yankee-hippie-activist area.

While an enormous amount of effort has been invested in creation of meditation retreat centers, it must also be recognized that an equally significant amount of substantial Buddhist scholarship has been accomplished in North America. Japan apart, arguably the cream of modern Buddhologists are today at work there: people like Luis Gomez, Robert Thurman (the first Westerner to take the robe as a Gelugpa monk after the Second World War, though he later resumed lay life), Donald Lopez, Philip Yampolsky, Jeffrey Hopkins (who has translated for H. H. the Dalai Lama), and Robert Buswell, Jr. (who spent time as a monk in Korea), to name only a few. There has been much translation work too, notably by the Cleary brothers—Thomas Cleary has, for instance, accomplished the almost superhuman task of rendering the vast and highly esoteric *Avatamsaka Sutra* into English. Academic research has also been conducted into the dynamics of meditation, and there has been experimentation with its applications in the medical sphere as a method of pain control, for instance.

Finally, as Buddhism interacts with the dynamic culture of North America, a number of crucial issues and trends have come to the fore. Arguably the most prominent is the issue of women in Buddhism. As we have seen, traditionally in Buddhist countries women were not accorded a very high status because only men were thought to have a fighting chance of being able to achieve anything substantial spiritually. Indeed, the tendency seems often to have been to see women not as neutral but as downright *anti*-spiritual: as "daughters of Mara," bent on hindering the enlightenment project. Since the order of nuns has died out in most traditions, moreover, opportunities for women to embark on monastic training have been very limited, and even where they do exist, women of long-standing religious practice may still find themselves subordinated to men. In today's cultural climate, where women and men exist on a more equal footing, this kind of situation obviously cannot be sustained. Both sexes therefore tend to train alongside each other in modern North American groups and centers, and women also fulfill the role of teachers—Sharon Salzburg, Jiyu Kennett Roshi, Pema Chödron, Toni Packer, Joko Beck, and Henrietta Rogell are examples—though not perhaps in such numbers as feminists might wish. In addition, ways of resurrecting the lost tradition of female ordination are also being actively explored. This area is seen to contain so much energy, in fact, that some commentators go so far as to suggest that the re-emergence of a long-suppressed "female spirituality" may be a vital creative factor in the formation of a distinctively Western *dharma*. For instance, Joanna Macy said in an interview in *Inquiring Mind:*

> In the Buddhist tradition, we talk about the Turning of the Wheel of the Dharma. When the old Buddhist teachings came in new form in Mahayana Buddhism it was called the Second Turning of the Wheel. This [gender] balancing of Buddhism in the late twentieth century (not just in America but for Buddhists around the world) is another Turning of the Wheel.
>
> For a wheel to turn it must be empty in the middle.
>
> I suggest to you who have been chosen to be women in this incarnation and have been fortunate enough to encounter the Dharma, that we have a particularly rewarding mission. We can bring to our time—to our practice and our world—a heightened sense of interrelatedness. By our conditioning as well as our biology, we tune to relationships, can intuitively grasp the relational nature of the universe, the Net of Indra.

It is also a question whether the old hierarchic forms of Buddhism will predominate in North America in the long run or whether more free and democratic forms will evolve. These would not require submission to a *guru* or master, as in the case of traditional forms based on feudal models, but would invest greater responsibility and initiative in the individual. As we have noted, the special status accorded to teachers who, as feminists will not be slow to point out, are usually male, is in any case open to abuse, and it also in a sense disempowers those who submit to it. For these reasons it can be said to be out of key with the way things are developing in society in general.

Another contemporary issue concerns the intervention that Buddhists might usefully make in the social and political arenas to combat such dire causes of *dukkha* as war, injustice, torture, poverty, and so forth. Traditional Buddhism has often had a poor record of social and political concern, both lay and monastic Buddhists having been prepared quietly to continue their spiritual work under feudal and repressive regimes whose functionaries have, to coin a contemporary phrase, flagrantly violated human rights. The rationale for this was that the world was *samsara,* and hence by definition beyond reform; beings who were suffering were furthermore merely reaping the fruits of past misdeeds; all that could be done, therefore, was to work for one's own salvation and offer others, to the best of one's ability, opportunities for doing the same. Many contemporary Buddhists feel that this is just not good enough; it is moreover definitely out of accord with the Mahayana spirit of compassion and concern. But at the same time so-called "engaged Buddhists" are keenly aware of the dangers of lapsing into confrontational attitudes and rhetoric. An important mentor in this area has been Thich Nhat Hanh, who coined the term "Engaged Buddhism," and Robert Aitken Roshi, who in 1978 founded the Buddhist Peace Fellowship to introduce awareness of social, ecological, and peace issues into the Buddhist community. Mention must also be made of the work of Joanna Macy, in particular her Despair and Empowerment Workshops, which seek to do something about the impotence that many (most? all?) individuals feel before the enormities of contemporary social, political, and ecological dilemmas.

Ancillary to this is the question of whether in the long run the traditional monastic forms of Buddhism will flourish in North America as they once did in Asia, or whether new and more evolved forms of lay Buddhism will predominate. In some American centers there are married "monks" and "nuns." This, of course, is a contradiction in terms, but it is also indicative of the way things are going. Many contemporary practitioners feel that they neither want nor need to secede from the mainstream of ordinary life and dedicate themselves to permanent celibacy and poverty in order to gain profound spiritual insight. Indeed, if Buddhism is going to have any useful effect and help solve our potentially lethal global problems, it must emerge from its monastic seclusion and extensively infiltrate the ordinary, everyday life of the world. Attempts have been made in the past to do this, without lasting success. But merely because something has been attempted and failed does not mean that it will not work sometime. In fact, it often means that it is a project that particularly begs to be addressed.

Buddhism and Psychotherapy

Many of those who have undertaken the study and practice of Buddhism have also taken an interest in the Western psychotherapies that developed from the pioneering work of Sigmund Freud. As well as Freudian psychoanalysis and its derivatives, this includes the analytical psychology of Freud's great but errant pupil, Carl Gustav Jung, as well as subsequent developments right down to the present time, where we find Buddhism and Western psychology coming together in a remarkable synthesis.

These modern Western psychotherapies and the theories underpinning them arose towards the end of the last century and in the early part of the present one partly as a response to the dilemma caused by the decline of conventional religion in the West. The great discovery made by the pioneers of this movement was of the existence of the unconscious: an area, or perhaps more accurately, a range of aspects of the human psyche falling outside the normal range of conscious awareness. William James, the psychologist brother of the novelist Henry James and author of *Varieties of Religious Experience* wrote:

> Our normal waking consciousness is but one special type of consciousness, while all about it, parted from it by the flimsiest of screens, there lie potential forms of consciousness entirely different. We may go through life without suspecting their existence,

but apply the requisite stimulus and at a touch they are there in all their completeness.*

Sigmund Freud (1856–1939), the great "nerve doctor of Vienna," was basically interested in the therapeutic aspects of this unconscious: what bearing it might have on the cure of his patient's neurotic and psychotic symptoms. His tendency, therefore, was to view the unconscious as a kind of cellar containing, in Erich Fromm's phrase, "mainly man's vices," that is, all those aspects of himself that a person does not wish to confront—unacceptable desires, aggressive impulses, painful memories, and so forth. Cure consisted in reclaiming this exiled material from the abyss of unknowing and restoring it to the province of consciousness, or in Freudian terminology, restoring it to the Ego from the Id, a process that the great man compared to reclaiming land from the sea, as in the case of the Zuyder Zee in Holland.

Carl Gustav Jung (1875–1961) of Zürich, on the other hand, tended to take a wider and less negative view of the unconscious. Certainly it had its "lumber-room of dirty secrets," but this was but a tiny fragment of the full picture. The unconscious was a vast "unglimpsable completeness of all subliminal psychic factors, a 'total exhibition' of potential nature," he wrote.† "It constitutes the entire disposition from which consciousness takes fragments all the time." It embraces not only personal elements, but collective and even cosmic possibilities as well. It could be a source of profound wisdom, too, if only we could become sensitive to its signals: for instance, by learning how to interpret dreams.

If Freud's tendency had been essentially secular (his negative attitude to religion is well-known), Jung's ideas brought the new psychology into the area once regarded as the preserve of religion. Indeed, he began to see the role of analysis not merely as directed towards curing neurotic symptoms but of assisting harmonious development, the flowering of individual potential, and ultimately towards securing a transformation that would take the individual beyond himself:

> The fact is that the approach to the numinous is the real therapy and inasmuch as you attain to the numinous experiences you are released from the curse of pathology.††

* Quoted in *Beyond Health and Normality*, ed. Walsh and Shapiro (New York: Van Norstand Rehinholt, 1983), 45.

† Carl Jung, foreword to *An Introduction to Zen Buddhism*, D. T. Suzuki (London: Rider, 1957), 22.

†† William James as quoted in Walsh and Shapiro, *op. cit.*, 55.

In the Freudian view, the psychoanalyst was a sort of medical doctor; in Jungian terms, he was that and more as well—a kind of priest. Jung's analytical psychology still operated on the basic Freudian principle of "making the darkness conscious"; however, there were differences too, for instance, of method.

Jung had a keen appreciation of the significance of the burgeoning interest in Eastern spirituality that he saw taking place in his own time. As he wrote in his essay, "The Spiritual Problem of Modern Man":

> Let us beware of underestimating it! So far, indeed, there is little of it to be seen on the intellectual surface: a handful of orientalists, one or two Buddhist enthusiasts, and a few sombre celebrities like Madame Blavatsky and Annie Besant with her Krishnamurti. These tiny manifestations are like tiny scattered islands in the ocean of mankind; in reality they are the peaks of submarine mountain ranges.*

But for Jung, the East was ultimately not a "Tibetan monastery full of Mahatmas," but a reality that "in a sense lies within us." This reality consisted precisely of those spiritual potentials that once Western religion had sought to foster, but, sadly, no more, leaving Western man in his deep dilemma. He did not, however, see salvation in abandoning one's native cultural heritage and recklessly adopting ideas, symbols, and practices that had developed in an alien milieu. Indeed, he thought this particularly risky and branded those who did it—the Theosophists were the worst offenders in his book—as "pitiable imitators." In particular he warned against the dangers of any Westerner jettisoning reason and its brainchild, science. If one were going to explore the undiscovered country of psyche and spirit, which was fraught with all manner of perils and pitfalls, it would be quixotic and foolhardy to do without this "one safe foundation of the Western mind."

The challenge Jung posed, then, was not merely one of self development; one's own native traditions had to be revitalized at the same time:

> It is not a question of our imitating, or worse still, becoming missionaries for what is organically foreign, but rather a question of building up our own Western culture, which sickens with a

---

* Carl Jung, "The Spiritual Problem of Modern Man," in *The Portable Jung,* ed. Joseph Campbell (1928; reprint, New York: Penguin, 1978), 470.

thousand ills. This has to be done on the spot, and by the real European as he is in his Western commonplaces, with his marriage problems, his neuroses, his social and political delusions, and his whole philosophical disorientation.*

These general caveats aside, Jung investigated the "Wisdom of the East" fairly extensively and wrote "psychological commentaries" to the W. Y. Evans-Wentz/Kazi Dawa Samdup renderings of *The Tibetan Book of the Dead* (1939/53) and *The Tibetan Book of the Great Liberation* (1939/54); also a foreword to D. T. Suzuki's *Introduction to Zen Buddhism* (1939). Important too are his commentaries on the Richard Wilhelm translations from the Chinese of the classic *I Ching* (1950) and *The Secret of the Golden Flower* (1929). Generally speaking, he found little to disagree with and much to celebrate in these writings, but always he was cautious about any venture into actual practice. Zen Buddhism, for instance, had great value "for the understanding of the religious transformation process"; however, "its use among Western people is very improbable. The spiritual conditions necessary to Zen are missing in the West."

Was Jung unnecessarily cautious? Certainly there is sound sense in most of what he has to say, but he was writing in and for a particular time and developments have proceeded apace since then. There is an enormous amount of cross-cultural traffic in our contemporary Global Village, far more perhaps than Jung could have envisaged. In this climate people *do* practice various forms of Buddhism and at the same time hold down executive jobs in business in Western cities like London and New York, nor do they have to be pseudo-Japanese or Tibetan or abandon Western rationality and science in order to do so.

In fact, the wheel has almost now turned full circle and Eastern mysticism is becoming quite respectable in certain forward-thinking scientific quarters. Dr. Fritjof Capra, author of *The Tao of Physics* and *The Turning Point,* has written of the fascinating correspondences between modern theories of atomic and sub-atomic physics and the insights of the Eastern mystics; and Professor David Bohm, a leading theoretical physicist, has had illuminating conversations with the sage J. Krishnamurti, some of which have been published.

To accord due credit to Jung, however, it must be said that many Western Buddhists have found that his ideas represent a useful bridge

---

* R. Wilhelm, trans., commentary to *The Secret of the Golden Flower* (London: Routledge & Kegan Paul, 1962), 84.

into the exotic world of Eastern spirituality. Some have gone so far as to undertake Jungian analysis and have found it helpful, particularly in dealing with specifically psychological problems. (Freudian analysis might be equally helpful in this regard, especially in dealing with problems that have their origin in early life.) It is open to question, however, whether Jungian analysis can offer any contribution towards higher spiritual development that could not equally well be found in Buddhism itself—and, as is often said, at considerably less cost, analysis being strictly for the well-heeled.

In England during the 1930s, the Harley Street psychiatrist, Eric Graham Howe, author of *She and Me* and *War Dance,* was also an early appreciator of the wisdom of the East and a supporter of the Buddhist Lodge which Christmas Humphreys had started in 1924. Howe was a formative influence upon the young Alan Watts, who was quick to see the fruitful cross-connections that could be made between the Eastern religious traditions (including of course Buddhism) and psychotherapy. By his own account, Watts had been reading the works of Jung while still at school; other, slightly later, influences upon him in this direction were a Dutch psychiatrist named Philip Metman and Dimitrije Mitrinovic, a "rascal guru" who had studied the psychotherapeutic techniques of Alfred Adler and Trigant Burrow and evolved an early form of encounter group.

As a powerful communicator, Alan Watts was able to express these cross-connections lucidly and persuasively in his books, pamphlets, and magazine articles. His first major work which brought his psychotherapeutic interests into primary focus was the pamphlet *Seven Symbols of Life* (1936). Here, in dealing with the symbol of the lotus, Watts points out that the pristine flower has its roots sunk into the "primeval slime," from which it also draws sustenance. Although Watts talks of the racial and cosmic dimensions of the unconscious, he does rather tend to dwell upon its "dark" or shadow aspects, thus making it smack more of Freud's cellarful of vices than Jung's repository of higher things. Then in 1937 Watts published his second full-length book, *The Legacy of Asia and Western Man,* in which he sought to relate Eastern thought and mysticism to Christianity and "that young but swiftly-growing science—psychology" (Christmas Humphreys). Watts went on to develop these themes in his later writings, including *Psychotherapy East and West* (1961). At one stage he propounded the idea that Buddhism has more in common with psychotherapy than with religion as the term is currently understood in the West.

The interest in Buddhism generally and in Zen Buddhism in particular became more widespread among psychotherapists, especially in

the United States, following the Second World War. This interest was
no doubt stimulated by Dr. D. T. Suzuki (1870–1966). In the early
1950s, Suzuki began lecturing at Columbia University in New York,
and his lectures were attended by psychoanalysts and therapists like Karen
Horney and Erich Fromm (neo-Freudians both), and Richard DeMartino.
In 1957, Suzuki spent the summer months in Mexico with Fromm and
participated in a workshop on Zen Buddhism and psychoanalysis held
under the auspices of the Department of Psychoanalysis of the Medical
School of the Autonomous University of Mexico. Nearly fifty psychologists and psychiatrists from both Mexico and the United States took
part, and a book resulted, *Zen Buddhism and Psychoanalysis* (New York,
1960), with contributions from Suzuki, Fromm, and DeMartino.

In re-examining this record of what was undoubtedly the first major
encounter between Buddhism and Western psychotherapy, one cannot help wondering to what extent the two parties understood, or
misunderstood, each other. Suzuki's use of the term "unconscious"
was, for one thing, very particular,* and he himself gave voice to the
thought that psychoanalysts might mean something entirely different.
Fromm, on the other hand, had never practiced Zen, and, as he readily
admitted, what he knew about it was derived entirely at second hand,
mainly from Suzuki, and presumably this went for just about all the
Western participants, barring perhaps DeMartino.† Nevertheless, the
encounter does seem to have been stimulating, and perhaps set the
scene for fruitful future developments.

In his contribution to the resulting book, *Psychoanalysis and Zen Buddhism,* Fromm follows in Jung's footsteps in proposing that psychoanalysis might have altogether more radical aims than those defined by
Freud. Instead of being basically concerned with securing the absence

---

* Suzuki preferred the term Cosmic Unconscious. In his view, this is a vast
mystery, "not known in the way relative things are known," which itself gives
birth to consciousness and "once recognized, enters into ordinary consciousness
and puts in good order all the complexities there which have been tormenting
us to greater or lesser degrees." This is the source of creativity "whereby not
only artists nourish their inspirations, but even we ordinary beings are enabled
each according to his natural endowments, to turn his life into something of
genuine art." See Erich Fromm, R. De Martino, et. al., *Zen Buddhism and Psychoanalysis* (paperback ed., London: Souvenir Press, 1974), 16–17.

† DeMartino was in Japan immediately after World War II, working with the
International Military Tribunal in Tokyo. In 1947 he visited D. T. Suzuki with
Philip Kapleau. See Rick Fields, *How the Swans Came to the Lake* (Boulder and
London: Shambhala Publications, 1986), 195ff.

of sickness, positive well-being might become the goal—a view given added force by the admittedly "disappointing results of character analysis (which have never been expressed more honestly than by Freud in his 'Analysis, Terminable or Interminable?')." No fundamental departures from basic Freudian theory or practice were being advocated, however, rather Fromm was calling for a logical extension of them, and, if "one carries Freud's principle of the transformation of unconsciousness into consciousness to its ultimate consequences, one approaches the concept of enlightenment." In other words, in ultimate terms the aims of Zen Buddhism and psychoanalysis are identical. Suzuki meanwhile had expressed the aims of Zen Buddhism thus:

> Zen in its essence is the art of seeing into the nature of one's being, and it points the way from bondage to freedom. . . . We can say that Zen liberates all the energies properly and naturally stored in each of us, which are in ordinary circumstances cramped and distorted so that they find no adequate channel of activity. . . . It is the object of Zen, therefore, to save us from going crazy or being crippled. This is what I mean by freedom, giving free play to all the creative and benevolent impulses inherently lying in our hearts. Generally, we are blind to this fact, that we are in possession of all the necessary faculties that will make us happy and loving towards one another.*

"This description of Zen's aim could be applied without change as a description of what psychoanalysis aspires to achieve," Fromm declared. Their methods remained entirely different, however. The method of Zen consisted of a "frontal attack on the alienated way of perception" by means of *zazen, koan,* and "the authority of the Master"; psychoanalysis, on the other hand, was "psychoempirical" in method and "trains consciousness to get hold of the unconscious in a different way." And from there on seemingly never the twain shall meet; for, like Jung, Fromm does not go so far as to suggest that any Westerner, psychoanalyst or layman, should actually experiment with the Zen method. He does, however, concede that students of Zen Buddhism might derive benefits from psychoanalysis.

Logically, the next phase had to be that a significant number of heroic pioneers from the Western world would venture across the dread abyss and actually embark upon Buddhist spiritual practice in earnest. Only

---

* D. T. Suzuki, *Zen Buddhism* (New York: Doubleday Anchor, 1956), 3.

then would the true nature of the higher spiritual development that had hitherto been contemplated only intellectually be known at first hand; also the effects and effectiveness of the various practices involved (e.g., meditation) gauged. This process began to get under way in earnest during that great era of innovative energy, the sixties. There was a tremendous upsurge in interest in Eastern religion at that time and tens of thousands of Westerners, mostly young and long-haired, journeyed to the East. Most perhaps were moved by collective forces whose true nature they only dimly discerned—or totally misconceived. This was after all the age of "Make Love Not War"—and the love proclaimed was of a distinctly carnal variety. Sexual orgasm was the *summum bonum* and, through the writings of D. H. Lawrence, Wilhelm Reich, Norman Mailer, and others, it had become imbued with quasi-spiritual connotations. Alternative—and better—orgasms were also sought elsewhere: in drugs, for instance, which were considered a sure source of alternative orgasmic highs, and then the word got about that spiritual practices could engineer even better and more durable highs than drugs. It may seem ironic now, but many Westerners who at this time undertook serious spiritual discipline in the East, and to their lasting credit saw the process through (or at least to advanced stages), were led to do so by these kinds of very mixed motives.

With the hippie horde went a few psychotherapists. R. D. Laing, for instance, who had pioneered new approaches to schizophrenia, spent a time at a temple in Sri Lanka; and Richard Alpert, a former psychology professor at Harvard University who, with Timothy Leary, had attained some notoriety as luminaries of the fashionable psychedelic drug culture that had arisen in the sixties. Alpert returned to the West gloriously reborn as Baba Ram Dass after having spent some months in India with Neem Karoli Baba. Later he studied *vipassana* mediation with, among others, U Pandita, a Burmese teacher. At the same time trained teachers and meditation masters from Tibet, Japan, Thailand, Burma, Korea, China, Sri Lanka—even from Mongolia—have come to the West and numerous centers have been established. Thus no longer did one have to go to the East to study its wisdom and to find facilities for practice.

All this activity inevitably spilled over into psychology, where great changes were afoot anyway. A new "humanistic" psychology had been evolving which was rather more preoccupied with promoting "growth" than with specifically curing psychological ills. Growth was very much about liberating energies, bringing potentialities to maximum fulfillment, and generally securing optimum well-being, but it only reached as far as the outer limits of the ego stage.

A "fourth force"* in Western psychology was also emerging that was explicitly concerned with extending the parameters to encompass the upper reaches of psychospiritual development. As such, it aspired beyond ego, or beyond the personal, hence its name: Transpersonal Psychology. Insofar as these mysterious shores, which were virtually blanks on most Western maps of the psyche, had been more thoroughly charted in the East, Eastern maps were given serious study by researchers. At the same time, it became clear that the practical methods—meditation, yoga, and so forth; the transpersonal term for them is consciousness disciplines—that had been shown in the East to provide access to a "broad range of states of consciousness" would have to be studied as well. This could only be done if they were actually practiced, and here of course the innovators ran up against the classic prejudice of the Western scholarly orthodoxy that any researcher getting actively and sympathetically involved in his field of research would jeopardize his precious objectivity. Investigations into "altered states of consciousness" using LSD and other substances were also begun, a direct inheritance of the sixties, it would seem.

The book, *Beyond Ego,* gives a fair idea of the range of interests encompassed by transpersonal psychology; it also includes contributions from many of the leading researchers in the area: Roger Walsh, Daniel Goleman, Duane Elgin, Frances Vaughan, Stanislav Grof, Charles Tart, Ram Dass, and the doyen of them all, Ken Wilber.

To conclude, we will briefly look at the work of Ken Wilber, which in a sense is a consummation of the ever deepening relationship between Buddhism (and the Eastern spiritual traditions generally) and Western psychotherapy. In his various writings Wilber has charted a panoramic "spectrum of consciousness" stretching from the most primitive level of undifferentiated embeddedness in nature (the blissful ignorance of Eden), right up through various expanding levels to the ego stage, and then on beyond up to the most exalted state of spiritual realization (the bliss of conscious unity). This is a process through which the human race itself is collectively evolving, and which its most advanced members (such as the Buddha) have completed. Each one of us also recapitulates the process of our own lives, from birth on up to . . . however far we want or are able to take it. Simply put, it is a progress from prepersonal (or pre-egoic) to personal (or egoic) to

* The other three "forces" in modern Western psychology are (1) psychoanalysis; (2) behaviorism (with which we have not been concerned here); and (3) humanistic psychology.

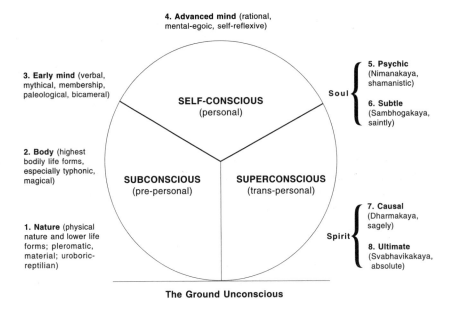

The Great Chain of Being

transpersonal (or trans-egoic). It can also be graphically represented as a Great Chain of Being.

Wilber's map is compounded of elements drawn from both East and West. In general, the phases up to and including the ego stage have been well charted by Western developmental psychologists, while the upper reaches have been charted in the spiritual psychologists of the East, though also to a lesser extent in Western mysticism. What we have here then is a massive work of synthesis or integration: a marriage of East and West.

As regards the dynamics of the Great Chain of Being, they may be described as follows. All there really is is primal Unity or *Brahman* (Wilber likes the Hindu term) but "for the sport and play of it all" *Brahman* throws itself out, as it has done untold times, and loses itself in its myriad manifestations. Once cast into this bitter exile, each fragment longs to return to the Unity whence it came. This is *Atman* Project in its positive form, and it is the drive that keeps the Great Chain of Being in motion. Everything might work like clockwork and the multiplicity be smoothly restored to the One, but there are complicating factors. Progress from each stage of development to the next implies self-overcoming, which is a kind of death, hence fears, resistances, and other symptoms arise. On the human level, for instance, we all intuit the truth: that our proper evolutionary function is to transcend ourselves and attain conscious unity. But we balk at this, and so instead of working towards *transformation*—i.e., progress to the next stage in the Great Chain—we syphon off the reintegrative energy and dissipate it in the pursuit of substitute goals (e.g., power, pleasure, fame, etc.). This Wilber calls *translation:* false *Atman* Project—in Buddhist terms it is dilly-dallying around in *samsara* instead of getting on with the task of seeking the deathless.

Basically all the different stages in the Great Chain of Being result from the drawing of boundaries. Boundaries are all basically battle lines because they create pairs of warring opposites (self versus not-self, the conscious versus the unconscious persona versus shadow). Hence problems—or in Buddhist terms, *duhkha*—inevitably arise. Problems are transcended by tearing down the boundaries that created the particular dualism from which they arose in the first place. As boundaries are basically illusory anyway, this just involves *seeing through* them. What was once disowned, cast "out there," is accepted and embraced. This "converts enemies into friends, wars into dances, battles into plays"; and so therapy and growth go hand in hand as the boundaries are pushed further and further back until ultimately a state of no boundary is attained, which is conscious unity with the totality.

As well as defining the various stages of psychospiritual development, Wilber also defines the therapy or method of transformation appropriate to each. His book, *No Boundary,* lays out his views in this regard. And here arguably he makes his most important contribution, for, as he himself points out, disagreement and often conflict have arisen as a result of a failure to understand that therapies and methods are strictly phase-specific; that is, each is designed to work on a particular developmental phase and is not only unworkable but potentially harmful if applied to another.

Wilber isolates a particularly regrettable example of this in "In Praise of Ego,"* an article that he wrote for *The Middle Way* in 1983. Here he laments the abyss of misunderstanding that has arisen between many Buddhists and psychologists. "After working with neurotics—who don't have enough ego-strength—and psychotics—who have no ego-strength at all—the average psychologist is dumbfounded to find us Buddhists recommending, indeed actively encouraging, 'no-ego' states," Wilber writes (*ibid.* p. 152). Both the Buddhist and the average psychologist are right when they speak in the context of the particular phase with

---

* Ken Wilber, "In Praise of Ego: An Uncommon Buddhist Sermon," *The Middle Way* vol. 58, no. 3 (Nov., 1983): 151ff.

which they are appropriately concerned, wrong when they generalize what maintains there to other phases. Thus there is due season for working to strengthen ego, for ego is a valid phase-specific structure on the road to nirvana. In fact one cannot develop *beyond* ego until one has developed a firm ego to transcend: a "self strong enough to die in nirvanic release." This is precisely a point emphasized by Jung:

> You cannot destroy a rationalist intellect that was never present. . . .
> Hence even with us it happens not infrequently that a conscious ego
> and a conscious, cultivated understanding must be produced by therapy
> before one can even think of abolishing I-ness or rationalism.*

Wilber sees the problem for Buddhists as lying with the *anatman* doctrine, which he strongly emphasizes should be treated as trans-egoic rather than pre-egoic. And hence only those with a "more-or-less intact ego" should undertake full Buddhist training, for applying methods like intensive meditation to subjects lacking the necessary ego strength can be disastrous:

> . . . meditation, far from being a cure-all, can be *extremely detri-*
> *mental* to borderline and narcissistic disorders (simply because the
> person is desperately attempting to create a strong and viable ego
> structure, and intensive meditation tends to dissolve what little
> structure the borderline has).†

Clearly, then, meditation should be approached with a certain amount of caution and with proper guidance. Even with the most gentle basic forms, the mind is being opened and material will enter consciousness, for in a sense meditation operates on the classic Freudian principle of making the unconscious conscious. If all goes well, what arises will be observed choicelessly and in due course will pass away. In this way the practitioner will see that problems are vagrant and incidental visitors, not an indissoluble part of the self. In other words, identification will cease. There is great relief and release in this, which is very real therapy. If the process becomes disturbing, however, it is wise to abandon, at least temporarily, whatever meditation practice has been undertaken and seek wise guidance. Another approach might be indicated.

---

* D. T. Suzuki, Foreword to *Introduction to Zen Buddhism,* reprinted in *Psychology & the East.* (London: Arkana, 1986), 154 (translation slightly different from the one quoted in the text).
† Wilber, "In Praise of Ego," 152.

Ken Wilber is also very cautious about optimistic predictions of a New Age and a general raising of the level of consciousness, for "the vast majority of humanity . . . has not yet stably reached the rational egoic level" let alone placed itself in any position to transcend that level. Even in Western societies where the New Age is most vociferously vaunted, social conditions are generally inimical to proper personal development and the resulting stresses cause many promising people to regress to prepersonal phases while masquerading as progressing towards transpersonal ones:

> This was perfectly prefigured in the "Dharma Bum" period of the Sixties, when an influential number of otherwise highly intellectual people, incapable of supporting rational and egoic responsibility in a culture clearly stressful and drifting, began championing typhonic, narcissistic, regressive freedom from the ego level, through pre-egoic license, while intellectually claiming to be actually pursuing the trans-egoic Zen of spontaneous freedom. . . . They often took as their heros a handful of truly trans-egoic souls, pointed to Krishnamurti and Ramana and Zen, and thus managed to front an otherwise undeniable rationalization for their regress to Eden.*

There is absolutely no going back to the blissful ignorance of the prepersonal unity of Eden, then. Transpersonal unity is the only valid goal for human beings who wish to fulfill their potential, and it differs from its prepersonal counterpart in that it is fully conscious. Psychotherapy and Buddhism both point in this direction and each has its part to play in assisting in its full realization, psychotherapy in helping to develop a sound ego, Buddhism in taking the process on from there.

---

* Ken Wilber, *Up From Eden* (London: Routledge & Kegan Paul, 1983), 323ff.

A·P·P·E·N·D·I·X·E·S

A·P·P·E·N·D·I·X I

Who's Who in Buddhism:
A Modern Western Perspective

The following represents a highly selective listing of those Buddhist writers, teachers, and practitioners with whom the contemporary Westerner is likely, directly or indirectly, to come in contact. Biographical and bibliographical details are necessarily brief. Neither inclusion nor exclusion in any way represent a value judgment on the relative importance or spiritual attainments of any particular figure.

There are sections on each of the traditions—Theravada, Tibetan, Zen, Pure Land, and Nichiren—and an additional Miscellaneous section. There is inevitably overlap, as some people have been involved with more than one tradition. However, one long homogenized listing would present other disadvantages.

Some of the details included here were obtained at source, others obliquely. In particular the following books were of considerable help:

Fields, Rick. *How the Swans Came to the Lake,* rev. ed. Boston and London: Shambhala, 1986.

Oliver, Ian P. *Buddhism in Britain*. London: Rider, 1979.

Humphreys, Christmas. *Sixty Years of Buddhism in England*. London: The Buddhist Society, 1968.

Rinpoché, Karma Thinley. *The Sixteen Karmapas of Tibet*. Boulder: Shambhala, 1981.

Zen Buddhism in North America: A History & A Directory. Toronto: Zen Lotus Society, 1986.
Kornfield, Jack. *Living Buddhist Masters*. Reprint. Boulder: Shambhala, 1984.
Sunim, Kusan. *The Way of Korean Zen*. Translated by Martine Fages. Edited with an Introduction by Stephen Batchelor. New York and Tokyo: John Weatherhill, 1985.

Many individuals helped compile this list. The following were astonishingly kind: Patrick Gaffney (RIGPA) and John Stevens (Tohoku Fukushi University), Rosie Warwick (Sakya Thinley Rinchen Ling), Marcia Seymour (ZCLA), Philip Kapleau Roshi (Rochester Zen Center), Maurice O'C Walshe, Nick Ribush (Wisdom Publications), Rev. Chushin Passmore (Throssel Hole Priory) James Y. Nagahiro (Buddhist Churches of America), Alan James (House of Inner Tranquility), and Jim Belither (Manjushri Institute).

To simplify matters, even though before 1972 Sri Lanka was known as Ceylon, references are given as "Sri Lanka," except where proper names are cited, e.g. Ceylon High Commissioner.

To save space, abbreviations have been used extensively, and titles and honorifics have been reduced to a minimum (no disrespect implied!). The abbreviations are as follows:

aka—also known as
assn—association
BA—Bachelor's degree
Bdsm—Buddhism
Bdst—Buddhist
C—Central
dept—department
E—East, eastern
ed(s)—editor, edited by, or edition(s)
esp—especially
govt—government
HH—His Holiness
incl—include, including
loc cit—at the place cited
MA—Master's degree

N—North, northern
NE—northeast
op cit—in the work cited
Prof—Professor
(qv)—quod vide (referenced elsewhere in book)
S—South, southern
SE—southeast
soc—society
tr(s)—translator, translated by, translation(s)
U—University
Ven—the Venerable
vol(s)—volume(s)
W—West, western

THERAVADA BUDDHISM
Notes on Titles

Ajahn (also Achaan): Thai pronunciation of the Sanskrit Acharya ("teacher"). In lay contexts can denote a senior school or college teacher; in the Thai Sangha a meditation master.

Anagarika: lit, "Homeless One"; one who enters the homeless life without formally ordaining as a monk.

Bhikkhu: fully ordained Bdst monk.

Bhikkhuni: fully ordained Bdst nun (this order has technically died out within the Theravada tradition).

Chao Khun: roughly "noble lord"; a title granted to important Thai bhikkhus, broadly equivalent to an honorary bishophood, with which a new name also goes.

Dasa Sila Mata: woman who has become a "homeless one" and adheres to Ten Precepts (a nun in all but name).

Dhammaduta: Bdst missionary work.

Dhutanga: ascetic practice.

Mahanayaka: patriarch or high-ranking Thera.

Mahathera (or Maha Thera): bhikkhu of 20 years' standing. Mahatheras generally just call themselves "Thera." The prefixed title "Maha" when used in Thailand also denotes having passed a certain examination in Pali.

Phra: Thai equivalent of Thera; also prefixed to names of successful Pali examination candidates.

Samanera: postulant or novice who adheres to the Precepts but has not as yet received full ordination.

Sayadaw: Burmese equivalent of "Maha Thera"; also given to highly respected Burmese bhikkhus.

Tan (properly Than): Thai title roughly equivalent to "Venerable."

Thera: "elder"; a bhikkhu of 10 years' standing. *Sthavira* is the rather less used Sanskrit equivalent.

Tudong: Pali equivalent for dhutanga. "Tudong monk" is a wandering ascetic.

Amritananda Thera (1918–90): *Senior Nepalese bhikkhu.* Born in Nepal. Entered Sangha at age 18. Ordained in Sri Lanka; returned to Nepal; established Bdst center at Svayambhunath, near Kathmandu. 1956: organized 4th WFB (World Fellowship of Bdsts) Conference, Kathmandu. Has traveled in W, USSR, Japan. In his last years he translated Pali texts into Newari and Nepali and wrote in both languages and in English, notably *A Short History of Theravada Buddhism in Modern Nepal.*

Ananda Maitreya Mahanayaka Thera: *Senior Sri Lankan monk and scholar active in W.* Born 1896, Sri Lanka; 1911: initial ordination. *c* 1911–20: studied Pali, Sanskrit, Bdst philosophy; also Sutta and Vinaya Pitakas. 1916: higher ordination. 1920: joined Ananda College. 1924: first missionary tour of India. 1924–26: lecturer in Pali and Sinhalese, at Nalanda College, Colombo. 1926–35: lecturer in Pali, Sanskrit, Sinhalese, and Bdsm at Ananda College. 1935: opened Sri Dharmananda Pirivena, an institute for Bdst monks, at Balangoda. 1956: appointed President of Sri Lankan contingent at 6th Sangha Council held in Rangoon. 1954: appointed Mahanayaka Thera of Suddharma school of Sri Lanka. 1959: appointed Professor of Mahayana Bdsm in

Vidyodaya U (now Sri Jayewardhenapura University). 1963: appointed Dean of the Faculty of Bdsm in same U. 1966: appointed Acting Vice Chancellor of same. 1967: appointed President and Mahanayaka of the United Amarapura school. 1960: to Manila (Philippines) for Pax Romana Conference as representative of Vidyodaya University 1973: stayed 3 months in UK. 1967: to Mahabodhi Center, Sarnath (near Benares) to teach Bdsm. 1980: to England, then to Moscow and Ulan Ude (Mongolia) with other Sri Lankan monks of the World Peace movement. 1981–86: visited England, Scotland, France, Sweden, Canada, and USA. Publications include numerous works in Sinhalese: complete translation of *Digha Nikaya;* abridgement of *Digha Nikaya, Life of the Buddha* (for children); *Life of the Buddha* (in pictures); *Khuddakapatha;* ed and tr *Dhammapada;* tr *Udana; Buddhism; Sanskrit Grammar and Composition; Pali Grammar and Composition; Easy Steps to English; English Grammar.* In English: versified tr of *Dhammapada,* 1975–78. Ed Bdst newspaper in Sinhalese *(Buddha Rasmi).*

Ananda Metteyya (Charles Henry Allan Bennett, 1872–1923): *First Bristish bhikkhu and Bdst missionary.* Born London, son of electrical engineer. Trained as analytical chemist. Involved in Golden Dawn (magic) movement, with W. B. Yeats et al. 1890: Arnold's *Light of Asia* kindled an interest in Bdsm. 1898: "Ill-health drove me from England to the East." Initially studied Dhamma in Sri Lanka and determined to lead Bdst mission to Europe. 1901: samanera ordination in Akyab (Burma), 1902: bhikkhu ordination. 1903: founded International Bdst Society (Buddhasasana Samagana) in Rangoon. 1908: led first mission to England; returned to Burma after 6 months. 1914: ill health compelled him to disrobe and return to UK; continued Bdst propaganda work, which he attempted to finance by his inventions. Books include an *Outline of Buddhism* and *The Wisdom of the Aryas.*

Ba Khin, Sayaji U Ba Khin (1899–1971): *Lay Burmese meditation master.* 1937: began practicing vipassana under Saya Thet Gyi. Mastered several types of concentration meditation and developed powerful vipassana technique. "This . . . involves sweeping the mind through the body, giving special attention to the ever-changing play of sensations . . ." (Jack Kornfield). 1941: began teaching individuals and small groups; at the same time held down various important posts in lay life, having entered Accountant General's office and achieved promotion. 1948–53: Accountant General of Burma; offered vipassana instruction to staff. 1952: founded and taught at International Meditation Center, Rangoon, where intensive 10-day courses given on regular basis. After retirement (1953), was active as a meditation teacher, developed his center, and was also acting head of several govt depts. Married young and raised 6 children. His style, which emphasizes intensive practice rather than theoretical understanding, is taught elsewhere in the world by his disciples, e.g. S. N. Goenka (qv), Ruth Dennison, Robert Hover. For further information see *Tranquility & Insight* (1986), A. Solé-Leris, London: Rider, pp. 136–41.

Bodhi, Bhikkhu (Thera), (Jeffrey Block): *American-born bhikkhu.* Born 1944, New York City, of Jewish parentage. Educated Brooklyn College. 1972: PhD in Philosophy from Claremont Graduate School. 1967: formally took Three Refuges. 1972: left for Sri Lanka, intending to enter Sangha. 1972: received samanera ordination, 1973: bhikkhu ordination. 1977: returned to USA and spent nearly 2 years at Lamaist Bdst Monastery of Geshe Wangyal (qv) and 3 years at Washington Bdst Vihara. 1982: returned to Sri Lanka. 1984: after periods of meditation training at Mitirigala Nissarana

Vanaya, accepted the editorship of the Bdst Publication Society upon the retirement of Ven Nuanaponika Mahathera (qv). Now lives together with Ven Nyanaponika at the Forest Hermitage, Kandy. Publications incl *Nourishing the Roots; Transcendental Dependent Arising; The Noble Eightfold Path; The Discourse on the All-embracing Net of Views; The Brahmajala Sutta and its Commentarial Exegesis; The Discourse on the Root of Existence; The Mulapariyaya Sutta and its Commentarial Exegesis; The Great Discourse on Causation; The Mahanidana Sutta and its Commentarial Exegesis.*

Boowa: see **Maha Boowa, Ajahn.**

Buddhadasa Bhikkhu (1906–93): *" . . . perhaps the best-known Dharma master in Thailand at this time"* (Jack Kornfield). Born Chaiya, son of well-to-do merchant; ordained at 21. Having completed Bdst studies, taught for some years and then lived alone as tudong monk in the forest for 6 years, studying Pali and avoiding all human contact. Then became Abbot of Wat Phra Data at Chaiya; later moved to Wat Suanmokkhabalarama, 2 ½ miles outside Chaiya. Influenced by Zen, Christianity, etc. "—teaches a more active outlook towards life and maintains that Nibbana can be attained 'here and now'" (*Buddhist Forum,* London). Books incl *Anapanasati Buddha Dhamma for Students; Towards Buddha-dhamma; The Right Approach to Dhamma; Exchanging Dhamma while Fighting; Dhamma—the World Saviour; In Samsara Exists Nirvana; Why Were We Born?; Two Kinds of Language; No Religion; Handbook of Mankind; Christianity & Buddhism (Sinclaire Thompson Memorial Lecture, Bangkok, 1967); Emancipation of the World;* and *Toward the Truth.* qv. Louis Gabaude "Une Hermeneutique—Bouddhique Contemporaire de Thailand: Buddhadasa Bhikku" (EFEO CL, Paris 1988).

Buddharakkhita Bhikkhu: *Founder of numerous social welfare organizations.* Born 1922, Imphal, Manipur State, India. Educated Institute of Engineering Technology, Calcutta. WWII: service as officer. 1946–48: Ramakrishna monk. 1949: bhikkhu ordination. 1949–52: Bdst studies in Sri Lanka. 1952–55: Bdst studies in Burma under Mahasi Sayadaw (qv) et al. Editorial board, Tipitaka Translation, 6th Bdst Synod, Burma. 1955–56: taught at Nalanda Postgraduate Institute. 1956: founded Maha Bodhi Soc, Bangalore. Later founded: International Meditation Center, school for indigent Bdst boys, Buddha Vachana Publishers and Tripitaka Press, Maitri Mandala, Mahabodhi Burns & Casualty Center (Bangalore), Institute of Buddhology & Pali Studies (Mysore), Artificial Limb Center (Bangalore), and Arogya Center. 1980 to present, has taught and conducted retreats in UK and USA. Publications incl over 50 books.

Cha, Ajahn (also spelled Chah, Chaa): (See note on name below.) *Meditation master of the Thai forest tradition.* Born in rural village in Lao part of NE Thailand. Ordained as a novice in early youth; at 20 took bhikkhu ordination. Studied basic Dhamma, discipline, and scriptures as a young monk; later practiced meditation under several masters of the forest tradition. Lived ascetic life for several years, wandering, sleeping in forests, caves, cremation grounds, then spent a short but enlightening period with Ajahn Mun (qv). Eventually settled in a thick forest grove near birthplace; a large monastery grew up around him there (Wat Pah Pong) from which numerous branch temples have sprung in NE Thailand and elsewhere. 1975: Wat Pah Nanachat established as special training monastery for Westerners. 1977 and 1979: visited UK. 1979: visited USA. (Note on name: Cha was his first lay name. Original bhikkhu name—Subhatto. Was later appointed Chao Khun with new name, Bodhinyana; does not use Chao Khun title but keeps name that goes with it.) Books incl *A Taste of Freedom; A Still Forest Pool;* and *Bodhinyana.*Died in 1992.

Coleman, John: *Vipassana teacher trained by U Ba Khin.*

Dharmapala, Anagarika (David Hewavitarne, 1864–1933): *Bdst propagandist.* Born Colombo, Sri Lanka; joined Theosophical Soc at early age; met Mme. Blavatsky and Col. Olcott. Studied Pali. 1888: visited Japan with the Theosophists. 1891: founded Maha Bodhi Society; became very vigorous re the restoration of Bodh Gaya to Bdst hands (this not achieved until 1949). 1893: attended World Parliament of Religions in Chicago. 1896–97: again in USA. 1926: founded British Maha Bodhi Soc in London, then went on to USA. 1928: established Bdst Mission (later London Bdst Vihara). 1931: ordained a bhikkhu as Sri Devamitta Dhammapala. (Biography in "Wheel" Series, BPS, Sri Lanka).

Dhiravamsa: *Thai-born lay meditation teacher.* Born NE Thailand *c.* 1934; became samanera at 13 and a bhikkhu (Tissadatto) at 21.1964: arrived London. 1966: became head of Buddhapadipa Temple as Chao Khun Sobhana Dhammasudhi. 1971: disrobed and established himself as a lay teacher. Had a center in UK (The Chapter House, Wisbech, Cambs), but later departed for USA. 1977: settled in N California. Runs courses in meditation and Abdhidhamma. In recent years has experimented with combining meditation with modern psychotherapeutic techniques. Books incl *The Real Way to Awakening; The Beneficial Factors for Meditation Practice; Insight Meditation; A New Approach to Buddhism;* and *The Dynamic Way of Meditation.*

Feldman, Christina: *Western vipassana teacher.* 1970–75: study and practice under various Bdst teachers in India, incl Geshe Rabten (qv). 1975–77: participated in various intensive vipassana retreats and personal retreats for development of insight meditation pratice. 1974–86: guided meditation retreats in Europe, USA, England, and Australia. Now lives in Devon where she teaches and is a guiding teacher at Gaia House, Denbury, Devon, which she also helped to found. In recent years has also led retreats which focus upon communication skills, women's spirituality, and family retreats. Books incl *Women Awake.*

Goenka, Satya Narayan: *Vipassana meditation teacher.* Born 1924, Burma. For many years a high-powered businessman with family responsibilities; also performed social good works. 1955: experimented with U Ba Khin's vipassana method hoping to gain migraine relief: was completely cured and achieved deep spiritual insight as well. For next 14 years an energetic student of U Ba Khin. 1969: returned to India; conducted own first vipassana course in Bombay; others followed in many parts of India—his "camps" attended by all sorts of people. 1976: Vipassana International Academy (VIA) established at Igatpuri (Maharashtra state); other centers later established at Hyderabad and Jaipur, smaller ones at Dharamsala, Barachakia, and in Nepal. In W, Vipassana Meditation center inaugurated at Shelburne Falls, Mass, USA in 1982; other centers planned for GB and Australia. Has latterly retired from business to devote himself to teaching meditation and now holds courses every year in Europe, USA, Canada, Japan, Australia, and New Zealand.

Goldstein, Joseph: *American vipassana teacher.* Ex-Peace Corps, trained with Anagarika Munindra (qv) in Bodh Gaya. Invited to teach by Ram Dass (Richard

Alpert) in Boulder. Met Jack Kornfield there. The two were peripatetic teachers for a few years until they became involved in the establishment of the Insight Meditation Society at Barre, Mass. Has also trained with S. N. Goenka in India. Books incl *The Experience of Insight*.

Horner, I. B. (Isaline Blew, 1896–1981): *English Pali scholar*. Met the Rhys Davids (qv) when young. 1936: commented Pali studies when the American scholar Kenneth J. Saunders introduced her to the *Dhammapada*. 1923–36: Librarian of Newnham College, Cambridge; was also a Fellow of the College. 1942–59: Secretary of Pali Text Soc; afterwards President. Also Vice-President of Bdst Society. 1980: OBE. Books incl *Women Under Primitive Buddhism; The Early Buddhist Theory of Man Perfected;* and *Gotama the Buddha* (with Ananda K. Coomaraswamy). Also many trs from Pali, incl *Vinaya Pitaka; Majihima Nikaya; Milindapanha; Buddhavamsa; Cariyapitaka;* and *Vimanavatthu*. Biography by R. E. and C. W. Iggleden in *Buddhist Studies in Honor of I. B. Horner, D. Reodel, Dordrecht, 1974.*

James, Alan: *Vipassana teacher*. Born 1940. Read Physics at London U; became dissatisfied with pure science and began studying philosophy and psychology. 1962–63 and 67: to India to study Oriental philosophy and meditation. 1968: ordained at Wat Buddhapadipa (London) as Dipadhammo Bhikkhu. 1967–70: trained under guidance of Ven Kapilavaddho (qv) at Wat Dhammapadipa, Hampstead (London). 1971–73: took over as teacher in residence at Dhammapadipa after death of Ven Kapilavaddho. 1972: married Jacqueline Randall. 1975–85: worked as Lecturer in Computer Programming in London and Bristol. With Jacqui James (qv) founded House of Inner Tranquility Meditation Center, Wilts, UK (1980); The Aukana Trust, a registered charity (1985); and Monastery of Absolute Harmony, Wilts, UK, (1986). Co-author with Jacqui James of *A Meditation Retreat* and *Modern Buddhism*.

James, Jacqui (1946–89): *Vipassana teacher*. Born 1946. 1968: attended Wat Dhammapadipa, Hampstead (London) and practiced intensive samatha and vipassana meditation under Ven Kapilavaddho (qv); conducted meditation classes and assisted with general admininistration. 1970–73: took up residence at Dhammapadipa; became Secretary and helped edit bi-monthly journal, *Sangha*. 1971: married Kapilavaddho, then Richard Randall. 1971–73: after death of Kapilavaddho, taught and helped administer Dhammapadipa. 1972: married Alan James (qv); with him co-founded House of Inner Tranquility (1980), Aukana Trust (1985), and The Monastery of Absolute Harmony (1986). Co-author with Alan James of *A Meditation Retreat* and *Modern Buddhism*.

Kapilavaddho, Ven (Wm Purfurst, 1906–71): *Founder of English Sangha Trust*. Born Hanwell, Middlesex (UK). Dissatisfied with business life, began studying psychology, philosophy, etc.; went to London (on foot) and became photographer in Fleet St.; found a teacher to instruct him in Yoga and Vedanta; developed a color printing process; took up sculpture. 1939: official war photographer, then fireman during Blitz; met U Thittila whose pupil he became; got married; finally photographer with RAF. After war began serious Bdst studies with U Thittila at Bdst Soc (then in Gt Russell St) covering Sutta, Vinaya, and Abhidhamma. Began lecturing on Bdsm; founded Manchester Bdst Soc. 1952: adopted anagarika status (with permission of wife); later became Samanera Dhammananada under U Thittila; worked for Bdst Soc; continued lecturing and founded societies in Oxford and Cambridge, also Bdst Summer School.

Later resigned samanera status and took job in Surrey hotel as barman to raise finance to go to Thailand. 1954: received lower and higher ordinations (single ceremony) in Thailand (name based on "Kapilavatthu," Buddha's home town; means "he who spreads the Dhamma"); surprised Thai Sangha with his knowledge, esp of Abhidhamma and Pali languages; successfully practiced intensive samatha and vipassana meditation. Returned to UK, to London Bdst Vihara, Knightsbridge, with intention of establishing English Sangha. 1955: to Thailand with 3 British samaneras (Robert Albison, George Blake, and Peter Morgan). 1956: triple ordination at Wat Paknam under Ven Chao Khun Bhavanakosol—the core of an English Sangha. Returned to UK; acquired house in London; English Sangha Trust founded; period of great activity. 1957: due to ill health, disrobed; changed name to Richard Randall; married Ruth Lester; remained 10 years in obscurity. 1967: returned to robe at Wat Buddhapadipa under Ven Chao Khun Sobhana Dhammasudhi; took over Hampstead Bdst Vihara (then renamed Wat Dhammapadipa). Again disrobed. 1971: married Jacqueline Gray.

Khantipalo, Phra (Lawrence Mills): *Pioneer British bhikkhu and Pali scholar.* Born 1932, near London. At Suez Canal with British Army, received book on Bdsm. Later joined Bdst Soc in London; 3 years later took samanera ordination under Ven Dr H. Saddahtissa (qv) at London Bdst Vihara. After 1 year in the robe in UK, left for 3 years in India, studying Pali, traveling and teaching Dr Ambedkar's new Bdsts. Took bhikkhu ordination under Abbot of Wat Cakkapat, Bangkok; studied at Wat Bovoranives; also practiced meditation under various distinguished teachers. After 11 years in Thailand went to Australia with senior Thai bhikkhu to set up wat (temple) in Sydney. Later moved to Sri Lanka; worked at Bdst Publication Soc (Kandy). Subsequently returned to Australia and taught at Wat Buddha-Dhamma, Wiseman's Ferry, NSW 2255. Disrobed after 30 years in the Sangha, married a young Sinhalese woman and lives in Cairns, Queensland, trying to create a Buddhist community in a former hippie area. Books incl *Banner of the Arahants; A Life of the Buddha; Calm & Insight; Nanamoi; Tolerance;* and *What is Buddhism?;* also tr of *Dhammapada* and ed of Nanamoli's tr of *Majihima Nikaya.*

Khema, Sister (Ilse Ledermann): *Pioneering Theravada nun.* Born 1923, Berlin. 1938: obliged to leave Germany due to Jewish origins. After long spiritual search, trained in vipassana under Robert Hover; subsequently led courses in USA, Australasia, and W Germany. 1978: became assistant to Ven Khantipalo (qv) at Wat Buddha-Dhamma, New South Wales, Australia (founded on land purchased by herself). 1979: ordained a nun by Narada Mahathera at Vajirarama, Colombo, Sri Lanka. Founder of Parappuduwa Nun's Island, Dodanduwa, Sri Lanka. Patron of planned International Bdst Womens' Center. Tours Europe and Australia teaching and lecturing on Bdsm. 1989: Returned to Germany and F. Buddha-Haus nr. Munich and conducts residential courses. Books incl *Buddha Ohne Geheimnis.*

Khemadhammo Bhikkhu: *British thera and teacher.* Born 1944, Portsmouth. 1967: became interested in Bdsm; began to attend Hampstead Vihara (instruction from Ruth Walshe and Ven Kapilavaddho). Also small involvement with FWBO. Took up training seriously under Ven Maha Boonchuay, a Thai bhikkhu resident at Hampstead. At Wat Buddhapadipa, co-founded Lay Bdst Assn and Honorary Secretary until 1971. 1971: to Thailand; began vipassana training under Ven Chao Khun Thep Siddhimuni at Wat Mahadhatu, Bangkok. 1971: samanera ordination. 1972: went to stay with Ven Ajahn Cha (qv); for next few years either resident at Wat Pah Pong or various branch wats. 1972:

bhikkhu ordination. 1977: to England with Ajahn Cha and Ven Sumedho Bhikku; stayed at Hampstead Vihara. 1977: began visiting prisons. 1978: moved to Birmingham Vihara. 1979: established vihara on Isle of Wight, first at Little Duxmore, later at Newport (Naradipa Vihara). 1984: established Buddha-Dhamma Vihara at Kenilworth. 1985: launched Angulimala, the Bdst Prison Chaplaincy (with Yann Lovelock); became its Spiritual Director. 1985: moved to The Forest Hermitage, Lower Fulbrook, Warwick, and became resident Ajahn; also Spiritual Adviser to Buddha-Dhamma Fellowship; lectures at Warwick U in Open Studies program and occasionally to trainee teachers; in addition teaches Herefordshire Bdst Group and still travels extensively to many prisons.

Kornfield, Jack: *American lay vipassana teacher, writer, and editor.* Began Asian & Bdst Studies at Dartmouth College. 1963–69: in Asia, studying and practicing Bdsm; Ven Ajahn Cha one of his main teachers; has also trained with S. N. Goenka (qv) in India. 1969: returned to US and disrobed. Drove taxi for a time, then returned to clinical psycholgy studies. Invited by Trungpa Rinpoché (qv) to teach Theravada meditation at Naropa Institute. Also taught at Esalen Institute. Peripatetic teacher for some years. Co-founder, Insight Meditation Society, Barre, Mass (USA). Publications incl *Living Buddhist Masters; A Guide to the Meditation Temples of Thailand; Dharma Talks* (with Joseph Goldstein); also compiled and ed selection of Ajahn Cha's discourses, *A Still Forest Pool.*

Maha Boowa, Ajahn: *Meditation master of the forest tradition of NE Thailand.* Born *c* 1914. Studied basic Dhamma and mastered Pali before embarking upon meditation training. Spent many years practicing meditation as a forest monk; received much instruction from Ajahn Mun (qv), who sternly lectured him on the difference between bliss states (jhanas) and the wisdom of Enlightenment. He "emphasizes the development of strong and steady concentration in practice as a forerunner to the arising of wisdom" (Kornfield). For further information see *Living Buddhist Masters,* by Jack Kornfield, chapter 9.

Mahasi Sayadaw (U Sobhana Mahathera, 1904–82): *Burmese meditation master.* At age 6 began studying at monastic school. Became samanera at 12 and bhikkhu at age 20. At Thaton, studied with U Narada (Mungun Sayadaw); after intensive meditation course returned to Moulmein and resumed working as teacher of Bdst scriptures. Later passed govt sponsored Pali and scholastic exams with flying colors. 1949: requested to give meditation instruction in Rangoon by Prime Minister of Burma, U Nu, and Sir U Thwin, both of Buddha Sasananuggaha Assn. Held intensive training courses at Thathana Yeiktha, headquarters of Buddha Sasananuggaha Assn. Thousands received training (est 45,000 at center; 600,000 in all Burma); many ancillary centers set up in Burma and method also spread abroad to Thailand, Bangladesh, India, Sri Lanka, Europe, S. Africa, Australia, and USA. 1954–56: Questioner (Pucchaka) at 6th Bdst Council in Rangoon to celebrate Buddha Jayanti. Died Rangoon. Books incl *Guide to the Practice of Meditation; Progress of Insight;* and *Practical Insight Meditation.* For further information see *Living Buddhist Masters,* Jack Kornfield, chapter 5.

Malalasekera, Dr Gunapala Piyasena (1899–1973): *"One of the most brilliant Buddhist savants produced by Ceylon and a warm friend of the Buddhist cause throughout the world"* (Buddhist Quarterly). Educated St Johns College, Panadura, and London U where he gained MA, PhD, and DLitt degrees. Taught at Ananda College and Nalanda Vidyalaya, Colombo. 1927–57: Dean of Faculty of Oriental Studies at U of Ceylon; also Prof of Pali. 1950: Founding President of World Fellowship of Bdsts (WFB). Also President,

Ceylon Bdst Congress. Hon Secretary and Treasurer of Pali Text Soc (PTS) in Sri Lanka. Participated in UNESCO projects worldwide. 1957: appointed Ambassador for Ceylon to USSR; also represented his country at UN and was High Commissioner for London for 3 years. Magnum opus—*Dictionary of Pali Proper Names;* also first Editor-in-Chief of *The Encyclopedia of Buddhism* (1966–). Other publications incl *Pali Literature of Ceylon.*

Mun, Ajahn (Phra Mun Bhuridatta Thera, 1870–1949): *Meditation master of the Thai forest tradition.* Born into Kankaew in Ubol Rajadhani, NE Thailand. Took samanera ordination in Khasmbong at age 15. Disrobed after 2 years for family reasons but returned to robe at age 22, taking bhikkhu ordination at Wat Liab. Afterwards trained with Phra Ajahn Sao Kantisilo of Wat Liab. "Under his guidance the Ascetic Forest Tradition became a very important tradition in the revival of Bdst meditation practice. The vast majority of recently deceased and presently living meditation masters in Thailand are either direct disciples of . . . (his) . . . or were substantially influenced by his Teachings" (footnote in *Bodhinyana*). "One of the most renowned of the Thai-Lao forest teachers of this century, known for his mastery of concentration and insight practices, for his great powers, and for the fierceness of his teaching style" (Jack Kornfield). Biography: *The Venerable Phra Achaan Mun Bhuridatta,* compiled by Achaan Maha Boowa (English tr Siri Buddhasukh).

Munindra, Anagarika: *Indian meditation teacher.* Bengali active in Maha Bodhi Society, who in 1949 was requested by the new govt of India to take charge of the Bdst Temple at Bodh Gaya. 1957: 6 months leave to study with Mahasi Sayadaw (qv) in Burma; remained Burma 7 years reading entire Pali Canon and training as monk-teacher with Mahasi Sayadaw. Afterwards returned to Bodh Gaya; ordained as anagarika; set up international meditation center. Occasionally teaches at Insight Meditation center, Barre, Mass., USA.

Nanamoli Bhikkhu (Osbert Moore, 1905–60): *Pioneer British bhikkhu and Pali scholar.* Educated Exeter College, Oxford. Discovered Bdsm via Julius Evola's *The Doctrine of Awakening* while serving in Italy during WWII. Joined BBC after War. 1949: went to Sri Lanka and ordained samanera with friend, Harold Musson. 1950: bhikkhu ordination at Vajirarama Temple (Colombo), then studied with Nyanatiloka Mahathera (qv) at Island Hermitage, Dodanduwa. By 1960: had translated *Visuddhimagga* into English as *The Path of Purification;* also tr *Nettippakarana* ("The Guide") and *Patisambhidamagga* ("Path of Discrimination"), most of the suttas of the *Majjhima Nikaya* and several from the *Samyutta Nikaya.* Died suddenly while on pilgrimage at Maho; cremated at Vajirarama Temple. Other books incl *The Life of the Buddha* and *A Thinker's Note Book.*

Narada Mahathera (Sumanapala Perera, 1898–1983): *Prominent English-educated Sinhalese bhikkhu.* Born Colombo suburb; educated SPCK School, St. Benedict's College (RC), and Paramananda Vihara Sunday School. Entered Sangha at 18; teacher Pelene Vajirañana Mahanayaka Thera; received traditional monastic education but also studied philosophy, logic, and ethics at U College (Colombo). Gained experience of Dhammaduta work with Servants of the Buddha Soc. 1929: first journey abroad (to India); later traveled widely in SE Asia and developed closest ties with Indonesia and Vietnam; also promoted Theravada Bdsm in W Europe. Was elected President of the Bdst Vihara Soc (founded London 1948). A few short stays in London. Also visited Australia. Publications incl *Buddhism in a Nutshell; The Buddha and His Teachings; The Buddhist Conception of Mind or Consciousness; The Buddhist Doctrine of Kamma and Rebirth; Brahma Viharas or The Sublime States; The Way to Nibbana; The Life of the Buddha; The Bodhisatta Ideal;* and *An Elementary Pali Course.* Translations incl *The Dhammapada* and *Abhidhammatthasangaha—A Manual of Abhidhamma.*

Nyanaponika Mahathera (Siegmund Feniger, 1901–94): *Pioneer European bhikkhu.* Born 1901 Hanau-am-Main, W Germany of Jewish parents. Converted to Bdsm via books while living in Upper Silesia. 1922: moved to Berlin and met other German Bdsts. Later formed a Bdst study circle in Königsberg (E Prussia). 1936: to Sri Lanka; samanera ordination at Island Hermitage Dodanduwa. 1937: bhikkhu ordination. WWII: interned as enemy alien in Dehra Dun (N India). 1951: went to Burma with Nyanatiloka Mahathera for 6th Bdst Council. Has served as delegate to World Fellowship of Bdsts (WFB) conferences at Rangoon, Bangkok, and Phnom Penh; has also served as one of the Vice-Presidents of WFB for a term. 1952 and after: resident at Forest Hermitage, Kandy. 1958–84: major founding force behind the Bdst Publication Soc (BPS); is its President and ex-Editor. Books in English incl *The Heart of Buddhist Meditation* and *Abhidhamma Studies.*

Nyanatiloka Mahathera (Anton Gueth, 1878–1957): *Pioneer European bhikkhu and notable Pali scholar.* Born Wiesbaden (Germany). After high school devoted himself to music in Frankfurt and Paris, then journeyed to India via Greece, Middle East, and Ceylon. 1903: samanera ordination in Rangoon; bhikkhu ordination the following year (the first non-British Western one). 1910–11: left Sri Lanka and traveled to Europe; stayed mainly in Switzerland (Lausanne area) and brought many to Bdsm; ordained first samanera on European soil. 1911: returned to Sri Lanka; thereafter lived at the Island Hermitage in Ratgama Lake, Dodanduwa. Interned during WWI as enemy alien. 1916: given passport to return to Germany via USA; traveled to Honolulu and then went to China but was arrested in Chungking and imprisoned in Hankow until 1919, then exchanged by the International Red Cross and sent back to Germany. Unable to return to Sri Lanka in 1920, so went on to Japan, became professor at Komazawa U. 1926: finally got back to Sri Lanka. WW II: again interned. 1946: returned to Dodanduwa. Nyanaponika Thera one of his disciples. Books incl *A Buddhist Dictionary; Guide Through the Abhidhamma; Path to Deliverance;* and *The Word of the Buddha.*

Paññavaddho, Ven (Peter Morgan): *Senior British-born bhikkhu.* Born 1925, Mysore, S India. 1955: samanera ordination at London Bdst Vihara (Knightsbridge). 1956: bhikkhu ordination at Wat Paknam, Thailand, under Ven Chao Khun Bhavanakosol; returned to London; helped found English Sangha Trust (also 1956). 1957: took over leadership of vihara at Alexandra Rd, London NW8, from Ven Kapilavaddho (qv). *c* 1961: left for Thailand and has since trained with Ajahn Maha Boowa (qv) at Wat Pa Barn Tard.

Rahula, Ven Walpola: *Sri Lankan scholar monk.* Born 1907, Galle dist, Sri Lanka. Educated privately. At 13 or 14, entered Sangha; studied Sinhalese, Pali, Sanskrit, Bdsm, and Bdst History according to traditional monastic curriculum. 1936: entered Ceylon U College; then to Calcutta U; later returned to U of Ceylon and gained PhD in 1950; also worked with G. P. Malalasekera (qv) on History of Bdsm in Ceylon. 1930s: well-known preacher criticizing some popular Bdst practices and publishing pamphlets; took special interest in social and economic matters; entered struggle for political freedom. 1940s: supported working class movement and was jailed for 3 days in 1947. 1947: attended Inter-Asian Relations Conference, New Delhi; met many Indian political leaders (Nehru, et al). Sometime Senior Teacher at Vidyalankara Pirivena; also held other posts there. 1950: to Sorbonne (Paris) on French govt fellowship to do research on Mahayana Bdsm (esp works of Asanga). Worked with Paul Demiéville of Collège de France; met André Bareau et al; tr *Abhidharmasamuccaya* into French as *Le Compendium de la Super-Doctrine (Philosophie) (Abhidharmasamuccaya) d'Asanga*. 1958: member of Ceylon Delegation to UNESCO General Conference; met the future Pope John XXIII. 1964: first Bishop Brashares Prof of History and Literature of Religions at Northwestern U, Evanston, Ill., USA. 1965: made *Tripitakavagisvacarya* (Supreme Master of the Bdst Scriptures). 1966: became Vice-Chancellor of Vidyodaya U of Sri Lanka. 1969: resigned to resume studies in Paris. 1970: Honorary Membership of Sri Lanka Academy of Letters. 1974: left Paris for London; worked with Miss I. B. Horner (qv) for Pali Text society. 1977: Cornell Visiting Prof, Swarthmore College, Penn., USA. 1978: Hon DLitt degrees from Us of Sri Lanka, Nava Nalanda Nahavihara (Bihar, India), and Los Angeles (Oriental Studies). 1979: Regent's Lecturer and Visiting Prof of Anthropology, U of California, Los Angeles. Has lectured widely elsewhere, incl Japan. Latterly Chancellor of Kelaniya U and President of Paramadhamma Bdst Institute of Sri Lanka. 1980: Hon DLitt, U of Kelaniya. Other books incl *The Heritage of the Bhikkhu; What the Buddha Taught; and Zen and the Taming of the Bull*. Festschrift: *Buddhist Studies in Honor of W. R.*

Rewata Dhamma Mahathera, Ven Dr: *Senior Burmese bhikkhu teaching in UK.* Born 1929, Thamangone, Henzada district, Burma. Joined local monastery at 5 and studied under various teachers. Age 11: samanera ordination. Age 20: bhikkhu ordination; preceptor—Myint Kwet Sayadaw of Henzada. Studied Pali and Theravada Bdsm at Aung Mingala Thidthi monastery, Rangoon; passed all exams to final Dhammacariya grade. Later went to Dakkhi Narama monastery, Mandalay, to study canon and commentaries under various eminent teachers. Afterwards appointed a teacher at Aung Mingala Thidthi. Age 23: awarded title of Sasanadhaja Siripavaradhammacariya by President of Burma. 1956+: studied at Banaras Hindu and Varanasi U's. 1964: obtained MA in sanskrit. 1967: PhD from Banaras Hindu U. Honorary Lecturer at both universities. 1972: resigned to develop vipassana meditation under S. N. Goenka (qv); had previously practiced with and been appointed a teacher by Mahasi Sayadaw. 1975: came to England at invitation of W Midlands Bdst Center (Birmingham); appointed Spiritual Director by Gyalwa Karmapa (qv). Helped set up other Bdst centers in Birmingham, London, and Isle o Man. Since 1975: has traveled widely in UK, Europe, USSR, Far E, and USA, teaching and lecturing. 1982: appointed member of University Court of Birmingham U. Publications incl ed of *Abhidhammatthasangaha* (with commentary); a 3 vol ed of *Visuddhimagga* (with commentary); ed of First Sermon of the Buddha (in Hindi). To 1975: Chief Editor of *Parami* (English/Hindi periodical). 1969: appointed Chief Editor of *Encyclopedia of Buddhist Technical Terms* by Sanskrit U Varanasi.

Rhys Davids, Caroline (née Foley, 1858–1942): *Pioneer Pali scholar.* Educated U College London; MA and DLitt degrees; also became Fellow. Later Reader in Pali at School of Oriental and African Studies and Lecturer in Indian Philosophy at Manchester U. 1894: married T. W. Rhys Davids (qv); issue—2 daughters, 1 son. Collaborated with husband in Pali Text Society (PTS); succeeded him as President.

"Interested in isolating in the Pali Canon the actual teaching of the Buddha . . . " (Christmas Humphreys). Numerous trans and eds; books incl *Gotama the Man; Sakya or Buddhist Origins;* and *Wayfarer's Words.*

Rhys Davids, Dr T. W. (Thomas William, 1843–1922): *Pioneer Pali scholar.* Born Colchester, son of Congregationalist minister. Educated Brighton and U of Breslau (Germany), where he gained PhD. 1864: entered Ceylon Civil Service. Drawn to Pali studies when work as magistrate produced a case involving a point of Bdst ecclesiastical law; learned Pali from Sumangala Thera (Yatramulle Unnanse). 1872: resigned from CCS; returned to London and studied law. 1977: called to Bar; law practice did not flourish, so concentrated upon Pali and Bdst studies. 1881: delivered Hibbert Trust Lectures; also announced the formation of the Pali Text Society. 1894: married Caroline Augusta Foley, who had similar academic interests. 1882: Professor of Pali at London U. 1885–1904: Secretary and Librarian of Royal Asiatic Society; also a founder of School of Oriental & African Studies (London U). 1894: lectured at Cornell U. 1889–1900: visited Bodh Gaya and other Bdst holy places in India. 1904–10: Prof of Comparative Religion, Victoria U Manchester. 1907: President of Bdst Soc of Great Britain and Ireland. 1910: elected President of India Soc. Retired to Chipstead, Surrey. Numerous eds and trans; books incl *The Ancient Coins & Measures of Ceylan; Manual of Buddhism; Buddhism, Its History & Literature;* and *Buddhist India.* Co-author with Dr Wm Stede of *Pali-English Dictionary.*

Saddhatissa, Ven Dr Hammalawa Mahanayaka Thera, MA, PhD, DLitt (1914–90): *Senior Sri Lankan-born bhikkhu and scholar.* Born 1914, Hammalawa, Satkorale province, Sri Lanka. 1926: bhikkhu ordination. Undergraduate studies at Vidyodaya Pirivena and Prachina Bhasopakara Samagama (Sri Lanka); also studied Banaras, London (SOAS, 1958–61), and Edinburgh (PhD 1965). Proficient in Pali, Sanskrit, Prakrit, Sinhala, and Hindi. 1940–73: held various academic posts, incl Prof of Pali, Banaras Hindu U (1956–57); Lecturer in Sinhala at SOAS, London (1958–60); Professor of Buddhism & Pali at Toronto U (1966–69); visiting lecturer at Oxford (1973). Has also conducted lecture tours in Europe, USA, and Japan. 1956: at Nagpur (India) as adviser to Dr Amdedkar (qv) during mass conversions of former "untouchables" to Bdsm. 1957: Head of London Bdst Vihara. 1966: revived British Mahabodhi Society (defunct since WWII); became its President. Has helped establish other centers, incl new London Bdst Vihara (1964); Bdst Center, Oakenholt, Oxford (1971); Bdst Research Library, Nugegoda, Sri Lanka (1984); Buddha Vihara, Handsworth, Birmingham (1986). Current appointments incl President, Sangha Council of Great Britain (1966); Sanghanayaka Thera (Bdst Primate) of UK (1980); Vice-President, Pali Text Society (1984). Books in English incl *The Buddha's Way; Buddhist Ethics; Essence of Buddhism; Handbook for Buddhists; Introduction to Buddhism;* and *The Life of the Buddha.* Various eds of Pali texts.

Silacara Bhikkhu (J. F. McKechnie, 1871–1950): *Pioneer British bhikkhu.* Born Hull; worked in garment industry, then emigrated to USA and worked on farms. Later went to Rangoon, Burma to help Ananda Metteyya (qv) edit journal *Buddhism.* 1906: ordained by U Kumara Thera at Kyundagon temple. 1925: health broke; disrobed and returned to UK. Worked with Anagarika Dharmapala at Mahabodi Soc. 1932: health broke again; left London for Surrey. During WWII: retreat at Wisborough Green sold; entered old folks home at Bury until death. Publications incl *The Four Noble Truths; The Noble Eightfold Path; Kamma; Lotus Blossoms;* and *Young People's Life of the Buddha.*

Sircar, Réné: *Vipassana teacher.* Former Burmese nun, disciple of Taungpulu Sayadaw, who teaches vipassana and Bdst psychology at the California Institute for Asian Studies.

Story, Francis (1910–71): *Influential English writer.* Born Croydon, Surrey (UK) and became Bdst at 16. Qualified in medicine and served in RAMC in WWII. 1948 became Anagorika Sugotananda at Bodh Gaya, India. 1950: helped form Burma Bdst World Mission, Rangoon, Burma. 1954: Director-in-Chief and joined English Editorial Board of *The Light of the Dhamma* (foremost Theravada periodical 1952–63). 1957: 10 years in Sri Lanka lecturing and broadcasting. Specialized in researching doctrine of rebirth with Prof Ian Stevenson (Virginia U, USA). 1968: lecture tour of USA on same theme. Books incl *The Four Noble Truths; Dialogues on the Dhamma; The Buddhist Doctrine of Nibbana* (with P. Vajirañana); *The Case for Rebirth; Rebirth as Doctrine and Experience;* and 2 vols of collected essays, *The Buddhist Outlook* and *Dimensions of Buddhist Thought.*

Sumedho, Ajahn: *American-born Theravada meditation master; founder of various W monasteries.* Born 1934. Began Far E Studies at U of Washington; studies interrupted by spell of service in US Navy during Korean War; visited Japan and encountered Bdsm. Later returned to U of Washington to complete degree; then to U of California for MA in Asian Studies; this completed 1963. 1964: to Borneo with Peace Corps; then to Thailand; taught English part-time at Thammasat U, Bangkok and practiced meditation. On vacation in Laos recommended to ordain in temple in Nong Kai (NE Thailand); practiced solo for 1 yr; later became a disciple of Ajahn Cha (qv) at Wat Pah Pong in Ubon province. 1973: after 7 Vassa (Rains Retreats) allowed to visit India as dhutanga monk. 1974: established and became Abbot of the international Wat Pah Nanachat at Bung Wai. 1976: first return visit to USA; visited UK and contacted English Sangha Trust. 1977: came to UK with Ajahn Cha at invitation of English Sangha Trust; resided at Hampstead Bdst Vihara. 1979: established Chithurst Forest Monastery (Wat Pah Cittaviveka) with 108 acres of forest in rural W Sussex (UK) and became first Abbot. Various other centers have sprung from this: Amaravati (Hemel Hempstead), Harnham Vihara (Northumberland), and the Devon Vihara. Presently Abbot of Amaravati, but teaches elsewhere and goes on regular world tours. Honorary President of the Bdst Society (London). Books incl *Cittaviveka (Teachings from the Silent Mind)* and *The Path to the Deathless.*

Sunlun Sayadaw (1878–1952): *Burmese meditation master.* Born U Kyaw Din in Myingyan, middle Burma. At 15 became office boy in District Commissioner's office, Myingyan. Married Ma Shew Yi. At 30, resigned job; became farmer. Disturbed by intimations of imminent death; interested in vipassana meditation by a mill clerk; began to practice. After certain insights, wished to become a monk; obtained wife's permission to do so. Afterwards practiced diligently until Oct 1920, when he is reputed to have achieved arahantship. Though barely literate, won great respect; many disciples. His practices, which emphasize intense effort, are taught by a number of meditation masters and in several centers in or near Rangoon, Burma (e.g., Sunlun Monastery). Further information: see *Living Buddhist Masters,* Jack Kornfield, chapter 6.

Taungpulu Sayadaw (Taungpulu Tawya Kaba Aye Sayadaw): *Burmese meditation master.* Trained with Mahasi Sayadaw's teacher and spent many years in austere practice. 1978: invited to USA; set up temporary forest monastery in Palo Alto. 1981: again returned to USA to found permanent vihara on W Coast. Main monastery is in the Meiktila District of Burma.

Thittila, Sayadaw U: *Senior Burmese bhikkhu.* Born 1896, Pyawbwe, C Burma. Samanera at 15 under U Kavinda; bhikkhu ordination at 20 under Ashin Adicca Vamsa. At 25 passed doctoral exams with highest honors; taught and lectured in Rangoon for 12 years. 1938–52: in UK; spent war years there; worked as stretcher bearer in Blitz. Onetime Librarian at Bdst Soc. Lectured widely, esp on Abhidhamma. 1952: returned to Burma; became Prof of Pali at Rangoon U. Has again visited UK and USA. Tr incl *Vibhanga* (Book of Analysis).

Tiradhammo, Ajahn: *Canadian-born bhikkhu active in UK.* Born 1949, New Westminster, Vancouver, British Columbia, Canada. 1967–69 and 1971–72: attended U of British Columbia, studying engineering, geology, geography. 1970: traveled in Europe and Middle East. 1970–71: to India and Sri Lanka; meditation retreat at Kanduboda. 1972–73: to Thailand. 1973: novice ordination. 1974: bhikkhu ordination. 1975–82: practiced with Ajahn Cha (qv) at Wat Pah Pong. 1982: to Chithurst Forest Monastery. 1984: senior incumbent at Harnham Vihara. 1987: established forest monastery near Berne, Switzerland.

Titmuss, Christopher: *British meditation teacher, spiritual counselor, and social activist.* Born 1944. 1962–69: reporter and photojournalist in London, Turkey, Thailand, Laos, and Australia. 1970–76: a monk in Thailand and India; studied and practiced under Ajahn Dhammadaro at Wat Chai Na and with Ajahn Buddhadasa (qv) at Wat Chaiya; 8-month period of solitary meditation practice at Ko Pha Nga, Thailand. Meditation teacher and lecturer in India, incl 6-month intensive at Dalhousie. 1977–present: international meditation teacher, lecturer, psychological and spiritual counselor in England, USA, Australia, India, and Europe. Co-founder of various spiritual communities and centers; Founder and ed of *Reality* (newspaper). "Presently, meditation practice and teaching emphasizes complete integration of awareness into daily life. In the silence and stillness of intensive practice, the emergence of transcendent understanding and the true significance of the nature of reality is experienced." Active in various engaged organizations, incl Bdst Peace Fellowship. Green Party candidate in S Devon. Publications incl 100 taped lectures: *Let All Things Be New* (published in Germany). Books incl *The Profound and the Profane* and *The Green Buddha*.

Vajiragnana, Ven Medagama: *Head of London Bdst Vihara.* Born 1928, Maha-Medagama, Sri Lanka. 1943: ordained and received traditional bhikkhu training. Also studied at Vidyodaya (BA 1961), Banaras (Diploma 1962), and Jadaipur (Calcutta, MA 1965) Us; subsequently awarded DLitt in Bdst Literature by Sangha Council of Sri Lanka for contribution to Bdst education in UK. After completing studies, worked in education and was principal of a monastic college and later of a Bhikkhu Teacher Training College in Sri Lanka; has since lectured in Asia, Europe, and America. 1966: appointed Kammacariya (Master of Acts of Vinaya) by Sangha Council of Sri Lanka. 1967: established himself in London; was Religious Director of the British Bdst Assn. Is a Vice President of World Sangha Council and Bdst Patron of UK & Ireland Group of World Conference of Religions for Peace. In Sri Lanka was Joint Secretary of United Religions Organization and a Committee Member of Standing Conference of Inter-Faith Dialogue in Education. Is currently head of London Bdst Bihara and author of a number of publications.

Vimalo, Anagarika (Walter Kulbarz): *German-born meditation teacher.* Born 1931. 1958: samanera ordination at former Thai Embassy, London with twin brother

(Dhammiko) by Chao Khun Vimaladhammo, Abbot of Wat Mahathat, Bangkok. Both trained as samaneras under Ven Paññavaddho (qv). Bhikkhu ordination in Rangoon. 1967–76: resident in Thailand. Returned to Germany, disrobed and was attached to Haus der Stille, Rosebürg, near Hamburg. Spent some years at Sharpham North Community in Devon. Currently in Germany.

Viradhammo, Ajahn: *Canadian bhikkhu now active in new Zealand.* Born 1948 (Vitauts Akers) of Latvian parents in W Germany. 1952: family emigrated to Toronto, Canada. 1971: met first teacher—American bhikkhu in India. 1973: samanera in Bangkok. 1975: bhikkhu at Wat Ba Pong, NE Tailand, under Ajahn Cha (qv). After training, resided in Forest Monastery, Chithurst, Sussex (UK), and was abbot of Wat Bodhinyanatama, New Zealand. Currently abbot of Amarvati Buddhist Monastery, successor to Ajahn Sumedho (qv).

Walshe, Maurice O'Connell: *British scholar and translator of Pali texts.* Born 1911, London, educated London U; also Berlin, Göttingen, Vienna. Twice married: (1) Ruth Meisel (b. Vienna) 1941, (2) Florence Knight 1973. Reader in German and Deputy Director, Institute of Germanic Studies, U of London; retired 1979. Sometime Vice-President, The Bdst Soc; also Chairman, English Sangha Trust. Author of *Buddhism for Today;* tr incl 3 vols of sermons by Meister Eckhart; also *Digha Nikaya.*

Webb, Russell: *Editor.* Born 1941, Worthing, Sussex (UK). Profession: Lloyd's insurance broker. 1964–66: Honorary Secretary and Librarian, London Bdst Assn. 1966–84: Honorary Secretary and Librarian, London Bdst Vihara (LBV). 1984–86: Dhammaduta Secretary, LBV. 1964–68: ed, *Buddhist News.* 1968–83: Joint Ed, *Buddhist Quarterly.* 1976–82: Ed, *Pali Buddhist Review.* 1983–: Ed, *Buddhist Studies Review.* Publications incl *An Analysis of the Pali Canon* and *A Buddhist's Manual* (with H. Saddhatissa). Joint Secretary and Ed of *Buddhist Studies in Honour of Hammalava Saddhatissa.*

Woodward, F. L. (Frank Lee, 1871–1952): *Pioneer English Pali scholar.* Born Saham, Norfork. Educated Christ Hospital and Sidney Sussex College, Cambridge. Became schoolmaster; began to study Pali and Sanskrit, also E and W philosophy and comparative religion. 1902: joined Theosophical Society. 1903–c 1919: headmaster, Mahinda College, Galle, Sri Lanka. 1919: left for Tasmania and dedicated remainder of life to producing translations for Pali Text Society. Best remembered for anthology, *Some Sayings of the Buddha.*

TIBETAN BUDDHISM

Notes on Titles:

Chögyal: lit, "Dharma Raja": Religious King or "Protector of the Bdst Religion."
Chujé: lit, "Lord of Dharma."
Gelong: monk.
Getsül: novice (samanera).
Geshe: Gelugpa title corresponding to Doctor of Divinity.
Gyalwa: lit, "Conqueror" (over delusion); i.e. one who has become a buddha. As a title, is used only for the highest spiritual leaders, such as the Dalai Lama (often called "Gyalwa Rinpoché") and the Karmapa.
Kazi: a high-ranking Sikkimese.

Khamtrul: title given to a tulku from Kham district of Tibet.
Khenpo: generally "Abbot"; title indicating high scholarship in Nyingma, Sakya, and Kagyu schools.
Khyentse: lit, "One in whom Wisdom and Compassion are perfectly combined"; a name carried by a number of exceptional Nyingma lamas during the last 200 years.
Kongtrul: title given to a tulku from the Konpo district of Tibet.
Kyabje: lit, "Protector" or "Lord of Refuges"; a lofty title equivalent to "His Holiness."
Lama: important religious teacher or guru; not necessarily a monk.
Lharampa: First Class Honors in the Geshe degree examinations. See *Tibet Journal*, vol 2, No 3, 1977, p. 67— "The Structure of the Gelug Monastic Order."
Ngakpa: lit, "a practitioner of mantras"; shamanistic practitioner of the Nyingma school, adept at exorcising spirits, making rain, etc.
Rinpoché: lit, "Precious One"; honorific suffixed to the name of a high lama.
Tertön: Nyingma lama who discovers a terma or (hidden) "treasure" teaching.
Tulku: voluntary re-incarnation of a religious figure of some distinction.
Yeshe: Wisdom (equivalent of Jñana).

Akong Rinpoché, Ven Chujé: *Tulku of Karma Kagyu and Nyingma lineages; Spiritual Director of Samyé Ling Tibetan Center.* Former Abbot Drolma Lhakhang monastery and retreat complex, Tsawa Gang, E Tibet. Received teachings from Jamgön Kongtrül of Shechen and other great teachers. Came to Britain in 1960s. 1967: with Trungpa Rinpoché (qv) established Kagyu Samyé Ling Tibetan Centre in Johnstone House, Langhom, Dumfries-shire, Scotland. After departure of Trungpa Rinpoché for USA (*c.* 1970), took charge of the centre; has since founded centers in Spain, South Africa, and other parts of the world.

Ato Rinpoché (Tendzin Tulku): *Karma Kagyu lama; 7th Incarnation of the Tendzin Tulku of Nehzang monastery, Kham, E Tibet; currently residing in UK.* Born 1933 at Ato Shokha, Gatöd, Kham; son of VIIth Tendzin Tulku. Claimed as tulku by both Jontang monastery (Gelug school) as well as by Nehzang; status confirmed by VIth Panchen Lama. Formally enthroned at age 8 years; received usual exhaustive religious training; received initiations and teachings from Dingo Khyentse Rinpoché (qv) et al and underwent various retreats practicing Vajra Yogini, Chakrasamvara, Mahakala, and the Six Doctrines of Naropa. 1957: spent 1 year at Tsurphu serving Gyalwa Karmapa, with whom he took novice vows; also received various teaching and initiations from both Karmapa and Dingo Khyentse. 1958: attended Sera monastery. 1959: sought refuge in India. 1960–63: Kagyupa representative in Dharamsala on Dalai Lama's Council for Religious & Cultural Affairs. 1963–66: assistant to Sister Palmo (Freda Bedi-qv) at Young Lama's School, Dalhousie. 1966: put in charge by Dalai Lama of new monastery created out of Young Lama's School. 1967: married Alethea Martineau; settled in Cambridge (UK). 1967 to present: taught privately; also Visiting Teacher at various groups in UK. 1986: began a monthly meditation group Cambridge. 1970–81; nursing assistant at Fulbourne Mental Hospital, Cambridge.

Ayang Rinpoché: *Tulku of the Drigung Kagyu lineage; a mind emanation of Chögyal Dorge.* Born 1941, Gaba province, Kham, E Tibet. Many termas of Chögyal Dorje are preserved in his family. 1949–59: lived in the main Drigung monastery near Lhasa. 1959: sought refuge in India. Founded monastery at Byalkuppe, S India. A specialist in Phowa (Transmission of Consciousness) practices; carries blessings of the three Phowa lineages: Nyingma, Drigung, and Namchö Phowa. At request of HH the Dalai Lama, taught Phowa in Japan; also a frequent visitor to Europe and USA, where he conducts Phowa courses and teaches in his various centers.

Batchelor, Stephen: *Writer and translator.* Born 1953, Scotland. Traveled in the East. 1971: began Tibetan Bdst studies. 1974: ordained as Gelugpa monk (Gelong Jhampa Thabkay); studied with Geshe Rabten (qv) in India and Switzerland. 1981–85; ordained as Popch'on Sunim and trained in Korean Zen with Kusan Sunim (qv) at Songgwang Sa Monastery. Presently at Sharpham North Community, S Devon (UK) and conducts retreats there as well as elsewhere in UK and Europe. Publications incl *Along with Others (Outlines for an Existential approach to Buddhism); Flight (An Existential Conception of Buddhism);* and *The Jewel in the Lotus (A Survey of the Buddhism of Tibet).* Tr incl Shantideva's *Bodhicaryavatara* (from the Tibetan) and Geshe Rabten's *Echoes of Voidness.*

Bedi, Freda (Sister Karma Khechog Palmö, 1911–77): *Late English Tibetan Bdst nun and refugee worker.* Educated Oxford; married Baba Bedi and lived many years in India; active in Indian Independence movement and later fought for women's rights in Punjab. Appointed head of Social Welfare Board by Nehru; responded wholeheartedly to plight of Tibetans post 1959; became Principal of Young Lama's School, Dalhousie. Studied with Sayadaw U Thittila and Mahasi Sayadaw (both qv) in Rangoon. 1966: samaneri ordination by Gyalwa Karmapa. 1972: bhikshuni ordination in Hong Kong. 1976: (International Women's Year) National Award from Indira Gandhi. Resided at Rumtek, Sikkim until death.

Beer, Robert: *Western thangka painter.* Born 1947, Cardiff, UK. Studied thangka painting in India and Nepal with Jhampa, thangka-painter to HH the Dalai Lama, and with Khamtrul Rinpoché. Illustrator of *Masters of Enchantment: The Lives and Legends of the Mahasiddhas.* Lives in London.

Beru, Sherapalden: *Resident thangka painter at Samyé Ling Tibetan Center, Scotland.* Main lineage holder of Karma Gadri tradition of fine art and temple decoration.

Berzin, Dr. Alexander: *Translator and teacher.* Born 1944, New Jersey, USA. 1972: PhD, Harvard. 1969: to India, initially as Fulbright scholar. 1972: joined Library of Tibetan Works & Archives, Dharamsala; studied with various Tibetan masters. Since 1975 has translated for various Tibetan masters, incl Dalai Lama and his late tutors. Trs incl *An Anthology of Well-spoken Advice; Mahamudra; Eliminating the Darkness of Ignorance; Dzogchen, the Four-themed Precious Garland;* and *The Wheel of Sharp Weapons, a Compendium of Ways of Knowing.*

Chhimed Rigdzin Rinpoché (Khordong Terchen Tulku Chhimed Rigdzin Rinpoché): *Nyingma lama; incarnation of Nuden Dorje Drophang Lingpa.* Born 1922; recognized as tulku by various important lamas. At age 4, enthroned at Khardong Gompa; overall charge of 12 gompas. At 10 discovered 2 important termas; also pilgrimage to Lhasa. *c* 1932–34: various empowerments, instructions, and practice; then returned to Khardong; trained under various lamas. Later given important instructions and predictions by Tulku Tsurlo: that at 18 he would wander in the mountains of Nepal, Bhutan, and Sikkim, then enter 2 years solitary retreat. *c* 1959: to Italy at invitation of G. Tucci (qv). 1984: received requests to return to Tibet; accordingly visited Tibet and proposes returning. Married with issue.

Chime Youndong Rinpoché, Lama: *Karma Kagyu lama active in UK.* Born Kham; recognized as a tulku of Benchen monastery. From his abbot, Nyentrul Rinpoché, received instruction in Mahamudra; and in Dzoghen from Dingo Khyentse Rinpoché (qv). Sent to W by Gyalwa Karmapa. 1972: resigned monk status and married Celia Jane Pertwee. 1973: set up Kham Tibetan House, Saffron Walden, Essex (UK); and 1987, Karma Kagyu Chö Khor Ling, London. Works for the British Library with their Tibetan manuscripts.

Chögyam, Ngakpa Chögyam ögyen Pogden: *British Nyingma shaman.* Born 1952, Farnham, Surrey, UK. Trained as illustrator in Bristol. Traveled in E to study and practice under several Tibetan Tantric masters, incl Chhimed Rigdzin Rinpoché; completed number of retreats; has also studied Tibetan art. 1983: initiated as a ngakpa. 1985: with wife founded Sang-ngak-chö-dzong (Tibetan Tantric Periphery) in Cardiff. Professional counselor and healer, works with psychologists and people in the caring professions. Books incl *Rainbow of Liberated Energy*.

Csoma de Körös, Alexander (1784–1842): *Hungarian pioneer of Tibetan studies.* Born Transylvania; son of Calvinist border guard. Inspired to look for "racial homeland" of Magyars. 1816–18: studied Arabic, Turkish, English, and Ethnology at Göttingen. 1819: set out for E on foot; never reached Tibet but traveled and researched in frontier regions (e.g. Ladakh). Obtained modest British govt sponsorship; compiled first Tibetan-English dictionary and a Tibetan Grammar (both published 1834). 1837–42: Librarian of Asiatic Society, Calcutta. 1842: set out again on quest for Magyar racial home; died Darjeeling of malaria. His analysis of the Kanjur and Tanjur was included in Waddell, L.A., *The Buddhism of Tibet or Lamaism* (1894). Various contributions to *Journal of the Asiatic Society of Bengal*. Dictionary, Grammar and Collected Writings reprinted Budapest 1984. 1920: founded Körösi Csoma Tarsasag [Society], Budapest.

Dalai Lama: "Dalai"—"Ocean." Title conferred by the Mongol Altan Khan upon Sönam Gyatso (1543–88) in 1578 and retrospectively on his two predecessors. The first Dalai Lama therefore became (posthumously) Gendun-drup (1391–1474), a principal disciple of Jé Tsongkhapa. The title has passed on by the tulku system to the present. Until 1959, the Dalai Lamas were at apex of Tibetan religio-political hierarchy.

Dalai Lama, HH the XIVth, (Gyalwa Tenzin Gyatso): *Exiled spiritual and temporal leader of the Tibetan people.* Born 1935, Taktser, Amdo, E Tibet of humble origins. Located and recognized as Dalai Lama incarnation 2 years later via portens discerned at the oracle lake (Lhama Lhatsö). 1939: brought to Lhasa. 1940: formally enthroned. Began education at 6 years; at 24 years took preliminary exams at Sera, Drepung, and Ganden monastic universities; final exams held at Jokhang ("Cathedral" of Lhasa) during Mönlam Festival; awarded Geshe Lharampa degree with honors at age 25. At age 16 assumed full temporal powers early because of Chinese Communist threat. 1954: went to Peking to hold discussions with Chinese Communist leaders. 1956: visited India for 2500 Buddha Jayanti celebrations; held political discussions with Pandit

Nehru and Chou En-lai. 1959: left Tibet following the Lhasa Uprising. Made unsuccessful appeals to United Nations on behalf of Tibetan people. 1963: promulgated draft democratic constitution for Tibet; since then has conducted government-in-exile at Dharamsala, N India, in accordance with this. Has also very successfully worked to resettle 100,000 Tibetan refugees and to preserve Tibetan religion and culture. In 1989 he was awared the Nobel Peace Prize. Widely traveled in both E and W (though has never returned to his native Tibet), has met political and spiritual leaders (incl two Popes and an Archbishop of Canterbury), scientists, doctors, writers, philosophers, and ordinary people. Has impressed people everywhere with his (very Buddhist) message of peace and kindness: "My religion is very simple—my religion is kindness . . . " A spiritual leader of world rank. Books incl *Opening the Eye of New Awareness; Kindness, Clarity & Insight; My Land and My People* (autobiographical) and *Freedom in Exile*. Biographies: *Great Ocean* by Roger Hicks and Ngakpa Chögyam and *The Last Dalai Lama* by Michael Harris Goodman.

Damcho Yonten, Geshe: *Gelugpa Lama active in UK.* Born 1930, Lhasa. Entered Drepung monastery at age 6. For next 23 years studied Bdst philosophy, psychology, logic, debate, and scriptural subjects. Also practiced meditation under guidance of distinguished lamas. Received Geshe degree while still at Drepung. 1959: left Tibet; continued studies in India and Ladakh; became abbot of Samtenling Gompa (Ladakh). 1966: began teaching W students. 1976: came to W. 1978: founded Lam Rim Buddhist Center, S Wales.

David-Neel, Alexandra (1868–1969): *Pioneering French mystic, traveler, and author.* Born Saint-Mandé (E suburb of Paris). Discovered E religion and philosophy at Musée Guimet (Paris) at age 23: "My vocation was born there and then." Became singer with Opéra Comique; later turned to journalism. 1894: married Philippe Neel in Tunis; soon separated. In E for next 20 years. Met exiled XIIIth Dalai Lama in Darjeeling. In Sikkim met Lama Yongden, her future traveling companion and adopted son. Went into retreat in Himalayan cave-hermitage; met Tibetan teachers who taught her Tibetan language and Bdst philosophy. Ventured 3 times into Tibet, once reaching Shigatse before being turned back. Subsequently left for Burma, Sri Lanka, and Japan, accompanied by Yongden; then to Korea, China, and Mongolia. Studied at Kumbum monastery (E Tibet). 1924: became first European woman to enter Lhasa (in disguise). 1925: returned to Europe; bought house in Digne (Haute Provence). 1937: returned to Asia, traveling via Transiberian Railway to China. Japanese invasion of Manchuria forced her westwards to Tatsienlu; spent most of WWII there. Later returned to France via India; subsequently engaged in study and writing at Digne until death at age 100+. 1964: made Commandeur de la Légion d'Honneur. Books in English incl *With Mystics & Magicians; My Journey to Lhasa; Tibetan Journey; A Tibetan Tale of Love & Magic; Secret Oral Traditions of Tibetan Buddhism;* and *Initiations & Intiates in Tibet.*

Dhargyey, Geshe: *Gelugpa Lama with W students.* Born 1925, Kham, E Tibet. Entered local monastery at 7 years; at 16 years entered Sera Monastery and remained until 1959. Completed studies in India and appointed resident teacher in Library of Tibetan Works & Archives (Dharamsala) 1971. Has taught many Westerners. Books incl *Advice from a Spiritual Friend* (with Geshe Rabten).

Dilgo Khyentse Rinpoché (1910–91): *Important Nyingma Master and exponent of Dzogchen Meditation.* Born in Kham, E Tibet. Recognized as mind incarnation of

Jamyang Khyentse Wangpo (1820–92). Studied under many distinguished lamas of all four schools, notably Jamyang Khyentse Chökyi Lodrö, and spent 20 years in retreat. A Tertön, also wrote many meditation texts and commentaries notable for their poetic beauty. Traveled extensively giving teachings in Bhutan, Nepal, India, and the W. 1976: to USA on invitation of Trungpa Rinpoché (qv), his pupil. 1983: to London at invitation of Sogyal Rinpoché (qv). Also visited France, where he supervised students undergoing long retreat. Transmitted teachings to Dalai Lama. Rebuilt Shechen Monastic University (formerly one of the great Nyingma centers in Tibet) at Bodh Nath, Nepal.

Dodrupchen Rinpoché (Thubten Trinley Pal Zangpo): *The Holder of the Dzogchen Teachings of Longchen Nyingthig*. Born 1927, Golok, E Tibet; 4th incarnation of Jigme Trinley Ozer (1745–1821), chief disciple of Jigme Lingpa (1729–98). Studied with Khomey Khenpo, Khenpo Kangnam, Khenpo Chochog, and Khenpo Thubnyen. Received transmissions from Jamyang Khyentse Chökyi Lödro, Khenpo Kunpal, Sechen Kongtrul, and Dzogchen Rinpoché; received final teachings on Dzogchen from Yuthog Chatralwa and Apang Tertön. Built scriptural college at Dodrupchen monastery; printed and distributed the *Seven Treasuries of Longchenpa* (1308–63). Traveled widely, teaching tens of thousands of students. 1957: made Gangtok, Sikkim, his home; again subsidized the printing of Longchenpa's *Seven Treasuries* and his *Trilogy of Finding Comfort & Ease*. 1973: to USA; established Mahasiddha Nyingma Center in Massachusetts; has since visited USA a number of times. 1975: taught in London and France.

Donden, Dr. Yeshe: *Notable Tibetan medical practitioner*. Born 1929, Lhoga district of C Tibet, near Lhasa. At 6 years entered a monastery. At 11 went to Chakpori Medical College, Lhasa; exhibited considerable ability in memorization and memorized four medical tantras; entered training with Kyenrab Norbu, Director of the College. At 20 years came out top of his exams. 1951: began practice in home district. 1959: left Tibet for India. 1960–80: Physician to Dalai Lama. Founded Tibetan Medical Center, Dharmsala. 1969 to present: engaged in private practice in addition to other duties; frequently travels to W to teach; has given a series of lectures at U of Virginia. Books in English incl *Health Through Balance*.

Dorji, Gyurmé: *British Nyingma scholar*. Tr *History of the Nyingma School* by Dudjom Rinpoché (qv).

Dorjiev, Khampo Agvan Lovsan (1853–1938): *Buryat Mongol Lama of some political notoriety*. Born Baikal region of E Russia. 1880: went to Lhasa; settled at Drepung monastery and acquired a reputation for scholarship. Became tutor to XIIIth Dalai Lama and gained influence with him. 1889: went on a journey to Russia to collect funds for his college. 1901: visit to St. Petersburg: returned to Lhasa laden with gifts and political overtures. News of this exacerbated existing British fears of Russian designs on Tibet and led directly to the Younghusband Expedition (1904). Before British troops reached Lhasa, fled with Dalai Lama to Mongolia. Was again seen in Lhasa after Dalai Lama's return from second period of exile (1913). 1920s: worked among Mongolian Bdsts. Died during Stalinist purges. Root guru of Geshe Wangyal (qv).

Dowman, Keith: *British translator*. From *c* 1979 at Varanasi and in Himalayan region studying and practicing Tibetan Bdsm. Trs incl *Divine Madman* (The Life and

Teachings of Drukpa Kunley); *The Legend of the Great Stupa; Sky Dancer: The Secret Life & Songs of the Lady Yeshe Tsogyel;* and *Masters of Enchantment: The Lives and Legends of the Mahasiddhas.*

Dudjom Rinpoché (HH Jigdral Yeshe Dorje, 1904–87): *Late Supreme Head of the Nyingma order of Tibetan Bdsm. Outstanding yogi, tertön, and meditation master.* Born Pemakö, SE Tibet. Recognized as incarnation of Dudjom Lingpa (1835–1904), yogi and tertön. Studied initially at Pemakö with Khenpo Aten, later in monastic universities of C Tibet (Mindroling, Dorje Drak, and Tarjé Tingpoling) and E Tibet (e.g. Kathok and Dzogchen); principal teachers incl Phungong Tulku Gyurmé Ngedön Wangpo, Jedrung Trinlé Jampa Jungne, Gyurmé Phendei özer, and Minling Dordzin Namdrol Gyatso. A meticulous scholar and prolific writer of more than 40 volumes elucidating the teachings and practice of the Nyingma lineage; writings acknowledged by all schools to be unsurpassed in their knowledge of traditional poetics, history, medicine, astrology, and philosophy. A married lama, settled in Darjeeling after leaving Tibet; later lived in Kathmandu, Nepal. 1972: invited to USA by Sonam Kazi; visited Berkeley and New York and conducted refugee and bodhisattva ceremonies and gave public talks. 1976: longer visit to USA on invitation of poet John Giorno; established Orgyen Cho Dzong in New York City. Has also established centers in Hong Kong and France, where European seat of Nyinmapas (Orgyen Samyé Chöling) established 1975. Visited London 1972, 76 and 79. Books incl a *History of the Nyingmapas* and a complete survey of Buddhadharma; also a *History of Tibet* written at request of Dalai Lama. Revised canonical teachings (kama) of Nyingmapas. Died at home in France. Extended bio-obituary, *The Middle Way,* vol. 62, p 25ff, 1987.

Dzogchen Rinpoché (Jigme Losel Wangpo): *Young Nyingma tulku; incarnation of Dzogchen Pema Rigdzin.* Born 1964, Sikkim. Recognized by Dodrupchen Rinpoché (qv) as VIIth incarnation of Dzogchen Pema Rigdzin (1625–97). 1972: enthroned. Has received teachings from Dudjom Rinpoché and Dingo Khyentse Rinpoché; education closely supervised by Dalai Lama. Has completed a course at the Bdst School of Dialectics, Dharamsala. Currently rebuilding Dzogchen Monastery (formerly foremost center of Nyingma study and practice in Tibet) in Mysore, S India. 1985: visited Europe and USA on invitation of Sogyal Rinpoché (qv); bestowed empowerments. Thought to have great potential as a future Nyingma teacher.

Dzongsar Khyentse Rinpoché (Jamyang Thubten Chökyi Gyatso): *Nyingma tulku; incarnation of Jamyang Khyentse Chökyi Lodrö.* Born 1960; recognized by Dalai Lama. Received training in all lineages to Tibetan Bdsm under 12 great masters, incl Dalai Lama, Karmapa, Sakya Trizin, Dudjom Rinpoché, and Dingo Khyentse Rinpoché. 1986: first visit to Europe and USA. Has thriving center in Australia.

Elliott, Neil: *British Gelug monk; teacher at Madhyamaka, the Yorkshire Bdst Center.*

Evans-Wentz, Dr Walter Yeeling (1878–1965): *Pioneer translator of Tibetan Bdst texts.* Born USA, educated Us of Stanford, Oxford, and Rennes, specializing in folklore; met W. B. Yeats. 1911: first book: *Fairy Faith in Celtic Countries.* An interest in the rebirth doctrine took him to E. 1919: met Kazi Dawa-Samdup in Sikkim; collaborated on translation of several texts, incl *The Tibetan Book of the Dead; The Tibetan Book of the Great Liberation; Tibetan Yoga and Secret Doctrines;* and *Tibet's Great*

Yogi Milarepa. Died near Encinitas, California at age 88 yrs. Biography: *Pilgrim of the Clear Light* by Ken Winkler.

Fletcher, Frederic (Lama Dorje Prajñananda, 1879–1950): *First Westener to be ordained in Tibetan Bdsm.* Born London, educated Oxford, read *Light of Asia*; traveled in E. WW I: Major in Army; sickened by carnage; decided to enter Sangha after war. 1922–23: with McGovern, Ellam, and Knight on British Bdst Mission to Tibet. Reached Shigatse; novice ordination (Gelug); obliged to leave Tibet. 1924: bhikkhu ordination in Sri Lanka. Traveled in India; once returned UK; lived out life in Burma.

Ganden Tripa or **Tri Rinpoché of Ganden:** *Supreme Head of Gelug Order.* See **Ling Rinpoché** and **Jampäl Shenpen.**

Govinda, Lama Anagarika (Anagarika Khamsum-Wangchuk; E. L. Hoffmann, 1898–1985): *Pioneer Western exponent and expositor of Tibetan Buddhism.* Born Waldheim (old kingdom of Saxony) of German father and Bolivian mother (family had mining interests in Bolivia). Invalided out of WWI. Studied Philosophy and Architecture at U of Freiburg, later Archeology; research in Mediterranean area and N Africa. 1928: to Sri Lanka. 1929: anagarika ordination in Burma. 1929–31: studied Pali. 1931: decisive turning point—encountered Tibetan Bdsm in Darjeeling and met main guru, Tomo Geshe Rinpoché. When TGR died, founded Arya Maitreya Mandala in his memory. 1930s: pursued Bdst studies in Sikkim, Ladakh, and Tibet; also taught, lectured, and practiced art (was gifted artist). During WW II: interned. 1947: married British-educated Parsi photographer Li Gotami; took Indian nationality. 1947–49: traveled to C Provinces and W Tibet; visited mounts Kailas and Gu-gé, as described in his *Way of the White Clouds.* Subsequently devoted himself to *magnum opus: The Foundations of Tibetan Mysticism.* As his reputation grew, traveled and lectured in USA, Japan, and Europe. Latterly based at Kasar Devi Ashram, near Almora (N India). 1980–81: went to USA for medical treatment; lived until death in Mill Valley. Other books incl *The Psychological Attitude of Early Buddhist Philosophy; Creative Meditation and Multidimensional Consciousness; the Psycho-Cosmic Symbolism of the Buddhist Stupa;* and *The Inner Structure of the I-Ching.*

Guenther, Prof Herbert: *Academic Tibetologist.* Born 1917, Bremen (W Germany) of Austrian parents. Holds PhDs from Munich and Vienna Us. Virtuoso linguist, is said to have learned Chinese at age 9 and later embarked on Sanskrit. Originally learned Tibetan in order to study Tibetan translations of lost Sanskrit texts; became acknowledged expert. 1959: appointed to teach Russian at Lucknow U, India. 1958: made Head of Dept of Philosophy and Bdst Studies at Sanskrit U, Varanasi (India). Became interested especially in literature and philosophy of Nyingma school. 1954: became Head of Far E Studies at U of Saskatchewan (Canada). Has also taught at Tarthang Tulku's Nyingma Institute and Trungpa Rinpoché's Naropa Institute. Often criticized for obscurity and for confusingly mingling jargon of various disparate disciplines; has nevertheless been described as "a true fortress of Tibetan Buddhism— so large it seems unassailable" (Hugh Richardson). Publications incl *The Life & Teachings of Naropa; Buddhist Philosophy in Theory and Practice; The Tantric View of Life; Tibetan Mysticism in a Western Perspective; Treasures of the Tibetan Middle Way; The Dawn of Tantra* (with Trungpa Rinpoché); and *Matrix of Mystery (Scientific and Humanistic Aspects of Dzogs-chen Thought).*

Hookham, Michael: *British Nyingma teacher.* Born 1935, London. Mathematician by profession; interested in possible relationships between Bdsm and W science and psychotherapy. Studied Theravada Bdsm for 9 years before meeting his Tibetan guru, Trungpa Rinpoché (qv), in 1965. 1975: asked by Trungpa Rinpoché to begin teaching. Established Longchen Foundation under Trungpa Rinpoché's overall direction; also established Nitartha School. Currently resides Oxford. Publications incl *On Freeing the Heart.*

Hookham, Shenpen (Shenpen Zangmo): *British Karma Kagyu / Nyingma teacher.* Born 1946, Essex. Studied and practiced as a nun of the Kagyu school for 9 years. Spent over 5 years in India before being requested by Gyalwa Karmapa to return to W to teach. 1977: met principal guru, Khenpo Tsultrim Gyamtso Rinpoché. Has acted as interpreter to various eminent lamas while continuing to undertake retreat and pursue studies. Obtained DPhil at Oxford with dissertation on Tathagatagarbha Doctrine according to Shentong interpretation of Ratnagotravibhaga.

Hopkins, Prof Jeffrey: *American scholar, writer, and translator; interpreter to Dalai Lama.* Born 1940. 1963: graduated Harvard. Studied for 6 years at Lamaist Bdst Monastery of America (Freewood Acres, New Jersey); entered Bdst Studies Program at U of Wisconsin. 1966: received PhD. 1973: began teaching at U of Virginia; founded a graduate program in Bdst Studies. Has accompanied HH the Dalai Lama as official interpreter since 1979, touring N America, Europe, Australia, and SE Asia. Publications incl *The Tantric Distinction; Meditation on Emptiness; Death, Intermediate State and Rebirth in Tibetan Buddhism; The Buddhism of Tibet & the Key to the Middle Way; The Precious Garland & the Song of the Four Mindfulness* (both with Lati Rinbochay); *Tantra in Tibet;* and *Yoga of Tibet.*

Jamgön Kongtrül Rinpoché (Karma Lodrö Chökyi Senge): *High Karma Kagyu Tulku.* Born 1954, C Tibet. Recognized as incarnation of Jamgön Kongtrül the Great via Jamgön Kongtröl of Palpung by Gyalwa Karmapa; taken under Karmapa's special care from early age. Received education and complete transmission of Karma Kagyu lineage from Karmapa et al. Left Tibet with Karmapa, Dingo Khyentse Rinpoché, and Tai Situ Rinpoché (all qv) in face of Chinese invasion. Has traveled extensively and been instrumental in bringing the Dharma to W. At present one of the four Regents for absent Karmapa.

Jampäl Shenpen, HH: *Current Tri Rinpoché of Ganden Monastery; Supreme Head of Gelug School.* Born 1921, Kham, E Tibet. At age 12 became monk; studied at Ganden Monastery (Thangtse College); gained Geshe Lharampa degree at age 35. Later became Abbot of Gyüme Tantric College. 1984: appointed by Dalai Lama to succeed Kyabje Ling Rinpoché (qv) as Ganden Tripa.

Jamyang Khyentse Chökyi Lodrö (1896–1969): *Authority and master of all the schools of Tibetan Bdsm.* Recognized as activity incarnation of Jamyang Khyentse Wangpo (1820–92), notable pioneer of Ri-mé movement. 1st teacher: Kathuk Situ Chókyi Gyatso. Assumed throne at Dzongsar monastery, seat of Khyentses. Studied and practiced teachings of all schools of Tibetan Bdsm under more than 80 masters. A leading light in Ri-mé movement, opened Dzongsar Khamje U and Karmo Tagtsang Retreat Centre, as well as restoring other monasteries, constructing images, printing books, and teaching extensively. Two pilgrimages to C Tibet. 1958: settled in Sikkim; became Chaplain to Maharaja; died there. Master of many notable Tibetan lamas (Dingo Khyentse Rinpoché, Dezhung Rinpoché, Kalu Rinpoché, Sogyal Rinpoché, Trungpa Rinpoché, and Tarthang Tulku).

Kalu Rinpoché (Karma Rangjung Kunkyab) (1905–89): *"A modern Milarepa."* Born in Hor region of Kham, E Tibet. Both parents students of Jangön Kongtrül Lodrö Thaye, Jamyang Khyentse Wangpo, and Mipham Rinpoché (all prominent in Ri-mé movement). Recognized as tulku but not ordained, instead wandered freely; education supervised by father. At 13 years began formal studies at Palpung monastery. Received getsül ordination from XIth Tai Situpa (Karma Rangjung Kunchap). At Palpung and elsewhere studied sutra and tantra teachings; received instruction and empowerments from many great lamas. At age 16 undertook 3-year retreat at Kunzang Dechen ösel Ling under the direction of root lama, Norbu Tondrup, from whom he received complete transmission of teachings of Karma Kagyu and Shangba Kagyu traditions. At age 25 embarked on 12-year solitary retreat in mountains of Kham. At request of Tai Situpa, returned to Palpung to become Director of 3-year retreats. Recognized by XVIth Gyalwa Karmapa as incarnation of Jamgön Kontrül Lodrö Thaye. 1940s: toured Tibet; in Lhasa, gave teachings to Regent (Reting Rinpoché). 1955: asked to leave Tibet by Karmapa; established two centers in Bhutan and ordained 300 monks. Made pilgrimages to Bdst holy places in India. 1965: established Samdrup Tarjay Ling at Sonada near Darjeeling (now his headquarters); at once embarked on another 3-year retreat. 1971: visited France and N America; founded several centers for practice of Chenrezi Sadhana. 1974, 77–78: second and third US visits. Gave Kalachakra Empowerments in New York City, San Francisco, and Boulder. Principal N American center is at Vancouver; Dezhung Rinpoché takes charge there in his absence. 1976: began 3-year retreats for Westerners in France, where he had established two centers. 1983: gave Rinchen Ter Dzö empowerments at Sonada to the "Four Great Heart-sons" of late Gyalwa Karmapa and others. Publications incl *The Writings of Kalu Rinpoché* (with Kenneth McLeod); *The Chariot for Travelling the Path to Freedom;* and *The Dharma that Illuminates all Beings like the Light of the Sun and Moon.*

Karma Thinley Rinpoché: *Sakyapa lama active in the West.* Born 1931, Nangchen, Kham, E Tibet. Recognized as incarnation of Beru Kunrik at age 2 ½ years. Teachers: Khen Rinpoché, Tashi Chopel, Tenpai Nyingpo, and Chogay Trichen Rinpoché. Special initiations: Hevajra, Vajarayogini, Vajrapani, and Chakrasamvara. Has made a special study of basic Sakya text known as lam-dre ("The Path and Its Fruit"). Specialization: tshogs-shay transmission of Sakya Lam-dre teachings and Kagyu Mahamudra teachings. Holds Khenpo degree. 1959: left Tibet. 1973: founded Kampo Gangra Drubgyud Ling in Toronto, Canada. 1977: inspired establishment of Sakya Rinchen Ling in Bristol (UK). Books incl *A History of the Sixteen Karmapas of Tibet.*

Karmapa, HH the XVIth Gyalwa (Rangjung Rigpe Dorje, 1923–81): *Late supreme head of the Karma Kagyu subschool of Tibetan Bdsm.* Born Denkhok, Derge district, Kham, E Tibet. Speedily recognized as new incarnation on evidence left in a letter by previous Karmapa. At age 7 years received ordination from Tai Situpa and Jamgön Kongtrül of Palpung; one year later Vajra Crown and Karmapa robes brought to him from Tsurphu (Karmapa seat). Enthroned by Situ Rinpoché at Palpung. In 1931, set out with grand entourage (Karmapa Garchen) for Tsurphu; en route performed Vajra Crown (Black Hat) Ceremony for first time at Nangchen. Afterwards visited XIIIth

Dalai Lama in Lhasa; underwent hair-cutting ceremony; then returned to Tsurphu and underwent second Golden Throne Ceremony. For next four years studied with Beru Khyentse Rinpoché and Bo Kangkar Mahapandita. 1937: visited Situ Rinpoché at Derge and received empowerments and transmissions. 1940–41: returned to Tsurphu. 1941–44: intensive practice. 1944: pilgrimage to Samyé and Lhodrak; also visited Bhutan at invitation of Maharaja. 1945: given further teachings by Situ Rinpoché and received full monk ordination. 1947–48: traveled in W Tibet, Sikkim, Nepal, and India. 1948: teachings from Jamgön Kongrül of Palpung; became master of Mahamudra. Early 1950s: occupied with teaching and administrative duties. 1954: visited Beijing with Dalai Lama. On return to Tibet, enthroned new Situ Rinpoché and tried to improve morale in Kham, then being occupied by Chinese communists. Entertained XIVth Dalai Lama at Tsurphu; Dalai Lama gave him empowerment of 1000-armed Avalokiteshvara; Karmapa performed Vajra Crown Ceremony in return. 1956: visited Druk Dechen Chokhor Ling (principal Drukpa Kagyu monastery), gave teachings and performed purification rite; visited Sikkim, Nepal, and India for Buddha Jayanti Celebrations. 1957: began to send lamas out of Tibet. 1959: left Tibet himself and found refuge in Bhutan, then in Sikkim. Headquarters set up at Rumtek (monastery completed 1966). 1974: world tour; visited centers established in W (e.g., Samyé Ling in Scotland and Trungpa Rinpoché's centers in Vermont and Colorado). Performed Vajra Crown Ceremony in London, New York, and Boulder. Subsequently established number of centers, notably Dhagpo Dagyu Ling (Montignac, France) in 1977. 1981: dedicated main US center, Karma Triyana Dharmachakra. Died Chicago after illness. Further biodata available in *Karmapa, The Black Hat Lama of Tibet* by Nik Douglas and Meryl White and *The History of the Sixteen Karmapas of Tibet* by Karma Thinley Rinpoché.

Kelsang Gyatso, Geshe: *Gelugpa lama active in UK.* Born 1932, W Tibet. 1940: ordained and entered Jampa Ling monastery; later graduated to Sera monastery, Lhasa (Jé College). 1959: left Tibet. 1959–77: intensive meditation retreats in Nepal and N India. 1972: awarded Geshe degree at New Sera Monastery, S India. 1977: became Director of General Studies at Manjushri Institute, Cumbria, UK. Established other centers in UK and Spain: Madhyamaka (York), Vajravarahi (Preston), Tara (Buxton and Macclesfield), Chenrezig (Lancaster), Tharpa Retreat Center (Dumfriesshire), and Instituto Dharma (Menorca, Spain). Spiritual Director, Instituto Vajra Dharma, Spain. Publications incl *Meaningful to Behold* (A Commentary on Shantideva's *Bodhicaryavatara*); *Clear Light of Bliss (Mahamudra in Vajrayana Buddhism); The Heart of Wisdom; and Buddhism in the Tibetan Tradition: A Guide.*

Khambo Lama: Title accorded to most senior lamas in Mongolia and Buryatia (E Siberia). The Head of Mongolian Bdsts is The Most Venerable Khambo Lama K1. Ganden (sic), whose seat is at Gandentheckchenling monastery, Ulan Bator. He is President of Asian Bdsts Conference for Peace (periodical—*Buddhists for Peace*). Buddhist patriarch of Buryatia— Bandido Khambo Lama; he is also titular head of all Soviet Bdsts. Chief Buryat monastery is Ivolginsky Datsan, near Buryat capital of Ulan Ude.

Konchog Tsewang, Geshe: *Gelugpa lama active in UK.* Born 1928, U Lam, E Tibet. 1940: ordained a monk at Zer Dru monastery, E Tibet. Later went to Drepung monastery, Lhasa (Loseling College). Studied Du-ra ("Collected Topics") and Lo-rig ("Mind and Cognition"); *The Ornament for Clear Realisations,* a text by Conqueror

Maitreya, and Candrakirti's *Guide to the Middle Way;* also logic by Jam Yang Gun Cho; finally passed on to Vinaya studies and a commentary thereon by Gunaprabha. 1959: left Tibet. 1970: entered Gyutö Tantric College; received Geshe Ngagrampa degree. 1974: Geshe Lharampa degree. Principal teachers: Khensur Yeshe Thubten, the late Khensur Pema Gyaltsen, and Nyima Gyaltsen, all former Abbots of Drepung Loseling College; and Shargön Khen Rinpoché. 1982: came to UK to become Resident Teacher and Director of Philosophical Studies (Geshe Training Program) at Manjushri Institute, Cumbria, UK.

Landaw, Jonathan: *Writer, translator, teacher.* Born New Jersey, USA. 1970 and after: extensive travels in E and elsewhere, studying and teaching Bdsm. Has written and edited several books for Library of Tibetan Works & Archives, Dharamsala. Other books incl *Prince Siddhartha.* Currently lives in California.

Lhalungpa, Lobsnag: *Tibetan scholar.* Born 1924, Lhasa. Studied Bdsm under various Tibetan masters. Took refuge in India after Chinese invasion; has since lived there and in W. A onetime teacher of Tibetan Buddhist Classics at U of British Columbia (Canada). Publications incl *The Life of Milarepa* and *Mahamudra: The Quintessence of Mind & Meditation.*

Ling Rinpoché, Kyabje (97th Ganden Tripa, 1903–83): *Late senior tutor to Dalai Lama; Head of the Gelug Order.* Born near Lhasa; educated Drepung monastery. After obtaining Geshe Lharampa degree, became Abbot of Upper Tantric College, Lhasa. Later became debating partner (Tsenshab) of present Dalai Lama; accompanied him to China (1954) and to India for Buddha Jayanti Celebrations (1956). 1965: enthroned as Ganden Tripa (Abbot of Ganden Monastery and Head of Gelug School) in exile. Visited and taught in W countires. Succeeded by HH Jamphäl Shenpen (qv).

Lobsang Tenzin, Geshe: *Abbot of Gyumé Tantric College.*

Lodö, Lama: *Karma Kagyu lama active in the West.* Born 1941, Sikkim. At age 8 entered monastery. At age 15, met guru, Drupon Tenzin Rinpoché, meditation master of Deyak monastery and a teacher of 16th Gyalwa Karmapa. Began 3-year retreat in cave but contracted tuberculosis and had to discontinue; later recovered and resumed retreat under direction of Kaly Rinpoché (qv), his master having died of same disease in the interim; contracted tuberculosis again but persevered and recovered; completed retreat. Afterwards taught in Ladakh; also spent 7 years as Meditation Master at Sonada. 1974: sent by Kalu Rinpoché to Europe; guided several students on 3-year retreat at Plaige (France). 1976: became resident lama at Kagyu Droden Kunchab in San Francisco. Travels extensively in Bay area and elsewhere. Publications incl *Bardo Teachings; Quintessence of the Animate & the Inanimate; Attaining Enlightenment; Maintaining the Bodhisattva Vow; Prayers for Generating Guru Devotion;* and *Radiant Wisdom.*

Losang Pende, Geshe: *Gelupa Lama active in UK.* Born 1941, Trognang, near Lhasa. 1953: ordained and entered Ganden monastery (Shartse College). 1959: left Tibet; went to refugee camp at Buxaduar; later moved to Ganden Shartse monastery, Mungod, S India. 1985: received Geshe degree. Has studied all aspects of Bdst philosophy; also Tibetan culture, chanting, and ritual music. Principal teacher: Lungrig Namgyal Rinpoché, Abbot of Gyutö Tantric College.

Mullin, Glenn H.: *Canadian writer, editor, and translator.* Born 1949, Gaspe, Quebec. 1972–76: joined Bdst Studies Program at Tibetan Library, Dharamsala. Later studied at the Dialectic School for 6 years. Tutors incl Geshes Ngawang Dhargyey and Rabten (both qv) and both late tutors of Dalai Lama. Presently engaged on a 10-volume series of collections of the writings of the 14 Dalai Lamas for Snow Lion Publications, Ithaca, New York, of which four have appeared to date: *Selected Works of Dalai Lama I: Bridging the Sutras & the Tantras; Selected Works of Dalai Lama II: Essence of Refined Gold; Selected Works of Dalai Lama III: The Tantric Yogas of Sister Niguma; Selected Works of Dalai Lama IV: Songs of Spiritual Change.* Other books incl *Death & Dying: The Tibetan Tradition* and *Atisha and Buddhism in Tibet* (with Doboom Tulku).

Namkhai Norbu Rinpoché: *Dzogchen master and scholar.* Born 1938, Derge district, E Tibet. At 2 years recognized as reincarnation of Adjom Drukpa, a great Dzogchen master of early 20th century. Later also recognized by the XVIth Gyalwa Karmapa and Situ Rinpoché as mind reincarnation of Shabdung Ngawang Namgyal, founder of line of Dharma Rajas (monk-kings) of Bhutan. Received initiations from two uncles, both Dzogchen masters, and from others. Age 5–9, educated at Derge Gonchen monastery, and later went on to Dzongsar monastic college for *c* 6 years. At 14 received Vajrayogini initiations according to the Sakya school and later received transmissons from 113-year-old woman teacher. At 16 went to China as representative of Tibetan youth; became instructor at SW U of Minor Nationalities, Chengdu (Szechuan, China). Back in Tibet, at 17 met Root Master, Chanchub Dorje (1926–1978). Afterwards went on long pilgrimage to C Tibet, Nepal, India, and Bhutan. Returning to Tibet, forced to flee the country due to violent political upheavals. 1958–60 lived in Gangtok, Sikkim; employed as author and editor of Tibetan text books by govt. 1960: invited to Italy by G. Tucci (qv). 1960–64: research associate at IsMEO, Rome. 1965–date: Professor in Oriental Institute of U of Naples. 1983: hosted first International Convention on Tibetan Medicine in Venice. For past 10 years has been active informally teaching in various countries, incl Italy, France, UK, Austria, Denmark, Norway and, since 1979, USA. The Dzogchen Community, an informal association of students practicing under his guidance, has arisen. Speaks English though prefers Italian. Married with two children. Books incl *The Crystal and the Way of Light; The Necklace of Gzi (A Cultural History of Tibet); Dzogchen and Zen; The Cycle of Day and Night; The Mirror (Advice on Presence and Awareness); On Birth and Life (A Treatise on Tibetan Medicine); Primordial Experience (Manjushrimitra's Treatise on the Meaning of Bodhicitta in Dzogchen);* and *Zer-Nga: The Five Principal Points (A Dzogchen Upadesha Practice).*

Nyoshul Khen Rinpoché (Jamyang Dorje): *One of the foremost Khenpos of the Nyingma school and a leading exponent of Dzogchen.* Studied with *c* 25 main teachers, Dudjom Rinpoché and Dingo Khyentse Rinpoché; holds special lineage of Patrul Rinpoché (1808–87). 1960: sought refuge in India; taught large numbers of monks; lived for a time in Bhutan. 1980: came to Europe; spent much time guiding retreat practitioners. Also visited USA. 1985–86: visited UK at invitation of Sogyal Rinpoché. Notable for his remarkable poetry.

Palden Sherab, Khenpo: *One of the most qualified scholars and meditation masters in the Nyingma tradition.* Born E Tibet. Joined Gonchen monastery and studied there; also at Riwoche, where he was invested with rank of Khenpo. Teachers incl Dudjom Rinpoché, Khenpo Acho, Kontrol Rinpoché, and Jedrung Rinpoché. 1967–80: Abbot in charge of Nyingma Dept of C Institute of Higher Studies, Sarnath, India.

Has written books on poetry and Tibetan Language; also a notable scholar. Has taught in London at request of Sogyal Rinpoché; also in Paris.

Pallis, Marco: *Writer.* Born 1895, Liverpool (GB) of Greek parents. After serving in WWI, became professional musician; also engaged in mountaineering. 1933: first came in contact with Bdsm in Sikkim; studied it and Tibetan in Ladakh with Konchog Gyalten of Phiyang. 1937: invited Geshe Wangyal (qv) to England for private tuition. 1947: studied with a Tibetan teacher in S Tibet (Sakya region); accompanied by Ronald Nicholson. 1970s: active as a member of the Shin Bdst Assn in London. Books incl *Peaks and Lamas* (1939—a classic); *The Way and the Mountain* (1960); and *A Buddhist Spectrum* (1980).

Panchen Lamas: *High-ranking Tibetan Bdst patriarchs.* Title an abbreviation of *Pandita Chenpo* ("Great Scholar"), given to abbots of Tashilhunpo monastery, near Shigatse, S Tibet (hence sometimes called Tashi Lamas). Lineage transmitted by tulku system from Chökyi Gyaltsen (1570–1662), tutor to Vth Dalai Lama. Used by Chinese as foil to power of Dalai Lamas. 1728: Emperor made PLs rulers of Tsang province. 1923: VIth PL fled to China; never returned; died 1937, Jyekundo. 1943: tulku (VIIth) discovered Litang, Sikiang; married and lived in China until his death.

Pawo Rinpoché, HE (Tsuglag Mawai Wangchuj): *Kagyupa lama; an Emanation of Amitabha and Vairocana.* 10th incarnation. Born 1912, C Tibet. 1917: from age 6 resided at Tsurphu Monastery with Gyalwa Karmapa Khakhyab Dorje and received empowerments, transmissions, explanations of sutra, tantra, and terma of Kagyu and Nyingma lineages. 1925: met XIIIth Dalai Lama who performed hair-cutting ceremony and gave him name Tsuglag Thubten Kunsel. Then went into long retreat. 1940: began 4-year residence at Palpung Monastery; received by Tai Situ Rinpoché, Padma Wangchuk Gyalpo, and Jamgön Kongtrül Rinpoché of Sechen. 1959: left Tibet; settled in India (Kalimpong). 1962–66: instructor in Bdst philosophy at Sanskrit U., Varanasi. 1966: retired due to illness and settled in Bhutan. 1975: to France for treatment and settled in Dordogne. Is sponsoring the construction of a new monastery, Nehnang Pungtsog Chodar Ling, at Bodh Nath, Nepal.

Phendé Rinpoché (Jamyang Kunzang Chö-chi Gyamtso): *Head of the Ngor subschool of the Sakya order; a teacher active in France.* "A personality of great wisdom and exemplary faith." Born 1934. 1974: founded Evam Phendé Ling at Les Ventes, Normandy. 1975: founded Pratique du Bouddhisme Mahanaya at Fresnes. Married Marie-Helène Ahni, who administers main residential center. Tr *L'Histoire des Enseignements Sakyapa.*

Rabten, Geshe (1920–86): *Gelugpa lama with many Western students.* Born Kham (E Tibet) into farming family. At age 18 entered Sera Monastery (Jé College); teacher was Geshe Jhampa Khedup. Became adept at rigorous philosophical debate; also went into frequent meditation retreat. Suffered poverty and undernourishment until appointed tutor to Gonsar Tulku. 1959: fled Tibet, settled first at Buxaduar; instrumental in setting up courses of study. 1963: awarded geshe Lharampa; shortly afterwards moved to Dharamsala to become personal assistant to Dalai Lama; lived at Namgyal Monastery and began to instruct Westerners. *c* 1970: into retreat near Dharamsala to contemplate meaning of sunyata. 1974: invited to Europe. 1975: returned to Switzerland as Abbot of Tibetan Monastic Institute at Rikon. 1977:

founded Tharpa Choeling Center for Higher Tibetan Studies at Mont Pèlerin, near Lausanne; also taught in USA and other European countries; established centers in Germany, Italy, Austria. "He adhered strictly to the Vinaya and placed great emphasis on a systematic and gradual training in the Gelugpa tradition . . . " (Stephen Batchelor). Books incl *The Preliminary Practices; Advice from a Spiritual Friend* (with Geshe Dhargyey); *The Life & Teaching of Geshe Rabten; Echoes of Voidness;* and *The Essential Nectar.*

Rampa, T. Lobsang (pseudonym of Cyril Henry Hoskins, 1911–81): *Novelist.* Plumber from Cornwall who had only visited Tibet in the pages of books; enjoyed great vogue for a while with a series of nearly 20 novels on Tibet (e.g., the bestselling *The Third Eye*) which catered to the public's perennial hunger for magic and mystery.

Richardson, Hugh Edward: *British authority on Tibet.* Born 1905; educated Oxford. Last British (and first Indian) representative in Lhasa. Was present when XIVth Dalai Lama brought to Lhasa. A Tibetan speaker and scholar, studied the culture of Tibet closely, especially various ancient inscriptions. Presently retired to St. Andrews, Scotland (also his birthplace). Books incl *Tibetan Précis; Tibet & Its History; Ancient Historical Edicts at Lhasa;* and *A Cultural History of Tibet* (with David Snellgrove).

Sakya, HE Jigdal Dagchen: *Head of Phuntsog Phodrang Palace of royal Sakya lineage.* Seat is at Sakya Tegchen Chöling in Seattle, Wash., USA.

Sakya Trizin, HH: *41st Patriarch of Sakya order.* A married lama, considered an incarnation of Manjushri and Padmasambhava. Born 1945, Tsedong, S Tibet. 1953: enthroned. Teachers; Ngawang Lodro Shenpen Nyingpo, Jamyang Khyentse Chökyi Lodrö (qv), Chogay Trichen, and Khenpo Appey. Special initiations: Hevajra, Chakrasamvara, Vajrayogini, and Vajrakilaya. Studies of special texts: *lam-dre* ("The Path and its Fruit"). Specializations: *tsog-shay* and *lob-shay* transmissions of the Sakya *lam-dre* teachings and the Khön lineage Vajrakilaya meditation and rituals. 1959: escaped to Sikkim. Began to learn English; went to Darjeeling to continue religious studies (Madhyamika, Prajnaparamita, and Abhidharma philosophy and logic). Spent 1 year in Mussoorie recovering from tuberculosis. 1964: founded Sakya center in Mussoorie. Has also since founded Sakya centers at Rajpur and Puruwala, and is head of all Sakya centers throughout the world. 1967: gave *lam-dre* teaching for first time to *c* 400 monks and 100 lay people. Now fluent in English, has taught in Europe, incl UK.

Scott, David (Ngakpa Jampa Thaye): *English Sakyapa teacher.* Born 1952, Bolton, Lancs. 1971: began training. Teachers: Karma Thinley Rinpoché, Ngor Phende Rinpoché, and Sakya Trizin. Special initiations: Hevajra, Vajrayogini, Chakrasamvara, and Amitabha. Studies of special texts: *Lam-dre* ("The Path and Its Fruit"). Specializations: Vajrayogini meditation. 1977: appointed Dharma Regent of Karma Thinley Rinpoché. 1985: further qualifications bestowed by Sakya Trizin. 1986: PhD U of Manchester on History & Teachings of the Dagpo Kagyu Tradition. 1977: founded Sakya Thinley Rinchen Ling (center) in Bristol, UK under inspiration of Karma Thinley.

Serkong Rinpoché (Kyabje Tsenshab Tserkong Tugse Rinpoché, 1914–83): *Late Tutor to Dalai Lama.* Born Loka region, S Tibet; recognized as incarnation of Marpa's son, Darmadodey. Studied with masters of all four traditions. Trained at Ganden (Jagtze College); received Geshe Lharampa degree after 14 years of study.

Spent 9 years at Gyüme Tantric College; passed all exams; appointed Master of Discipline. 1948: appointed Debating Partner to HH the Dalai Lama (qv); continued in this capacity throughout life; imparted many lineages, oral transmissions, and initiations to Dalai Lama. 1954: to China with Dalai Lama. 1959: to India (and exile). Helped to establish Office of Religious & Cultural Affairs; continued as tutor and close advisor to Dalai Lama. Traveled extensively; made 2 tours of Europe and N America.

Shamar ("Red Hat") Rinpoché (The Shamarpa): Has often acted as Regent and lineage-holder during the minority of a Karmapa.

Shechen Rabjam Rinpoché: *Young Nyingma Lama.* Recognized by Gyalwa Karmapa and other Heads of the Tibetan Bdst Schools as VIIth Incarnation of the Founder of Sechen Monastery, Kham, E Tibet. Since age 5 years with Dingo Khyentse Rinpoché, receiving teachings and empowerments.

Shenphen Dawa Rinpoché: *Youngest son and Darma-heir of late Dudjom Rinpoché.* Born Tibet. Studies closely supervised by father; has received empowerments and transmissions of all the Nyingma lineages from an early age. Has played a major role in establishing centers and in the spread of the Dharma worldwide; in particular will ensure continuance of Dudjom Lingpa's lineage.

Snellgrove, David R.: *British academic Buddhologist.* Born 1920. *c* 1950–82, Lecturer/Reader/Professor of Tibetan at SOAS (London U). Widely traveled in India and Himalayas. Overseas University posts and consultancy at Vatican. Fellow of British Academy. Books incl *Buddhist Himalaya; Himalayan Pilgrimage; The Hevajra Tantra* (2 vols); *Four Lamas of Dolpo* (2 vols); *A Cultural History of Tibet (with Hugh Richardson* [qv]; *A Cultural History of Ladakh* (with T. Skorupski); and *Indo-Tibetan Buddhism.* Ed *The Image of the Buddha.*

Sogyal Rinpoché, Lama: *Incarnate lama of Ri-mé tradition based in London.* Born mid-1940s, Kham, E Tibet; recognized as tulku of famous lama and mystic, Tertön Sogyal; also of Do Khyentse, great Dzogchen master. Raised as a son by Jamyang Khyentse Chökyi Lodrö (qv) at Dzongsar Monastic U (E Tibet); received complete training in sutras and tantras with transmissions and empowerments of all four schools of Tibetan Bdsm (esp Nyingma) from Khyentse and other great masters. Mid-1950s: with Khyentse on long pilgrimage to C Tibet; visited inter alia Lhasa, Samyé, and Sakya. 1958: accompanied Khyentse to Sikkim; later attended school in India; continued to receive spiritual teachings from Dingo Kyentse Rinpoché and Dudjom Rinpoché. Then undertook BA studies in Philosophy at St. Stephen's College, Delhi U; from there won scholarship to Trinity College, Cambridge. 1973: accompanied Dalai Lama on first European tour; also accompanied Dudjom Rinpoché on US tour as translator and aide. 1974: began to teach in London. 1975: established Dzogchen Orgyen Chöling in London. 1976–77: began to teach in Paris, later in USA. 1981: founded Rigpa Fellowship in London. Currently directs Rigpa centers in London, Paris, and Santa Cruz (Ca., USA). Teaches widely with special emphasis on Dzogchen. Has made death and dying a specialty, working with hospices and near-death researchers.

Sonam Kazi: *Sikkimese Dzogchen teacher (Nyingma school) active in USA.* A layman, received a Roman Catholic education; later studied psychology in Delhi. Suffered from depression in early life; this led to an interest in meditation. Posted to Lhasa with

Sikkimese diplomatic legation; studied with various gurus; referred to Dudjom Rinpoché (his root guru); became devoted follower of Dzogchen. 1970: arrived in US. Later invited to New York, where the Longchen Nyingthig Bdst Soc developed around him.

Sopa, Geshe Lhundup: *Gelugpa lama working in US.* Born 1923, Tsang province, Tibet. At 9 years began monastic training locally. At 18 joined Sera monastery, Lhasa, and studied for Geshe degree. One of the examiners when Dalai Lama took Geshe exams in 1959. 1959: sought refuge in India. 1961: completed studies and attained Geshe Lharampa degree. 1963: to Lamaist Bdst Monastery of America, New Jersey; became President. 1967: invited by Prof Richard Robinson, founder of Bdst Studies Program at U of Wisconsin, to teach at the Madison campus; became Prof in SE Asian Studies Dept. 1978, 1987: awarded Fulbright scholarships to study in India and Tibet. Is currently Abbot of Evam monastery and main teacher at Deer Park, Wisconsin. Travels widely on teaching engagements. Publications incl *The Theory and Practice of Tibetan Buddhism* and *The Wheel of Time.*

Tai Situ Rinpoché, HH: *Notable Karma Kagyu tulku.* Born 1954, Kham, E Tibet. Recognized as 12th incarnation of Tai Situpa by 16th Gyalwa Karmapa. (First of line, who are regarded as emanations of Maitreya, received honorific title Kenting Tai Situ Rinpoché from Emperor of China in 1407). At age 18 months enthroned at Palpung monatery, the traditional seat of the Situpas and headquarters of a monastic grouping comprising some 180 major monasteries and numerous smaller ones. 1954: left Tibet; went first to Bhutan and then to Rumtek monastery, Sikkim; completed training, receiving transmissions from Gyalwa Karmapa et al. Has since traveled widely. Presently engaged in building Sherab Ling (Land of Wisdom), a religious and educational center in Himalayan foothills, N India.

Tara Tulku: *Gelugpa lama; former Abbot of Gyutö Tantric College.* Born 1927, E Tibet. Studied for nearly 30 years at Sendru and Drepung monasteries. 1959: sought refuge in India. Has now retired as Abbot of Gyutö Tantric Monastery. Among other things, currently teaches Westerners at Bodh Gaya, India.

Tarthang Tulku: *Nyingma lama active in US.* Born 1935, Golok, E Tibet. Left home at 17 to travel in Kham; studied with many famous teachers of all schools but mainly Nyingma. 1958: left Tibet for Bhutan and India; later to Sikkim to study with root guru Jamyang Khyentse Chökyi Lodrö (qv). *c* 1962: appointed to represent Nyingma tradition at Sanskrit U, Varanasi; founded Dharma Publishing. 1968: to USA; established Tibetan Nyingma Meditation Center (Berkeley, Cal.), Nyingma Institute, and Odiyan Retreat Center. Married to French-Egyptian woman. Books incl *Gesture of Balance; Openness Mind; Hidden Mind of Freedom; Skillful Means; Kum Nye Relaxation I and II; Sacred Art of Tibet; Time, Space and Knowledge; Knowledge of Freedom; Love of Knowledge;* and *Copper Mountain Mandala.* Trs incl *Calm and Clear* and *Mother of Knowledge.* General ed of *Crystal Mirror* series; *Ancient Tibet;* and of new Nyingma ed of *Kangyur and Tangyur.*

Tendzin, Ösel (Thomas Rich, 1944–90): *Vajra Regent of Chögyam Trungpa Rinpoché.* From Passaic, New Jersey. Former student of Swami Satchidananda. 1976: became first Westerner to be empowered as a holder of the Karma Kagyu lineage. As the foremost student of Chögyam Trungpa, lectured widely in America and Europe. Book: *Buddha in the Palm of Your Hand.*

Thondup, Tulku: *Incarnation of Komey Khenpo, one of the principal teachers at Dodrupchen monastery.* Studied under Khenpo Chochog at Dodrupchen monastery; subsequently traveled to USA where, firstly as Visiting Scholar and later as Research Fellow, was attached to the Center for the Study of World Religions at Harvard U.

Thrangu Rinpoché: *Karma Kagyu lama active in W.* Born 1933, Kham, E Tibet. Recognized as 9th tulku of his lineage of Gyalwa Karmapa and Situ Rinpoché. Traditional education at Thrangu monastery. At 16, began to study "inner wisdom" (incl Abhidharma, Madhyamika, religious dialects, *Bodhicaryavatara, Prajñaparamita, Uttara Tantra,* and *Hevajra Tantra*) under Khenpo Lodro Rapsel. At 23, given monk ordination by Karmapa with Surmang Gawang Rinpoché and Trungpa Rinpoché (qv). Many retreats and initiations followed; also introduced to absolute nature by Khenpo Gangshar Wangpo. 1959: from Tibet to Rumtek, Sikkim; further teachings incl Six Yogas of Naropa and Mahamudra. 1967: after exams, awarded degree of Geshe Rabjam; praised by Dalai Lama; made khenpo by Karmapa and has since taught Shamar Rinpoché, Situ Rinpoché, Jamgön Kongtrül Rinpoché, and Gyaltsap Rinpoché; became Yarnay Khenpo (director of rainy season retreats) and published many texts. 1976: moved to Nepal; established retreat center at Namo Buddha and monastery at Boudha near Kathmandu. 1979: visited UK, Germany, Belgium, Denmark, Norway, and USA. 1981 and 84: to Europe again. 1982: pilgrimage and teaching tour of Sri Lanka, Thailand, Indonesia, Malaysia, the Philippines, and Hong Kong. 1984: several months in Tibet; visited Thrangu monastery and ordained more than 100 monks and nuns.

Thubten Ngawang, Geshe: *Gelug lama active in Germany.* Born 1931 of nomad family on pilgrimage to Mt. Kailas. From age 14, studied at Dhargyey monastery, Tehor-Kham, E Tibet, with Geshe Jampa Khedrup. At 25, to Sera monastery; taught by Geshe Rabten (qv). 1959: from Tibet; in refugee camp at Buxaduar. 1969: to new Sera monastery, Bylakuppe, Mysore, S India. 1975–79: Geshe Lharampa degree. 1979–: spiritual head of Tibetisches Zentrum, Hamburg. Various publications in German.

Thurman, Robert Alexander Farrar (Upasaka Tenzin Chotrag): *President, American Institute of Bdst Studies; translator and academic.* After Harvard and Asian travels, studied with Geshe Wangyal (qv) (mainly Tibetan language and texts), then to Dharamsala (*c* 1963); was ordained by Dalai Lama and spent time at Namgyal monastery. Became fluent in Tibetan and studied Nagarjuna and Tsongkhapa. Later resigned monk status and returned to academic life. 1972: PhD at Harvard with a translation of a Madhyamika text by Tsongkhapa. Currently Professor of Religion at Amherst College. Trs incl *The Holy Teaching of Vimalakirti; The Life & Teachings of Tsong Khapa;* and *Tsong Khapa's Speech of Gold in the Essence of True Eloquence.*

Trogawa Rinpoché: *Tibetan lama doctor.* Born 1931 in Tibet; recognized as tulku of famous lama doctor; underwent traditional medical apprenticeship in Lhasa. 1954: left Tibet. Has since practiced Tibetan medicine throughout Himalayan region; has also taught at School of Tibetan Medicine and Astrology, Dharamsala. Principal guest speaker at 1st International Conference on Tibetan Medicine held in Italy. Founder of Chakpori Institute of Medicine, USA, and France.

Trungpa Rinpoché, Vidyadhara Chögyam (Karma Ngawang Chökyi Gyatso Künga Zangpo, 1939–87): *One of the first lamas to come to the West; meditation master* *of the Kagyu and Nyingma lineages and writer.* Born Geje, E Tibet. Recognized and enthroned as 11th Trungpa Tulku by Gyalwa Karmapa at 1½ years. Became Abbot of Surmang monasteries. Took sramanera precepts at 8 years; also went into 3-month retreat (to meditate on Manjushri). At 9 met principal guru, Jamgön Kongtrül II of Sechen. At 11 years, began ngondro (preliminary practices for Vajrayana teachings). At 14, conducted first full empowerment (wangkur), which lasted 3 months. Later left Tibet for India. Became protégé of Freda Bedi (Sister Palmo—qv). 1963: came to W as Spaulding Fellow at Oxford U; studied W philosophy, psychology, art, and comparative religion. 1967: co-founder with Chujé Akong Rinpoché (qv) of Samyé-Ling Tibetan Center in Scotland, the first Tibetan Bdst meditation center in W. Late 1960s: married Diana Judith Pybus (Lady Diana Mukpo); several children born. 1970: left for USA; established important centers in Vermont (Tail of the Tiger), Colorado (Karma Dzong in Boulder and Rocky Mountain Dharma Center), and Nova Scotia (Gampo Abbey). Numerous other centers (Dharmadhatus) in USA and Europe. Headed Vajradhatu, a world-wide organization. Died Halifax, Nova Scotia. Books incl *Meditation in Action; Cutting Through Spiritual Materialsim; The Myth of Freedom; Mudra; Shambhala—The Sacred Path of the Warrior;* and *Journey Without Goal.* Autobiography: *Born in Tibet* (with Esmé Cramer Roberts).

Tsultrim Gyamtso, Khenpo: *Senior Karma Kagyu lama.* Born *c* 1937. Ordained young after completing rigorous 9-year course; took Khenpo degree; afterwards went into 3-year retreat, practicing rituals and meditation practices of the Mahamudra teachings. 1977: at instruction of his main guru, Gyalwa Karmapa, moved to Europe; also, alternating with Thrangu Rinpoché, serves as chief teacher at the monastic college (shedra) at Rumtek monastery, Bhutan. Books incl *Progressive Stages of Meditation on Emptiness.*

Tucci, Prof Giuseppe (1894–1984): *Pioneer Italian Tibetologist.* Born Macerata. 1919: D.Litt from U of Rome, where he became a Lecturer, soon rising to Professor of the Religions and Philosophies of India (to 1969). 1929: elected to Italian Academy. 1933: founded IsMEO (Instituto Italiano per il Medio ed Estremo Oriente) in Rome. 1927–48; traveled, researched, and collected manuscripts and artifacts on several expeditions to Tibet. "A man of outstanding wealth, social position and power" and "a believing and to some extent even practicing Buddhist" (E. Conze). Books in English incl *The Religions of Tibet; The Theory & Practice of the Mandala; Tibet; Secrets of Tibet; Transhimalaya; Indo-Tibetica; To Lhasa & Beyond;* and *Tibetan Painted Scrolls.*

Urgyen, Tulku: *Senior Nyingma lama noted for Dzogchen teachings; special holder of a Terma lineage of Chogyur Dechen Lingpa.* Resides in Ka-Nying Shedrup Ling monastery, Bodh-Nath, Kathmandu, Nepal; spends most of this time in retreat. 1981: visited W to teach his son, Chökyi Nyima Rinpoché. Died in 1996.

Wangchen, Geshe Namgyal: *Gelugpa lama teaching in UK.* Born mid-1930s. 1948: entered Drepung monastery (Loseling College) at 13. 1959: fled from Tibet; spent next 10 years in Indian refugee center (Buxaduar), continuing Geshe studies. 1972: received Geshe degree. "Geshe Wangchen studied the vast range of Mahayana Buddhist thought under the guidance of his main Guru, Khensur Pema Gyaltsen Rinpoché, and other special masters of the tradition" (Manjushri London program). Lived for a time at the new Drepung Loseling in Karnataka, India; later moved to Delhi to work as Librarian at Tibet House. Instructed American students under the auspices of U of

Wisconsin at Sarnath. 1981 (April): came to UK and became Resident Teacher at Manjushri London. Fluent in English. Is working on several books. Currently in Drepung, India.

Wangyal, Geshe (1901–83): *Late Gelugpa lama of Kalmuk origin active in USA.* Studied at Drepung. Root guru: the Buryat Lama Agvan Dorjiev. At 19, with Lama Dorjiev in St. Petersburg. In Peking during the 1930s; also traveled with Sir Charles Bell in C Asia. 1937: invited to Britain by Marco Pallis (qv). 1951: when Chinese entered Kham, left Tibet. Visited Paris, Hanoi, and Hong Kong. 1955: to Freewood Acres, New Jersey (USA) to minister to community of Kalmuk refugees brought over after WW II by Tolstoy Foundation. Brought over four lamas from India, incl Geshe Sopa (qv) and Lama Kunga. Taught 1-day weekly in Dept of Altaic Languages at Columbia U (New York). Books incl *The Door of Liberation* and *The Jewelled Staircase*.

Wylie, Turrell V., (1927–84): *Originator of the Wylie System of Tibetan Transcription.* Born Durango, Colorado, USA. Onetime Professor of Tibetan Studies at U of Washington, Seattle. Studied with G. Tucci (qv) in Rome. Following invasion of Tibet (1959), helped with relief work via Rockefeller Foundation. Traveled in India and met Tibetan scholars, some of whom he brought to Seattle. Books incl *The Geography of Tibet according to Dzam-gling-rgyasbshad.* Many articles, incl "A Standard System of Tibetan Transcription" (*Harvard Journal of Asiatic Studies,* 22: pp. 261–7. Dec. 1959). Anonymous co-author of Shakabpa's *Tibet: A Political History*.

Yeshe, Lama Thubten (1935–84): *Gelugpa Lama and influential teacher of Westerners.* Born near Lhasa; educated Sera Monastery (Jé College). 1959: to India; settled at Buxaduar. Began teaching Westerners with principal disciple, Wopa Rinpoché (qv), in Darjeeling and later Kathmandu. 1971: helped found Kopan Monastery at Bodh Nath in Kathmandu Valley, Nepal. In subsequent years he and his students established 28 centers in 13 countries under auspices of FPMT (Foundation for the Preservation of the Mahayana Tradition). Also instrumental in establishing Wisdom Publications, The Universal Education Association, a couple of monasteries for W monks and nuns as well as supporting leper colony in India. Toured and lectured annually in N America, Asia, Australia, and Europe. Books incl *Wisdom Energy* (with Lama Zopa).

Yeshe, Lama (new incarnation: Lama ösel): Born 1985, Granada, Spain, 5th child of Maria Torres and Paco Hita, students of late Lama Yeshe who helped found ösel Ling, retreat center near Granada. First met by Lama Zopa at age 6 months; confirmed by Dalai Lama, 1986.

Zong Rinpoché, Kyabje (Zongtrul Jetson Losang Tsondu Thubten Gyaltsen, 1904–84): *Revered Gelug lama.* Born Kham, E Tibet; recognized as reincarnation of Zongtrul Tenma Chöphel (1836–99). Came to C Tibet at age 12 and entered Ganden monastery (Shartse College). Late Trijang Rinpoché became first mentor. Soon displayed skill in debate and scholarly talents. At 25, passed Geshe exams with honors; passed exams at Gyutö Tantric College similarly well. Appointed Abbot of Ganden Shartse by Regent (Reting Rinpoché) and instituted reforms and useful new developments. Resigned after 9 years to go on pilgrimage. Left Tibet; found refuge in India at Buxaduar; became Principal of Tibetan Teachers' Training Program. 1969: first Principal of new C Institute for Tibetan Higher Studies at Sarnath (near Varanasi). On retirement, devoted himself to practice. Gave teachings to both Tibetans and Westerners. Visited Europe and USA. Died S India following tour of N America and Europe.

Zopa Rinpoché, Lama: *Gelug lama; teacher of Westerners.* Born 1946 of Sherpa stock at Thami, NE Nepal, near Everest. At age 5 recognized as tulku of Lawudo Lama, great Nyingma practitioner. Educated Solu Khumbu region (Nepal). Taken on pilgrimage to Tibet by uncle while still young and decided to remain. Studied first at Dungkar monastery, later at Sera (Jé College). 1959: to India; lived in refugee camp at Buxaduar; there met Lama Thuben Yeshe (qv), his guru. Remained several years studying under various Tibetan masters. 1965: he and Lama Yeshe met their first W student (Zina Rachevsky). 1969: with LTY and ZR, founded small center at Kopan in Kathmandu Valley, Nepal; taught intensively there in following years. 1971: helped found FPMT with Lama Yeshe. 1974: made first visit to W, visiting USA and Australia. Co-author with Lama Thubten Yeshe of *Wisdom Energy*.

ZEN BUDDHISM

Notes on Titles

Daisho: (Jap) lit, "great priest."

Dharma Heir: disciple to whom a Master has given Dharma Transmission(qv).

Dharma Transmission: the transmission of Truth or the OneMindfrommaster to disciple, heart to heart (i.e. beyond words and concepts).

Dojo: (Jap) training hall.

Inka: (Jap) lit, "seal"; signifies that the Master has formally certified the disciple's understanding.

Kensho: (Jap) first glimpse of one's nature.

Osho: (Jap) priest.

Roshi: (Jap) lit, "old teacher"; signifies a Zen Master.

Sesshin: (Jap) intensive retreat.

Sensei: (Jap) teacher

Sunim: (Kor) formal title for Korean monks and nuns.

Transmission: see Dharma Transmission.

Zendo: (Jap) Zen training hall.

Aitken Roshi, Robert: *Hawaii-based Zen teacher of the Sanbo Kyodan lineage and writer.* Captured on Guam by Japanese and interned as enemy alien for duration of WW II. Preceding interest in Japanese literature, esp haiku poetry, given new impetus by encounter with R. H. Blyth (qv) in POW camp (1944); also became interested in zazen, though unable to practice. After War, began Zen practice with Nyogen Senzaki (qv) in California. 1950: returned to Japan to continue haiku studies; also began practice as lay student at Ryutakuji under Yamamoto Gempo Roshi and Nakagawa Soen Roshi (qv). Later also studied with Yasutani Hakuun Roshi (qv) and Yamada Doun Roshi. 1974: received title roshi from Yamada Doun Roshi. Currently closely associated with the Diamond Sangha, which has zendos on various of the Hawaiian islands as well as elsewhere in USA and Australia. Wife, Anne Aitken, has been partner in all Zen work. Books incl *A Zen Wave: Basho's Haiku & Zen* (a study of Basho's *haiku*); *Taking the Path of Zen;* and *The Mind of Clover: Essays in Zen Buddhist Ethics.* Writes regularly in the journal *Blind Donkey.*

Awakawa, Yasuoichi (1902–79): *Scholar of Zen art.* Trained as an economist with PhD from Kyoto U; devoted life to collecting and cataloging Zen art. Books incl the classic *Zen Art.*

Baker Roshi, Richard: *Dharma Heir to Shunryu Suzuki Roshi.* A Harvard graduate and one-time head of San Francisco Zen Center; now operating independently.

Blyth, Reginald H. (1898–1964): *Writer and translator.* Born London; went to Korea via India; taught English and studied Zen under Kayama Taigi Roshi. 1940: moved to Japan; taught English; tutored Crown Prince. Interned during WWII as enemy alien. Books incl *Zen & Zen Classics* (5 vols); *Japanese Humour; Japanese Life & Character in Shenryu; Edo Satirical Verse Anthologies; Haiku* (4 vols); and *History of Haiku* (2 vols).

Chisan Zenji (Koho Keido Chisan Zenji, 1879–1968): *Japanese Soto master.* Born Toyama prefecture; ordained by Koho Hakugan of Yoko-ji. 1901: Dharma transmission from Kyoto Hakugan. 1904: graduated from Soto Ken U and entered Soji-ji. 1948: became Chief Abbot of Soji-ji and of Kanto Plains; also received honor of Daikyosei ("Great Teacher") from Emperor. 1950s: 2 world tours; while in England met Jiyu Kennett Roshi (qv) and invited her to train with him in Japan. First Founder of Shastazan Chisan-ji (Shasta Abbey) posthumously.

Deshimaru Roshi, Taisen (1914–82): *Japanese Soto Zen teacher active in Europe.* Lived layman's life for many years; later trained with Kodo Sawaki; received Dharma transmission. 1967: settled in France; became based in Paris. 1970: founded L'Association Zen d'Europe; dojos and zazen centers established in France, Belgium, W Germany, N America, N Africa, and S America. Died Tokyo; cremated Soji-ji temple, Yokohama. Books incl *Vrai Zen; Zazen; La Pratique du Zen; Zen-Geist; Zen-Bdsmus und Christentum; Zen im den Kampfkünsten Japans; Zen et Arts Martiaux; La Pratique de la Concentration; Questions à un Maître Zen;* and *Le Bol et le Baton.* Autobiography: *Autobiographie d'un Moine Zen.*

Dumoulin, Heinrich, S. J.: *Author born 1905.* 1929: PhD, Gregorian U, Rome. 1941: Prof of Philosophy & History of Religions, Sophia U, Tokyo. 1970: Director, Institute of Oriental Religions, Sophia U, Tokyo. Books incl *The Development of Chinese Zen after the VIth Patriarch in the Light of the Mumonkan; Ostliche Meditation und Christiche Mystik; Christianity Meets Buddhism; Zen Enlightenment: Origins & Meaning;* and *A History of Zen Buddhism* (the definitive work). Ed *Buddhism in the Modern World* (UK ed *Buddhism Today*).

Eido Tai Shimano Roshi—*see* **Shimano Roshi, Eido.**

Freedgood, née Stuart, Roshi, Maurine (1922–90): *Canadian-born Zen master.* Trained as pianist. Early 1960s: began formal Zen practice with Yasutani Roshi (qv) in New York. 1977: ordained Rinzai priest by Eido Roshi (qv); participated regularly in retreats at Dai Bosatsu Zendo (Catskill Mts.) 1982: authorized to teach by Nakagawa Soen Roshi (qv). 1979: resident teacher and president of Cambridge, Massachusetts Bdst Assn until death. See Lenore Friedman, *Meetings with Remarkable Women: Buddhist Teachers in America* (Boston: Shambala, 1987).

Furukawa Roshi, Gyudo (1872–1961): *Important early 20th century Rinzai Zen master.* A disciple of Soyen Shaku (qv); while Soyen in USA studied with Nantembo (qv). Succeeded Soyen as Abbot of Engaku-ji. 1930: following retirement, visited USA at request of Chisaki Nyogen. 1935: re-elected Abbot of Engaku-ji.

Glassman Sensei, Bernard Tetsugen: *Dharma heir of Maezumi Roshi (ZCLA).* Born 1939, Brooklyn, New York. Educated Polytechnic Institute of Brooklyn and U of California; PhD in applied mathematics 1970. Worked as administrator and engineer in US space program for 15 years. 1958: began studying Zen. 1963: began zazen practice at Zenshu-ji (Soto) Zen Mission, Los Angeles, guided by Sumi Roshi. 1968: began practicing with Maezumi Roshi (qv). 1970: ordained Zen Bdst monk at ZCLA. Undertook and completed koan study with Maezumi. 1977: received Shiho or Dharma transmission from Maezumi Roshi. At present is Abbot of Zen Community of New York (ZCNY) Zenshin-ji, a Soto Zen temple and training center in Riverdale, New York. Early 1980s: started Greyston Bakery as "livelihood practice" of ZCNY.

Goto Roshi, Zuigan (?–1965): *Rinzai Zen master.* Zen master in the lineage of Imagita Kosen Roshi (qv) and Soyen Shaku (qv). Graduated in Philosophy from Imperial U, Tokyo. 1906: accompanied Sokatsu Shaku, Sokei-an Sasaki et al to USA. Later became Abbot of Myoshin-ji (Kamakura), later still of Daitoku-ji (Kyoto). Teacher of Oda Sesso Roshi, Morinaga Soko Roshi, Ruth Fuller Sasaki, Walter Nowick (to whom he gave inka) et al. (All qv.) Retired to Daishu-in; succeeded as Abbot of Daitoku-ji by Sesso Oda Roshi (qv). On death succeeded at Daishu-in by Morinaga Soko Roshi (qv).

Harada Roshi, Sogaku (1870–1961): *Japanese Zen master.* Trained in both Rinzai and Soto traditions, entered Soto temple as novice at age 7. Continued training in Soto temples during primary and high school years. At 20 became monk at Shogen-ji, a Rinzai monastery; after 2 ½ years of strenuous training, attained kensho. At age 27 enrolled at Soto-sponsored Komazawa U. Continued to do research under well-known scholars for 6 years after graduation. Then trained with Dokutan Roshi of Nanzen-ji, Kyoto for 2 years; later moved into Nanzen-ji as Dokutan's assistant and applied himself wholeheartedly to zazen and koans; completed all koans and received inka from Dokutan Roshi. At this time, recalled to Komazawa U; spent 12 years teaching there, part of the time as full professor; combined Zen teaching with academic work. Afterwards became Abbot of Hosshin-ji, a post he retained for 40 years. Until almost age 90, conducted week-long sesshin at Hosshin-ji 6 times a year; also held sesshin elsewhere. "Nominally of the Soto sect, he welded together the best of Soto and Rinzai and the amalgam was a vibrant Buddhism, which has become one of the great teaching lines in Japan today"; "His commentary on *Shushogi,* a codification of Dogen's *Shobogenzo,* is recognized as one of the most penetrating of its kind" (Philip Kapleau).

Herrigel, Eugen (1884–1955): *Author and translator.* With August Faust, responsible for introducing Zen to Germany. Educated Heidelberg; read Philosophy with Shuei Ohasama (Jap Rinzai Master) and together tr Zen texts based on W philosophical terminology. Books incl *Zen in the Art of Archery* and *The Method of Zen.*

Hisamatsu, Shin'ichi (1889–1980): *Zen philosopher.* Disciple of Nishida Kenji, studied Zen under Ikegami Shozan of Myoshin-ji. Became Prof of Bdsm at Kyoto U; also taught at Harvard and traveled widely abroad. Active as tea master, founded

FAS Society in Kyoto to promote philosophical and practical understanding of Zen. Major work in English: *Zen & the Fine Arts*.

Hsü Yün, Ch'an Master (1840–1959): *"Universally regarded as the most outstanding Buddhist of the Chinese Sangha in the modern era" (Richard Hunn).* Dharma successor of all five Ch'an schools; main reformer in Chinese Bdst Revival (1900–50). Born Chuan Chou, Fukien province. Left home at 19; took Refuge at Yung Chuan Ssu on Mt. Ku; head shaved there by Master Chang Kai. At 20 took precepts with Master Miao Lien and received Dharma name Ku Yen; remained on Mt. Ku 4 years. *c* 1868–71: lived in wilderness on Mt. Ku on grass, nettles, etc. At 31 began traveling; given kung-an "Who is dragging this corpse about?" by Master Yung Ching of Luang Chuan Temple on Mt. T'ien T'ai. At 43: extensive pilgrimage on foot carrying incense and prostrating every third step to P'u T'o Shan, Wu T'ai Shan, Omei Shan, Tibet, Bhutan, India, Sri Lanka, Burma, back to China by sea, then visits to more holy sites in Yunnan, Hunan, and Anhwei. In 56th year achieved final awakening at Kao Min Ssu in Yang Chou. Thereafter began revival and teaching work. 1934; while Abbot of Ku Shan Ssu, had visions of 6th Patriarch; eventually invited to take charge of 6th Patriarch's temple (Ts'ao-Ch'i), then very run down; restored it along with other temples and monastaries; also in his life founded many schools and hospitals. Spent last years in cowshed near Chen Ju Ssu, Mt. Yun Chu, where he died in 120th year. Had also traveled in Malaysia and Thailand, and taught King of Thailand. Autobiography: *Empty Cloud,* tr Charles Luk. *Ch'an & Zen Teaching,* Series 1, tr Charles Luk contains his "Discourses & Dharma Words." Chinese sources incl Hsu Yun Ho Shang Shih Chi *("Records of Master Hsu Yun")*and Hsu Yun Ho Shang Nien Pu *("Autobiography of Master Hsu Yun")*.

Hsüan Hua, Tripitaka (or Dhyana) Master (Dharma names An Tz'u and Tu Lun): *Abbot of Gold Mountain Dhyana Monastery (California) and Chairman of Sino-American Bdst Assn.* Born 1908, Shuang-Ch'eng district, NE China. Trauma at age 11: encountered death; resolved to become a monk right away but delayed by family duties, though did take refuge in 3 Jewels; Ven Master Ch'ang became teacher. Well (though not formally) educated in Chinese classics, Bdst scriptures, medicine, physiognomy, and astrology. At age 19 mother died; took sramamera ordination; mourned by mother's grave for 3 years; meditation intensive; Hui Neng (6th Patriarch) also appeared, predicting future journey to W. After WWII, traveled 3000 miles to Nan Hua monastery in Canton province to visit Ven. Hsü Yün (qv). Received bhikshu ordination at Mt. P'u T'o during journey. Hsü Yün transmitted mind seal; made him 9th patriarch of Wei Yang lineage; asked him to be Director of Nan Hua Institute for the Study of Vinaya. 1950: resigned post at Nan Hua monastery; traveled to Ta Chiao monastery where Ven Hsü Yün had become Abbot. Soon after left for Hong Kong; lived in cave in the New Territories until requested by refugees from mainland China to help establish temples; remained in Hong Kong 12 years. 1962: to USA (San Francisco). Awaited developments. 1968: declared that the "flower of Buddhism would bloom that year in America with 5 petals"; in summer conducted a Surangama Sutra Dharma Assembly lasting 96 days; 5 people took ordination subsequently. Has delivered lectures on other sutras; more people have ordained. 1971: established Gold Mountain Monastery; subsequently also set up Bdst Text Translation Soc, International Institute for the Tr of Bdst Texts, Instilling Virtue Elementary School, City of 10,000 Buddhas and Dharma Realm Bdst U (both at Talmage, Cal). Has delivered extensive commentaries to canonical texts; published as *The Shurangama Sutra; The Heart Sutra; The Diamond Sutra; The 6th Patriarch's Platform Sutra; The Amitabha Sutra; The Sutra of the Past Vows of Earth Store Bodhisattva [Ksitigarbha];*

The Great Compassion Heart Dharani Sutra; The Sutra in 42 Sections; The Dharma Flower Sutra [Avatamsaka]; also The Shramanera Vinaya; The Awakening of Faith in the Mahayana Shastra; and several series of *Ch'an & Pure Land Dharma Talks*.

Hyobong Sunim (1888–1966): *"One of the most remarkable Buddhist teachers of this century in Korea"* (Stephen Batchelor). Born near present capital of N Korea. Studied law; became judge during Japanese occupation. Resigned after *c* 10 years, on grounds of conscience, left home and became wandering toffee seller. At 39 years commenced intensive monastic meditation practice. At age 43: into solitary retreat; after 1½ years achieved insight. For next 30 years was widely known and respected teacher at Songgwang-sa, Tongwa Sa, Haein Sa, and other monasteries and hermitages. Became head of the Chogye Order. Conferred Dharma transmission on Kusan Sunim (qv). Died in meditation posture while staying at P'yoch'ung monastery.

Imagita Roshi, Kosen (1816–92): *Major 19th century Rinzai master.* Born Osaka; studied to become Confucian scholar; at age 25 decided to become Zen monk; divorced wife and entered Shokuku-ji (Kyoto). Awarded inka at age 36 by Gisan. As Abbot of Engaku-ji (Kamakura) staunchly defended Bdsm during troubled Meiji years. A mentor of D.T. Suzuki (qv), who wrote a biography.

Kapleau Roshi, Philip: *American Zen teacher.* Born 1912, New Haven, Connecticut. 1946: Chief Court reporter, International Military Tribunal, Nuremberg. 1947: court reporter, International Military Tribunal, Tokyo. 1953-66: trained in various Rinzai and Soto Zen monasteries and temples in Japan. Teachers—Harada Roshi, Yasutani Roshi, and Nakagawa Soen Roshi (all qv). Also spent 1 year in SE Asia living at ashrams in India, Burma, and Sri Lanka. Centers established in Rochester, New York (1966– headquarters); Toronto and Montreal, Canada; Evanston, Illinois; Denver, Colorado; Santa Fe, New Mexico; Madison, Wisconsin; Mexico City; San Jose, Costa Rica; Poland (3 centers); Stockholm, Sweden; W. Berlin, Germany. Makes periodic visits to all, conducting sesshin and workshops. Holds two 3-month formal training periods annually at Rochester. Has also for 20 years spoken at colleges, universities, growth centers, and symposia. Books incl *Three Pillars of Zen; Zen Dawn in the West; Wheel of Death; To Cherish all Life (The Buddhist Case for Vegetarianism); A Pilgrimage to the Buddhist Temples and Caves of China; The Private Encounter with the Roshi: Its Hazards and Rewards;* and *The Passage of the Flame: Practical Guidance in Death, Dying, Karma & Rebirth*.

Katagiri Roshi, Dainin: *Soto Zen Master of the Eihei-ji line who works in the USA.* Born 1928. 1963: came to USA to serve at Zenshu-ji Soto Zen Mission, Los Angeles. 1964-71: assisted Shunryu Suzuki Roshi (qv) at Soko-ji Soto Zen Mission, San Francisco; later helped establish San Francisco Zen Center and Tassajara Mountain Center. 1972: moved to Minneapolis; founded Minnesota Zen Meditation Center; has since worked all over midwest. 1976: helped found Catching the Moon Zen Mt. Center in SE Minnesota (near New Albin, Iowa). Has ordained a number of Westerners into Bdst priesthood.

Kennett Roshi, Jiyu (Peggy Teresa Nancy Kennett 1924–96): *British-born Soto Zen master working in the USA.* Born 1924, England. Educated Trinity College of Music, London, and Durham U. Early Bdst studies at London Bdst Vihara and Bdst Society. 1962: ordained by Seck Kim Seng, Abbot of Cheng Hoon Teng Temple in Malacca, Malaysia; went on to study Soto Zen in Japan at Soji-ji under Chisan Koho Zenji (qv);

received transmission from Koho Zenji; installed as Abbess of Unpuku-ji (Mie Prefecture); granted Sanzen license. 1969: to San Francisco on lecture tour. 1970: Zen Mission Soc founded; moved to Mt. Shasta and became Abbess and Spiritual Director at Shasta Abbey; also Instructor at U of California Extension in Berkeley since 1972; sits on the faculty of the California Institute of Transpersonal Psychology and has lectured at universities worldwide. Has also founded numerous Zen temples and meditation groups through US, Canada, and in England (esp Throssel Hole Priory). Founder of Order of Bdst Comtemplatives (OBC). Books incl *Zen is Eternal Life* (first issued as *Selling Water by the River*); *How to Grow a Lotus Blossom, or How A Zen Buddhist Prepares for Death; The Wild White Goose, Diaries of Years in Japan* (2 vols); and *The Book of Life*.

Kitaro, Nishida (1870–1945): *Japan's premier modern philosopher.* Became Prof at Kyoto Imperial U in his 40s and 50s. 1927: retired early but retained status as Japan's foremost thinker; published a great deal—collected works run to 19 vols.

Kusan Sunim (1909–83): *Korean Zen Master.* Born Namwon, SW Korea of farming stock. Worked as farmer and married; then at 26, severe illness cured by reciting Bdst mantra; 3 years later left home to dedicate himself to Bdsm. Became student of Hyobong Sunim (qv) at Songgwang Sa monastery. At 31 bhikshu ordination at T'ongdo Sa. Not interested in sutra study; instead dedicated himself to meditation practice in meditation halls and hermitages. First important experience at Sudo Am hermitage and another major breakthrough at Popwang Dae hermitage in 1946. During Korean War escaped to UN controlled territory; lived in temples in or near Chungmu. After war accepted number of administrative posts; chief inspector at National Sangha headquarters in Seoul and later head of general monastic affairs in Cholla Namdo province. Also founded Milae Sa temple near Chungmu and was abbot there 1954–57. To deepen meditation practice, resigned and went to small hermitage (Paegun Am); achieved another awakening; then received Dharma transmission from Hyobong Sunim. 1962–66: Abbot of Tonghwa Sa monastery. 1966: visited SE Asia, India, and Nepal. 1967: founded Bul-il International Meditation Centre at Songgwang Sa for foreign monks and nuns. Latterly made several visits to US and founded centers in Los Angeles and Carmel; also visited Europe and founded center in Geneva. Died in meditation posture after short illness. Books incl *Nine Mountains* and *The Way of Korean Zen*.

Kyungbo Sunim: *First Korean Zen teacher to visit USA.* 1964: visited USA and toured various Bdst groups. 1965–69: studied at Temple U, Philadelphia; PhD for study of early history of Korean Zen. 1969: returned to Korea and became Dean of the Bdst College, Dongguk U, Seoul. Has visited USA regularly since 1973, but set up no teaching organization, though the Il Bung Zen Bdst Assn is umbrella organization for his groups. His disciple, Gosung Sunim, has also visited the USA. A prolific writer.

Leggett, Trevor Price: *Writer on Zen, the martial arts, and Vedanta.* Born 1914. LIB degree at London U. Lived and worked for 10 years in E (India, Japan); studied traditional Yoga of the Self under Hari Prasad Shastri; studied Japanese language. Bdsm and Judo in Japan. Did Zen training at Daitokuji (Kyoto). Was first foreigner to obtain 6th Dan (senior teacher's degree) in Judo from Kodakan. 1946–70: Head of BBC Japanese service. 1984: Order of the Sacred Treasure (third class) for services to Anglo-Japanese relations. 1987: Bukkyo Dendo Kyokai literary prize for trs of Bdst classics. Lives in London. Books incl *A First Zen Reader; The Tiger's Cave; Zen & the Ways;*

Encounters in Yoga & Zen; and *The Warrior Koans;* also four books on Judo (including *Demonstration of Throws*); and *Shogi* (Japanese Chess). From Sanskrit: first translations of Shankara's *Chapter of the Self* and the (newly discovered) *Commentary on the Yoga Sutras*. On panel of trs of Prof Nakamura's *The Development of Vedanta Philosophy*.

Luk, Charles (Upsaka Lu Ku'an Yü, 1898–1978): *Translator and writer on Ch'an*. Born Canton. Studied with Hutuktu (– Tulku) of Singkang (a Vajrayana teacher of both Kagyu and Gelug Lineages) and Master Hsü Yün (qv), who urged him to translate Chinese Bdst texts. Dedicated the last 20 years of his life (from 1956) to this cause. Lived in exile in Hong Kong, maintaining a world-wide correspondence. First visited Europe in 1930s; visited London and met Christmas Humphreys (qv) in 1935. Publications incl *Ch'an & Zen Teachings* (3 vols); trs of various sutras (*Surangama, Vimalakirti, Diamond, Heart*); *Secrets of Chinese Meditation; Taoist Yoga; The Transmission of the Mind Outside the Teaching;* and *Practical Buddhism*.

Maezumi Roshi, Hakuyu Taizen(1931–95): *Founder of Zen Center of Los Angeles*. Born 1931, Otawara, Tochigi prefecture, Japan. Age 11: ordained a Zen monk. Received degrees in Oriental literature and philosophy from Komazawa U. Afterwards studied at Soji-ji. 1955: received Dharma transmission from Hakuun Kuroda Roshi. Also received inka from Koryu Osaka Roshi and Hakuun Kuroda Roshi, thus also becoming Dharma successor in two major lines of Rinzai Zen. Holds Sanzen Dojo Shike (Training Master's credentials). 1956: came to Los Angeles as priest of Zenshuji temple. 1967: founded Zen Center of Los Angeles (ZCLA). 1976: established Kuroda Institute for Transcultural Studies (now called Kuroda Institute for the Study of Bdsm & Human Values). Also founding influence behind Zen Arts Center, Mt. Tremper, New York. Books incl *On Zen Practice* (I and II, both eds with B.T. Glassman); *The Hazy Moon of Enlightenment* (with B.T. Glassman); and *The Way of Everyday Life*.

Merzel Sensei, Dennis Genpo: *Dharma heir of Maezumi Roshi (ZCLA):* Born 1944, Brooklyn, New York. Raised and schooled in S California. Holds undergraduate degree in economics and MS in educational administration. Taught school for 8 years before moving to ZCLA. 1972: began studying with Maezumi Roshi (qv). 1973: ordained a Zen monk. 1978: assisted Maezumi Roshi in guiding student practice. 1979: completed koan study and appointed Dharma Holder. 1980: received Dharma Transmission. 1981: traveled to Japan for installation as Zen priest. Resided with wife Hobai at ZCLA until 1984; held post of ZCLA executive vice-president. Since June 1984 has been guiding the Kanzeon Sangha, an international organization of groups in Holland, England, Poland, Germany, and USA. Recently resided Amsterdam, currently in Maine.

Morgan, Daishin: *Abbot of Throssel Hole Priory*. Born 1951, London. 1974: ordained and began monastic training at Throssel Hole Priory. 1977: to Shasta Abbey, California, to train under Jiyu Kennett Roshi (qv). 1980: received certification as teacher of Bdsm. 1981: certification as Master (Roshi). 1982: appointed Abbot of Throssel Hole Priory; continues as its spiritual director while running retreats and lecturing all over UK.

Morinaga Roshi, Soko: *Rinzai Zen master*. Born 1925, Uotsu, Toyama prefecture. Conscripted into WW II at c age 19. 1947: graduated Toyama High School. Loss of faith following the Japanese defeat in War pointed him towards Zen; became disciple of Goto Zuigan Roshi (qv). 1948: ordained a monk. 1949: undertook training at

Daitoku-ji (Kyoto). On death of Zuigan Roshi, became incumbent of Daishu-in, a sub-temple in the Daitoku-ji complex. Has visited London and taught at the Zen Centre and the Bdst Soc. Books incl *Pointers to Insight*.

Myokyo-ni (Dr Irmgard Schloegl): *Austrian-born teacher of Rinzai Zen in UK.* Born Feldbach, near Graz. PhD in natural sciences; later specialized in mining. 1950: Assistant Lecturer in Geology, Imperial College (London); joined Bdst Soc. Early 1962: to Japan for 10 years Rinzai Zen training at Daitoku-ji (Kyoto) under Oda Sesso Roshi and Morinaga Soko Roshi (both qv). Returned to UK and began teaching at Bdst Soc, where she worked for a time as Librarian. Later founded The Zen Center in Christmas Humphrey's house in N London (house subsequently dedicated as Zen temple, renamed Shobo-an). 1984: ordained a Zen nun by Morinaga Soko Roshi. Books incl *The Zen Way* and *The Wisdom of the Zen Masters;* has also tr the *Rinzairoku* as *The Record of Rinzai*. Numerous contributions to *Zen Traces,* journal of the Zen Centre.

Nantembo (Nakahara Toju, 1839–1925): *One of the most colorful Zen priests of the modern era.* Famed for giving students a taste of his heavy Nanten-staff whether they "spoke or not" and for taking on other Zen Masters in "Dharma combat." Had over 3,000 students, incl famous generals Nogi and Kodama; bestowed inka on 6 priests and 25 laymen. Wrote many books and produced large number of Zen paintings and calligraphies.

Nakagawa Soen Roshi—see **Soen Roshi, Nakagawa.**

Nhat Hahn, Thich: *Exiled Vietnamese monk, peace activist, and poet; proponent of "Engaged Bdsm."* One-time student at Columbia U; recalled to native Vietnam, then at war, to help with third Way of Reconciliation, an attempt at a viable alternative to the corruption of Saigon and the communism of Hanoi. Established Van Hahn U; also School of Youth for Social Service, which went out to help the peasantry in the war-torn rural areas. Coined term "Engaged Bdsm" in his book *Vietnam: Lotus in a Sea of Fire*. Other books include *The Miracle of Mindfulness*. Presently lives in exile at Plum Village, Meyrac, France.

Nowick Roshi, Walter: *First American to receive full Dharma transmission in orthodox Rinzai Zen Lineage.* Studied piano under Henriette Michelson (onetime member of First Zen Institute, New York) at Julliard School, New York. Later became lay student of Rinzai Zen at Daitoku-ji (Kyoto) under Goto Zuigan Roshi (qv), who eventually conferred inka on him after *c* 17 years training. Supported himself in Japan playing concerts and teaching piano. Later spent 10 years working on his farm in Maine (USA) and teaching music before beginning to teach Zen. Life at his isolated and austere center in Maine described in *A Glimpse of Nothingness* by Janwillen van der Wetering.

Oda Roshi, Sesso (1901?–66): *Rinzai Zen master.* Brother senior disciple with Morinaga Soko Roshi (qv) under Goto Zuigan Roshi (qv). One time Abbot of Daitoku-ji (Kyoto).

Omori Roshi, Sogen: Born 1904, Yamanashi prefecture. Originally a teacher of kendo (swordsmanship), became Zen priest of Tenryu-ji school in his early 40s. 1948: established Tesshu Society in Tokyo; this became influential and attracted a number of foreign trainees. 1970s and early 80s: professor and later President of Hanazono

U (Kyoto). Author of a score of books of Zen theory and practice, incl *Zen & the Art of Calligraphy* (with Terayama Katsujo). Now retired.

Prabhasa Roshi, Dharma (formerly Gesshin Myoko): *German-born Zen teacher.* Born 1931 near Frankfurt. One-time painter. 1967: emigrated to USA. Became disciple of Joshu Saaki Roshi (qv). 1970: appointed first Head, Mt. Baldy Zen Training Center. 1972: ordained teacher of Rinzai Zen. Thereafter founded and directed International Zen Institute of America (Los Angeles). Often visits Europe.

Samu Sunim: *Korean Zen master active in USA.* Born 1941. 1967: to USA; stayed New York City until 1968, working as parcel sorter on night-shift and practicing meditation in the daytime; started Zen Lotus Society in Manhattan room. 1968: to Montreal, Canada; applied for refugee status; studied French and conducted meditation session. 1974: into 3-year retreat in basement flat following instructions of teacher, Solbong Sunim (1890–1969); afterwards began to teach Zen. 1979: purchase of Toronto property to become Zen Bdst Temple of Toronto (home of Zen Lotus Society); journal *Spring Wind* inaugurated. 1981: branch temple in Ann Arbor, Michigan. 1985: El Centro Zen Loto de Mexico inaugurated.

Sasaki Roshi, Joshu: *Zen master currently based in USA.* Born 1907; entered Rinzai Zen (Yoshenji line) training at 14. 1962: came to USA having been resident monk of Shoju-an, a small mountain temple in Nagano prefecture. Began to teach in the Los Angeles area. 1966: established Cimarron Zen Center. 1970: established Mt. Baldy Zen Center. 1974: established Jemez Bodhi Mandala in New Mexico. Umbrella organization—Rinzai-ji. Travels extensively each year teaching and conducting sesshin. Currently visits First Zen Institute of America, New York. Books incl *Zen: Center of Gravity.*

Sasaki, Ruth Fuller (1883–1967): *Pioneer of Zen Bdsm in USA.* Early 1930s: to Japan; zazen at Nanzenji (Kyoto) for a few months. 1938: settled New York City; became supporter of Sokei-an Sasaki's Bdst Society of America (later The First Zen Institute of New York, later still of America). 1944: married Sokei-an Sasaki (death 1945). 1949: returned to Japan with 3-fold purpose: (1) to find a teacher to take over First Zen Institute; (2) to complete translations of Rinzairoku and other Zen texts; (3) to complete her own Zen training. Studied at Daitokuji with Goto Zuigan Roshi (qv). 1956: allowed to build a small zendo and library, Ryosen-an, at Daitoku-ji; this a branch of First Zen Institute of America; believed that the only authentic way to study Zen was in Japan. 1958: ordained a Zen priest at Daitoku-ji, sponsored by Sesso Oda Roshi. Books incl *Zen—A Religion; Zen—A Method for Religious Awakening; Zen Dust* and *The Zen Koan* (with Isshu Miura); *The Recorded Sayings of Layman P'ang* (reprinted as *A Man of Zen,* with Iriya Yoshitaka and Dana R. Fraser); and *Recorded Sayings of Lin-chi* (with Yoshitaka).

Sasaki, Sokei-an (Sokei-an Shigetsu Osho, 1882–1945): *Pioneer teacher of Zen in USA.* Born Japan and trained as a dragon carver. Served in Manchuria during Russo-Japanese War. Encouraged to "carve a Buddha statue" (i.e. become a Buddha himself) by Soyen Shaku (qv). 1906: to USA with group aiming to found Rinzai Zen monastery in California and begin teaching Zen to Americans. After mission left, stayed in US and eventually established himself as a Zen teacher in New York. 1931: Bdst Society of America formed (later First Zen Institute of New York, later still of America). Group slowly grew and in 1938 joined by Ruth Fuller Everett. Her son-in-law, Alan Watts, also studied with Sokei-an for a short time. 1942: internment camp as enemy alien. 1944: married Ruth Everett.

Schloegl, Dr. Irmgard—see **Myokyo-ni.**

Senzaki Sensei, Nyogen (1876–1958): *Pioneer teacher of Rinzai Zen in USA.* Born and orphaned in Siberia; finally came under patronage of Soto Zen priest and Kegon scholar who began his education in Chinese Classics and Bdsm at *c* age 5. Studied Soto Zen, Shignon, and Vinaya School teachings. Met Soyen Shaku. 1896: entered Engaku-ji, despite having tuberculosis. 1901: left Engaku-ji. Influenced by "kindergarten" ideas of Froebel, set up nursery school (Mentorgarten). *c* 1905: went to USA; joined Soyen Shaku at home of Mr. and Mrs. Alexander Russell in San Francisco. Soon discharged; parted from Soyen Shaku in Golden Gate Park; told to work with Americans and not "utter the B of Bdsm" for 17 years. To 1922; worked variously mostly in hotel business, then hired a hall in San Francisco and gave first lecture; thus began his "floating zendo." 1927: small financial aid from Japan. 1931: moved to Los Angeles and set up zendo (Mentorgarten Meditation Hall, a.k.a. Tosen Zenkutsu). Lived austere monkish lifestyle. 1934: began correspondence with Nakagawa Soen Roshi (qv). 1943: interned as an enemy alien. 1945: took top floor apartment at Miyako Hotel in Little Tokyo, Los Angeles; Mentorgarten meetings took place there; students included Robert Aitken (1947) and Garry Snyder (briefly). 1955: brief return visit to Japan; met Eido Tai Shimano Roshi (qv). Books incl *The Iron Flute* (ed Ruth McCandless); *Zen Flesh, Zen Bones* (with P. Reps); and *Buddhism and Zen.*

Seung Sahn (Soen Sunim, alt. Soen Sa Nim): *Korean Zen master based in USA.* Born 1927, Korea, as Lee Duk An during Japanese occupation. Parents Christian. Joined underground movements. After WW II, studied W philosophy at Dongguk U; became disenchanted with both politics and scholarship. 1948: became Bdst monk and embarked upon intensive meditation. At 32 received Dharma Transmission from Zen Master Ko Bong. During Korean War spent 5 years in S Korean Army; afterwards returned to monastic life; became abbot of temple in New Seoul. Then spent 9 years in Japan and Hong Kong, founding temples and teaching. 1972: went to US; at first worked in a laundry in Providence, Rhode Island; began to gather students from Brown U; Providence Zen Center developed, now head temple for many sub-centers and affiliated groups both in N America and in Europe (Poland, W Germany, etc.). Books incl *Only Don't Know; Dropping Ashes on the Buddha;* and *Bone of Space: Zen Poems.*

Shimano Roshi, Eido Tai: *Zen master active in USA.* Born 1932. Responsible for guiding Zen Studies Soc. 1976: International Dai Bosatsu Zendo founded in Catskill Mts., New York State (first traditional Zen monastery in N America).

Soen Roshi, Nakagawa (1907–84): *Japanese Zen Master and noted poet.* Educated Tokyo U; majored in Japanese literature; then became Zen monk and trained under Yamamoto Genpo Roshi at Ryutaku-ji. Went with Genpo Roshi to Kyoto; Genpo briefly Abbot of Myoshin-ji; then to Manchuria, where Genpo Abbot of branch monastery of Myoshin-ji during WW II. 1951: became Abbot of Ryutaku-ji, Mishima. 1974: retired. "He was known particularly for his innovative and creative changes in ritual, and for his interest in the development of Zen Buddhism in the West. He was also a nationally known poet . . . " (Robert Aitken). Late 1930s: began to correspond with Nyogen Senzaki (qv). 1948: first of series of visits to USA; led various sesshin after Senzaki's death. Instrumental in establishment of Diamond Sangha in Hawaii; encouraged other US Zen centers in Los Angeles and New York, where disciples Eido Tai Shimano Roshi and Nakagawa Khudo Roshi continue to teach.

Soen Sunim — see **Seung Sahn.**

Soyen Shaku (1859–1919): *"The first modern Zen master of Japan."* Pupil of Imagita Kosen Roshi and teacher of D.T. Suzuki. Received inka at 25. Afterwards sent by Kosen Roshi to Keian U to study W subjects, then on to Sri Lanka to study Theravada Bdsm. Returned to Japan after 2 years as Theravada bhikkhu (later disrobed); on death of Kosen Roshi (1892) became Master of Engaku-ji. 1893: at World Parliament of Religions in Chicago. Is reputed to have said: "Following history, it will take 300 years for Zen to come to its full flowering in America." 1905–6: taught in San Francisco and adjacent cities with D.T. Suzuki (qv) translating: talks collected, issued as Sermons of a Bdst Abbot. Was a man with a progressive, modern outlook, who wished to revitalize Bdsm and make it relevant for the coming age. "His attitude was something like that of a free thinker, grounded on Buddhist idealism, hopeful of joining with other religious leaders in forging a world class way of mutual benefit for the sentient beings of the future" (Mary Farkas). Two pupils also taught in USA: Nyogen Senzaki Sensei and Sokei-an Sasaki (both qv).

Stevens, John: *Bdst scholar, translator, calligrapher, and Aikido instructor.* Born 1947, Chicago. 1975: ordained a Soto Zen priest. 1978: graduated, Bdst Seminary Tohoku Social Welfare U, Sendai, Japan. 1984: resigned from the priesthood. Holds 5th dan black belt in Aikido. Current posting: Professor of Bdst Studies and Aikido Instructor, Tohoku Social Welfare U. Director, Zen Art Soc. Publications incl *One Robe, One Bowl: The Zen Poetry of Ryokan; Mountain Tasting: Zen Haiku by Taneda Santoka; Sacred Calligraphy of the East; Aikido: The Way of Harmony; The Sword of No-Sword: Life of Master Warrior Tesshu; Zen Guide, Where to Meditate in Japan; Shobogenzo,* English tr with K. Nishiyana et al; *Adundant Peace: The Life of Morihei Ueshiba, Founder of Aikido;* and *Marathon Monks of Mt. Hiei.*

Suzuki, Beatrice Erskine (née Lane): *American pioneer of Bdst studies.* Graduate of Columbia U. 1911: married D.T. Suzuki (qv); collaborated with him in his work— co-ed of *The Eastern Bdst.* Student of Soyen Shaku (qv); latterly drawn to Shingon. Onetime Professor of English at Otani U (Kyoto). Died 1939. Books incl *Buddhist Readings* and *Mahayana Buddhism.*

Suzuki, Daisetz Yeitaro (1870–1966): *"The man who brought Zen to the West."* Born Kanazawa, Japan. After school, taught English. 1891: entered Tokyo Semmon Gakko (Waseda U). 1891: began Zen training under Imagita Kosen Roshi and Soyen Shaku (qv) at Engaku-ji (Kamakura). 1897: to USA (LaSalle, Ill.) to work for Open Court Publishing Co. 1909: returned to Japan; became lecturer at Peers' School and at Tokyo Imperial U. 1911: married Beatrice Erskine Lane. 1912: visited England at invitation of Swedenborg Soc. 1921: began publication of *The Eastern Buddhist;* also moved to Kyoto to Chair of Bdst Philosophy at Otani U. 1936: attended World Congress of Faiths in London and lectured on Zen and Japanese culture at various British and American universities. 1946: founded Matsugaoka Bunko ("Pine Hill Library") in Kamakura, near Engaku-ji; began publication of *The Cultural East.* 1947: lectured on Bdsm to Emperor of Japan. 1950–58: lectured and toured extensively in the W, notably in USA; held posts at Columbia U. Books incl *Essays in Zen Buddhism* (3 series); *Studies in the Lankavatara Sutra; Introduction to Zen Buddhism; Manual of Zen Buddhism; Japanese Buddhism; The Essence of Buddhism; The Zen Doctrine of No-Mind; Living by Zen; A Miscellany on the Shin Teaching of Buddhism; Studies in Zen; Mysticism: Christian and Buddhist; Zen & Japanese Buddhism; Zen and Japanese Culture; Zen Buddhism & Psychoanalysis; The Field of Zen; Shin Buddhism; What Is Zen?; Sengai the Zen Master;* and *Collected Writings on Shin Buddhism.* Trs incl *The Lankavatara Sutra; The Awakening of Faith* (Asvaghosha); *Sermons of a Buddhist Abbot* (Soyen Shaku); *The Life of Shinran Shonin;* and *The Kyogyoshinsho.* Biography by A. Irwin Switzer III. Memoir: *Suzuki Remembered,* ed Masao Abe.

Suzuki Roshi, Shunryu (1904–71): *Eminent teacher of Soto Zen in USA: founder of San Francisco Zen Center.* Born Japan; father a Zen Master; at early age began Zen training under Gyokujun Soon-daiosho, a Soto Master, and other teachers. Recognized as a Zen Master *c* 30; became responsible for many temples and a monastery. During WW II led a pacifist group. 1959: to USA intending only short visit but settled in San Francisco area, where a group formed. 1962: San Francisco Zen Center formally inaugurated; this grew to occupy a number of California locations, incl Zen Mountain Center at Tassajara Springs (first Zen monastery in USA with facilities for long-term practice; established 1967). 1971: installed Richard Baker (qv) as Dharma Heir. Author of the classic *Zen Mind, Beginner's Mind.*

Suzuki Roshi, Sochu: *Soto Zen master with W connections.* Born 1921, Tochigi prefecture. 1931: entered Seitai-ji temple, Mino, Gifu prefecture after death of parents. Stayed for some years in Taiwan where his Master established a school of Zen. 1939: entered a Rinzai school; soon drafted into Army; survived WW II at Saipan Island. 1947: entered Hanazono College. 1957: ordained as monk and entered Ryutaku-ji; studied under Genpo Yamamoto Roshi and Soen Nakagawa Roshi (qv). 1977: became Abbot of Ryutaku-ji. Has traveled abroad to W Germany, Israel, and Italy and has visited London on a number of occasions.

Takashina Roshi, Rosen: *Primate of the Soto Zen sect.* One-time President, Japan Bdst Assn. Writings incl *A Tongue-tip Taste of Zen (Zetto Zemmi).*

Terayama, Katsujo (Tanchu): Born 1938, Saitama prefecture. Studied for many years with Omori Sogen (qv), receiving inka in 1971. 1965: pilgrimage to Bdst sites in India. Currently Head of Zen Calligraphy Soc (Hitsuzenkai) and professor at Nishogakusha U (Tokyo). Has instructed many foreign students and given exhibitions and workshops in Europe. Author of several imp studies of Zen art; in English *Zen & the Art of Calligraphy* (with Omori Sogen).

Tesshu, Master Warrior (Yamaoka Tesshu): *Zen master , calligrapher, and swordsman.* Widely regarded as savior of Japanese Bdsm in general and Zen in particular during Meiji period. Founded and restored scores of temples; protected Bdst treasures from thieves and vandals; defended Dharma against anti-Bdst forces; supported a small army of priests and nuns, down-and-out samurai, beggars, and stray animals. Established "No-Sword" School; was also one of the greatest Zen artists of modern times, producing over one million works, mostly to raise finance for noble causes. Biography: *The Sword of No-Sword* by John Stevens.

Thien-An, Thich (1926–80): *Late Vietnamese Zen master and scholar active in USA.* Trained in Lin-chi (Rinzai) tradition but adopted ecumenical approach. 1966: came to USA; lectured at UCLA. 1967: began to teach in Hollywood. Founded International Bdst Meditation Center and, 1973, College (later U) of Oriental Studies, Los Angeles. 1975: after fall of Saigon, active in helping Vietnamese refugees to USA.

Tsuji Somei: *Present-day Zen master.* Born *c* 1903. Studied at Tokyo U of Commerce (now Hitotsubashu U); later went into business, working as accountant for big oil company. 1925: began Zen training at Engakuji under Furukawa Gyodo Roshi (qv). Currently incumbent at Funi Zendo, Tokyo.

Uchiyama Roshi, Kosho. *Former Abbot of Antai-ji.* Has had many foreign students; author of 2 books in English—*Refining Your Life* and *Approach to Zen.*

van de Wetering, Janwillem: *Dutch-born writer on Zen.* Born 1931, the Netherlands. Wrote two books on experiences in Zen centers: *The Empty Mirror* describes 1½ year stay at Daitoku-ji (Kyoto), and *A Glimpse* (in US *A Touch*) *of Nothingness* represents his participation in an obscure settlement on E Coast of US. Also writer of thrillers; spent 7 years on active duty with Dutch Special Constabulary. Currently resides in Maine, USA.

Yamada Roshi, Mumon: *Japanese Rinzai master.* Born 1900, Aichi prefecture. Ordained a Bdst priest at 19 by Kawaguchi Ekai (adventurer-monk-scholar who was first Japanese to enter Tibet and spent 3 years there prior to dramatic flight). Was President of Hanazono U for 30 years; trained many of the current generation of Rinzai priests. Also served as Primate of Myoshin-ji Rinzai school prior to retirement. Several foreign students have trained with him; has also visited main Zen centers overseas. Perhaps the most prolific modern Zen teacher; his huge corpus of work being published by Zen Culture Institute, Kyoto (which he helped found).

Yamahata Roshi, Hogen Daido: *Japanese Zen master.* Abbot of Chogenji (Japan). Trained in both Rinzai and Soto schools. Now leads Soto-style sesshin in Europe each year that incorporate hatha yoga in addition to traditional elements. "Hogensan's teaching imparts the classic Zen flavor of transcendental understanding coupled with a direct down-to-earth approach to life's realities" (press release). In UK teaches at Gaia House, Devon.

Yasutani Roshi, Hakuun (1885–1973): *Japanese Zen master.* At age 5 years, head shaven and sent to live in a temple. Remained there until 12. At 13, became novice at large Soto temple; then, after 2 more years of primary school, went on to a Soto seminary and later spent 4 years in teachers' training school. At age 30, married and begot 5 children; remained nominally a priest but worked as schoolteacher for *c* 10 years and continued zazen practice. At 40 began training with Sogaku Harada Roshi (qv); relinquished principalship of school; became temple priest and began attending sesshin at Hosshin-ji. Attained kensho during second session using koan Mu. Received inka from Harada at 58 and appointed Dharma Heir. Held periodic sesshin at his temple in the suburbs of Tokyo and elsewhere in the vicinity; also in Hokkaido and Kyushu. 1962–69: traveled annually to USA. At 80, undertook extended stay in USA. "Husband, father, schoolmaster, and ultimately Zen Master, Hakuun Yasutani did not achieve his distinction by avoiding the pains and joys incident to the life of the ordinary man but in experiencing and then transcending them. In this his life reflects the Mahayana ideal that Self-realisation is for the householder no less than the celibate monk" (Philip Kapleau). Wrote and published 5 vols of commentary on the *Mumonkan*, the *Hekiganroku*, the *Shoyoroku* and the *Denkoroku*; also on the *Five Degrees of Tozan*.

PURE LAND BUDDHISM

Austin, Rev Jack: *Pioneer of Shin Bdsm in UK.* Born 1917, Caerleon, Gwent (S Wales, UK). With Richard Robinson, founded Dharma Study Group for studying Mahayana sutras. 1946–52: a member of first ad hoc council of Bdst Soc. 1952: with Richard Robinson, ordained by Ven Sumangalo (qv) in London. 1953: launched *Western Buddhist* to promote Mahayana Bdsm. 1954: initiated into Arya Maitreya Mandala (founded by Lama Govinda (qv) in Das Buddhistische Haus, W Berlin. 1966: initiated into Soto Zen by Chisan Koho Zenji (qv) in London. With others founded the Hannyakai (later London Zen Soc). Served as Bdst representative on various committees. 1976: co-founder of Shin Bdst Assn in London (Patron: Chief Abbot Kosho Ohtani). 1977: ordained a Hongwan-ji priest in Kyoto. Has also visited Shin temples in Hawaii, San Francisco, and New York.

Bloom, Alfred: *Dean, Institute of Buddhist Studies; author.* Born 1926, Philadelphia. 1951: Eastern Baptist Theological Seminary, AB and ThB; married; 2 children. 1953: Andover-Newton Theological Seminary, BD and STM. 1953: ordained Baptist minister. 1957–59: Fulbright scholar. 1963: Harvard, PhD. 1970: Prof Religion, U of Hawaii. Member, American Academy of Religion. Publications incl *Shinran's Gospel of Pue Grace; The Life of Shinran; The Journey of Self-Acceptance; Indian and Far Eastern Religious Traditions; Resource of Modern Living—Tannisho;* and *Shoshinge: The Heart of Shin Buddhism.*

Chevrier, Rev Jodo A.: *Swiss Shin leader.* Has produced many French trs of important Shin texts.

Clifton, Robert: —see **Sumangalo.**

Eracle, Rev. Jean: *Swiss Shin leader and translator.* Curator and researcher in Asiatic Dept, Ethnographical Museum, Geneva. 1970: President, Société Bouddhique Suisse Jodo-Shinshu, with chapel near Geneva linked to Nishi Hongwan-ji. Publications incl first complete tr of three Pure Land sutras. Also *La Doctrine Bouddhique de la Terre Pure, Un Bouddhisme pour tous: l'Admisme.*

Fenzl, Friedrich: *Leader of Shin movement in Austria.* Born 1932. Although read Bhikshu Subhadra's *Buddhist Catechism* in 1949 did not formally become Bdst until 1955. Became associated with Bdst Soc of Vienna and George Grimm's Old Bdst Community (Bavaria). 1960: under the influence of H. Pieper, converted to Jodo Shinshu; set up Austrian branch in Salzburg (where he works at U). 1965–75: edited newsletter *Mahayana*. Established social welfare body along Bst lines.

Hunt, Ernest (Rev Shinkaku Hunt, 1876–1967): *Possibly first Western Shin propagator.* Born Hoddesden (UK), educated Kensington, Eastbourne; later went to sea. 1915: emigrated to Hawaii; worked in plantations; joined local Jodo Shin temples. 1924: ordained a priest of the Hongwan-ji by Bishop Imamura; became active in imparting (via English language) the authentic Bdst teachings to young generation of Japanese immigrants (Nisei); founded and became headmaster of schools and won popularity through social welfare activities among Bdst community. 1932: Founded International Buddhist Institute of Hawaii. 1952: joined Soto Zen temple in Honolulu. 1962: "choro"ordination from Vice Abbot Iwamoto of Sojiji; later received Dharma succession from Zenkyo Komagata, was given name Daiko and later still made daiosho. Books incl *An Outline of Buddhism; The Religion of Wisdom & Compassion; Buddhismin Hawaii;* and numerous works for children.

Inagaki, Rev Prof Hisao: *Executive Secretary of International Assn of Shin Buddhist Studies (founded 1984).* Currently Prof of English at Ryukoku U. 1970s: lectured at SOAS (London U); the (British) Pure Land Bdst Fellowship initiated in his house at that time. Editor of *The Pure Land.* Member of the English and Portuguese Translation Centres at Hongwanji International Centre. Editor of Ryokoku Translation series. Publications incl *A Dictionary of Japanese Buddhist Terms* and *A Glossary of the Sukhavativyuha Sutras; The Three Pure Land Sutras; The Amida Sutra Mandala;* and *The Way of Nembutsu Faith.*

Inagaki, Rev Zuiken Saizo (1885–1981): *Shin Bdst Priest.* A prime inspirer of the development of Jodoshinu in Europe. Born Himeji, taught English, became student of Riken Katsura and ordained priest of Nishi Hongwanji in 1945. Publications incl more than 70 books in Japanese, Anjin and Tannisho into English.

Kell, Gerhard: *Second leader of German Shin movement.* Born 1948, Halle; studied modern languages and law at Free U (W Berlin) and privately E religions. 1978: joined German Jodo Community; confirmed at Nishi Hongwan-ji. 1978: succeeded H. Pieper (qv) as leader. Specializes in tr Shin Bdst texts.

Murakami, Toshio: *Bishop, Buddhist Churches of Canada.* Born 1931, Kita Kyushu-shi, Fukoaka, Japan. 1959: MA from Ryukoku U, Kyoto; ordained Jodo Shinshu minister, Bdst Churches of America. 1959–60: orientation at Berkeley. 1960–62: Oregon. 1963–68: San Jose. 1964: married Yoko Murakami; 2 daughters. 1968–71: Monterey. 1971–77: Director, BCA Bureau of Education. 1981–83: Executive Assistant to Bishop. 1982–83: Executive Director, Inst of Bdst Studies. 1984–86: Oakland.

Ohtani, Lord Kosho: *Chief Abbot Emeritus, Nishi Hongwan-ji, Kyoto.* President of the International Assoc of Bdst Studies. Has visited Europe several times and conducted ordinations and consecrations. Currently oversees the development of Shin Buddhism in Europe.

Peel, Shitoku Adriaan: *Chairman, Federation des Associations Bouddhiques de Belgique/ Federatie van Boeddhistische Verenigingen Belgie; ed, Dutch Shin journal* Eko. 1956–57: ed Theravada oriented periodical *Magga.* 1976: became active in Jodo Shinshu; founded 1st Belgian branch in Antwerp. 1977: initiated as Shaky Shitoku in London by Lord Kosho Ohtani (qv) of Nishi Hongwan-ji. Chairman, Belgian branch of World Congress of Faiths; Belgian representative of Intl Assn of Shin Bdst Studies (Kyoto). Dean, Faculty of Comparative Study of Religions, Antwerp. Publications incl *Shin-Boeddhisme—De Simpele Weg; Problems of Shin Buddhism in Europe and Its Relations to Other Buddhist Denominations;* and *Some Fundamental Differences between Buddhism and Christianity.*

Pieper, Rev Harry (1902–78): *Seminal leader of German Shin movement.* Born Berlin; attended Das Buddhistische Haus. 1946: formed a Mahayana group. 1951: joined Arya Maitreya Mandala; received ordination and became Secretary. Met Prof Osamu Yamada: invited him to lecture on Shin Bdsm. 1954: on visit of Kosho Ohtani (qv), received initiation in Nishi Hongwan-ji lineage; resigned from AMM. 1956: founded first Pure Land Assn in Europe (Buddhistische Gemeinschaft Jodo-Shin). 1962: founded first Bdst prison chaplaincy in German-speaking world. Tr many US and Japanese books on Shin Bdsm.

Pym, Jim: Founding member of the Shin Bdst Assoc and The Pure Land Bdst Fellowship, a non-sectarian network of those interested in Other Power/Pure Land Buddhism. Studied Jodoshinshu with Rev Austin, initiated into Jodoshinshu 1976. Currently contact for P.L.B.F. and editor of *Pure Land Notes.*

Saski, Rev Prof Esho: Secretary of International Assoc of Bdst Culture, which promotes Shin Buddhism worldwide, particularly in Europe. Professor of Buddhism at Kyoto Women's University.

Snow Elson: English ed of *The World of Dharma,* newspaper of Bdst Churches of America. Publications incl *Blue Tiles, Women at Yoshizaki,* translation of Kisamboge and Ogon-ge.

Sumangalo, Ven (Robert Stuart Clifton, 1903–63): *Pioneering W Shin Priest in US.* Born Birmingham, Alabama, USA as Harold Amos Eugene Newman. Traveled in E. First Westerner to be ordained a priest of Nishi Hongwan-ji by Ven Kosho Ohtani (qv). Returned to US; performed priestly functions while working as probation officer. 1951: founded W Bdst Order, "an organization dedicated to interpreting the Dharma to the W and to establishing groups where none existed" *(The Western Buddhist).* Later moved to Malaya and worked vigorously for Bdsm there until his death.

Tabrah, Rev Ruth: Shin Bdst minister, author and lecturer. A director of Bdst Study Center Press, Hawaii. Publications incl *The Monk Who Dared; The Natural Way of Shin Buddhism;* and *Ajatasatru: The Story of Who We Are* (with Shoji Matsumoto).

Tsuji, Kenryu Takashi: *Minister, Buddhist Churches of America.* Born 1919, Mission City, BC, Canada. 1946: m Sakaye Kawabata; 5 children. 1937: U of BC, Canada. 1942: U of Toronto. 1948: Ryukoku U, Kyoto. 1958: ordained minister, Jodo Shinshu, Bdst Churches of America. 1968: Bishop, Bdst Churches of America. 1941–42: minister, Vancouver Bdst Church. 1942–45: Slocan Bdst Church. 1945–58: Toronto Bdst Church. 1958–68: National Director of Bdst Education, BCA. 1968–81: Bishop, BCA; President of Bdst Studies. 1981–: Eko-ji Bdst Temple. Ed, *Program of Studies of Buddhist Sunday Schools.* Publications incl *Three Lectures on Tannisho.* Has made documentary films, incl *In the Footsteps of Shinran; The Story of Hongwan-ji; A Bdst Pilgrimage;* and *Sri Lanka, Where the Dhamma is Preserved.*

Tsumura, Junjo: *Bishop, Honpa Hongwan-ji Mission of Hawaii.* Born 1924, Osaka, Japan. Married Teruko Ogata; 2 children. Graduated Ryukoku U, Kyoto. 1952: ordained. 1952–56: minister, Sacramento. 1956–72: Watsonville. 1972–75: BCA,

Exec Assistant to Bishop (BCA 75th anniversary). 1975–82: San Mateo. 1982–85: San Jose. 1985–87: Monterey. 1987–: Bishop, HHMH.

Yamaoka, Seigen Haruo: *Bishop, Buddhist Churches of America (1981); President, Institute of Buddhist Studies.* Born 1934, Fresno, California. 1966: married Shigeko Masuyama; 2 children. 1956: BA from California State U, Fresno. 1961: MA from Ryukoku U, Kyoto. 1969: MRE, and 1979, PhD (Ministry in Religious Education) from Pacific School of Religion, Berkeley, Cal. 1964: ordained, Bdst Churches of America; minister, Bdst Church of Oakland. 1971–81: Stockton Bdst Temple. 1969–71: Registrar, Inst of Bdst Studies, Berkeley, Cal. 1970–75: member, Research Committee, BCA. 1971–75 and 1979–81: member, IBS Board of Trustees. 1972–75: English Secretary, Ministers Assn. 1977: member, Board of Bdst Education. 1979–81: Chairman, Ministers Assn. Publications incl *Compassion in Encounter; Teaching & Practice of Jodo Shinshu; Jodo Shinshu—Religion of Human Experience; Meditation—Gut Enlightenment; The Way of Hara;* and *Six Aspects of Jodo Shinshu.* Office: San Francisco.

NICHIREN TRADITION

Causton, Richard (1920–95): *Chairman and Director General of Nichiren Shoshu (UK).* Born *c* 1920. Educated at Sandhurst. Joined Border Regiment; remained a professional soldier to age 38. WW II: served in Burma. 1958: retired from Army with rank of Lieut. Col. Joined Harrods; later became General Sales Manager for Dunhill cigarettes; moved to Far East to set up Dunhill operation there; discovered Soka Gakkai Buddhism. After many years of "trying to be a good Christian," this was "an electrifying experience." 1971: committed himself to NS. 1974: returned to UK. 1977: gave up business to join permanent staff of NSUK. 1975: became Ch and DG; also Vice President of Nichiren Shoshu European Institute and Vice President of Soka Gakkai International.

Fujii, The Most Ven Nichidatsu (1884–1985): *Founder and preceptor of the Nipponzan Myohoji order.* 1903: became a monk. 1918: began to preach Bdsm publicly, traveling widely through China, Korea, Manchuria, and Japan. Warned of the growing militarism in Japan. Disciples joined him in the practice of beating the hand-drum and chanting the prayer for peace *(Namu myoho renge kyo).* 1924: first Nipponzan Myohoji formed at Tagonoura, near Mt. Fuji. 1931–33: traveled in India to regenerate Bdsm there; met Gandhi. Throughout WWII, prayed and regularly fasted for early peace. After war, began promoting construction of peace pagodas in Japan and later elsewhere. In UK, pagodas built at Milton Keynes and Battersea Park (London). Books incl *Buddhism for World Peace; Beating Celestial Drums; Ichienbudai;* and *The Time Has Come.*

Hasegawa, Hiromi: *Founder of Reiyukai in UK.* Born 1947, Kyoto. Became a teacher. Mid-1970s: visited UK for study purposes; stayed in Norfolk; later returned to Japan and converted to Reiyukai. 1976: returned to Norfolk to (successfully) establish Reiyukai in England.

Ikeda, Daisaku: *Current (third) President of Soka Gakkai (Nichiren Shoshu).* Born 1928, Omori, Tokyo, 5th son of edible seaweed farmer. Childhood dogged by poverty and ill health. 1940: left school at age 12; persevered to read in spare time and later to write. *c* 1947: introduced to SG "and knew instantly that this was a way of life he must follow." Greatly influenced by Josei Toda (qv), second President of SG, his "master in life." 1960: on Toda's death, became third President of SG. Set out to raise membership to 3 million, to erect a large reception hall at Head Temple, and "to arouse an awakening in religious circles." 1962: first goal realized. 1964: second goal realized. Third is "forever in his heart and actions." 1975: Soka Gakkai International formed; began international activities, holding dialogues with eminent world leaders and leading intellectuals, arranging cultural exchanges, etc. 1972: Sho Hondo, Grand Main Temple, opened at Head Temple (Taiseki-ji). 1983: presented with UN Peace Award by UN Sec. Gen. Perez de Cuellar, Books include *The Living Buddha; My Recollections; Dialogue on Life (A Buddhist Perspective on Life and the Universe); Life an Enigma; A Precious Jewel; A Lasting Peace; Buddhism: The First Millennium; Choose Life (with Arnold Toynbee); and The Human Revolution (5 vols)*.

Kotani, Kimi (1901–71): *Co-founder of Reiyukai.* Born Miura, Kanagawa prefecture, Japan. 1925: married Yasukichi Kubo, elder brother of Kakutaro Kubo (qv), founder of Reiyukai. Worked with Kubo to expand movement and eventually became its Honorary President (1930). After death of Kubo, widened scope of Reiyukai as social welfare organization, created many youth programs. 1963: Kotani Scholarship established.

Kubo, Kakutaro (1890 or 92–1944): *Founder of Reiyukai.* Born Kominato, Japan, the birthplace of Nichiren Daishonin. A carpenter, later in life taken up by Baron Sengaku, a fervent follower of Nichiren. Lived in Tokyo; employee in Imperial Household Ministry. 1919: began formulating own philosophy. 1920s and 30s: worked to attract support for his vision of a lay Bdst society. 1930: installed as Chairman of Board of Directors. 1940: registered his organization with the city of Tokyo. Until death worked with Kimi Kotani (qv). 1958: Kubo Memorial Hall completed in Tokyo and dedicated as socil welfare facility.

Kubo, Dr Tsungunari: *Current President of Reiyukai.* Took over Presidency following death of Kimi Kotani (qv) in 1971.

Matiguchi, Tsunesaburo (1871–1944): *Founder and first President of Soka Kyoiku Gakkai (forerunner of Soka Gakkai).* Born Niigata prefecture, NW Japan. At 14, went to Hokkaido; educated Sapporo Normal School (now Hokkaido University of Education). Later served as teacher and principal of several elementary schools in Sapporo and Tokyo. Formed small organization of educators. 1928: converted to Nichiren Shoshu. 1930: established Soka Kyoiku Gakkai (literally "Value-creating Education Society"); worked to spread knowledge of Nichiren's teachings. 1943: arrested together with other leaders for opposing Shintoism and criticizing war effort. Died in prison at age 73. Publications incl *Soka Kyoikugan Taikei* (The System of Value-Creating Pedagogy) and *Kyodaka Kenkyu* (Research Studies in Folk Culture of Local Communities).

Naganuma, Mrs Myoko (1899–1957): *One of the founding inspirations of Rissho Kosei-Kai.* Born of farming stock in Saitama prefecture. Came to Tokyo; worked in factory; married man in ice business. Due to disease, had to drink much milk; met N. Niwano (qv), then in the milk business. Joined Reiyukai. 1938: with Niwano set up Dai Nippon Rissho Kosei-Kai; became first Vice-President.

Niwano, Rev Nikkyo: *Founder of Rissho Kosei-Kai.* Born 1906, Tokamachi, Niigata prefecture, Japan, of farming stock; named Shikazo. Saw military service in Japanese Navy. No higher education. 1923: went to Tokyo; apprenticed to shopkeeper; studied religion, divination, Chinese classics. Daughter's sickness led him to join Reiyukai. 1934: set up milk shop in order to meet people. 1938: seceded from Reiyukai, not because of doctrinal differences, but due to growing awareness of his own powers of leadership and consequent desire for independence; with Mrs. M. Naganuma (qv), established Dai Nippon Rissho Kosei-Kai; became first President. Membership has grown to *c* 5 million with branches throughout Japan and overseas. Practices incl Hoza (Circle of Compassion) and the discipline of Veneration. 1979: won Templeton Prize. Books incl *Buddhism for Today.*

Toda, Josei (1900–58): *Second President of Soka Gakkai.* In 1920s, joined staff of school where Tsunesaburo Makiguchi (qv) headmaster; joined Makiguchi's small organization. *c* 1928: followed Makiguchi in converting to Nichiren Shoshu, joined Makiguchi's small embryo organization. Interned with Makiguchi during WWII. Took over Presidency after death of Makiguchi. Had powerful spiritual experience in Sugamo Prison. 1945: "Toda emerged at the end of the war fired with the determination that he would rebuild and develop the lay society" (Nichiren Shoshu leaflet). Health very poor but began new organization and called it Soka Gakkai. At death, counted more than 750,000 households in membership.

Wilde, Julian: *Secretary of British branch of Reiyukai.* Born 1951, Norwich (UK). Attracted to Bdsm at *c* 11 years; studied Zen, Tibetan Bdsm. 1976: encountered Hiromi Hasegawa (qv); joined Reiyukai; visited Japan. Books incl *The Grimoire of Chaos Magick.*

Williams, George: *General Director of Nichiren Shoshu of America (NSA).* Of Japanese origin, changed his name from Massayasu Sadanaga. Came to UCLA in early 1950s to study politics; set about creating NSA.

MISCELLANEOUS

Ambedkar, Dr Bhim Rao (1891–1956): *Founder of the Indian movement for converting harijans (untouchables) from Hinduism to Bdsm.* Member of Bombay Legislative Assembly, later Law Minister in the Central Government at Indian independence. 1956: at Nagpur, he and his wife along with *c* 500,000 followers formally renounced the Hindu religion and espoused Bdsm. Work carried on by Indian Bdst Society, which he founded. Book: *The Buddha and His Dhamma.* See *Ambedkar & Buddhism* by Sangharakshita.

Arnold, Sir Edwin (1832–1904): *English poet and journalist.* Born 1832, Gravesend, Kent, UK. Educated King's School, Rochester; King's College, London, and U College, Oxford. 1852: won Newdigate Prize. 1853: first book of poems published. 1854: married Katherine Biddulph. Became master at King Edward VI School, Birmingham; afterwards Principal of Deccan College, Poona (India). Mastered Sanskrit; produced translations. 1861: became Asian Affairs correspondent of *Daily Telegraph;* worked for the paper for *c* 40 years. 1979: *The Light of Asia* appeared—"'the best seller' of all Buddhist books in the West" (Christmas Humphreys). Later drew attention to the poor state of the Bdst holy places in N India; initiated scheme for buying

Bodh Gaya from its (then) Hindu owner. Honors: Companion of (Order of) the Star of India (British), and Order of the White Elephant (Thai); knighted by Queen Victoria.

Batchelor, Stephen: *Writer and translator.* Born 1953, Scotland. Travelled in the East. 1971: began Tib Bdst studies. 1974: ordained as Gelugpa monk (Gelong Jhampa Thabkay); studied with Geshe Rabten (wv) in India and Switzerland. 1981–85: ordained at Popch'on Sunim and trained in Korean Zen with Kusan Sunim (qv) at Songgwang Sa Monastery. At Sharpham North Community, S Devon (UK) till 1990 and conducts retreats in UK, Europe, and USA. Publications incl *Alone with Others (Outlines for an Existential Approach to Buddhism); Flight (An Existential Conception of Buddhism);* and *The Jewel in the Lotus (A Survey of the Buddhism of Tibet), The Faith to Doubt, The Awakening of the West, The Tibet Guide,* and *Buddhism Without Beliefs.* Tr include Shantideva's *Bodhicaryavatara* (from the Tib), Geshe Rabten's *Echoes of Voidness.*

Blavatsky, Helena Petrovna (1831–91): *Co-founder of the Theosophical Soc in New York 1875.* 1880: declared herself a Bdst in Galle (Sri Lanka). Credited with inspiring Bdst revival in Sri Lanka. Books incl *Isis Unveiled; The Secret Doctrine;* and *The Voice of the Silence.*

Blofeld, John (Chu Ch'an, 1913–87): *English writer and translator specializing in Bdsm and Toaism.* Educated Haileybury College and Cambridge (Downing College); read natural sciences at latter; did not take degree but left in second year and went to China. 1933–39: in China; visited many Bdst monasteries; formally became pupil of Master Hsü Yün (qv) but actually received training in Ch'an meditation from his pupils at Hua T'ing Monastery, near Kunming, Yunnan; also received Vajrayana teachings. 1939–40: taught at School of Oriental Studies, London U. 1940–42: War service as Army Captain at War Office, London. 1942–45: Cultural Attaché, British Embassy, Chunking. 1947–49: Chinese National Govt scholarship to study T'ang dynasty Bdsm in Peking; translations of Huang Po and Hui Hai drafted; married Chang Meifang. 1949–61: taught in Hong Kong and Bangkok. Also visited Darjeeling to study with Nyingma teachers incl Dudjom Rinpoché (qv) and Dodrupchen Rinpoché (qv). 1961–74: worked for UN (ECAFE), Bangkok 1974–79: taught English at Kasetsart and Chulalongkorn Us, Bangkok. 1978–80: Extensive lecture tours of USA and Canada. Latterly engaged in studying Chinese composition and literature. Books incl *The Jewel in the Lotus; Red China in Perspective; The Wheel of Life* (autobiography); *People of the Sun; The Zen Teaching of Huang Po; The City of Lingering Splendour; The Zen Teaching of Hui Hai; The Book of Change; The Way of Power; The Tantric Mysticism of Tibet; Mahayana Buddhism in South-East Asia; The World of Buddhism; King Maha Mongkut of Siam; The Secret and the Sublime; Beyond the Gods; Mantras; Compassion Yoga; Taoism: Quest for Immortality; Gateway to Wisdom; The Chinese Art of Tea;* and a book of reminiscences written in Chinese.

Conze, Dr Edward Julius Dietrich (1904–79): *Pioneer naturalized British Buddhist scholar and translator; authority on the Prajnaparamita literature.* Born London, son of German Vice-Consul, educated Germany; PhD Cologne 1928. 1933: emigrated to UK due to dislike of Nazis. 1937: chance discovery of book by D.T. Suzuki revived an earlier interest in Bdsm; thereafter devoted himself tirelessly to Bdst studies and produced a steady flow of books, incl Mahayana translations and anthologies. Held academic posts at Us of Wisconsin, Washington, Lancaster, California, Bonn, and at Manchester College, Oxford. Also sometime Vice-President of The Bdst Society and Custodian of C Asian manuscripts at Indian Office Library. "In his writings he was that *rara avis*: a man deeply versed in technical scholarship yet at the same time both loving and striving to live the religion of which he was such an able exponent" (Christmas Humphreys). "He was in my view the most important scholar of Buddhism in post-war Britain . . ." (Ninian Smart). Books incl *Buddhism Its Essence & Development; Thirty Years of Buddhist Studies; Further Buddhist Studies; Selected Sayings from the Perfection of Wisdom; The Buddha's Law Among the Birds; Buddhist Meditation; Buddhist Wisdom Books; Buddhist Scriptures; Buddhist Texts through the Ages; A Short History of Buddhism; Buddhist Thought in India;* and trs of the *Abhisamayalankara* and the *Astasahasrika*. Autobiography: *Memoirs of a Modern Gnostic* (2 vols).

Dahlke, Dr Paul (1865–1928): *Pioneer German Bdst.* E Prussia; studied medicine and became homeopath in Berlin. Came to Bdsm via writings of A. Schopenhauer. 1900: to Ceylon; studied with Sumangala Thera, W.O.C. Wagiswara, et al. Commuted between E and W for many years. Eventually built Das Buddhistische Haus, one of the first Bdst vihare in Europe in garden of house at Frohnau, near Berlin; here he "lived in ascetic conditions, observing the Rules of the Sangha" (Christmas Humphreys). Books in English incl *Buddhist Essays; Buddhism & Science; Essays and Poems; Buddhist Stories;* and *Buddhism & Its Place in the Mental Life of Mankind;* edited and largely wrote *Die Brockensammlung*. Tr *Dhammapada* into German.

Grimm, George (1868–1945): *Pioneer German Bdst.* Born Rollh bei Lauf. Destined for priesthood but took to Law instead. Attracted to Schopenhauer's philosophy; became close friend of Dr. Paul Deussen (1845–1919); began to study Bdsm. After retirement from Supreme Court Bench, spent remaining 37 years of life on study, practice and propagination of Bdsm in Germany. Wrote books and articles and lectured widely (e.g., at U of Munich). 1921: formed Old Buddhist Community at Utting am Ammersee in Bavaria (with Dr. Karl Seidenstrucker). Books in English incl *The Doctrine of the Buddha (The Religion of Reason & Meditation)*.

Harding, Douglas E.: *Discoverer and proponent of the Headless Way.* Born 1909 into an Exclusive Plymouth Brethren family in Lowestoft, Suffolk (UK). Left Brethren while architectural student at London U (Bartlett School). Disowned by family. Later went into architectural practice in India and in England. While walking in the Himalayas had a profound seeing into his own self-nature that is recounted in his book, *On Having No Head*. Has taught his Way, through a variety of skillful means, in Britian (e.g., at The Buddhist Soc Summer School) and in the USA (e.g., under the auspices of EST). Other books incl *The Hierarchy of Heaven and Earth* and *Religions of the World*. An occassional journal, *Share It,* is produced by those following his Way. Lives near Ipswich in Suffolk (UK).

Humphreys, Travers Christmas QC (1901–83): *Great propagator of Bdsm in the West.* Born London. Educated Malvern and Trinity College, Cambridge. Called to the Bar in London and like his father, Sir Travers Humphreys KC, enjoyed a long and distinguished career in criminal law. As First Treasury Counsel, led for the prosecution in many famous murder trials held in courtrooms of London's Central Central Criminal

Court (Old Bailey); e.g., those of Ruth Ellis and Craig and Bentley. After WW II wen to Japan to sit on International War Crimes Tribunal. 1927: married Aileen Faulkner (known as "Puck"); no issue. Member and in 1956 elected Master of the Worshipful Company of Saddlers. Also a poet and a pundit in the debate over the authorship of the plays ascribed to William Shakespeare. Founded The Bdst Lodge, later The Bdst Society, in 1924. Great public speaker, broadcaster, and writer on Bdsm. Books incl *The Great Pearl Robbery of 1913; Buddhist Poems; The Mountain Side (poems); Poems of Peace and War; Seagulls & Other Poems; Shadows & Other Poems; Via Tokyo; The Field of Theosophy; Buddhism; The Buddhist Students' Manual; The Buddhist Way of Life; Concentration & Meditation; Exploring Buddhism; Karma & Rebirth; A Popular Dictionary of Buddhism; The Search Within; Sixty Years of Buddhism in England; Studies in the Middle Way; Teach Yourself Zen (Zen, a Way of Life); Thus Have I Heard; Walk On! The Way of Action (The Buddhist Way of Action); A Western Approach to Zen; What is Buddhism?; Zen Buddhism;* and *Zen Comes West.* Autobiography: *Both Sides of the Circle.* See also special Christmas Humphreys memorial issue of *The Middle Way,* vol. 58, no. 2 (Aug, 1983).

Huyên-Vi, Thich: *Important Vietnamese Bdst leader in the W, propagator and writer.* Born 1924, Ninh-Thuan, S Vietnam. 1935: entered Sangha, 1940, Srāmanera, 1946 bhiksu, graduated from An-quang Bdst. Inst. Saigon. Lecturer there and in 1955 became Director. 1961 enrolled at Nalanda Pāli Post-Grad Research Inst Patna. 1967: MA thesis. Magadh University—*The Four Abhidhammic Reals,* 1971: PhD, Magadha U (Patna) for "A Critical Study of the Life & Wks of Sariputta Thera." Directs Monastère Bouddhique Linh-Son (Paris), which is center of worldwide network of temples. Publications incl *The Four Abhidhammic Realms; La Vie de Bouddha Sakyamuni;* and *Dharma Talks.* 1973: Prof. at Van-Hanh University, Saigon. 1974: Prof of Bdst Studies, Saigon University. 1975: invited to Paris by Linh-So'n Bdst Assoc. 1977: Abbot. 1978: President. 1986: Vice President for France of World Bdst Sangha Sabhia. Translated Nāgārjuna's Sūtrasamuccaya, ed and tr multi-lingual version of Heart Sutra.

Ling, Trevor (1920–95): Learned Pali at school of Oriental Studies, London University, PhD *Buddhism and the Mythology of Evil* (Oxford 1977). 1971–84: Chair of Comparative Religion, Manchester University. Publications incl *Buddha; Marx and God; Religious Chance in the Secular World; Buddhist Revival in India;* and *The Buddha: Buddhist Civilization in India & Ceylon.* Tr Dīgha Nikāya, called *The Buddha's Philosophy of Man.*

Sangharakshita, Ven Maha Sthavira (D.P.E. Lingwood): *Founder of the Friends of the Western Bdst Order (FWBD); writer and poet.* Born 1925, Stockwell, S London. Little formal education but read widely. Joined Bdst Soc at 18. 1943: joined Royal Corps of Signals; served in India, Ceylon and Singapore during WWII. Left the service in India at end of war and pursued the homeless life. 1949: samanera ordination. 1950: bhikkhu ordination. Spent 1 year at Banaras U studying Pali, Abhidhamma, and logic with Ven Jagdish Kashyap. Settled in Kalimpong; founded Young Men's Bdst Assn and established Triyana Vardhana Vihara ("Monastery of the Three Vehicles.") Sat on ed board of *Maha Bodhi Journal* and founded journal *Stepping Stones.* 1950s: exodus of lamas from Tibet; received teachings from Dhardo Rinpoché, Jamyang Khyentse Rinpoché (qv), et al; also studied Ch'an. 1957: became active in Bombay area, working among "Untouchables"; advised Dr. Ambedkar (qv) and "personally officiated at the conversion of 200,000 people" (Subhuti). 1964: returned to UK, to Hampstead Bdst Vihara. 1967: established Friends of the Western Bdst Order (FWBO). 1970: conducted Hall Seminar at Yale. Publications incl *Messengers from Tibet and Other Poems; A Survey of Buddhism; The Three Jewels; Peace Is a Fire; Flame in Darkness; The Enchanted Heart; Crossing the Stream; The Path of the Inner Life; The Religion of Art; Travel Letters; Mind—Reactive and Creative; Aspects of Buddhist Morality; Buddhism; World Peace and Nuclear War; The Bodhisattva; Evolution and Transcendence; The Glory of the Literary World; Going for Refuge; Human Enlightenment; Alternative Traditions; Buddhism & Blasphemy;* and *The Eternal Legacy.* Autobiography: *The Thousand-Petalled Lotus.*

Tennisons, Karlis Alexis (1873–1962): *Onetime Bdst Archbishop of Lithuania, Estonia, and Latvia by decree of XIIIth Dalai Lama.* Born North Latvia. Traveled to E Siberia in search of Bdst teaching. Trained by HH Mahacariya Ratnavajra, a Lithuanian Bdst living in E Russia. Became "profound Sanskrit scholar and Indologist." Did Dhammaduta work beyond Arctic Circle among Yakuts, Samoyeds, etc, and in C Asia. Also studied in China. 1890s: with Friedrich Lustig (a Baltic German) et al, established first W Bdst community on European soil. Supervised building of Bdst temple in Leningrad/St Petersburg (opened 1915). During WWI: Bdst chaplain to Russian Army. 1917: went into exile. 1956: with Lustig in Delhi for Jayanti celebrations. Died Rangoon, Burma.

Watts, Alan Wilson (1915–73): *Writer and talker on Zen and religion in general.* Born Chiselhurst, Kent (UK). Educated King's School, Canterbury. 1930: began correspondence with Christmas Humphreys of Bdst Lodge; introduced to writings of D. T. Suzuki. 1931: first article published. 1932: left school; did not go on to university instead took daytime job and pursued spiritual interests in spare time. 1963–68: Editor of *Buddhism in England.* 1936: first book, *The Spirit of Zen.* 1938: married Eleanor Everett, daughter of Ruth Fuller Everett (later Salaki); emigrated to USA. 1944: ordained Episcopalian priest in Chicago; became Chaplain at Nothwestern University (Evanston). 1950: left Episcopalian Church. 1951: married Dorothy De Witt. 1951–57: taught at American Academy of Asian Studies, San Francisco; served as Dean 1953–56. Involved in Californian Counterculture (fictionalized as Arthur Whane in Kerouac's *Dharma Bums*). Took part in experiments with LSD in UCLA Dept of Neuropsychology. After 1957 worked independently ("lived by my wits") as lecturer, writer, and broadcaster. 1958: Honorary Doctorate degree, U of Vermont; visited Europe; lectured at C. G. Jung Institute and had discussions with D. T. Suzuki. *c*1959: married Mary Jane Yates. 1961: went to live on houseboat Vallejo in Sausalito. 1960–65: visited Japan, escorting parties to Kyoto. Died of heart failure in home at Druid Heights, Mt. Tamalpais, California, after exhausting lecture tour of Europe. Books incl *The Spirit of Zen; The Legacy of Asia & Western Man; The Meaning of Happiness; Behold the Spirit; Theologica Mystica of St. Dionysius; The Supreme Identity; Myth & Ritual in Christianity; Nature, Man & Woman; The Wisdom of Insecurity; Easter—Its Meaning & Story; The Way of Zen; This Is It; The Book on the Taboo Against Knowing Who You Are; Psychotherapy East and West; The Joyous Cosmology; The Two Hands of God; Cloud-hidden; Whereabouts Unknown; Does It Matter?; Man's Relation to Materiality;* and *Tao: The Watercourse Way.* Autobiography: *In My Own Way.* Biographies: *Alan Watts* by David Stuart and *Genuine Fake* by Monica Furlong.

Wei Wu Wei (Terrence Gray, 1895–1986): *Zen/Taoist writer.* Born of wealthy Anglo-Irish ancestry at Felixstowe, Suffolk. Completed education at Cambridge and much involved in setting up a theater in the town. Latterly lived in Monte Carlo and owned vineyard in Rhone Valley where produced own wine. At one time kept a string of race horses and won Ascot Gold Cup one year. A member of the Carlton Club, he ran a Rolls Royce. Married twice. 1960s: traveled in East; visited Lama Govinda (qv) in Almora and Arthur Osborne in Turuvannamalai; met John Blofeld (qv) in Bangkok and visited Taiwan and Hong Kong in search of remnants of the Ch'an tradition; in Japan, stayed with Ogata San and visited D.T. Suzuki (qv) and Nakagawa Soen Roshi (qv). Books incl *All Else Is Bondage; Why Lazarus Laughed; Ask the Awakened; OOO; Fingers Pointing at the Moon;* and *Posthumous Papers.*

Wilber, Ken: *American scholar and writer on Bdsm, transpersonal psychology, meditation, and allied topics.* Born 1949, Oklahoma City. BA in biochemistry; MAs in biochemistry/biophysics (both U of Nebraska). At age 23: left graduate school to write first book, *Spectrum of Consciousness.*" I just kept on writing, basically, and since then have written 10 books and close to 100 articles/reviews." Co-founder and ed-in-chief of *ReVision;* consulting ed for *Journal of Transpersonal Psychology;* general ed of New Science Library/Shambala Publications. 1971: began Zen practice; was particularly influenced by Philip Kapleau, Eido Roshi, Katagiri Roshi, and Maezumi Roshi. Later began to study and practice Vajrayana Bdsm under Trungpa Rinpoché and Kalu Rinpoché. "My spiritual studies have also been strongly influenced by Krishnamurti, Ramana Maharshi, Aurobindo, and Da Free John." Married to Treya Killam Wilber. Books incl *The Spectrum of Consciousness; The Atman Project; Up from Eden; Eye to Eye; No Boundary; A Sociable God;* and *Transformations of Consciousness.* Ed *The Holographic Paradigm* and *Quantum Questions.*

A·P·P·E·N·D·I·X II

Useful Addresses

The following selection of addresses should be useful to readers wishing to explore the world of Buddhism in the U.S.A. and Canada:

THERAVADA

American Buddhist Seminary, 2717 Haste St., Berkeley, CA 94704. Phone: (510) 845-4843. Fax: (510) 644-9739. E-mail: abs@slip.net. Web site: www.slip.net./~abs.

Bhavana Society, Bhavana Center, Rt. 1, Box 218-3, High View, WV 26808. Phone: (304) 856-3240. Fax: (304) 856-2111. E-mail: bhavanasoc@aol.com

Buddhist Vihara Society (Ven. Dr. Gunaratana), 5017 16th St. NW, Washington, DC 20011. Phone: (202) 723-0733.

Dhammakaya International Society of California, 5950 Heliotrope Circle, Maywood, CA 90270. Phone: (213) 771-7435 or 771-7436. Fax: (213) 771-7437. E-mail: dhammakaya@aol.com.

Green Mountain Sangha, c/o Ann Barker, PO Box 78, East Middlebury, VT 05740. Phone: (802) 388-7329 or 247-3479. Fax: (802) 388-6406. E-mail: asbarker@sover.net. Web site: www.sover.net/ ~asbarker/sangha.html.

International Buddhist Meditation Center of Canada, 6926 St. Vallier, Montreal, Quebec H2S 2P9, Canada. Phone: (514) 948-3950. Fax: (514) 879-8329. E-mail: ibmcc@panorama.net.

International Meditation Center-USA, 438 Bankard Rd., Westminster, MD 21158. Phone: (410) 346-7889. Fax: (410) 346-7133. E-mail: IMCUSA@compuserve.com.

Khemara Buddhikaram (Cambodian Buddhist Temple), 2100 West Willow St., Long Beach, CA 90810. Phone: (310) 595-0566. Fax: (310) 426-4870.

Los Angeles Buddhist Vihara. 1147 North Beechwood Drive, Hollywood, CA 90038. Phone: (213) 464-9698.

Maha Dhammika Temple, 435 Hopewell Ave., Toronto, Ontario M6E 2S4, Canada. Phone: (416) 785-7497.

New York Buddhist Vihara (Sri Lankan), 84–32 124th St., Kew Gardens, NY 11415. Phone and Fax: (718) 849-2637.

Southwest Sangha, Black Range Station, San Lorenzo, NM 88041. Phone: (505) 536-9847.

Taungpulu Kaba-Aye Monastery, 18335 Big Basin Way, Boulder Creek, CA 95006. Phone: (408) 338-4050.

Toronto Mahavihara Buddhist Center, 4698 Kingston Rd., Scarborough, Ontario M2E 2P9, Canada. Phone and Fax: (416) 208-9276.

Vajiradhammapadip Temple (Thai), 110 Rustic Rd., Centereach, NY 11720-4070. Phone (516) 471-8006. Fax: (516) 588-2482.

Wat Dhammabucha, 6201 Sawyer Rd., San Antonio, TX 78238-2206. Phone: (210) 521-7622 (mornings) or 520-5022. Fax: (210_ 520-5042. E-mail: bucha@connecti.com. Web site: www.connecti.com/~bucha.

Wat Dhammagunaram. 644 East 10000 N. Layton, UT 84041. Phone and Fax: (801) 544-7616. E-mail: ThaiPal@aol.com.

Wat Phrasiraratanaram (Thai), The Buddhist Temple of Great St. Louis, 890 Linsay Lane, Florissant, MO 63031. Phone: (314) 839-3115.

Wat Prasriratanamahadhatu of Chicago, 4735 North Magnolia Ave., Chicago, IL 60640. Phone: (773) 784-0257.

Wat Promgunaram of Arizona, 17212 West Maryland Ave., Waddell, AZ 85355. Phone: (602) 935-2276. Fax: (602) 935-1174.

Wat Yarna Rangee, 22147 Cedar Green Rd., Sterling, A 20164. Phone: (703) 406-8290. Fax: (703) 406-4705. E-mail: klom@erols.com.

VIPASSANA MEDITATION CENTERS

Bodhi Tree Dhamma Center, 11355 Dauphin Ave., Largo, FL 34648. Phone: (813) 392-7698.

California Vipassana Center (U Ba Khin; S. N. Goenka tradition), PO Box 1167, North Fork, CA 93643-1167. Phone: (209) 877-4386. Fax: (209) 877-4387. E-mail: Mahavana@aol.com.

Cambridge Insight Meditation Center (Larry Rosenberg), 331 Broadway, Cambridge, MA 02139. Phone: (617) 491-5070. Fax: (617) 491-5070.

Durham Meditation Center (John Orr), 1214 Broad St. No. 2, Durham, NC 27705. Phone: (919) 286-4754.

Fondation Vipassana Foundation, CP 32083, Les Atriums, Montreal, Quebec H2L 4Y5, Canada. Phone: (514) 481-3504. Fax: (514) 879-8302.

Insight Meditation Center (U Pandita, Joseph Goldstein, Sharon Salzburg, and others), 1230 Pleasant St., Barre, MA 01005. Phone: (617) 355-4378. Fax: (508) 355-6398.

Insight Retreats, 128 Durham St. W, Lindsay, Ontario K9V 2R5, Canada. Phone: (705) 799-6992.

Las Vegas Vipassana, Southwest Center for Spiritual Living, 715 Sperry Drive, Las Vegas, NM 87701. Phone (505) 454-1671.

Mongomery Dhamma Society, 528 Seminole Place, Montgomery, AL 26117. Phone: (334) 277-6987. E-mail: jiml@mont.mindspring.com. Web site: www.mindspring.com/~jiml/home.htm.

Northwest Vipassana Center, Dhamma Kunja, PO Box 345, Ethel, WA 98542-5434. Phone and Fax: (360) 978-5434. E-mail: DhKunja@aol.com.

Rocky Mountain Vipassana Association, c/o Judi Sammons, 760 NW Birch St., Cedaredge, CO 81413. Phone: (970) 835-8295.

Southwest Vipassana Meditation Center, Dhamma Siri, PO Box 190248, Dallas, TX 75219-0248. Phone: (214) 521-5258 (course information), (214) 932-7868 (meditation center). Fax: (214) 522-5973. E-mail: vip@onramp.net.

Spirit Rock Meditation Center, PO Box 909, Woodacre, CA 94973. Phone: (415) 488-0164. Fax: (415) 488-0170. E-mail: srmc@spiritrock.org. Web site: www.spiritrock.org.

Vipassana Meditation Center (VMC), Dhamma Dhara, PO Box 24, Shelburne Falls, MA 01370-0024. Phone: (413) 625-2160. Fax: (413) 625-2170. E-mail: VmcDhara@aol.com. Web site: www.dhamma.org.

ZEN

Berkeley Zen Center, 1931 Russell St., Berkeley, CA 94703. Phone: (510) 845-2403.

Dai Bosatsu Zendo Kongo-ji (Rinzai; Eido Shimano Roshi), HCR 1 Box 171, Livingston Manor, NY 12758. Phone: (914) 439-4566. Fax: (914) 439-3119. E-mail: zen@daibotsatu.org. Web site: www.daibotsatu.org.

Diamond Sangha (Soto-Rinzai; Robert Aitken Roshi), 2119 Kaloa Way, Honolulu, HI 96822. Phone: (808) 946-0666.

First Zen Institute of America (Rinzai), 113 East 30th St., New York, NY 10016. Phone: (212) 686-2520.

Green Gulch Farm (San Francisco Zen Center; Soto Zen; Tenshin Reb Anderson), 1601 Shoreline Highway, Sausalito, CA 94965. Phone: (415) 383-3134. Fax: (415) 383-3128.

Institute of Chung Hwa (Master Sheng Yen Chang), 90-56 Corona Ave., Elmhurst, NY 11373. Phone: (718) 592-6593. Fax: (718) 592-0717. E-mail: DDMBAny@aol.com.

Kwan Um Zen School and Providence Zen Center (Korean Chogye; Seung Sahn Sunim), 99 Pound Rd., Cumberland, RI 02864. Phone: (401) 658-1476. Fax: (401) 658-1188. E-mail: kwanumzen@aol.com.

Minnesota Zen Meditation Center (Soto; Katagri Roshi), 3343 East Calhoun Parkway, Minneapolis, MN 55408-3313. Phone: (612) 822-5313. E-mail: mnzenctr@aol.com.

Morgan Bay Zendo, PO Box 188, Surry, ME 04684. Phone: (207) 667-7170, 374-9963, or 667-5428.

Mount Baldy Zen Center (Rinzai; Joshu Sasaki Roshi), PO Box 429, Mount Baldy, CA 91759. Phone: (909) 985-6410. Fax: (909) 985-4870. E-mail: mbzc@aol.com.

New York Zendo Shobo-ji (Rinzai; Eido Tai Shimano Roshi), 223 East 67th St., New York, NY 10021. Phone: (212) 861-3333. Fax: (212) 628-6968.

Providence Zen Center: *see* Kwan Um Zen School.

Ring of Bone Zendo, PO Box 510, North San Juan, CA 95960. Phone: (916) 292-3792.

Rochester Zen Center (Soto-Rinzai; Phillip Kapleau Roshi), 7 Arnold Park, Rochester, NY 14607. Phone: (716) 473-9180. Fax: (716) 473-6846.

San Francisco Zen Center (Soto Zen; Tenshin Reb Anderson), 300 Page St., San Francisco, CA 94102. Phone: (415) 863-3136. Fax: (415) 431-9220. Web site: http:\\bodi.zendo.com.

Shasta Abbey (Soto; Order of Buddhist Contemplates; Jiyu Kennett Roshi), 3724 Summit Drive, Mount Shasta, CA 96067. Phone: (916) 926-4208. Fax (916) 926-0428. Web site: www.OBCON.org.

Sonoma Mountain Zen Center (Soto; Jakusho Kwong Roshi), 6367 Sonoma Mountain Rd., Santa Rosa, CA 95404. Phone: (707) 545-8105.

Tassajara Mountain Center (San Francisco Zen Center; Soto Zen; Tenshin Reb Anderson), 39171 Tassajara Rd., Carmel Valley, CA 93924. Phone: Contact San Francisco Zen Center.

Vermont Zen Center, PO Box 880, Shelburne, VT 05482. Phone: (802) 985-9746. Fax: (802) 985-2668. E-mail: vzc-graef@worldnet.att.net.

Zen Affiliate of Vermont, 54 Rivermount Terrace, c/o Bob Tokushu Senghas, Burlington, VT 05401. Phone: (802) 658-6466.

ZCLA Mountain Center (Zen Center of Los Angeles; Soto-Rinzai; Taizan Maezumi Roshi), PO Box 43, Mountain Center, CA 92361. Phone: (714) 659-5272.

Zen Center of Los Angeles (Soto-Rinzai; Taizan Maezumi Roshi), 923 South Normandie Avenue, Los Angeles, CA 90006. Phone: (213) 387-2351. Fax: (213) 387-2377.

Zen Center of Ottawa Dainen-ji, 240 Daly Ave., Ottawa, Ontario K1N 6G2, Canada. Phone: (613) 562-1568. Fax: (613) 241-5731. E-mail: 70670.1514@compuserve.com or

White_Wind_Zen_Community@compuserve.com. Web site:
www.wwzc.org.
Zen Mountain Monastery, Doshin-ji (John Daido Loori Sensei), PO Box
197, Mt. Tremper, NY 12457. Phone: (914) 688-2228. Fax: (914)
688-2415. E-mail: dharmacom@mhv.net. Web site:
www1.mhv.net/~dharmacom.

PURE LAND

Brooklyn Buddhist Association, 211 Smith St., Brooklyn, NY 11201.
Phone: (718) 488-9511. Fax: (718) 797-1073. E-mail:
sjosephj@aol.com, bbajsk1@aol.com.
Buddhist Churches of America (Jodo Shin-shu), National Headquarters,
1710 Octavia St., San Francisco, CA 94109. Phone: (415) 776-
5600.
Buddhist Churches of Canada (Jodo Shin-shu), 918 Bathurst St.,
Toronto, Ontario M5R 3G5, Canada.
Eko-ji Buddhist Temple, (Jodo Shin-shu), 10301 Burke Land Rd., Fairfax
Station, VA 22039. Phone: (703) 569-2311. E-mail: tsuji@uno.com.
Institute of Buddhist Studies (Jodo Shin-shu), 1900 Addison St., Berke-
ley, CA 94704. Phone: (510) 849-2383. Fax: (510) 849-2158.
Yuk Fut Monastery, 3348 Mooheau Ave., Honolulu, HI 96816. Phone:
(808) 734-3021. E-mail: jlchang@hawaii.edu (Yu-Ling Chang).

NICHIREN TRADITION

Soka Gakkai International Association of Canada (SGI-Canada), Culture
Centers: 2050 Dufferin St., Toronto, Ontario M6E 3R6. Phone:
(416) 654-3211. Fax: (416) 654-3539; 5025 Buchan St., Montreal,
Quebec H4P 1S4. Phone: (514) 733-6633. Fax: (514) 733-7887;
8401 Cambie St., Vancouver, BC V6P 3J9. Phone: (604) 322-0492.
Fax: (604) 322-0491.
Soka Gakkai International-USA (SGI-USA), National Offices and Center,
525 Wilshire Blvd., Santa Monica, CA 90401. Phone: (310) 260-
8900. Fax: (310) 260-8917. E-mail: sguisa@aol.com. Web site:
http://www.sgi-usa.org.

TIBETAN BUDDHISM

The Deer Park (Gelug; Geshe Sopa), 4548 Schneider Drive, Oregon, WI
93575. Phone: (608) 835-5572. Fax: (608) 835-2964.
Diamond Way Buddhist Center, 110 Merced Ave., San Francisco, CA
94127. Phone: (415) 661-6467. Fax: (415) 665-2241. E-mail:
kclsf@best.com. Web site: www.diamondway.org.
Gampo Abbey (Vajradhatu Monastic Center; Trungpa Rinpoche tradition), Pleasant Bay, Cape Breton Nova Scotia B0E 2P0, Canada.
Phone: (902) 224-2752. Fax: (902) 224-1521. E-mail:
gampo@shambala.org.

Foundation for the Preservation of the Mahayana Tradition (FPMT–Gelug Organization), PO Box 1778, Soquel, CA 95073. Phone: (408) 476-8435. Fax: (408) 476-4823. E-mail: 76734.3620@compuserve.com (Holly Ansett).

Karma Dzong, Boulder Shambhala Center (Vajradhatu Center; Trüngpa Rinpoche tradition), 1345 Spruce St., Boulder, CO 80302. Phone: (303) 444-0190. Fax: (303) 443-2975. E-mail: sc@indra.com.

Karma Thegchen Ling (Karma Kagyu; Lama Karma Rinchen), 26 Gartley Place, Honolulu, HI 96817. Phone: (808) 595-8989.

Khandarohi Buddhist Center of Massachusetts, 34 Avon St., Somerville, MA 02143. Phone: (617) 628-2648.

Kurukulla Buddhist Center (FPMT; Gelug), PO Box 628, Astor Station, Boston, MA 02123. Phone: (617) 628-1953. Fax: (617) 536-1897. E-mail: persyn@law.harvard.edu or sr@math.bu.edu.

Los Angeles Karma Thegsum Choling, 3586 Tacoma Ave., Los Angeles, CA 90065. Phone: (213) 222-0479.

Milarepa Center (Gelug; Geshe Losang Jhampa), Barnet Mountain, Barnet, VT 05821. (802) 633-4136. Fax: (802) 633-3808.

The Naropa Institute, (A Contemplative College of the Arts and the Humanities, founded by Trüngpa Rinpoche), 2130 Arapahoe Ave., Boulder, CO 80302. Phone: (303) 444-0202.

Northampton Dharmadhatu, 518 Pleasant St. #2, Northampton, MA 01060. Phone: (413) 584-6415.

Nyingma Institute (Nyingma; Tarthang Tulku), 1815 Highland Place, Berkeley, CA 94709. Phone: (510) 843-6812. Fax: (510) 486-1679. E-mail: nyingma-institute@nyingma.org.

Rangrig Yeshe Center, PO Box 1167, Stockbridge, MA 01262. Phone: (413) 528-9932. Fax: (413) 448-7595.

Rashi Gempil Ling, First Kalmuk Buddhist Temple (Gelug; Geshe Losang Tharchin), 47 East Fifth St., Howell, NJ 07731. Phone: (908) 364-1824. Fax: (908) 901-5940. E-mail: acip@well.com.

Rigpa Fellowship Office for North America (Rimé tradition; Sögyal Rinpoche), PO Box 607, Santa Cruz, CA 95061. Phone: (408) 454-9103. Fax: (408) 454-0917.

Sakya Puntsok Ling (Sakya; Ven. Kalsang Gyaltsen), 608 Ray Drive, Silver Spring, MD 20810. Phone: (301) 589-3115. E-mail: sakya@erols.com or shiwa@aol.com. Web site: http://members.aol.com/shiwa/sakya.html.

The Tibet Center, 359 Broadway, New York, NY 10013. Phone and Fax: (212) 966-8504.

Tibet House, 421 East 32nd St., New York, NY 10012. Phone: (212) 213-5592. Fax: (212) 213-6408. E-mail: tibetkb@aol.com.

Tibetan Meditation Center, 34 Adams St., Newton, MA. Phone: (617) 332-1835. E-mail: jdean@mvinc.com. Web site: www.churchward.com/drikung.

Vajradhatu International (Karma Kagyu; Trüngpa Rinpoche tradition): *see* Karma Dzong.

Vajrapani Institute (FPMT; Gelugpa), PO Box 2130, Boulder Creek, CA 95006. Phone: (408) 338-6654. Fax: (408) 338-3666. E-mail: 76764.2256@compuserve.com.

Zuru Ling (Gelug; Zasep Rinpoche), PO Box 15283, Vancouver, BC V6B 5B1, Canada.

NON-SECTARIAN

Buddhist Association of the United States, Rd. 13, Route 301, Carmel, NY 10512. Phone: (914) 225-6470, 225-6117, or 225-1819. Fax: (914) 225-0447. E-mail: bausny@aol.com

Buddhist Council of New York, c/o Ven. Kurunegoda Pitatissa, New York Buddhist Vihara, 84-32 124th St., Kew Gardens, New York, NY 11415-3303. Phone: (718) 849-2637 or (212) 781-1947. Fax: (212) 795-8146. E-mail: Dimitri@aol.com.

Buddhist Council of the Midwest, 2400 Prairie, Evanston, IL 60201. Phone: (847) 869-4975.

Cloud Mountain Retreat Center, 373 Agren Rd., Castle Rock, WA 98611. Phone: (360) 274-4859 or Northwest Dharma Association (206) 789-5456. Fax: (360) 274-9119. E-mail: cloudmtn@teleport.com or cwdharma@accessone.com. Web site: www.teleport.com/~cloudmtn.

Dharma Center of Canada, RR 1, Galway Rd., Kinmount, Ontario K0M 2A0, Canada. Phone: (705) 488-2704. Fax: (705) 488-2215. E-mail: Dharma@halhinet.on.ca.

Gay Buddhist Fellowship, 2261 Market Street #44, San Francisco, CA 94114. Phone: (415) 974-9878.

Mindfulness Meditation Foundation, 3061 Merriam Lane, Kansas City, KS 66106. Phone: (913) 432-7787, ext. 109. Fax: (913) 432-9242.

Springwater Center (Toni Packer), 7179 Mill St., Springwater, NY 14560. Phone: (716) 669-2141. Fax: (716) 669-9573. E-mail: spwtrctr@servtech.com.

WOMEN AND BUDDHISM

Sakyadhita, International Association of Buddhist Women, 400 Habron Lane #2615, Honolulu, HI 96815. Fax: (808) 944-7070. E-mail: tsomo@hawaii.edu.

Rev. Bhikkuni Martha Dharmapali (Martha Sentnor), Cha-Nhu Buddhist Pagoda, 7201 West Bayaud Place, Lakewood, CO 80226.

ENGAGED BUDDHISM

Buddhist Peace Fellowship, PO Box 4650, Berkeley, CA 94704. Phone: (510) 655-6169. Fax: (510) 655-1369. E-mail: bpf@bpg.org. Web site: www.bpf.org.

WORLD AND EUROPEAN ORGANIZATIONS

World Fellowship of Buddhists, 33 Sukhumvit Rd., Bangkok 10110, Thailand. Phone: 66 11 284-89.

European Buddhist Union, via Pio Rolla 71, 10094 Giaveno, Torino, Italia. Phone: (011) 93 78 331.

The Buddhist Society, 58 Eccleston Sq., London SW1V 1PH, UK. Phone: (0171) 834-5858. Fax: (0171) 976-5238.

Office of H. H. the Dalai Lama, Thekchen Choeling, McLeod Ganj, Dharamsala, Dist. Kangra, Himachal Pradesh, India.

A·P·P·E·N·D·I·X III

Major Buddhist Festivals

Buddhist festivals vary from country to country, though the most important ones usually celebrate the major events of the Buddha's life. Mostly they fall on days in the local lunar calendar.

THERAVADA BUDDHIST FESTIVALS

In Theravada countries, the Birth, Enlightenment, and Parinirvana of the Buddha are celebrated on the full moon day of May. This festival is called *Wisakha Puja* in Thailand, *Wesak* in Sri Lanka. Other festivals include:

In Sri Lanka

Poya, full moon days, are of special significance. The five most important *poya* are named after the lunar months in which they fall: *Duruthu* (Dec/Jan), *Navam* (usually Feb), *Wesak* (May), *Poson* (June, celebrating the bringing of the Dhamma to Sri Lanka by Venerable Mahinda), and *Esala* (July/Aug). The distinctive Sri Lankan festivity is a colorful parade-pageant called a *perahera*. At the *Esala Perahera* in Kandy each year the Buddha's tooth relic is paraded through the streets on the back of a magnificently caparisoned elephant. The Sri Lankan New Year falls in mid-April.

In Thailand

Asalha Puja (June/July) celebrates the Buddha's First Sermon. The 3-month Rains Retreat (*Vassa*) starts immediately afterwards. It is followed by *Kathina* (Oct or Nov), a kind of Thanksgiving when the laity donate requisites to the Sangha. *Magha Puja* (Jan/Feb) celebrates various minor events in the Buddha's life, including his prediction of his *Parinirvana*. *Maha Jat* celebrates his past lives. The New Year Festival, *Songkran* (mid-April), includes a Water Festival. Finally, there are special observance days each month.

MAHAYANA BUDDHIST FESTIVALS

In Tibet

The Buddha's Birth is celebrated on the 9th day of the 4th month of the Tibetan calendar, his Enlightenment and *Parinirvana* on the 15th day of the same month. The New Year ceremonies are spectacular, and were even more so in the old days. *Gutor* is a pre–New Year festival when all the negative accumulations of the Old Year are put to rest. *Losar* is the New Year festival proper; it lasts for 4 days and is followed by a long religious ceremony, *Monlam Chenmo* (lit. "Great Prayer Festival"), which goes on for about 3 weeks and culminates in a Butter Festival. *Dzam Ling Chi Sang* (15th day, 5th month) is a day when offereings are made to local deities. Tibet National Uprising Day, commemorating the Lhasa Uprising (1959) has been fixed for March 10 in the Western Calendar, and the Dalai Lama's Birthday for July 6. *Chökhor Düchen* (4th day, 6th month) commemorates the Buddha's First Sermon and *Lha Bab Düchen* (22nd day, 9th month), his ascent into the Tushita Heaven to give teachings to his mother. *Ngachö Chenmo* (25th day, 10th month) is a festival of lights commemorating the death of Jé Tsongkhapa. There are numerous other festivals and auspicious days every month.

In Japan

Hana Matsuri (April 8) celebrates the Buddha's Birth, *Nehan* (Feb 15) his Enlightenment, and *Rohatsu* (Dec 8) his Death. The two equinoxes are celebrated at *Higan* (around March 21 and Sept 20), while *Obon* spans 4 days beginning July 13 and commemorates the release from one of the hells of the mother of one of the Buddha's foremost disciples. The object of *Setsubon* (early Feb) is to drive out evil spirits. Special Zen celebrations include Bodhidharma Day (Oct), and the anniversaries of Rinzai Zenji (Jan 10), Daito Zenji (Nov 22), Dogen

Zenji (Aug 28), and Keizan Zenji (Aug 15). The Jodo Shin school celebrates the birth of Shinran Shonin on May 21; his death commemoration (*Ho Om Ko*) varies between Jan 16 and Nov 16 according to the head temple followed.

THE WEST

Now that Buddhism is coming to the West there are moves afoot to bring Buddhists of all schools and traditions together in a single celebration of the life and teachings of the Buddha, called Buddha Day, on the full moon day of May.

A·P·P·E·N·D·I·X IV

Further Reading

THE BUDDHA

The Indian Background

The Rig Veda. Translated by Wendy O'Flaherty. Harmondsworth, U.K.:
  Penguin, 1981.
The Upanishads. Translated by Joan Mascaró. Hardmondsworth, U.K.:
  Penguin, 1965.
Early Indian Religious Thought. P.D. Mehta, 1965. London: Luzac, 1965.
Prehistoric India. Stuart Piggott. Harmondsworth, U.K.: Penguin, 1950.
A History of India. Vol. 1. Romila Thapar. Harmondsworth, U.K.: Penguin,
  1966.
Hinduism. K. M. Sen. Harmondsworth, U.K.: Penguin, 1961.

The Life of the Buddha

Reflections on the Life of the Buddha. Garry Thomson. London: The Buddhist
  Society, 1983.
The Life of the Buddha. H. Saddhatissa. London: Unwin Books, 1976.
The Life of the Buddha. Edward J. Thomas. London: Kegan Paul, 1949 (3rd
  edition).
The Life of the Buddha. Bhikkhu Nanamoli. Kandy, Sri Lanka: Buddhist
  Publication Society, 1971.
"The Legend of the Buddha Shakyamuni." In chapter 2 of *Buddhist Scriptures*.
  Translated by Edward Conze. Harmondsworth, U.K.: Penguin, 1959.
The Buddha. Michael Carrithers. Oxford: Oxford University Press, 1983.
The Buddha. Trevor Ling. Harmondsworth, U.K.: Penguin, 1973.

THE BASIC TEACHINGS

The Buddhist World View

"Buddhist Cosmogony and Cosmology," L. de La Vallée Pussin, and "Indian Cosmogony and Cosmology," H. Jacobi. In the *Encyclopaedia of Religion and Ethics*. James Hastings, ed. Edinburgh: J. Clark, 1921.
Buddhist Cosmology. Randy Kloetzli. Delhi: Motilal Barnarsidass, 1983.
Fundamentals of Mainstream Buddhism (Booklet no. 1: Samsara and Rebirth). Eric Cheetham. London: The Buddhist Society, 1985.

Buddhist Ethics

Ethics of Buddhism. S. Tachibana. London: Curzon Press, 1981 (reprint).
Buddhist Ethics. H. Saddhatissa. London: Allen & Unwin, 1970.
The Buddhist Case for Vegetarianism. Philip Kapleau. London: Rider, 1982.
Buddhism and Sex. (Sangha Guide no. 5) Maurice Walshe. London: Wat Dhammapadipa, 1972(?).

Buddhism and Death

Death and Dying: The Tibetan Perspective. Glenn H. Mullin. London: Arkana, 1986.
Death, Intermediate State and Rebirth. Lati Rinbochay and Jeffrey Hopkins. London: Rider, 1979.
Rebirth and the Western Buddhist. Martin Willson. London: Wisdom Publications, 1987.
The Tibetan Book of the Dead. Translated by Francesca Fremantle and Chögyam Trungpa. Berkeley and London: Shambhala, 1974.
The Tibetan Book of Living and Dying. Sogyal Rinpoche. San Francisco: HarperSanFrancisco, 1992.
Who Dies? Stephen Levine. New York: Anchor/Doubleday, 1982.

Meditation

The Heart of Buddhist Meditation. Nyanaponika Thera. London: Rider, 1983.
Living Buddhist Masters. Jack Kornfield. Boulder: Shambhala Publications, 1983 (reprint).
Meditation in Action. Chögyam Trungpa. London: Watkins, 1969.
The Path to the Deathless. Ven. Ajahn Sumedho. Hemel Hempstead, U.K.: Amaravati, undated (probably *c.* 1985).
Tranquillity and Insight A. Solé-Leris. London: Rider, 1986.
Visuddhimagga ("The Path of Purification"). Bhadantacariya Buddhaghosa, translated by Bhikkhu Nanamoli. Kandy, Sri Lanka: Buddhist Publication Society, 1979.
See also *The Atman Project*. Ken Wilber. Wheaton, Ill.: Theosophical Publishing House, 1980, chapter 12.

General Books

The Buddha and His Teachings. Narada Thera. Kandy, Sri Lanka: publisher not stated but probably Vajirarama, 1980.

The Buddha's Ancient Path. Piyadassi Thera. Kandy, Sri Lanka: Buddhist Publication Society, 1974.

Buddhist Dictionary. Nyanatiloka Thera. Kandy, Sri Lanka: Buddhist Publication Society, 1980.

Cittaviveka. Ven. Ajahn Sumedho. Petersfield, U.K.: Chithurst Forest Monastery, 1983.

What the Buddha Taught. Walpola Rahula. Bedford, U.K.: Gordon Fraser, 1972. Highly recommended.

THE DEVELOPMENT

Hinayana

Buddhism, Its Essence and Development. E. Conze, Oxford, U.K.: Cassirer, 1960.

Buddhist Thought in India. E. Conze. London: George Allen & Unwin, 1962.

Indian Buddhism. A.K. Warder. Delhi: Motilal Banarsidass, 1970.

An Analysis of the Pali Canon. Russel Webb. Kandy, Sri Lanka: Buddhist Publication Society, 1975.

The Central Conception of Buddhism, and the Meaning of the Word "Dharma." Th. Stcherbatsky. Delhi: Motilal Banarsidass, 1974 (reprint).

The Manual of Abhidhamma. Narada Maha Thera. Colombo, Sri Lanka: Vajirarama, 1956.

Mahayana

Indo-Tibetan Buddhism. David Snellgrove. Boston: Shambhala and London: Serindia, 1987.

A Short History of Buddhism. E. Conze. London: George Allen and Unwin, 1980.

The Central Philosophy of Buddhism: A Study of the Madhyamika System. T. R. V. Murti. London: George Allen & Unwin, 1955.

The Essentials of Buddhist Philosophy. J. Takakusu. Delhi: Motilal Banarsidass, 1975.

Mahayana Buddhism. Paul Williams. London: Routledge & Kegan Paul, 1989.

Studies in the Lankavatara Sutra. D.T. Suzuki. London: Routledge & Kegan Paul, 1930.

Tantra

Foundations of Tibetan Mysticism. Lama Anagarika Govinda. London: Rider, 1960.

An Introduction to Tantric Buddhism. S.B. Dasgupta. Berkeley and London: Shambala, 1974 (reprint).

"The Jewel in the Lotus: A Survey of the Buddhism of Tibet. Part 5: The Tantras." Stephen Batchelor in *The Middle Way.* Vol. 60, no. 1 (May, 1985), pp. 17ff.

Tantra in Tibet: The Great Exposition of Secret Mantra. Tsong-ka-pa, translated by Jeffrey Hopkins. Introduction by H.H. the XIVth Dalai Lama. London: Allen & Unwin, 1977.
The Tantric View of Life. (1976) Herbert V. Guenther. Boulder: Shambhala, 1976.
The Theory and Practice of the Mandala. Giuseppe Tucci, translated by A. H. Brodrick. London: Rider, 1969.

THE SPREAD OF BUDDHISM

Sri Lanka

Two Sinhalese records relate the early history of Buddhism in Sri Lanka: the *Mahavamsa* (a translation exists by Wilhelm Geiger) and the *Dipavamsa*.
The Heritage of the Bhikkhu. Walpola Rahula. New York: Grove Press, 1974.
History of Buddhism in Ceylon: The Anuradhapura Period. Walpola Rahula. Colombo, Sri Lanka: Gunasena, 1956.

Burma

A History of Burma. G. E. Harvey, 1925 (2 vols).
Religion and Politics in Burma. D. E. Smith. Cambridge, Mass: Princeton University Press, 1968.
Sanskrit Buddhism in Burma. N. Ray. Calcutta: University of Calcutta, 1936.
A Thousand Lives Away: Buddhism in Contemporary Burma. Winston L. King. Oxford, U.K.: Cassirer, 1964.

Thailand

Buddhist Monk, Buddhist Layman. A study of Buddhist monastic organization in central Thailand. Jane Bunnag. Cambridge: Cambridge University Press, 1973.
Sangha, State and Society. Yoneo Ishii. Honolulu: University of Hawaii Press, 1986.
Buddhism in Thailand. H. R. H. Prince Damrong. London: Information Service of Thailand, 1971.

The Northwestern Springboard

The Buddhist Art of Gandhara. Sir John Marshall. Cambridge: Cambridge University Press, 1960.
A Guide to Taxila. Sir John Marshall. Cambridge: Cambridge University Press, 1960.
The Real Tripitaka. Arthur Waley. London: George Allen & Unwin, 1952.
"Expansion to the North: Afghanistan and Central Asia." Oskar von Hinüber in *The World of Buddhism.* H. Béchert and R. Gombrich, eds. London: Thames & Hudson, 1984.
"Evidence of Buddhist Activity in the North Western Provinces of India."

Eric Cheetham in *The Middle Way*. Vol. 55, no. 1 (May, 1980), p.7.
"The Kashmiri Bridge." Eric Cheetham in *The Middle Way*. Vol. 56, no.1,
p.59.

The Silk Route

"Buddhism in Central Asia." R. E. Emmerick in *The Encyclopaedia of Religion*.
Mircea Eliade, ed. New York: Macmillan, 1987. Vol. 2, pp. 400ff.
Foreign Devils on the Silk Road. Peter Hopkirk. London: John Murray, 1980.
On Ancient Central Asian Tracks. Aurel Stein. London: Macmillan, 1933.
Reissued Chicago: University of Chicago Press, 1974. Jeannette
Mirsky, ed.
Buddhism in Central Asia. Kshanika Saha. Calcutta: Mukopadhyay, 1970.

China

Buddhism in China. Kenneth Ch'en. Princeton, N. J.: Princeton University
Press, 1964.
Buddhism in Chinese History. A. F. Wright. Stanford, Ca.: University of
California Press, 1965 (reprint).
The Buddhist Conquest of China. E. Zürcher. Leiden, Holland: E. J. Brill,
1959.
Chinese Thought: An Introduction. Donald H. Bishop, ed. Delhi: Motilal
Banarsidass, 1985.
The Essentials of Buddhist Philosophy. Junjiro Takakusu. Delhi: Motilal
Banarsidass, 1975.
Monkey. Wu Ch'en-en, translated by Arthur Waley. London: George Allen
& Unwin, 1942.
*A Record of the Buddhistic Kingdoms (Being an Account by the Chinese Monk Fa-
hien of his Travels in India and Ceylon [A.D. 399–414] in Search of the
Buddhist Books of Discipline)*. Translated by James Legge. Oxford: The
Clarendon Press, 1886. (Reprint: New York: Dover Publications,
1965.)
A Source Book in Chinese Philosophy. Translated and compiled by Wing-tsit
Chan. Princeton, N.J.: Princeton University Press, 1963.
The Wheel of Life. John Blofeld. London: Rider, 1959.

Vietnam and Korea

Buddhism and Zen in Vietnam. Thich Thien-An. Rutland, Vt.: Tuttle, 1975.
"Buddhism in Korea." Robert Evans Buswell Jr. in *The Encyclopaedia of
Religion*. Mircea Eliade, ed. New York: Macmillan, 1987.
The Korean Approach to Zen: The Collected Works of Chinul. R. E. Buswell Jr.
Honolulu: University of Hawaii Press, 1983
The Way of Korean Zen. Kusan Sunim, translated by Martine Fages. Edited
with an introduction by Stephen Batchelor. New York and Tokyo:
Weatherhill, 1985.

Japan

A First Zen Reader. Compiled by Trevor Leggett. Tokyo and Rutland, Vt.: Tuttle, 1960.
A History of Zen Buddhism. Heinrich Dumoulin. London: Faber & Faber, 1968.
Nichiren Shoshu Buddhism. Richard Causton. London: Century, 1988.
Plain Words on the Pure Land Way. Translated by Dennis Hirota. Kyoto: Ryukoku, 1989.
The Religions of Japan. H. Byron Earhart. San Francisco: Harper & Row, 1984.
Shinran's Gospel of Pure Grace. Alfred Bloom. Tucson: University of Arizona Press, 1965.
Sources of Japanese Tradition. Compiled by R. Tsunoda. William T. de Bary and Donald Keene, eds. New York: Columbia University Press, 1964 (2 vols).
Taking the Path of Zen. Robert Aitken. San Francisco: North Point Press, 1982.
"This World and the Other Power: Contrasting Paths to Deliverance in Japan." Robert K. Heinemann in *The World of Buddhism.* H. Bechert and R. Gombrich, eds. London: Thames & Hudson, 1984.
Unsui. A Diary of Zen Monastic Life. Giei Sato and Eshin Nishimura. Honolulu: University of Hawaii Press, 1973.
Zen Action, Zen Person. T. P. Kasulis. Honolulu: University of Hawaii Press, 1981.
Zen and Japanese Buddhism. D. T. Suzuki. Tokyo: Japan Tourist Bureau, 1970.
Zen and Japanese Culture D. T. Suzuki. New York: Pantheon Books, 1959.
The Zen Life. Sosei Kuzunishi and Koji Sato. New York: Weatherhill and Tokyo: Tankosha, 1977.
Zen and the Ways. Trevor Leggett. London: Routledge & Kegan Paul, 1978.

Tibet

Advice from a Spiritual Friend. Geshe Rabten and Geshe Dhargyey, translated and edited by Brian Beresford. London: Wisdom Publications, 1978 (revised edition).
A Cultural History of Tibet. David Snellgrove and Hugh Richardson. Boston and London: Shambhala, 1968 (revised edition).
Foundations of Tibetan Mysticism. Lama Anagarika Govinda. London: Rider, 1960.
The Jewel in the Lotus. A Guide to the Buddhist Traditions of Tibet. Stephen Batchelor. London: Wisdom Publications, 1987.
The Religions of Tibet. Giuseppe Tucci. London: Routledge & Kegan Paul, 1980.

Mongolia and Russia

"Der Buddhismus in Russland in Vergagenheit und Gegenwart." Friedrich Fenzl in *Bodhi Baum* (Austrian Buddhist journal). Vol. 10, no.2 (1985), pp. 91ff.

The Religions of Mongolia. Walter Heissig. London: Routledge & Kegan Paul, 1980.
The Empire of the Steppes. René Grousset, translated by N. Walfard. New York: Franklin Watts, 1970.
The Kalmyk Mongols. Paula G. Reubel. Bloomington: Indiana University Press, 1967.

BUDDHISM COMES WEST

Slow Beginnings

Both Sides of the Circle. Christmas Humphreys. London: George Allen & Unwin, 1978.
A Buddhist Student's Handbook. Christmas Humphreys, ed. London: The Buddhist Society, 1956
The Early Writings of Alan Watts. Vol. 1. John Snelling, ed. Los Angeles: Celestial Arts, 1987.
Genuine Fake. Monica Furling. London: Heinemann, 1986.
In My Own Way. Alan Watts. New York: Vintage Books, 1973.
Sixty Years of Buddhism in England. Christmas Humphreys. London: The Buddhist Society, 1968.
The Western Contribution to Buddhism. William Pieris. Delhi: Motilal Banarsidass, 1974.

After World War II

Born in Tibet. Chögyam Trungpa. Boulder: Prajña Press, 1981 (revised edition).
Buddhism in Britain. Ian P. Oliver. London: Rider, 1979.
The Buddhism of the Sun. Compiled by Jim Cowan. Richmond, Surrey, U.K.: Nichiren Shoshu, U.K., 1982.
Buddhism for Today. Dharmachari Subhuti (Alex Kennedy). Salisbury, U.K.: Element Books, 1983.
Memoirs of a Modern Gnostic. Vols. 1 and 2 (Vol. 3. not issued). Edward Conze. Sherborne, U.K.: Samizdat, 1979.
On Having No Head. Douglas Harding. London: Routledge & Kegan Paul (Arkana Books), 1986.
The Thousand Petalled Lotus. Ven. Maha Sthavira Sangharakshita. London: William Heinemann, 1976.

Buddhism in North America

Buddhist America: Centers, Retreats, Practices. Don Morrale, ed. Santa Fé: John Muir Publications, 1988.
How the Swans Came to the Lake. Rick Fields. 2nd revised and updated edition. Boston: Shambala, 1986. Highly recommended.
Nine-Headed Dragon River. Peter Mathiessen. Boston: Shambhala, 1986.
Zen Buddhism in North America, A History and a Directory. Toronto: Zen Lotus Society, 1986.

Buddhism and Psychotherapy

The Awakening of the Heart. John Welwood, ed. Boulder and London: Shambhala, 1983.

Beyond Ego: Transpersonal Dimensions in Psychology. Roger Walsh and Frances Vaughan, eds. Los Angeles, Ca.: J. P. Tarcher/Houghton Mifflin, 1980.

Beyond Health and Normality. Roger Walsh and Deane H. Shapiro, eds. New York: Van Nostrand Reinhold, 1983.

Beyond Therapy. Guy Claxton, ed. London: Wisdom Publications, 1986.

Buddhist and Western Psychology. Nathan Kats, ed. Boulder and London: Shambhala, 1983.

The Legacy of Asia and Western Man. Alan Watts. London: John Murray, 1937.

Psychotherapy East and West. Alan Watts. New York: Ballantine, 1961.

The Supreme Doctrine. Hubert Benoit. London: Routledge & Kegan Paul, 1955.

Zen Buddhism and Psychoanalysis. D. T. Suzuki, Erich Fromm, and Richard DeMartino. London: Souvenir Press, 1974.

By C. G. Jung:

Psychology and Religion: West and East. Vol. 2 of the collected works. London: Routledge & Kegan Paul, 1958. (Second edition, 1969.)

Psychology and the East. London: Arkana, 1986. See also *Jung and Tibetan Buddhism.* Radmila Moacanin. London: Wisdom Publications, 1987.

By Ken Wilber:

The *Atman Project.* Wheaton, Ill.: Theosophical Publishing House, 1980.

Eye to Eye. New York: Anchor/Doubleday, 1983.

No Boundary: Eastern and Western Approaches to Personal Growth. Boulder and London: Shambhala, 1981.

Spectrum of Consciousness. Wheaton, Ill.: Theosophical Publishing House, 1977.

Up From Eden. London: Routledge & Kegan Paul, 1983.

"In Praise of Ego." In *The Middle Way.* Vol. 58, no. 3 (Nov., 1983).

WOMEN AND BUDDHISM

Turning the Wheel: American Women Creating the New Buddhism. Sandy Boucher. San Francisco: Harper & Row, 1985.

Meetings with Remarkable Women. Lenore Friedman. Boston: Shambhala, 1987.

Women Awake. Christina Feldman. London: Arkana, 1989.

The Social Face of Buddhism: An Approach to Social and Political Activity. Ken Jones. London: Wisdom Publications, 1989.

Spirit for Change. Christopher Titmuss interviews Joanna Macy, A. T. Ariyaratna, U Nu, Sulak Sivarakla, Roger Walsh, et al. London: Green Print, 1989.
Being Peace. Thich Nhat Hanh. Berkeley: Parallax Press, 1987.

BUDDHIST JOURNALS

Buddhism Now, BPG, Shaarpham North, Ashprington, Totnes, S. Decon, TQ9 7UT, UK.
Buddhist Studies Review, 31 Russell Chambers, Bury Place, London WC1A 2JX, UK.
Chö Yang, The Voice of Tibetan Religion & Culture, c/o Jeremy Russell, Library of Tibetan Works & Archives, Ganchen Kyishong, Dharamsala 176215, Distt. Kangra, Hinmachal Pradesh, India.
Golden Drum, Journal of the Friends of the Western Buddhist Order, 51 Roman Rd., London E2 OHU, UK.
Inquiring Mind, A Journal of the Vipassana Community, PO Box 9999, North Berkeley Station, Berkeley, CA 94709.
Maha Bodhi, B. Dhammaratana Thera, ed. 90 Duku Rd., Singapore 1542.
The Middle Way, The Buddhist Society, 58 Eccleston Sq., London SW1V 1PH, UK.
The Mountain Record, Journal of Zen Mountain Monastery (John Daido Loori Sensei), PO Box 197 WS, Mt. Tremper, NY 12457.
Primary Point, Kwan Um Zen School, 528 Pound Rd., Cumberland, RI 02864.
Sangha Newsletter, The English Sangha Trust, Amaravati, Gt. Gaddessden, Hemel Hempstead, Herts HP1 3BZ, UK.
Ten Directions, ZCLA, 923 South Normandie Ave., Los Angeles, CA 90006.
WFB Review, Published by the World Fellowship of Buddhists, 33 Sukhumvit Rd., Bangkok 11, Thailand.
Wind Bell, Zen Center, 300 Page St., San Francisco, CA 94102.
Vajradhatu Sun, published by Vajradhatu (Chögyam Trungpa organization), 1345 Spruce St., Boulder, CO 80302, USA.
Zen Notes, published by the First Zen Institute of America, 113 East 30th St., New York, NY 10016.

Buddhist Book Service

Wisdom Publications, 361 Newbury St., Boston, MA 02115. Phone: (617) 536-3358. Fax: (617) 536-189.

Index

Tibet's Sacred Mountain

THE EXTRAORDINARY PILGRIMAGE TO MOUNT KAILAS

RUSSELL JOHNSON and KERRY MORAN

Spectacular color photography and vivid narrative lead you through the Himalayas to Mount Kailas, held sacred by both Hindu and Buddhist for more than 1,000 years. During the few years that Westerners were permitted to visit this area of Tibet, the authors joined a group of pilgrims on the path of devotion around Kailas and were able to record a rare glimpse of a region and a ritual almost unknown in the West.

ISBN 0-89281-847-6 • $25.00 paperback • 115 color photographs

"Both the vivid description and the awe-inspiring color photographs help to capture the mystical experience of this region and its religious significance."
Booklist

Power Places of Kathmandu

HINDU AND BUDDHIST HOLY SITES IN THE SACRED VALLEY OF NEPAL

Photography by KEVIN BUBRISKI • Text by KEITH DOWMAN

Award-winning photographer Kevin Bubriski captures in stunning detail the sacred places of Nepal's Kathmandu Valley.

ISBN 0-89281-540-X • $39.95 hardcover
144 pages, $10^3/_4$ x $13^3/_4$ • 108 color plates

Enlightened Management

BRINGING BUDDHIST PRINCIPLES TO WORK

DONA WITTEN with AKONG TULKU RINPOCHE

A management consultant teams up with a Tibetan lama to show how to create a successful and harmonious business environment by bringing Buddhist principles to the workplace.

ISBN 0-89281-876-X • $14.95 paperback • 176 pages, $5^3/_8$ x $8^1/_4$

Immortality and Reincarnation

WISDOM FROM THE FORBIDDEN JOURNEY

ALEXANDRA DAVID-NEEL

The first Western woman to visit the forbidden city of Lhasa examines Eastern concepts of the afterlife.

ISBN 0-89281-619-8 • $12.95 paperback • 176 pages, $5^3/_8$ x $8^1/_4$

Buddhist Masters of Enchantment
THE LIVES AND LEGENDS OF THE MAHASIDDHAS

Translated by KEITH DOWMAN
Illustrated by ROBERT BEER

These beautifully illustrated stories reveal a way through human suffering into a free state of oneness with the divine, by the example of the
Mahasiddhas—extraordinary men and women who attained enlightenment and magical powers.

ISBN 0-89281-784-4 • $24.95 paperback
208 pages, $8^1/_2$ x 11 • 30 color plates

The Doctrine of Awakening
THE ATTAINMENT OF SELF-MASTERY ACCORDING
TO THE EARLIEST BUDDHIST TEXTS

JULIUS EVOLA

Italian philosopher Julius Evola pares away centuries of adaptations to
reveal Buddhist practice in its original context.

ISBN 0-89281-553-1 • $16.95 paperback • 272 pages, 6 x 9

Nirvana Tao
THE SECRET MEDITATION TECHNIQUES OF THE TAOIST AND
BUDDHIST MASTERS

DANIEL ODIER

The author reveals techniques of meditation as practiced in the monasteries of India, Nepal, Sri Lanka, Thailand, and Japan.

ISBN 0-89281-045-9 • $12.95 paperback
208 pages, 6 x 9 • 50 black-and-white illustrations

Taming the Tiger
TIBETAN TEACHINGS ON RIGHT CONDUCT,
MINDFULNESS, AND UNIVERSAL COMPASSION

AKONG TULKU RINPOCHE

Founder of the oldest Tibetan Buddhist center in the West and an
accomplished meditation master, Dr. Akong Tulku Rinpoche explains
how true peace can be found in a practical program for cultivating
awareness and bringing the spiritual into everyday life.

ISBN 0-89281-569-8 • $12.95 paperback • 208 pages, $5^3/_8$ x $8^1/_4$

A Brief Tour of Higher Consciousness
A Cosmic Book on the Mechanics of Creation
ITZHAK BENTOV

A lighthearted yet profound guide to the realms of higher consciousness and the nature of reality.

ISBN 0-89281-814-X • $12.95 paperback
144 pages, $5^1/_4$ x $8^1/_4$ • 63 black-and-white illustrations

"A delightfully ingenious cosmic comedy on the nature and structure of ultimates. Here are travelers' tales such as you rarely find—metaphysical jaunts from one end of the universe to the other." **Jean Houston,**
The Foundation for Mind Research

Centering
A Guide to Inner Growth
SANDERS LAURIE and MELVIN TUCKER

A unique system of meditation techniques helps you increase personal learning power, reduce stress, and access healing energy.

ISBN 0-89281-420-9 • $9.95 paperback • 224 pages, $5^3/_8$ x $8^1/_4$
60-minute audiocassette: ISBN 0-89281-521-3 • $9.95
Also available in Spanish: ISBN 0-89281-579-5 • $9.95 pb

Creating the Work You Love
Courage, Commitment, and Career
RICK JAROW, Ph.D.

A career counselor presents an alternative approach to finding meaningful work and creating a life filled with purpose.

ISBN 0-89281-542-6 • $14.95 paperback • 216 pages, 6 x 9

"This wise and inspiring book can help you create a life that is a work of art."
Yoga Journal

The Meditator's Guidebook
Pathways to Greater Awareness and Creativity
LUCY OLIVER

"Rich in clear analysis, acute observations, and calm empathy. . . . treats meditation as a means rather than a sanctified set of rules." **Gnosis**

ISBN 0-89281-360-1 • $9.95 paperback • 160 pages, 5 x $7^3/_4$

The Invisible Player

CONSCIOUSNESS AS THE SOUL OF ECONOMIC,
SOCIAL, AND POLITICAL LIFE

MARIO KAMENETZKY

For every individual who has ever dreamed of running a successful business without having to sacrifice personal integrity, this book offers a blueprint for recovering our psychological and political health.

ISBN 0-89281-665-1 • $16.95 paperback • 336 pages, 6 x 9

"Profound and important—and a joy to read!" **Hazel Henderson, author of Building a Win-Win World**

Creative Visualization

USING IMAGERY AND IMAGINATION FOR SELF-TRANSFORMATION

RONALD SHONE

This comprehensive guide to harnessing the power of visualization for positive life changes explains the principles behind the visualization process and how each of us can awaken these abilities to realize our life goals.

ISBN 0-89281-707-0 • $12.95 paperback
176 pages, $5^3/_8$ x $8^1/_4$ • 12 black-and-white illustrations

Less Is More

An Anthology

Edited by GOLDIAN VANDENBROECK

This engaging anthology offers words of wisdom from the world's greatest thinkers on the virtues of simplicity. Included are writings from Ovid, Patañjali, St. Matthew, Milarepa, Rumi, Eckhart, Basho, Rousseau, Tagore, Suzuki, Illich, and many others.

ISBN 0-89281-554-X • $14.95 paperback • 334 pages, 6 x 9

These and other Inner Traditions titles are available at many fine bookstores or, to order directly from the publisher, send a check or money order for the total amount, payable to Inner Traditions, plus $3.50 shipping for the first book and $1.00 for each additional, to:

Inner Traditions, P.O. Box 388, Rochester, VT 05767
1-800-246-8648 • Fax (802) 767-3726
www.InnerTraditions.com

About the Author

John Snelling was born in Wales in 1943 and brought up there and in London and Canterbury. After graduating from university with degrees in English and Philosophy, he lectured for some years at a provincial English art school before leaving to travel in the East, where he became interested in Oriental religion and philosophy. He was involved in Buddhism since the early 1970s, practicing mainly in the Zen and Theravada schools. From 1980 until 1984 he was general secretary of the Buddhist Society, London, and from 1980 until 1987 editor of *The Middle Way*, the Society's quarterly journal. He wrote many books for adults and children and numerous articles as well as stories, plays, and features for radio and scripts for television. His books for adults include *The Sacred Mountain (Pilgrims & Travellers at Mt. Kailas in Western Tibet), Memoirs of a Political Officer's Wife in Tibet, Sikkim and Bhutan* (with Margaret D. Williamson), and *The Elements of Buddhism*. In addition, he edited two volumes of the early writings of Alan Watts. John Snelling lived at the Sharpham North Community in South Devon, England, for a number of years before his death in January 1992.